The Confucian *Four Books for Women*

The Confucian *Four Books for Women*

A New Translation of the *Nü Sishu* and the Commentary of Wang Xiang

Translated with introductions and notes by

ANN A. PANG-WHITE

OXFORD
UNIVERSITY PRESS

OXFORD
UNIVERSITY PRESS

Oxford University Press is a department of the University of Oxford. It furthers the University's objective of excellence in research, scholarship, and education by publishing worldwide. Oxford is a registered trade mark of Oxford University Press in the UK and certain other countries.

Published in the United States of America by Oxford University Press
198 Madison Avenue, New York, NY 10016, United States of America.

Library of Congress Cataloging-in-Publication Data
Names: Wang, Xiang, active 17th century, writer of added commentary. |
Pang-White, Ann A., translator, writer of added commentary.
Title: The Confucian Four books for women (Nü sishu) / with commentaries
by Wang Xiang and the translator ; translated and edited by Ann A. Pang-White.
Other titles: Nü sishu. English
Description: New York : Oxford University Press, 2018. |
Includes bibliographical references and index.
Identifiers: LCCN 2017042814 (print) | LCCN 2017061371 (ebook) |
ISBN 9780190460907 (updf) | ISBN 9780190460914 (epub) |
ISBN 9780190460884 (hardback) | ISBN 9780190460891 (paperback)
Subjects: LCSH: Women—Conduct of life—Early works to 1800. |
Women—China—Conduct of life—Early works to 1800. |
Confucian ethics—Early works to 1800. |
BISAC: RELIGION / Confucianism. |
PHILOSOPHY / Eastern. | HISTORY / Asia / China.
Classification: LCC BJ1609 (ebook) |
LCC BJ1609 .N813 2018 (print) | DDC 170.82—dc23
LC record available at https://lccn.loc.gov/2017042814

Contents

BOOK IV. The Ming Women: Madame Liu and the *Short Records of Models for Women* (*Nüfan jielu*): c. 16th century CE

Acknowledgments

THIS TRANSLATION AND commentary project is a result of many encouragements and helping hands. I would like to thank my colleagues in the greater Chinese studies and culture community whose inspiring works and encouraging words have been, and continue to be, invaluable to me, as well as the assistance from the editorial and production teams at Oxford University Press (OUP). Especially, I am grateful to Robin R. Wang for her tireless stimulating work on Chinese philosophy, women, and *yin-yang*, and her encouragement of my projects; and to Cynthia Read, the executive editor of religions at OUP, for her efficiency, faith, and unwavering support for this project. My first encounter and interest with the *Nü sishu* was through my reading of Li-Hsiang Lisa Rosenlee's *Confucianism and Women: A Philosophical Interpretation*; for this, I am indebted to her fine work.

I am also thankful to the University of Scranton for awarding me a research grant and one-year sabbatical leave; the Institute of Chinese Literature and Philosophy at *Academia Sinica* for allowing me to access an original copy of the 1885 Zhuangyuange edition of the manuscript; the National Central Library of Taiwan for all the resources it made available; the Chinese Text Project for its amazing array of digital resources; and my husband, David A. White, for his patient proofreading of hundreds of pages of my writings. All these are essential to the completion of this project.

I would finally like to thank the five women authors of the *Nü sishu* for their strong characters and pioneering arguments for women's education, intelligence, and wisdom. Without their work I would simply not be who I am. Through this translation and commentary project, they are no longer merely historical figures, but have come alive for me.

Note on Other Editions and on This Translation

THE *FOUR BOOKS for Women* (*Nü sishu*《女四書》) has been widely circulated since the late sixteenth century. The earliest edition known today is the 1624 Duowentang edition 多文堂刊本.[1] This collection was also published in Japan and Korea from the seventeenth century to the 1930s.[2] Several Chinese editions of the *Nü sishu* are available today, including the following:

1. *Zhuangyuange nü sishu jizhu*《狀元閣女四書集註》(Zhuangyuange Edition of the *Nü sishu* with Commentary) by Wenchengtang 文成堂, 1885 (in Chinese). This 1885 printing includes an extensive commentary by Wang Xiang 王相 (a Ming scholar, the compiler of the *Nü sishu*, and the son of Madame Liu, author of one of the *Four Books for Women*).[3] This edition also contains the 1580 imperial edict (萬曆八年) issued by Emperor Shenzong of the Ming dynasty 明神宗 (r. 1573–1620), commissioning a Confucian scholar-official (*ru chen* 儒臣) to compile Ban Zhao's 班昭 *Lessons for Women* (*Nüjie*《女誡》) and Empress Renxiaowen's 仁孝文皇后 *Teachings for the Inner Court* (*Neixun*《內訓》) in one volume and to promulgate it to the public. Thus, the Zhuangyuange edition has Ban Zhao's *Lessons for Women* (c. 100) and Empress Renxiaowen's *Teachings for the Inner Court* (c. 1405) as part I (*juan shang* 卷上), followed somewhat anachronistically by the Song sisters' (Song Ruoxin 宋若莘 and Song Ruozhao 宋若昭) *Analects for Women* (*Nü lunyu*《女論語》) and Madame Liu's 劉氏 *Short Records of Models for Women* (*Nüfan jielu*《女範捷錄》) as part II (*juan xia* 卷下). This edition is available both in print (archived at several research institutes and universities) and online.[4]
2. *Huitu nü sishu baihuajie*《繪畫女四書白話解》(Illustrated *Nü sishu*, with Explanations in Vernacular Chinese) (Taipei: Laoku Publishing 老古文化事業股份有限公司, 2012; a reprint of the 1908 text) (in Chinese). This illustrated edition contains four paintings by Li Wenquan 李文銓 depicting

the women authors of these four books. As suggested by its title, this edition intends to make the *Nü sishu* more accessible to the common public. The preface by Madame Shen-Zhang 沈張氏 immediately repudiates the received opinion that "without talent is a woman's virtue." She further states that she was educated by her mother, later became a widow at a young age, and single-handedly raised and taught her two sons. Now in her old age, she had the leisure to reread the *Nü sishu* and believes that their lessons are beneficial to all women. Through education, women can contribute significantly to the flourishing of the family and the state. She therefore requests her daughter-in-law, Mme. Shen Zhukun 沈朱坤, to provide commentary in vernacular Chinese so that the contents of the *Four Books for Women* can be easily understandable to teachers at girls' or women's schools (*nü xuetang* 女學堂) and to parents and young girls at home.

3. *Nü sishu jizhu yizheng*《女四書集注義證》(Four Books for Women with Selections from Traditional Commentaries) by Huang Yanli 黃嫣梨 (Hong Kong: Shangwu yinshuguan 商務印書館, 2008). In this 2008 book, Huang Yanli examines several editions of the *Nü sishu* and tracks down the origins of historical references and explanatory notes, including Wang Xiang's. This book also includes an essay by Huang exploring the meaning of the *Nü sishu* in the contemporary context. In contrast with the Zhuangyuange edition, Huang arranges the four books according to a historical timeline; thus, the Song sisters' *Analects for Women* comes second and Empress Renxiaowen's *Teachings for the Inner Court* comes third.

This English translation project bases its translation on the Zhuangyuange edition while consulting editions 2 and 3, listed here, for accuracy. To streamline our understanding of the historical development of social perception and expectation of women, women's education, virtue, and self-identity across the sixteen hundred years of Chinese history, I have arranged these four books in chronological order.

To keep the flow of the original text uninterrupted so that the reader can better appreciate the authors' arguments, and because Wang Xiang's commentaries are substantial and often exceed the length of the original text, I have placed his commentaries and my annotations in the "Commentaries and Annotations" section that immediately follows the original text, at the end of each chapter. Moreover, to differentiate my annotations from Wang Xiang's commentaries, Wang's commentaries are italicized and introduced with the phrase "Wang Xiang's commentary," whereas my annotations are set in roman and most are preceded with "Translator's annotation." I have also opted a more literal translation of the text so as to keep the texture of classic Chinese as much as possible.

---

1. Hu Wenkai 胡文楷, *Lidai funü zhuzuokao* 《歷代婦女著作考》 (*Verified Records of Women's Writings Through the Ages*) (Shanghai: Shanghai guji chubanshe 上海古籍出版社, 1985), 843. See also Huang Liling 黃麗玲, "*Nü sishu* yanjiu" 《女四書》研究 ("Research on the *Four Books for Women*") (MA thesis, Taiwan Nanhua University 臺灣南華大學, 2003), 36–37. According to Huang's research, scene five of a renowned Ming dynasty novel, Tang Xianzu's 湯顯祖 *Mudan ting* 《牡丹亭》, explicitly mentioned *Nü sishu* as one of the books studied by the main female character Du Liniang 杜麗娘. Since *Mudan ting* was published in 1598, Huang argues that *Nü sishu* must have already been popular by 1598 for it to be cited in a novel. *Mudan ting* is translated into English as the *Peony Pavilion: Mudan ting*, trans. Cyril Birch, 2nd ed. (Bloomington: Indiana University Press, 2002).
2. Japanese and Korean editions of the *Nü sishu* took varied forms. Some editions replaced the *Short Records of Model for Women* with the *Filial Piety for Women* or placed the former in the appendix. See Huang Liling, "*Nü sishu* yanjiu," 52–3.
3. Not much direct biographic records about Wang Xiang are available. However, in addition to *Nü sishu*, several other important texts for primary education, such as *Qianjiashi zhujie* 《千家詩註解》, also bore his name as a commentator.
4. Print copies are archived at Harvard University, Wuhan University (China), China's National Library, and Academia Sinica (Taiwan), among others. The digitized version is available through Google Books (however, it has several missing pages). Other online versions derived from the Zhuangyuange edition with modern punctuation in Chinese are also readily accessible.

Chronology of Chinese Dynasties and Republics

Legendary Ancient Period

Three Sovereigns and Five Emperors (*Sanhuang wudi* 三皇五帝)

Three Sovereigns (*Sanhuang* 三皇)
Fu Xi 伏羲 or Heavenly Sovereign (Tianhuang 天皇)
Shennong 神農 or Tai Sovereign (Taihuang 泰皇)/
Ren Sovereign (Renhuang 人皇)
Nüwa 女媧 or Earthly Sovereign (Dihuang 地皇)*

Five Emperors (*Wudi* 五帝)
Yellow Emperor (Huangdi 黃帝)
Emperor Zhuanxu (顓頊)
Emperor Ku (嚳)
Emperor Yao (堯)
Emperor Shun (舜)

Ancient Dynasties

Xia dynasty 夏 (c. 2100–1600 BCE)

Shang dynasty 商 (c. 1600–1046 BCE)

Zhou dynasty 周 (c. 1046–256 BCE)

- Western Zhou (Xizhou 西周) (c. 1046–771 BCE)
- Eastern Zhou (Dongzhou 東周) (c. 770–256 BCE)
  - Spring and Autumn period (Chunqiu 春秋) (770–476 BCE)
  - Warring States period (Zhanguo 戰國) (475–222 BCE)

* Some accounts replace Nüwa with Suiren 燧人, Zhurong 祝融, or Gonggong 共工.

Imperial Dynasties

Qin dynasty 秦 (221–206 BCE)

Han dynasty 漢 (206 BCE–220 CE)

- Western Han (Xihan 西漢 (206 BCE–8 CE)
    - Xin dynasty 新 (9–25 CE)
- Eastern Han (Donghan 東漢) (25–220)

Three kingdoms (Sanguo 三國) (220–265 CE)

Jin dynasty 晉 (265–420 CE)

- Western Jin (Xijin 西晉) (265–316)
    - Sixteen Kingdoms (Shiliuguo 十六國) (303–c. 420)
- Eastern Jin (Dongjin 東晉) (317–420)

Northern and Southern dynasties (Nanbeichao 南北朝) (420–589 CE)

Sui dynasty 隋 (581–618 CE)

Tang dynasty 唐 (618–907 CE)

Five dynasties and Ten kingdoms (Wudai shiguo 五代十國) (907–960 CE)

- Liao dynasty 遼 (907–1125)

Song dynasty 宋 (960–1279 CE)

- Northern Song (Beisong 北宋) (960–1126)
- Southern Song (Nansong 南宋) (1127–1279)
    - Western Xia dynasty (Xixia 西夏) (1038–1227)
    - Jin dynasty 金 (1115–1234)

Yuan dynasty 元 (1271–1368 CE)

Ming dynasty 明 (1368–1644 CE)

Qing dynasty 清 (1644–1911 CE)

Republics

Republic of China (Zhonghua Minguo 中華民國) (1911–Present)

People's Republic of China (Zhongguo Renmin Gongheguo 中國人民國共和國) (1949–Present)

Essential Classic Chinese Terms and Corresponding English Translations

THE FOLLOWING IS not meant to be an exhaustive list, but it includes words, terms, titles, and names frequently used in this volume.

ai 愛	love
Baihu tongyi 白虎通義	*Comprehensive Discussions in the White Tiger Hall*
Ban Zhao 班昭	Han woman scholar, historian, author of *Nüjie*
bei 卑	lowly
Beishi 北史	*History of Northern Dynasties*
bie 別	distinction
cai de 才德	talent and virtue
chong 寵	favorite, indulge, pamper, spoil
Chunqiu 春秋	*Spring and Autumn Annals*
Chunqiu fanlu 春秋繁露	*Luxuriant Dew of the Spring and Autumn Annals*
ci 慈	kindness, benevolence
cong 從	following, obedience; follow, obey
Daxue 大學	*Great Learning*
de 德	virtue
Dong Zhongshu 董仲舒	Han Confucian political thinker, author of *Chunqiu fanlu*
en 恩	favor, grace, kindness, loving-kindness
fu 夫	husband
fu 婦	wife, married woman, woman
fu 父	father
fufu 夫婦	husband and wife
fumu 父母	father and mother, parents
gang 剛	strong, firm
gu 姑	mother-in-law

Gujin tushu jicheng 古今圖書集成	*Collection of Illustrations and Books from Antiquity to the Present*
Guoyu 國語	*Discourses of the States*
Han 漢	name of a Chinese dynasty
Hanshu 漢書	*Book of Han*
he 和	harmony, harmonize
Houhanshu 後漢書	*Book of Later Han*
hui 惠	favor
jian 儉	frugality
jie 節	integrity, principledness
Jin silu 近思錄	*Reflection on Things at Hand*
jing 靜	quiet
jing 敬	respect
jingbiao 旌表	honor-commendation system
Jinshi 金史	*History of Jin* 金
Jinshu 晉書	*Book of Jin* 晉
jiu 舅	father-in-law
jiugu 舅姑	parents-in-law
Jiutangshu 舊唐書	*Old Book of Tang*
Kongzi 孔子	Confucius
Kongzi jiayu 孔子家語	*Family Discourse of Confucius*
kun 坤	paradigm, trigram, or hexagram representing Earth, female, woman, yin
lei 類	kind(s), category/categories
li 禮	ritual(s), rite(s), ritual propriety
li 理	principle, reason
Liji 禮記	*Record/Book of Rites/Rituals*
lie 列	row, list
lie 烈	ardent, passionate; ardency, passion
Lienü zhuan 列女傳	*Biographies of Women*
Liu Shi 劉氏	Madame Liu (also known as Wang jiefu 王節婦), author of *Nüfan jielu,* mother of Wang Xiang
Liu Xiang 劉向	Han scholar-official, author and compiler of *Lienü zhuan*
Lunyu 論語	*Analects*
Mengzi 孟子	Mencius, influential Confucian during the Warring States period
Mengzi 孟子	*Book of Mencius*, the *Mencius*
ming 明	enlightened, intelligent, clear, bright; enlightenment, intelligence

Ming 明	name of a Chinese dynasty
Mingshi 明史	*History of Ming*
mu 母	mother, female
mu 睦	friendliness
nan 男	male(s), man/men, boy(s)
nei 內	inner, internal
Neixun 內訓	*Teachings for the Inner Court*
neiwai zhibie 內外之別	inner–outer distinction
nü 女	female(s), woman/women, girl(s)
Nüfan jielu 女範捷錄	*Short Records of Models for Women*
Nüjie 女誡	*Lessons for Women*
Nü lunyu 女論語	*Analects for Women*
Nü sishu 女四書	*Four Books for Women*
Nüxian 女憲	*Decrees for Women*
Nü xiaojing 女孝經	*Classic of Filial Piety for Women*
Nüze 女則	*Regulations for Women*
qi 氣	vital energy, psycho-physical force
qi 妻	wife
qian 乾	trigram or hexagram representing Heaven, male, man, yang
Qianhanshu 前漢書	*Book of Former Han*, another name for *Book of Han*
qin 勤	diligence
qing 清	tranquility, serenity; tranquil, serene
Qing 清	name of a Chinese dynasty
qucong 曲從	conceding obedience
rang 讓	yielding
ren 仁	humaneness, benevolence; humane, benevolent, human-heartedness
Renxiaowen huanghou 仁孝文皇后	Empress Renxiaowen, author of *Neixun*
rou 柔	gentle
ru 儒	intellectual, scholar, literati
ruo 弱	weak
sangcong 三從	three obediences
sangang 三綱	three bonds
Sanguo yanyi 三國演義	*The Three Kingdoms*
Sanguozhi 三國志	*History of the Three Kingdoms*
Shangshu 尚書	*Book of Documents, Book of History*
sheng 聖	sage, sagely, holy
Shiji 史記	*Historical Records*, or *Historical Records of the Grand Historian*

Shijing 詩經	*Classic of Poetry, Book of Poetry, the Odes*
shun 順	compliance, obedience; comply, obey
Shun 舜	legendary sage king in pre-dynastic ancient China
side 四德	four (womanly) virtues
Siku quanshu 四庫全書	*Complete Library in Four Sections*
Sishu 四書	*Four Books*
sixing 四行	four (womanly) conducts
Song 宋	name of a Chinese dynasty
Song Ruohua 宋若華	another name of Song Ruoxin
Song Ruoxin 宋若莘	Tang woman scholar, author of *Nü lunyu*
Song Ruozhao 宋若昭	Tang woman scholar, author of *Nü lunyu*
Songshi 宋史	*History of Song*
Tang 唐	name of a Chinese dynasty
Tangshu 唐書	*Book of Tang*
Wangshi ji lienü zhuan 汪氏輯列女傳	*Wangshi's Biographies of Women*
wai 外	outer, external
Wang jiefu 王節婦	Chaste Widow Wang, maiden name Liu Shi 劉氏, author of *Nüfan jielu*
Wang Xiang 王相	Compiler and commentator of *Nü sishu*
wuchang 五常	five constant virtues
wulun 五倫	five relationships
wuxing 五行	five elements, five processes
xian 閒	leisurely composure
xian 賢	virtuous, worthy
xiao 孝	filialness, filial piety
Xiaojing 孝經	*Classic of Filial Piety*
xin 心	heart, mind
Xintangshu 新唐書	*New Book of Tang*
Xinyuanshi 新元史	*New History of Yuan*
xing 行	conduct
xing 性	nature
Xu jin silu 續近思錄	*Further Reflection on Things at Hand*
ya 雅	elegance
yang 陽	category/paradigm describing the strong, active, moving, etc., in comparison with yin
Yao 堯	legendary sage king in pre-dynastic ancient China
yi 義	righteousness
yi 易	change, changes

yi 儀	ceremony, model, mode
Yijing 易經	*Book/Classic of Changes*
Yili 儀禮	*Book of Ceremonial Rites, Book of Etiquette and the Ceremonial*
yin 陰	category/paradigm describing the gentle, receptive, still, etc., in comparison with yang
you 幽	solitude, seclusion, tranquility, serenity; deep, reclusive, hidden
Yuanshi 元史	*History of Yuan*
zhe 哲	wise, intelligent; wisdom, intelligence
zhen 貞	correct and firm, pure, chaste; purity, chastity
Zheng Shi 鄭氏	Madame Zheng, author of *Classic of Filial Piety for Women*
zhi 智	wise; wisdom
zhihui 智慧	wisdom
Zhouli 周禮	*Zhou Rituals, Rites of Zhou*
Zhu Xi 朱熹	Neo-Confucian scholar of Song dynasty
Zhuzi yulei 朱子語類	*Classified Conversations of Zhu Xi*
Zuozhuan 左傳	*Zuo Commentary* [to the *Spring and Autumn Annals*]

Introduction

Uncovering the Confucian Four Books for Women—*Why* Nü sishu? *Why Now?*

Yet only to educate men and not to educate women, are they not being partial in treating the two sides?
—Ban Zhao, *Nüjie* 《女誡》(*Lessons for Women*)

Although the great way of governing in peace rests on men, yet a wise woman surpasses a man.
—Liu Shi (Madame Liu), *Nüfan jielu* 《女範捷錄》(*Short Records of Models for Women*)

1. *Introduction*

Traditional China's gender-oppressive social practices in the past, such as foot binding, forced widowhood, female infanticide, and exclusion of women from the public realm, coupled with its refusal of women's equal access to social advancement even in the present, continue to generate the public perception that Chinese philosophy undermines liberal feminist causes.[1] Confucianism, in particular, is often regarded as the main instigator that legitimizes all this oppression. Not surprisingly, much Eastern and Western feminist critique in modern times tends to be anti-Confucian. Nonetheless, transcultural feminists (whether in the West or in the East) who uncritically endorse the values of liberalism have been heavily criticized in more recent feminist discourse as being neo-colonial and one-sided in their exclusive use of the liberal definition of equality as the universal—and only—measuring stick to judge cultural practices outside the West.[2] This neo-colonial mentality may have resulted from a lack of familiarity with women's traditions in other civilizations, which in turn may have been caused in part by the scarcity of primary texts—especially those authored by women—in English translation.

Culturally and philosophically, we must consider whether the term "feminism" (which is of Western origin) needs to be *broadened* and *redefined* if we are to treat non-Western cultures as true equals, true conversation partners, on this important subject. It should be noted that this chapter is not intended to conceal Confucianism's anti-feminist motif. Rather, it is to call attention to essential textual, cultural, and historical elements in the Confucian tradition, in particular the *Nü sishu* 《女四書》 (*Four Books for Women*), that modern readers may have bypassed owing to their cultural blinders. Uncovering these hidden elements is a critical step toward our fair assessment, as well as creative reconstruction, of Confucian philosophy and the *real* identity of Chinese women.

One thing to be sure is that Confucius (c. 551–479 BCE) never directly wrote any treatise on women nor did he formally teach any female students. Remarks about women historically attributed to him are found only a few times in the *Lunyu* 《論語》 (*Analects*) and in some other classic texts. Nonetheless, the infamous *Analects* 17.23 (in some versions, 17.25) has been a major target of the gender critique of Confucianism since the beginning of the twentieth century. Contemporary scholarship has demonstrated that the troubled history of Confucianism has much to do with the symbolic female subordination in the husband–wife relation and how it became entangled with the political symbolism of the ruler–minister relation by means of a politicized reading of the *yin–yang* metaphysics.[3]

Recent scholarship has been careful in separating *original* Confucianism from *politicized* Confucianism. Thus, if one is willing to reimagine the functions that Confucian norms play through the eyes of Chinese women when they are exercised authentically rather than abusively, the feminist potential of a depoliticized Confucianism is not out of bounds. We shall explore this possibility by closely examining a controversial set of four books, the *Nü sishu*, compiled and commented on by Wang Xiang 王相 (c. 16th–17th century), a Ming scholar and the son of Madame Liu (one of the authors of the *Nü sishu*). For some readers, the *Nü sishu* have perpetuated androcentric Confucian patriarchy, while for others these four books have contributed significantly to women's literary tradition.

The *Nü sishu* (*Four Books for Women*) were regarded as a counterpart to the famous *Sishu* 《四書》 (*Four Books*) grouped by Zhu Xi 朱熹 (1130–1200 CE), a Song Neo-Confucian. In the Confucian tradition, the four books for gentlemen's learning included: (1) the *Analects*, (2) the *Mencius*, (3) the *Great Learning*, and (4) the *Book of the Mean*. The *Sishu* exerted immense influence on Chinese society, thought, and culture, particularly in the period from 1313 to 1905 during which these four books were used as standard textbooks for the imperial civil service examination. Similarly, the *Nü sishu* were considered a very important collection of four didactic texts for the education of women. Unlike the *Sishu*, however, the *Nü sishu* were written by women and included:

1. *Nüjie* 《女誡》(*Lessons for Women*): by a Han dynasty woman historian Ban Zhao 班昭 (a.k.a. Cao Dagu 曹大家, c. 45–117)[4]
2. *Nü lunyu* 《女論語》(*Analects for Women*): by two sisters of the Tang dynasty, Song Ruoxin 宋若莘 (?–820) and Song Ruozhao 宋若昭 (?–825)
3. *Neixun* 《內訓》(*Teachings for the Inner Court*): by Empress Renxiaowen 仁孝文皇后 (1361–1407) of the Ming dynasty
4. *Nüfan jielu* 《女範捷錄》(*Short Records of Models for Women*): by Chaste Widow Wang 王節婦 of the Ming dynasty, also known by her maiden name Madame Liu 劉氏 (c. 16th century)

These four books spanned approximately 1,600 years from the first century to the sixteenth century, covering several Chinese dynasties. They provide readers with an invaluable view of the continuity and the longstanding tradition of Chinese women's writings, lives, education, history, and philosophy. The whole set is translated into English for the first time in this current volume. This collection provides *lived* narratives of *real* women that debunk the prevailing bias in several world philosophies and religions that women are more bound by their bodies than men are and, consequently, are more easily swayed by emotions and less capable of rational thinking.

Considering recent criticism directed toward the unidirectional discourse of transcultural feminism, this introduction aims to investigate the development of women's narratives and to what extent the *Nü sishu* may be argued to be a Chinese feminist response to traditional Confucian teachings from within. Furthermore, to enrich our understanding and to contrast the gender perspectives of the two sexes, we will first look at what Confucian men have said about the opposite sex before we turn our attention to what Confucian women have said about women.

2. *"The Master Says . . . ": What Did Confucius and Other Confucian Men Say About Women?*

2.1 Confucius's Encounters with Women

Even though Confucius never directly wrote a treatise on women nor did he formally teach any female students, his encounters with women can still shed light on his view of women. For example, according to historical records such as Kongzi shijia 孔子世家 ("Family Genealogy of Confucius") in the *Shiji* 《史記》(*Historical Records*) by Sima Qian 司馬遷 (145/139 BCE–87/86 BCE?) and the *Kongzi jiayu* 《孔子家語》(*Family Discourse of Confucius*) by Wang Shu 王肅 (195 CE–256 CE), we know that Confucius was born of an aging father Shuliang He 叔梁紇, known for his great physical strength, and Yan Zhengzai 顏徵在, a young lady from a noble family.[5] After Shuliang He's first wife passed away and his second wife did not beget a healthy son to carry on the family name, he married Ms. Yan. A selection from the *Kongzi jiayu* is translated here:

> The ancestors of Confucius were the descendants of Song 宋. . . . . [After many generations,] Fangsu 防叔 begot Boxia 伯夏. Boxia begot Shuliang He. The record said, "Although Shuliang He had nine daughters, he had no son." . . . Shuliang He therefore made a request of a marriage to the Yan family. The Yan family has three daughters. The youngest is Zhengzai. [After receiving the marriage request,] Mr. Yan, the father, spoke with his three daughters: "Although Sir Shuliang He's father and grandfather were only low-ranking governmental officials, he is a descendent of former sage kings. . . . I am fond of him. Even though he is old and his temperament strict, this is not something to be concerned about. Which one of you would be willing to marry him?" Two older daughters were silent. Zhengzai [, the youngest of the three,] stepped forward and said: "I will be willing to go. Is there any need to inquire further?" Mr. Yan replied: "Only you are able to do it" and married Zhengzai to Shuliang He. . . . Zhengzai then gave birth to Confucius and named him Qiu 丘 and gave him another given name Zhongni 仲尼. When Confucius was three years old, his father . . . passed away. . . . Later, when Confucius was at the age of nineteen, he married Miss Shangguan 上官氏. They had a son Boyu 伯魚.[6]

One learns from this anecdote that Confucius's mother Zhengzai was the youngest of the three Yan daughters. While her two older sisters hesitated, she alone looked past her future husband's old age and married him for his virtue. She became a widow when Confucius was only three years old and single-handedly raised Confucius. It seems unlikely that Confucius, a strong advocate of filial piety with such a close relation to his widowed mother who raised him, would hold a misogynist view against *all* women. Even though we do not know much about Confucius's wife, we do know that together they had a son Boyu, who was known for his love of learning.[7]

When Confucius traveled to various feudal states to promote the Way, he also encountered other women. The *Analects* 6.28 mentions Lady Nanzi 南子, who is known for her exceptional beauty: "When Confucius went to see Nanzi, Zilu 子路 [Confucius's student] was not pleased." Kongzi shijia, in the *Shiji*, provides us with further details about the actual event:

> Duke Ling [of Wei 衛] 靈公 had a concubine Nanzi. She sent a messenger to Confucius with the message that "No known gentlemen will insult [their hosts]: if a gentleman desires to become like a brother with my king, he must first come to me, the little king. I, the little king, am willing to receive you." Confucius declined Nanzi's request at first, but he later went to see her reluctantly. When the meeting took place, Nanzi stayed behind the curtain. Confucius entered the door, faced north, and bowed. Nanzi returned a bow behind the curtain—her jade jewelries and accessories made many sounds. [Later returning to his residence,] Confucius said: "I wished that I did not have to meet with Lady Nanzi. But since the meeting had to take place, I followed all ritual propriety during our meeting." Zilu was still displeased. Confucius sighed: "If I did anything contrary to rituals, may Heaven despise me! May Heaven despise me!" Confucius stayed in the State of Wei 衛 for over a month. One day Duke Ling and Lady Nanzi rode in the same carriage in an outing. They made official Yong Qu 雍渠 participate in the ride and asked Confucius to follow in the next carriage. The carriages drove passed the city and market ostentatiously. Confucius lamented: "I have yet to meet someone who desires virtues as much as he desires a woman's physical beauty." Feeling ashamed, he left the State of Wei.[8]

Clearly, Nanzi was eager to exercise her influence on state affairs—calling herself the "little king" (*xiao jun* 小君) and demanding Confucius to pay honor to her. Having heard that she engaged in inappropriate sexual relations with multiple men, including Duke Ling's son (a clear violation of proper rituals), Confucius declined the meeting at first; however, with a thin hope to meet with Duke Ling and to persuade him to govern by virtue, he reluctantly met with Nanzi. Confucius eventually left the State of Wei after realizing that Duke Ling was too corrupt to consider humane government. Confucius's lamentation that "I have yet to meet someone who desires virtues as much as he desires a woman's physical beauty" would provide the authors of the *Nü sishu* an important foundation in upholding that the real beauty of a woman (*fu rong* 婦容) rests on her inner virtue, not her outward appearance.

2.2 Liu Xiang's *Lienü zhuan* (*Biographies of Women*)

Another important source that informs us about Confucius's view of women is the *Lienü zhuan* 《列女傳》(*Biographies of Women*), composed by Liu Xiang 劉向 (77 BCE–6 BCE), a court historian and Confucian scholar of the Western Han dynasty.[9] Liu's *Lienü zhuan*, the first of its genre that has inspired many other writings of biographies of women in the following two millennia, provides quasi-historical records of 109 women, of which ninety-four are virtuous persons and fifteen are licentious characters.[10] Mencius's mother is among the ninety-four virtuous cases. *Lienü zhuan* originally comprises seven volumes: (1) *Muyi* 母儀 ("Model Motherhood"), (2) *Xianming* 賢明 ("Virtuous Intelligence"), (3) *Renzhi* 仁智 ("Humaneness and Wisdom"), (4) *Zenshun* 貞順 ("Chastity and Obedience"), (5) *Jieyi* 節義 ("Integrity and Righteousness"), (6) *Biantong* 辯通 ("Penetrating Rhetorical Skills"), and (7) *Niebi* 孽嬖 ("The Evil and Spoiled"). Later scholars added another twenty biographies as volume 8, called *Xu lienü zhuan* 續列女傳 ("Supplemental Biographies of Women").

While gender-oppressive practices often derived from ritual traditions, many women in these biographies exercised ritual propriety (*li* 禮) in innovative manners as powerful means to protect their autonomy and to counter the societal and familial pressure of marriage or remarriage. One reads, for example, that a woman of the State of Shen 申 in the Zhaonan 召南 region was about to marry a man of Feng 酆. But her future matrimonial family planned to bring her to the new household without properly following the six marriage rites.[11] She refused the marriage unyieldingly, arguing that the husband–wife relationship is the most fundamental of all human relations. If the root is incorrectly planted, the harm that is done will be insurmountable. Therefore, the marital ritual must be carried out completely and properly. Her future husband's family sued her in court. She firmly stated in response: "If one thing is incomplete or one rite is unprepared, my integrity shall not be compromised because of it. Even if death comes, I shall not marry."[12] In a similar vein, one reads that Woman Cai 蔡人之妻, Lady Boying 伯嬴, Widow Taoying of Lu 魯寡陶嬰, and Duke Weixuan's wife 衛宣夫人, among others, exercised personal integrity and ritual propriety in resisting their male suitors' requests, as well as family pressure to remarry.[13] We also learn in the *Lienü zhuan* that many women from different walks of life (whether they were young girls or elderly women) outsmarted men and emperors in political affairs, as well as in military strategy. Some of them—for example, Zhong Lichun 鐘離春, Woman "Large Tumor" (Suliunü 宿瘤女)—were extremely unattractive by conventional standards.[14] By exercising impressive rhetorical skills, these women not only confronted their husbands, sons, and emperors about their misdeeds and short-sightedness but also provided them with wise counsel on how to remedy these problems.[15]

Even though Liu Xiang's real intention may have been to use the *Lienü zhuan* as metaphor to criticize the political corruption of his time by means of citing historical examples of virtuous and licentious women, the value of *Lienü zhuan* in our study of the history and the philosophy of women in the Chinese tradition remains considerable. Furthermore, considering that the *Lienü zhuan* was composed more than two thousand years ago, it is worth noting that even though Liu Xiang was bound by the ultra-conservative values of *sancong side* 三從四德 (three womanly obediences and four womanly virtues), he was independent enough to author biographies for women and to acknowledge their exemplary wisdom, integrity, intelligence, and talents in the social and political realms.

The *Lienü zhuan* often cites Confucius. Volume 1, *Muyi* ("Model Motherhood"), chapter 9 (Lu Ji Jingjiang 魯季敬姜), for example, recorded that Confucius held Lady Jingjiang of the Ji clan in the State of Lu in high regard. She was the wife of court official Gongfu Mubo 公父穆伯 and the mother of Prime Minister Wenbo 文伯. Commenting on her frugality and diligence even after her son became the prime minister, Confucius said: "My students: remember this. This lady of Ji does not indulge in extravagance."[16] Lady Jingjiang's husband died early. Later, when her son passed away, she strongly admonished her daughters-in-law that they should not starve themselves to death and that the funeral must be simple, according to proper rituals. Upon hearing this, Confucius commented: "The wisdom of a young girl is not as great as that of an adult woman, and the wisdom of a young boy is not as good as that of an adult man. Gongfu's wife is wise. She wants to illuminate her son's virtue."[17] Lady Jingjiang mourned her husband in the morning and her son in the evening. Confucius heard about this and again praised her for knowing ritual, expressing affection without bias, and handling affairs with proper order.[18] Volume 6, *Biantong* ("Penetrating Rhetorical Skills"), chapter 6 (Agu chunü 阿谷處女), recorded that Confucius and his students encountered a young girl who was washing clothes in a mountain valley. Confucius sent his student, Zigong 子貢, to initiate a conversation. This young girl handled their questions calmly and wisely. According to the record, Confucius praised her: "This woman understands human feelings and proper ritual."[19] In both accounts, these women were praised for their wisdom and virtue, *not* for their domestic skills. In addition, Confucius advised his students (all male) to take note and learn from these women. Contrary to received opinion, these episodes support an *alternative* reading of Confucian philosophy of women—namely that women's intelligence was not necessarily frowned upon in early Confucianism. Rather, strong character, argumentative talent, and reasoning ability in a woman were valued just as highly as her skills in household management.

Nonetheless, one may still take issue with certain statements that were historically attributed to Confucius. There is, for example, the much-debated *Analects* 8.20:

> [Sage King] Shun 舜 had five ministers and all under Heaven was well governed, and King Wu 武王 [of Zhou 周] said: "I have ten ministers

> who are skilled in government." Master Kong commented: "Is it not true that talent is hard to find? At the time of Shun's accession things are thought to have flourished, and with a woman among King Wu's ministers, there were in fact only nine men [alternatively, ministers]."[20]

And, the infamous *Analects* 17.23:

> Only women (*nüzi* 女子, alternatively concubines or young girls) and morally inferior men (*xiaoren* 小人, or servants,) seem difficult to care for. If you keep them close, they become insubordinate; but if you keep them at a distance, they become resentful.[21]

It is easier, in my view, to defend *Analects* 8.20 than to defend *Analects* 17.23. One could argue that 8.20 is not necessarily a sexist statement. What Confucius meant was to point out that out of the ten ministers employed by King Wu, one was a woman or that a woman does not amount to a minister in the traditional sense whose role is essentially to administer "external" affairs while a woman's role is to manage "internal" affairs. This is a restatement of the codified division of labor. Thus, King Wu of Zhou only had nine ministers. *Analects* 17.23, however, is much more difficult to explain away. Even if one interprets this passage more charitably (taking *nüzi* as referring to concubines or young girls, not women in general), it is still puzzling why no similar comments are made about men or young boys.[22]

In addition to Confucius and Liu Xiang, what did other Confucians say about women and how did they influence society's perception of women?

2.3 Dong Zhongshu's Radical Transformation of Early Confucianism

Early Confucianism underwent a radical transformation in the Han dynasty (206 BCE–220 CE) due to Dong Zhongshu 董仲舒 (c. 179 BCE–104 BCE). Dong was not only a scholar but also a chief minister to Emperor Wu of Han 漢武帝 (r. 140 BCE–87 BCE). He played an instrumental role to convince Emperor Wu in making Confucianism the state philosophy (or, better, ideology) of Han in 136 BCE. But Dong's Confucianism was *not* the Confucianism presented by Confucius or Mencius; rather, it was deeply entrenched in the *Yinyang Wuxing* 陰陽五行 theory. For instance, a theoretical and political move of "honoring *yang*, denigrating *yin*" occurred in Han's attempt to legitimize its political authority as a mandate of Heaven, after defeating the short-lived Qin 秦 dynasty (221 BCE–207 BCE), by means of aligning Han with *yang* (and the earth, or fire, element) and distancing itself from Qin, which identified itself with *yin* (and the water element).[23] Moreover, based on classical Confucian texts before the early Han, the personal, the familial, the social, and the political are regarded as co-related concentric circles moving toward the goal of what Roger T. Ames calls a "radial and centripetal harmony."[24] Concurrently, the reciprocal familial relationships rooted in *ren* 仁 (humaneness) and their correspondingly manifested virtues are regarded as normative models for relations in the comparatively more distant public realm. Dong replaced these reciprocal relationships, best known in the form of Mencius's "five relationships" (*wulun*) (*Mencius* 3A:4), "there should be affection between father and son, righteousness between ruler and subject, distinction between husband and wife, proper order between the old and the young, and trustworthiness between friends" with the autocratic and patriarchal "three bonds" (*sangong* 三綱)—namely "the authority of the ruler over the minister, the father over the son, and the husband over the wife,"[25] by identifying the minister, the son, and the wife with *yin*.

This hierarchical alignment of *yang* with ruler/father/male/husband and *yin* with subject/son/female/wife only began in the Han dynasty, and *not* in any of the earlier ancient or Confucian texts. Formerly, *yin* and *yang* were presented as a contrasting but interdependent and complementary pair: *yin* (the shady side of a hill, rain, clouds, contraction, stillness, receptive force, etc.) and *yang* (the sunny side of a hill, dryness, sun, expansion, movement, active force, etc.).[26] *Yin* and *yang* were different but equal.[27] Dong's school of Confucianism, often called Han Confucianism, departs from the classic reading of the *yin–yang* relation as two co-relative and mutually generating, complementary, interdependent, and transformational paradigms in favor of a bleak hierarchical and oppositional interpretation. For example, Dong writes: "one should esteem *yang* and despise *yin*."[28] Han Confucianism deploys this recast *yin-yang* theory not merely to reinterpret natural phenomena but, more importantly, to justify the sociopolitical domination by the ruler, the father, and the husband over the minister, the son, and the wife, as both a law of nature and a mandate from Heaven. Dong's *Luxuriant Dew of the Spring and Autumn Annals* (*Chunqiu fanlu* 《春秋繁露》), chapter 43 ("*Yang* the Venerable, *Yin* the Lowly"), expresses this politicized *yin–yang* metaphysics just as much:

> [W]hen counting days, one bases it on day, not on night. When counting years, one bases it on *yang*, not on *yin*. . . . [T]his is using Heaven's way as the measurement. A husband is *yang* even if he is base; a wife is *yin* even if she is noble. . . . The *Spring and Autumn Annals*, therefore, does not call out rulers' shortcomings nor does it speak of the ministers-subjects' merits. All merits belong to the rulers; all shortcomings belong to the minsters-subjects. . . . Hence, a filial son's conduct and a loyal

> minister's righteousness all model after Earth. Earth serves Heaven just like how those of the lower position serve those of the higher position.... Everything bad is *yin*; everything good is *yang*. ... Thus, it is said, *yang* is Heaven's virtue, and *yin* Heaven's punishment. *Yang qi* is warm, while *yin qi* is cold; *yang qi* gives, while *yin qi* takes; *yang qi* is humane, while *yin qi* is hostile.

Chapter 53 ("Basic Meaning") further adds:

> The righteous meaning of the ruler-minister, father-son, husband-wife relations is all taken from the way of *yin* and *yang*. The ruler is *yang* and the minister[-subject] is *yin*; the father is *yang* and the son is *yin*; the husband is *yang* and the wife is *yin*. The way of *yin* cannot act on its own: neither can it arise on its own at the beginning, nor can it share merits at the end.

The politically motivated "three bonds" and its concomitant symbolic control embedded in the authoritarian "husband, the ruler" vis-à-vis "wife, the subject" over the reciprocal Mencian five relationships is thus fully solidified in Han Confucianism, placing the subject, the son, and the wife in uncompromising subservient roles. The Han and later dynasties all suffered from this ominous reversal of paradigms. Owing to its historical proximity, Dong Zhongshu's influence is most evident in Ban Zhao's *Lessons for Women* (even in her choice of chapter titles).

2.4 Neo-Confucians and Zhu Xi on Women

The movement of Neo-Confucianism, a Confucian revival and response to the challenges posed by the popularity of Buddhism and Daoism, began in the ninth century with Han Yu (768–824) and Li Ao (772–841), reached its climate in the Song (960–1279) and Ming (1368–1644) dynasties, and continued in the Qing dynasty (1644–1911) through the early twentieth century. Neo-Confucians absorbed and syncretized (while criticizing) multiple Buddhist and Daoist elements into the Confucian apparatus, purged Confucianism of superstitions, and reestablished Confucianism as a school of rational thought equipped with practical moral and social philosophy and backed by a sophisticated metaphysics. Song–Ming Neo-Confucianism is generally regarded as a hyper-conservative philosophy and, as Tak-Ling Terry Woo has insightfully noted, its syncretism gravely undermined diversity and pluralism and put greater restrictions on women than its preceding dynasties.[29] Repudiation of widow remarrying depicted in Cheng

Yi's 程頤 (1033–1107) infamous statement: "to starve to death is a very small matter[;] [t]o lose one's integrity, however, is a very serious matter" well illustrates Song Neo-Confucians' conservative view on women's chastity.[30] Not all Song Neo-Confucians however, Julia Ching reminds us, held the same position. For instance, famous Song scholars and reformers Fan Zhongyan 范仲淹 (989–1052) and Wang Anshi 王安石 (1021–1086) held somewhat more liberal positions in comparison to Cheng Yi and Zhu Xi 朱熹 (1130–1200).[31] And, *not* all women were expected to adhere to such a high moral mandate. Even Cheng Yi and Zhu Xi (the most conservative of Song scholars) demonstrated flexibility in applying their ideas to real-life situations. For example, contrary to his declaration that a widow should not remarry, Cheng Yi praised his father for arranging the remarriage of a widowed grandniece.[32] Zhu Xi also was less rigid in his treatment of *real* women (vs. idealized women). A case in point is that, contrary to his student's stricter opinion, Zhu supported the ruling of a local magistrate in allowing a woman, following her parents' wishes, to return to her natal home because "her husband was too poor to support her."[33] Integrity was regarded as a paramount virtue by the Neo-Confucians. Under the influence of Neo-Confucianism, women's chastity as a gendered expression of integrity gradually became not just one of the many essential virtues (as in previous dynasties) but also the very epitome of female virtues. Promulgated by the widely implemented governmental honor-commending system (*jingbiao* 旌表), chastity gained even great fervor among Ming–Qing women.

In terms of his impact on China and Chinese cultural regions, Zhu Xi is easily ranked first among Neo-Confucians of the Song, Yuan, Ming, and Qing dynasties. He is best known for his selection and commentary on the *Four Books* (*Sishu* 《四書》), which were used as the standard textbooks in preparation for the imperial civil service examinations from 1313 to 1905. In addition, Ming Taizu (the founding emperor of Ming) relied on Zhu Xi's philosophy to restore social order and morality after the fall of the Yuan dynasty (1271–1368). Zhu's influence was especially pronounced in the Ming dynasty—a historical period during which two of the women authors of the *Nü sishu* lived. Zhu's Neo-Confucianism focuses particularly on moral cultivation. Following Confucius and especially Mencius, Zhu Xi affirms the innate goodness in human nature and the effect of habits. He distinguishes "original nature" (endowed good nature) from "physical nature" (nature affected by external conditions):

> [O]riginal nature is perfectly good. This is the nature described by Mencius as "good." . . . However, it will be obstructed if [our] physical

> nature contains impurity. . . . When we speak of the physical nature, we refer to principle [*li* 理] and [psycho-physical] force [*qi* 氣] combined.[34]

Thus, the purpose of "learning is to transform this material endowment."[35] For this reason, Zhu Xi also encourages women's learning so that they can become virtuous models for their children, relatives, and villagers. In the *Zhuzi yulei* 《朱子語類》 (*Classified Conversations of Zhu Xi*), where elementary learning for children was discussed, a student asked: "Since girls should also be educated, in addition to teaching them the *Classic of Filial Piety*, how about also teaching them selections from the *Analects* that are clear and easy to understand?" Zhu Xi replied: "That will do. Ban Zhao's *Lessons for Women* and Sima Guang's *Family Precepts* are good too."[36]

He upheld women's equal capacity to achieve the paramount Confucian virtue of humaneness.[37] The subjects, however, were limited because Zhu Xi still sees the inner–outer distinction between men and women as a weighty ritual mandate, and obedience as women's primary virtue.[38]

Still influenced by the Han Confucians' *yin-yang* hierarchy that was so ingrained in the Song consciousness, Zhu Xi's teaching on the *yin–yang* relation was one of inconsistency. On the one hand, following Zhou Dunyi's *Taijitu shuo* 《太極圖說》 (*Explanations of the Diagram of the Supreme/Great Ultimate*), he upholds the complementarity of *yang*/activity/male and *yin*/tranquility/female. On the other hand, women are construed unfairly as the inferior sex because of their *yin* nature. He states in his *Reflections on Things at Hand*: "Between man and woman, there is an order of superiority and inferiority, and between husband and wife, there is the principle of who leads and who follows. This is a constant principle."[39] In the *Further Reflections on Things at Hand*, women are advised to strictly adhere to their domestic roles:

> To do wrong is unbecoming to a wife, and to do good is also unbecoming to a wife. A woman is merely to be obedient to what is proper. If a daughter does nothing wrong, that is enough. If she does good, then likewise, that is neither a favorable nor a desirable thing. Only spirits and food are her concern, and not to occasion sorrow to her parents is all that is called for.[40]

Because family plays such an important role in a Confucian society, enculturation of obedience to authority often begins in the household. The political purpose of "three bonds" and subordination of women to men is clear when mapped against the "husband-ruler" and "wife-subject" symbolism. How does one free Confucianism from the distortion that began in the Han dynasty and continues to exercise its influence? I venture to suggest that, after deconstructing, a more constructive approach to our creative task of rereading the canons is to turn our attention to the core teachings of Confucian philosophy that have not been distorted by later Confucians. In other words, if we are to regard the authors of the *Nü sishu* as forerunners of Chinese feminism, what could have inspired these woman authors and those who came before or after them? Since much comparative work has already been done on Confucian *ren* 仁 (humaneness) vis-à-vis the feminist ethics of care,[41] in what follows I will instead turn to the highly contentious notion of *li* 禮 (ritual) as an example in my appropriation of the feminist potential of Confucianism.

2.5 *Li* (禮 ritual) and the Image of the Feminine

Because of his belief that "human beings are by nature similar to one another; it is due to habits that they become far apart,"[42] Confucius is a strong advocate for the accessibility of education and learning. *Analects* 15.39 reads: "In education, there should be no class distinction."[43] A Confucian curriculum stresses moral education and the six arts (*liuyi* 六藝) and ritual is one of them. Among the principal virtues discussed in the *Analects, li* (ritual propriety, ritual, rites) is regarded as important as humaneness (*ren* 仁), righteousness (*yi* 義), wisdom (*zhi* 智), and filial piety (*xiao* 孝). *Li* is mentioned more than one hundred times in the *Analects*. One reads, for example, "if one is forthright but does without ritual, then one becomes rude" (*Analects* 8.2);[44] "to [control] oneself and return to ritual is to practice humaneness" (*Analects* 12.1);[45] "righteousness the gentleman regards as the essential stuff and the rites are his means of putting it into effect" (*Analects* 15.18);[46] "One is roused by poetry, established by ritual, and perfected by music" (*Analects* 8.8);[47] "If [one does] not study the rites, [one] will have no way of taking [one's] stand" (*Analects* 16.3);[48] "when parents are alive, serve them according to proper rituals; when they are dead, bury them according to ritual propriety" (*Analects* 2.5).[49]

Moreover, *li* is regarded as a superior way to govern as opposed to legal sanction or punishment. The latter is often regarded as having a masculine and militant undertone:

> If one leads the people by means of government and keeps order among them by means of punishments, the people will try to avoid the punishments but without shame. If one leads the people by means of virtue and keeps order among them by means of ritual, they will have a sense of conscience and moreover they will arrive at the good that one tries to lead them to. (*Analects* 2.3)[50]

Furthermore,

> If rituals and music do not flourish, then laws and punishment will not hit the mean. If laws and punishments do not hit the mean, then the people will not know where to put their hands and feet. (*Analects* 13.3)[51]

The importance of *li* to Confucian ethics and social-political philosophy is evident. One further point about *li* in the *Analects* warrants attention. *Analects* 3.8 clearly associates *li* with the image of the *feminine*:

> Zixia 子夏 asked: what is the meaning of this passage [from the *Book of Songs*]? "Fine looking smile is lovely. Beautiful eyes have an attractive gaze. Plain silk is to be adorned to become finery." Confucius said: "The work of painting comes after the plain silk." Zixia further asked: "Does ritual comes after?" Confucius replied, "Shang 商 [Zixia's other name] is the one who can penetrate my teaching. Now I can talk about the *Book of Songs* with him."[52]

The image of the feminine, the perfecting function of *li*, and the teaching on the continuity of the personal, the social, and the political as three concentric circles are repeated in the *Daxue* 《大學》 (*Great Learning*). Note how the images of the *feminine* (a *mother*, a *wife*, and a *young girl*) are explicitly deployed as symbols of *virtuous rulers* in the following passage. Moreover, in line with *Analects* 2.21, the normative priority of the *nei* 內 (the internal) over the *wai* 外 (the external)—thus the primacy of self-cultivation and the household preceding the social and the political—is also explicitly made.[53]

> What is meant by "In order to rightly govern the state, it is necessary first to regulate the family" is this: It is not possible for one to teach others, while he cannot teach his own family. Therefore, the ruler, without going beyond his family, completes the lessons for the state. . . . In the *Announcement to Kang* [*Kanggao* 《康誥》], it is said, "Act as if you were watching over an infant." If a *mother* is really anxious about it, even though *she* may not know exactly the wants of her infant, she will not be far from doing so. There never has been *a girl* who learned how to bring up a child so that she might afterwards marry. From the loving example of one *family* a whole *state* becomes loving, and from its courtesies the whole state becomes courteous; while, from the ambition and perverseness of the one man, the whole state may be led to rebellious disorder. Such is the nature of the influence. . . . Thus we see how the government

> of the state depends on the regulation of the family. In the [*Classic*] *of Poetry* [the *Shijing* 《詩經》], it is said, "That peach tree, so delicate and elegant! How luxuriant is its foliage! This *girl* is going to her husband's house. *She* will rightly order *her household*." Let *the household* be rightly ordered, and then *the people of the state* may be taught.[54]

These passages provide notable evidence that classical Confucian canons contain latent materials amenable to feminist concerns.

3. *The* Nü sishu*: What Did Confucian Women Say About Women?*

How do Confucian women perceive their own identity and how do these women teach other women about women's roles in the household and in the social and political realms of a Confucian society? It is true that the "inner–outer distinction" (*neiwai zhibie*), and the "three obediences and four womanly virtues" (*sancong side*), first appeared in the *Liji* 《禮記》 (*Record of Rites*).[55] Nonetheless, the *Liji* also made it clear that childhood education for both genders was essential. In addition, women played an important role in early childhood education as children's first teachers before these children reached the age of ten.[56] Unlike other Confucian canonical texts, the *Nü sishu* (*Four Books for Women*) are unique in that these texts were written by women authors specifically for women's education. Who were these women and why did they write?

The following sections (3.1 and 3.2) intend to provide a brief overview of the authors and the contents of the *Nü sishu*. A fuller biography of the authors, the cultural historical background in which each book is composed, and a more detailed guide for each book can be found in the translator's introductions immediately preceding each book.

3.1 The Authors of the *Nü Sishu* 《女四書》

The author of *Nüjie* (*Lessons for Women*) was Ban Zhao (c. 45–117), born of a family of scholars and officials. She was the first woman historian in Chinese history, and was quite knowledgeable in astronomy, geography, and poetry. Her father (Ban Biao 班彪) and older brother (Ban Gu 班固) were both famous historians, and her brother was the main author of the *Hanshu* 《漢書》 (*Book of Han*). But both passed away before this monumental work could be completed. Emperor He of the Eastern Han dynasty 漢和帝 summoned Ban Zhao to complete this unfinished work. She traveled to the imperial library to research and eventually brought the work to fruition. In addition to the *Hanshu* and *Nüjie*,

Ban Zhao authored many other works. She married her husband (surname, Cao) at the age of fourteen, and became a widow at a very young age. Owing to her broad learning and moral integrity, she was again called upon by Emperor He to serve at the imperial court as the teacher of the empress, imperial concubines, princes, and princesses. Ban Zhao was often referred to by her honorary title "Cao Dagu" 曹大家 (大家, pronounced as *da-gu*), which means "a great woman-teacher from the Cao family."[57]

Song Ruoxin (?–820) and Song Ruozhao (?–825) were the authors of the *Nü lunyu* (*Analects for Women*). They were two of the five daughters of a well-known Tang dynasty Confucian scholar, Song Tingfen 宋廷棻. Both sisters were famous Tang female scholars. Emperor Dezong of Tang often summoned them to participate in literary events and to expound the meaning of the classics and historical records at the imperial court. The two sisters were also charged with the tasks of managing the imperial library and documents. Over their lifetimes, the two sisters served five emperors and were given high-ranking official titles including *Xue Shi* 學士 and *Shang Gong* 尚宮. People also addressed them as *Xian Sheng* 先生 ("sir," "teacher"). Both sisters chose the untraditional path of remaining single, and they devoted their lives to teaching and their work in the imperial court.[58]

Empress Renxiaowen of Ming (maiden name Xu, 1361–1407) authored the *Neixun* (*Teachings for the Inner Court*). She was well-learned and known for her filial piety and her courage in protecting the capital city when it was under attack by the enemy force, while her husband and the troops were engaged in a battle in distant areas. She often advised her husband, Emperor Chengzu 明成祖 (i.e., the Yongle Emperor 永樂皇帝), known for his quick temperament in using force, to practice humane governance. Empress Renxiaowen was not only a Confucian but also a devout Buddhist. The *Neixun* was regarded by some scholars as the most comprehensive and well-reasoned work among the *Nü sishu*. In addition to the *Neixun*, she authored several other Confucian texts and Buddhist texts. When she passed away, Emperor Chengzu bestowed on her the honorary title of "Humaneness" (*ren* 仁) and "Filial Piety" (*xiao* 孝), in addition to her literary achievements (*wen* 文), thus the name Renxiaowen Empress.[59]

Chaste Widow Wang (also known as Madame Liu, c. 16th century), who composed the *Nüfan jielu* (*Short Records of Models for Women*), the last book of the *Nü sishu*, also lived during the Ming dynasty. Liu was the mother of Wang Xiang, a Ming scholar and the compiler and annotator of the *Nü sishu*. From her son's introduction, one learns that Liu's husband passed away early in their marriage when she was only thirty years old. She went through considerable hardship as a widow, raised the young Wang Xiang, and remained chaste for sixty years. To commemorate her virtue of chastity, some famous high-ranking officials honored her in public for her exemplary virtue.[60] Although not coming from an elite family, Liu was nonetheless well-versed in the classics, as evidenced by her writings and her citation of more than one hundred and fifty examples of women from Liu Xiang's *Biographies of Women* and other texts in her *Nüfan jielu*.

3.2 The Contents of the *Nü Sishu* 《女四書》

Ban Zhao mentioned in her introduction to the *Nüjie* (*Lessons for Women*) that it had now been over forty years since she married her husband at the age of fourteen. Therefore, Ban Zhao was probably in her fifties when she composed this work. Since Ban Zhao was born in 45 CE, the *Nüjie* can be dated to around the last decade of the first century or the first few years of the second century, approximately one hundred years after Liu Xiang's *Biographies of Women*.

The *Nüjie*, influenced by Dong Zhongshu (see section 2.3), is the most conservative of the *Nü sishu*. This is somewhat surprising when one considers Ban Zhao's quite unconventional life journey and career path as a woman in first-century feudal China. Ban Zhao explained that her motivation for writing the *Nüjie* was to provide marriage advice to her daughters. Thus, the contents of the work are limited to three areas: (a) how to serve one's husband, (b) how to serve one's parents-in-law, and (c) how to get along with one's sisters- and brothers-in-law. She endorsed strict adherence to the four womanly conducts (a.k.a. *side*, including woman's virtue, woman's speech, woman's appearance, and woman's work). She even cited an extremely conservative ancient text, the *Nüxian* 《女憲》 (*Decrees for Women*), stating that "to win the heart of one man is the completion of [a woman's] eternal end; to lose the heart of one man is to suffer the eternal separation from him" (*Nüjie*, chapter 5).[61] More progressive topics included in Liu Xiang's *Biographies of Women* that affirm women's wisdom, intelligence, and rhetorical skills—such as "virtuous intelligence," "humaneness and wisdom," and "penetrating rhetorical skills"—were dropped in Ban Zhao's *Nüjie* (see appendix). This is clearly a big step backward in the advance of women's causes. Still, one finds some insights in the *Nüjie* that could support feminist causes. For example, based on the Confucian emphasis on equal access to education and the importance of respecting proper rituals, Ban Zhao made a strong argument for woman's education:

> Yet only to educate men and not to educate women—are they not being partial in their treatment of the two sides? According to the *Record of Rituals*, at the age of eight, children should begin receiving instructions on the classics. At the age of fifteen, they should receive adult education. Why should [women's education] alone not follow this as a principle? (*Nüjie*, chapter 2)

Ban Zhao also argued against domestic violence, verbal abuse, and physical beating of a wife on the grounds of ritual respect and conjugal love (*Nüjie*, chapter 3). Furthermore, she insisted that beauty must come from within (not based on physical attraction that in part depends on luck and can easily disappear at an old age). She articulated firmly that "woman's appearance requires neither a beautiful nor a splendid look or form; . . . Wash clothes that are dusty and soiled, and keep one's clothing and accessories always fresh and clean. Take bath regularly, and keep one's body free from filth and disgrace. This is what is meant by woman's bearing" (*Nüjie*, chapter 4).

The Song sisters' *Nü lunyu* (*Analects for Women*) was composed approximately in the beginning of the ninth century, several hundred years after Ban Zhao's *Nüjie*. Although the Song sisters were among the elite women of Tang, they wrote the *Nü lunyu* to provide an education manual for the common people. This work expands the outlines of "four womanly virtues" laid out in Ban Zhao's *Nüjie* and codifies them in everyday conduct. Even though the *Nü lunyu* did not break much new ground, and the numerous precepts prescribed for women's proper behavior could be stifling at times, the *Nü lunyu*'s contributions were at least threefold: (1) The work was written in a simpler style and in idiomatic language; accordingly, it was more accessible to non-elite women. (2) The scope of its subjects was broader than Ban Zhao's *Nüjie*, covering instructions for women's self-cultivation, home economics, children's education, hospitality, and community relations. (3) It argued that in serving one's husband, "should he slide into evil ways, the wife ought to remonstrate with him repeatedly" (*Nü lunyu*, chapter 7); and, "the authority to instruct children belongs primarily to the mother" (*Nü lunyu*, chapter 8). The latter includes selecting good teachers, preparing honorariums, and so on. Item (1) promulgates literacy among non-elite women. Items (2) and (3) are welcome affirmations of women's relative autonomy, as well as comparative authority in the household and a rebuttal of blind obedience to one's husband or son. In addition, while *Nüjie* emphasizes spousal respect and marital hierarchy, *Nü lunyu* stresses conjugal love and mutual dependence.

The *Neixun* (*Teachings for the Inner Court*) was composed in the early fifteenth century, more than one millennium after Ban Zhao's *Nüjie* (*Lessons for Women*) and several hundred years after Song sisters' *Nü lunyu* (*Analects for Women*). In her preface to the *Neixun*, Empress Renxiaowen explained that education for both men and women are important. But proper education requires good methods.[62] And yet, a complete work that contains suitable teaching materials for girls and women was lacking. She wrote that Ban Zhao's *Nüjie* was too simple and some other ancient texts were no longer in existence. She lamented that even though Zhu Xi compiled a work called *Xiao xue* 《小學》 (*Elementary Learning*), it was not suitable for women's education. This is because women in feudal China were educated separately from men and the two genders had different realms of responsibilities based on the division of labor.[63] These concerns motivated her to write the *Neixun*, aiming at educating women of the imperial court. Later, this work was made available to the public by several emperors' decree.

In comparison with the *Lessons for Women* and the *Analects for Women*, the *Teachings for the Inner Court* broke new ground. In addition to being a much lengthier work, the topics ranged from personal cultivation and management of the household, to the social and the political. It explicitly cited Confucius and the *Analects* several times.[64] It also referenced the *Record of Rites* and Liu Xiang's *Biographies of Women*. For example, in chapter 3, even though Empress Renxiaowen affirmed the conservative "four womanly virtues" (*side*), she (like Ban Zhao) also argued that:

> [A] woman should not be haughty about her physical beauty; what matters is her virtue. Even though Wu Yan 無鹽 [i.e., Zhong Lichun] was physically unattractive, her words when used to govern the State of Qi 齊 brought peace and stability to the country. Confucius said: "One who has virtue will necessarily have words. One who has words may not necessarily have virtue." (*Neixun*, chapter 3)

In this passage, the empress cited Zhong Lichun from Liu Xiang's *Biographies of Women*, a commoner who was physically unattractive but known for her intelligence and rhetorical skills. Zhong Lichun dared to request an audience with King Xuan of Qi 齊宣王 in person. She criticized the king's mistakes in government during their meeting. Her words shamed the king and inspired him to correct his ways. Zhong later became the king's wife. Empress Renxiaowen also cited Confucius and *Analects* 14.5 in her praise of Zhong's forthrightness and integrity.

Several chapters in the *Teachings for the Inner Court* praise the importance of women's domestic work and how they contributed to the stability of the nation, linking the personal and the familial with the social and the political. One reads: "women assist the nation from the inside";[65] "the founding of a country has always relied on the virtue of inner helpmates";[66] "[l]ooking back at ancient times, it had never been the case that the rise and the fall of a nation did not depend on whether women were virtuous."[67] Therefore, "one can infer from this, inner harmony brings outer harmony. The harmony of a family brings the harmony of a country. The harmony of a country brings the harmony of the world. How can one not weigh it heavily?"[68] Thus, the teaching on the continuity of the inner and the outer and the normative priority of the household found in the *Analects* and the *Great Learning* discussed earlier in this chapter provides strong textual authority for Empress Renxiaowen not only to teach women the importance of self-cultivation and household management but also to acknowledge their contribution to the state by virtue of their domestic work.

Madame Liu's *Nüfan jielu* (*Short Records of Models for Women*) was composed in the sixteenth century, approximately one hundred years after Empress Renxiaowen's *Neixun*. She wrote the work to encourage women who are confined to the inner quarters not to despair but to draw inspiring lessons from historically exemplary women: "A person who uses a bronze as mirror can rectify her clothes and cap; a woman who uses history as her teacher can surely find worthy role models. If she can take the ancients as her teachers, there is no reason she should be worried that her virtue is not cultivated" (chapter 1). The *Short Records of Models for Women* cites more than one hundred and fifty cases of model women (far surpassing the number of cases quoted in the other three books) and is the most outspoken book of the *Nü sishu*. The opening chapter immediately argues for a bold thesis that women's education is *more important than* men's:

> If children are not educated when they are young, they will be disrespectful and will neglect rituals when they become adults. Males can still benefit from their teachers and friends [from outside] to complete their virtue. Where can females select good role models to correct their mistakes? Therefore, the way of women's education is even more important than men's. The correct model of the inner realm is prior to that of the external realm. (*Nüfan jielu*, chapter 1)

Chapter 2 ("Queenly Virtues") affirms the duty and the importance of an empress in wisely assisting the king (echoing Empress Renxiaowen's *Neixun*), "From the ancient times, great emperors who founded a nation must have had wise empresses." Chapter 3 ("Model Motherhood") illustrates the temporal priority of the maternal influence on the education of a child before a father's teaching: "From ancient times, when virtuous wise women are pregnant, they are prudent in prenatal education. Thus, model motherhood is prior to the teaching of a father."

The chapter on "Loyalty and Righteousness" makes a strong case with regard to women's courage. The chapter cites twenty-four examples of model women, including the following:

> The old saying goes: "all under Heaven are the ministers of the emperor." How could it be that in the inner quarters of women, there is no loyalty and righteousness? . . . When Jiang You 江油 surrendered to the [enemy] State of Wei, the defense general's wife would not survive [in shame] with him . . . Lady Zhu 朱夫人 helped build the city wall to defend the City of

> Xiangyang 襄陽 and warded off the Qin 秦 soldiers. Madame Liang 梁夫人 climbed Jin Mountain 金山 to beat the martial drums [to encourage the troop] and thus defeated the invading Jin 金 soldiers. . . . Lady Xie 謝夫人 was willing to be captured by the enemies in order to save her people. (*Nüfan jielu*, chapter 6)

Furthermore, citing multiple examples from Liu Xiang's *Biographies of Women*, Madame Liu argues that ritual propriety should apply to both men and women equally. At times a woman must use ritual propriety (*li*) as a means to defend her rights and to awaken her male counterparts.[69] Owing to women's sensitivity to context, Liu also asserts that in handling emergencies and sudden changes, "a wise woman surpasses a man."[70]

The book concludes with a chapter on women's talents and virtues where Liu skillfully debunks a commonly held sexist belief—"without talent is a woman's virtue" 女子無才便是德—often used by societies to deprive women's access to learning and opportunities. By a *reductio ad absurdum*, Liu adeptly exposed the absurdity of her opponents' position. She wrote that if the statement "without talent is a women's virtue" were true, then it would imply: (1) all women without talent are all virtuous, (2) all virtuous women must all lack talent, (3) all women without virtue must all be talented, and (4) all women with talent must all lack virtue. But surely, none of the above is true. To drive her point home, Liu argued that anyone who is familiar with history would see that Ban Zhao, Empress Renxiaowen, the Song sisters, and Madame Zheng 鄭氏 (author of the *Nü xiaojing* 《女孝經》, *Filial Piety for Women*), among many others, were examples of real-life women who were not only talented but also exemplary in their virtue.[71]

4. Conclusion

This chapter has examined Confucius's encounters with women, the *Analects*, the *Lienü zhuan*, and the *Nü sishu*. We find that Confucius's teaching, particularly on education and ritual respect, laid an important foundation for normative didactic writings by later authors, intended specifically for women's education. These later works acknowledge women's contributions to the well-being of society and the state. The contents, purposes, and emphases of the *Nü sishu* vary, at times quite considerably. Nonetheless, these women writers found inspiration from the Confucian canon in developing their own understanding of women's identity. Ranging from the first century to the sixteenth century, these women authors appropriated Confucian values and formulated arguments therein to defend women's rights and to empower women as much as each author saw fit, even under the constraints of an extremely conservative feudal society in imperial

China. One observes a progression from the earliest book of the *Nü sishu* to the latest of the four. The topics were broadened, the tones became firmer, and the arguments were sharpened. These works built on the lived experience of real women. Many others after them have found strength and encouragement in these lived narratives.

Some of the views in the *Nü sishu* may seem antiquated by today's standards. And yet, in finding our own ways amid the structural constraints even in modern times, we owe much to the pioneering work of these inspiring women thinkers. How should a modern woman recognize that her true worth and beauty lie in strong character, not in physical attractiveness? How does one negotiate sexual and gender equality when things do not necessarily work out in a fifty/fifty division of everything? How does one effect a structural change in a deeply seated patriarchal ideology from within? How does one persuade one's opponents in their own terms? The *Nü sishu* provides us with compelling thought that can inform our own creative strategies.

This is *not* to suggest that Confucius is a feminist or "Confucianism as is" is a feminist philosophy. We need to constantly reread, reappropriate, and reimagine canonical texts in order to enrich the dynamic growth of traditions. This is, however, quite different from suggesting the tradition's total eradication. In other words, we need to be careful in our critique of Confucian ideology, so as to separate politicized Confucianism from the essential teachings of classic Confucianism as a philosophy.

The argument presented in this chapter is that a rereading of the canons in consideration of contemporary feminist concerns does not do violence to these texts. Rather, there are hidden threads of thought in need of contextualized reappropriation in order to reveal their relevance to the audience of different times and ages. The women authors of the *Nü sishu* did exactly this with their own historically situated consciousness. It is therefore essential for modern readers to *see* these women (and their appropriation of Confucian traditions) not as helpless passive victims who could only perpetuate oppressive patriarchal values, but as independent thinkers who could articulate their aspirations in their own terms even under strenuous social constraints. To perceive these women writers simply as products of a patriarchal structure is to rob them of their voice, their struggle, and their triumph in their respective cultural and historical contexts. Such an attitude is self-defeating. It is self-defeating because it not only disrespects these women pioneers but also undermines the true spirit of sisterhood in feminist movement. This is why historical and cultural study is much needed in comparative philosophy in order to nourish a nuanced and ongoing discussion of gender dynamics in an intercultural setting. So far, little contemporary scholarship has been devoted to the *Nü sishu*. With this new translation, commentary, and annotations, I hope to excite a greater interest in this subject.[72]

---

1. An earlier, partial version of this introduction appeared in *Feminist Encounters with Confucius*, ed. Mathew A. Foust and Sor-hoon Tan (Leiden: Brill, 2016), 17–39. Materials reused here with Brill's permission per author's copyright.
2. See, for example, Audre Lorde, *Sister Outsider: Essays and Speeches* (Berkeley, CA: Crossing, 1984), repr., 2007; Gayatri Chakravorty Spivak, *In Other Words: Essays in Culture and Politics* (New York: Methuen, 1987); Chandra Talpade Mohanty, *Feminism without Borders: Decolonizing Theory, Practicing Solidarity* (Durham, NC: Duke University Press, 2003); Sandra Wawrytko, "Kongzi as Feminist: Confucian Self-cultivation in a Contemporary Context," *Journal of Chinese Philosophy* 27, no. 2 (2000): 171–86; Li-Hsiang Lisa Rosenlee, *Confucianism and Women: A Philosophical Interpretation* (Albany: State University of New York Press, 2006); Rosemarie Tong, *Feminist Thought: A More Comprehensive Introduction*, 3rd ed. (Boulder, CO: Westview, 2009). For important works on the history of Chinese women that aim to overturn the stereotypical view of medieval Chinese women as uneducated and weak, see Patricia Buckley Ebrey, *The Inner Quarters: Marriage and the Lives of Chinese Women in the Sung Period* (Berkeley and Los Angeles: University of California Press, 1993); Dorothy Ko, *Teachers of the Inner Quarter: Women and Culture in Seventeenth Century China* (Stanford, CA: Stanford University Press, 1994), among others.
3. See Julia Ching, "Sung Philosophers on Women," *Monumenta Serica* 42 (1994): 273–4; Wei-ming Tu, "Probing the 'Three Bonds' and 'Five Relationships' in Confucian Humanism," in *Confucianism and the Family*, ed. Walter H. Slote and George A. DeVos (Albany: State University of New York Press, 1998), 122–9; Sin Yee Chan, "The Confucian Conception of Gender in the Twenty-First Century," in *Confucianism for the Modern World*, ed. Daniel A. Bell and Chaibong Hahm (Cambridge: Cambridge University Press, 2003), 312–33; Ann A. Pang-White, "Zhu Xi on Family and Women: Challenges and Potentials," *Journal of Chinese Philosophy* 40, nos. 3–4 (2013): 439–40, rev. repr., in Ann A. Pang-White, ed., *The Bloomsbury Research Handbook of Chinese Philosophy and Gender* (London: Bloomsbury, 2016), 71–2.
4. There are various ways of pronouncing 曹大家. Here I follow the ancient pronunciation.
5. Even though the authenticity of the *Kongzi jiayu* 《孔子家語》 (*Family Discourse of Confucius*) and its authorship is widely debated among scholars, several newly unearthed archeological texts from China (e.g., the 1973 Hebei province Western Han tomb bamboo slips, the 1977 Anhui province Western Han tomb wood blocks), and the Shanghai Museum's Chu bamboo book of the Warring States

Period, demonstrate that the work is authentic. According to one account, the *Kongzi jiayu* was probably composed by students of the Confucian school. The earliest 27-volume version was lost during the imperially sanctioned book burning disaster of the Qin dynasty. During the Western Han dynasty, Confucius's descendants compared extant versions and edited the ten-volume version. Wang Shu of the Three Kingdoms period received this version, wrote an introduction, and provided notes and commentaries. This is the version that is in circulation now. For more information, see Wang Shu, *Kongzi jiayu* 《孔子家語》, trans. and ed. Pan Shuren 潘樹仁 (Hong Kong: Chunghwa shuju, 2013), 1–3; also Wang Shu, *Xinyi Kongzi jiayu* 《新譯孔子家語》, trans. and ed. Yang Chunqiu 羊春秋 (Taipei: Sanmin shuju, 2008), 1–4.

6. Wang Shu, *Kongzi jiayu*, volume 9, chapter 39, Benxingjie 本姓解 ("Explanation of the Origin of the Family Name"). See also Sima Qian, *Shiji* (*Historical Records*), volume 47, chapter 17, the Kongzi shijia ("Family Genealogy of Confucius"). Unless otherwise noted, all English translations (as well as any errors) throughout this introduction and this work are mine.
7. See Confucius, *Lunyu* (*Analects*) 16.13.
8. Chinese text is adopted from the Chinese Text Project, http://ctext.org/shiji/zh?searchu=%E5%8D%97%E5%AD%90#n6941.
9. An English translation of Liu Xiang's *Lienü zhuan* was recently published. See Ann Behnke Kinney, trans. and ed., *Exemplary Women of Early China: The Lienü Zhuan of Liu Xiang* (New York: Columbia University Press, 2014).
10. Most of the chapters contain biographies devoted to one individual. Occasionally, some chapters present two to three women. See, for example, volume 1, chapters 1 and 6; volume 4, chapter 12; volume 5, chapter 13.
11. See Chen Hao, *Liji jishuo*《禮記集說》(*Book of Rites with Collected Commentaries*) (Taipei: Shijie shuju, 2009), volume 10, chapter 44 (Hunyi), 324.
12. Liu Xiang, *Lienü zhuan* (*Biographies of Women*), volume 4, chapter 1 (Zhaonan Shennü 召南申女 ["Woman of Shen in the Zhaonan Region"]), in *Xinyi lienü zhuan* 《新譯列女傳》, 2nd ed., ed. and trans. Huang Qingquan 黃清泉 (Taipei: Sanmin shuju, 2008), 186.
13. Liu Xiang, *Lienü zhuan*, volume 4, chapters 3, 4, 9, 11, 13, and 15.
14. Ibid., volume 6, chapters 10, 11, and 12.
15. Ibid. See, for example, "Lady Fan of King Zhuang of Chu" 楚莊樊姬, "Queen Jiang of King Xuan of Zhou" 周宣姜后, and "Madame Liu Xiahui" 柳下惠妻 in volume 2 ("Virtuous Intelligence"); "Lady Jingjiang of Ji in Lu" 魯季敬姜, in volume 1 ("Model Motherhood").
16. Liu Xiang, in Huang Qingquan, *Xinyi leinü zhuan*, 42 (仲尼聞之曰：「弟子記之，季氏之婦不淫矣。」).
17. Ibid., 46 (仲尼聞之曰：「女知莫如婦，男知莫如夫，公父氏之婦知矣，欲明其子之令德。」).

18. Ibid., 47 (仲尼聞之曰：「季氏之婦可謂知禮矣，愛而無私，上下有章。」).
19. Ibid., 304 (孔子曰：「丘已知之矣。斯婦人達於人情而知禮。」).
20. Raymond Dawson, trans., *The Analects* (Oxford: Oxford University Press, 1993), 30. Some scholars have argued that this passage clearly denigrates women. See Xinyan Jiang, "Confucianism, Women, and Social Contexts," *Journal of Chinese Philosophy* 36, no. 2 (2009): 228–42. Others have argued otherwise. See Paul R. Goldin, "The View of Women in Early Confucianism," in *The Sage and the Second Sex: Confucianism, Ethics, and Gender*, ed. Chenyang Li (Chicago and La Salle: Open Court, 2000), 140; Lisa Raphals, "Gendered Virtue Reconsidered," also in *The Sage and the Second Sex*, 225.
21. Dawson, *The Analects*, 73 (with modification). Attempts to resolve the tension created by this text are many, including Chenyang Li's introduction to *The Sage and the Second Sex*, 3–4; Arthur Wiley, trans., *The Analects of Confucius* (New York: Random House, 1938), 217; Goldin, "View of Women," 139.
22. Here I agree with Jiang's assessment regarding the difficulty of *Analects* 17.23. See Jiang, "Confucianism," 230–1.
23. Depending on whether the mutual overcoming, or mutual generating, relation of the five elements is used, Han was identified with either the earth element or the fire element. For more, see Yuan Chen, "Legitimation Discourse and the Theory of Five Elements in Imperial China," *Journal of Song-Yuan Studies* 44 (2014): 328–9.
24. Roger T. Ames, "The Confucian World View: Uncommon Assumptions, Common Misconceptions," in *Asian Texts—Asian Contexts: Encounters with Asian Philosophies and Religions*, ed. David Jones and E. R. Klein (Albany: State University of New York Press, 2010), 45.
25. Tu, "Probing the 'Three Bonds,'" 122–9.
26. Robin R. Wang, *Yinyang: The Way of Heaven and Earth in Chinese Thought and Culture* (New York: Cambridge University, 2012), 1–39.
27. See, for example, the *Shijing*《詩經》, the *Zuozhuan*《左傳》, the *Guoyu*《國語》, the *Mozi*《墨子》, and the *Xunzi*《荀子》, the *Daodejing*《道德經》, the *Zhuangzi*《莊子》, the *Yijing*《易經》, the *Huainanzi*《淮南子》, the *Huangdi neijing*《黃帝內經》, among others. See also Rosenlee, *Confucianism and Women*, 50–5.
28. Dong Zhongshu, *Chunqiu fanlu*《春秋繁露》(*Luxuriant Dew of the Spring and Autumn Annals*), chapter 43, in Lai Yanyuan 賴炎元, ed. and tran., *Chunqiu fanlu jinzhu jinyi*《春秋繁露今註今譯》, 2nd edition (Taipei: Shangwu yinshuguan, 2010), 332.
29. Tak-Ling Terry Woo, "Discourses on Women from the Classical Period to the Song: An Integrated Approach," in Pang-White, *Bloomsbury Research Handbook*, 37–9, 61–2.

30. Wing-tsit Chan, trans., *Reflections on Things at Hand: The Neo-Confucian Anthology Compiled by Chu Hsi and Lu Tsu-Chien* (New York: Columbia University Press, 1967), 177.
31. Ching, "Sung Philosophers on Women," 260.
32. Chan, *Reflections on Things*, 179; Zhu Xi, *Zhuzi yulei* 《朱子語類》 (*Classified Conversations of Zhu Xi*) (Beijing: Zhonghua shuju, 1986), 2473.
33. Ibid., 2644; Ching, "Sung Philosophers on Women," 269–70; Pang-White, "Zhu Xi on Family and Women," 437–8.
34. Wing-tsit Chan, trans. and ed., *A Source Book in Chinese Philosophy* (Princeton, NJ: Princeton University Press, 1973), 624.
35. Ibid, 625.
36. Zhu Xi, *Zhuzi yulei*, 126–7.
37. Ibid., 57 and 1403. See also Wing-tsit Chan, *Zhuzi xintansuo* 《朱子新探索》 (*New Research on Zhu Xi*) (Taipei: Xuesheng shuju, 1988), 784.
38. This, however, does not mean women cannot reprimand their husbands. As will become clear, several women authors of the *Nü sishu* reappropriated the virtue of obedience.
39. Chan, *Reflections on Things*, 272.
40. Zhu Xi, *Xu jinsi lu* (*Further Reflections on Things at Hand*), in *Images of Women in Chinese Thought and Cultures: Writings from the Pre-Qin Period through the Song Dynasty*, ed. Robin R. Wang (Indianapolis: Hackett, 2003), 325.
41. See, for example, Chenyang Li, "The Confucian Concept of Jen and the Feminist Ethics of Care: A Comparative Study," *Hypatia: A Journal of Feminist Philosophy* 9, no. 1 (1994): 70–89; Lijun Yuan, "Ethics of Care and Concept of Jen: A Reply to Chenyang Li," *Hypatia* 17, no. 1 (2002): 107–29; Ranjoo Seodu Herr, "Is Confucianism Compatible with Care Ethics? A Critique," *Philosophy East and West* 53, no. 4 (2003): 471–89; Karyn L. Lai, *Learning From Chinese Philosophies: Ethics of Interdependent and Contextualised Self* (Aldershot and Burlington: Ashgate, 2006); Shirong Luo, "Relation, Virtue, and Relational Virtue: Three Concepts of Caring," *Hypatia* 22, no. 3 (2007): 92–110; Ann A. Pang-White, "Reconstructing Modern Ethics: Confucian Care Ethics," *Journal of Chinese Philosophy* 36, no. 2 (2009): 210–27; Ann A. Pang-White, "Caring in Confucian Philosophy," *Philosophy Compass* 6, no. 6 (2011): 374–84.
42. Confucius, *Analects* 17.2. My translation.
43. Chan, *A Source Book*, 44. See also *Analects* 7.7, where Confucius said that he never refuses teaching anyone who demonstrates some initiative.
44. Dawson, *Analects*, 28.
45. Ibid., 44 (with modification).
46. Ibid., 62 (with modification).
47. Ibid., 29 (with modification).
48. Ibid., 68. See also *Analects* 20.3.

49. My translation.
50. Dawson, *Analects*, 6 (with modification). A similar point is made in *Analects* 4.23.
51. Ibid, 49 (with modification).
52. My translation.
53. *Analects* 2.21: Someone said to Master Kong: "Why do you not take part in government?" The Master said: "*The Book of Documents* mentions filial piety, doesn't it? 'Only be dutiful towards your parents and friendly towards your brothers, and you will be contributing to the existence of government.' These virtues surely constitute taking part in government, so why should only that particular activity be regarded as taking part in government?" (Dawson, *Analects*, 8).
54. *Daxue* (*Great Learning*), paragraph 11, trans. James Legge, with modification, emphasis added, the Chinese Text Project, http://ctext.org/liji/da-xue.
55. See *Liji* (*Record of Rituals*), chapters 11, 12, and 44, English trans. by James Legge, *The Li ki,* in *Sacred Books of the East,* vols. 27–8, ed. F. Max Müller (Oxford: Clarendon Press, 1879–1910), available at http://ctext.org/liji.
56. Ibid., chapter 12. It is a misconception to think that ancient Chinese women were completely trapped in the inner quarters of the household and denied any access to education. See Ko, *Teachers of the Inner Chambers*.
57. See Fan Ye 范曄, *Houhanshu* 《後漢書》(*Book of the Later Han*), "Biographies of Women" (paragraphs 8–21), http://ctext.org/hou-han-shu/lie-nv-zhuan/zh; and Huang Yanli 黃嫣梨, ed., *Nü sishu jizhu yizheng* 《女四書集注義證》(*Four Books for Women with Selections from Traditional Commentaries*) (Hong Kong: Shangwu yinshuguan, 2008), 3–4.
58. Ibid., 33–4.
59. Ibid., 67–8.
60. Ibid., 167–8.
61. Ban Zhao, *Nüjie*, chapter 5.
62. Renxiaowen Huanghou, *Neixun* (*Teachings for the Inner Court*), preface and chapter 11, in *Nü sishu jizhu* (*Four Books for Women with Commentary*), edited by Wang Xiang (China: Wenchengtang, 1885).
63. Zhu Xi, too, was concerned that Ban Zhao's *Nüjie* was insufficient and had planned to commission his friend to edit a book for women's education. His friend unexpectedly passed away; the project therefore never came to fruition. See Zhu Xi, *Huian xiansheng Zhu wengong wenji*《晦庵先生朱文公文集》(*Collected Works of Sir Huian Zhu Wengong*) (Beijing: Beijing tushuguan chubanshe, 2006), book 35; Zhu Xi, *Zhuzi yulei*, volume 1, book 7; and Pang-White, "Zhu Xi on Family and Women," 443.
64. See Renxiaowen Huanghou, *Neixun*, chapters 3, 7, 12, and 16,
65. Ibid., chapter 8 (婦人內助於國家).
66. Ibid., chapter 10 (國家肇基，皆有內助之德。).
67. Ibid., chapter 13 (縱觀往古，國家廢興，未有不由於婦之賢否也。).

68. Ibid., chapter 17 (由是推之，內和而外和。一家和而一國和。一國和而天下和矣。可不重哉。).
69. Liu Shi, *Nüfan jielu*, chapter 8.
70. Ibid., chapter 9.
71. Ibid., chapter 11.
72. So far, only Robin R. Wang and Li-Hsiang Lisa Rosenlee have made brief references in their work to the *Nü sishu*. The only article-length research devoted to this subject is Terry Tak-Ling Woo's "Emotions and Self-Cultivation in *Nü Lunyu* 《女論語》 (*Women's Analects*)," *Journal of Chinese Philosophy* 36, no. 2 (2009): 334–47. However, Woo's article focuses only on the *Nü lunyu*, not on all four books of the *Nü sishu*.

BOOK I

The Han Women

Ban Zhao and the *Lessons for Women* (*Nüjie*): c. 45–117 CE

Translator's Introduction

1. The Author and the Work

By the late first century, and in addition to canonical Confucian classics, a few didactic texts considered especially suitable for teaching women, such as the *Decrees for Women* (*Nüxian* 《女憲》)[1] and Liu Xiang's *Biographies of Women* (*Lienü zhuan* 《列女傳》),[2] were in circulation. Nonetheless, Ban Zhao's 班昭 *Lessons for Women* (*Nüjie* 《女誡》), composed around 100 CE, was the earliest Chinese text known to be authored by a woman scholar and solely intended for women's education. The full text is included in Ban Zhao's biography in the *Book of Later Han* (*Houhanshu* 《後漢書》) and was widely studied following its publication.[3]

Later, several commentarial texts were produced, including one commissioned by Emperor Ming Shenzong 明神宗 (r. 1573–1620). Scholars generally agree that the *Lessons for Women* should be ranked as the *first* among all Chinese women's writings, in terms of both its chronology and its influence; later women writers either expanded its thesis or supplemented what was deficient in it. This work's long-lasting impact on Chinese women and culture is well attested by the number of existent commentarial texts and its inclusion in many important anthologies of later times, including Tao Zongyi's 陶宗儀 *Compendium of Famous Writings* (*Shuofu* 《說郛》), Wang Xiang's *Four Books for Women* (*Nü shishu* 《女四書》), Chen Hongmou's 陳宏謀 *Remaining Instructions for Teaching Women* (*Jiaonü yigui* 《教女遺規》), and Chen Menglei's 陳夢雷 *Collection of Illustrations and Books from Antiquity to the Present* (*Gujin tushu jicheng* 《古今圖書集成》) among others.[4] The text was also well-known in Japan and Korea well into the early twentieth century.[5]

Ban Zhao (c. 45–117 CE), who lived during the Eastern Han dynasty 東漢 (25–220 CE), was the first woman historian in Chinese history. Born into a family of noted scholar-officials, she was exceptionally gifted and knowledgeable in astronomy, geography, history, literature, mathematics, and the classics. According the *Book of the Later Han* and her own writings, she married her husband, Cao Shishu 曹世叔, at the age of fourteen. Her husband died young. She safeguarded her chastity for several decades, while raising one son and several daughters. Her father, Ban Biao 班彪, composed the *Supplemental Records to [Sima Qian's] Historical Records* (*Shiji houzhuan* 《史記後傳》). Her oldest brother, Ban Gu 班固, was the main author of the *Book of Han* (*Hanshu* 《漢書》), a one-hundred-volume record of the history of the Western Han dynasty (206 BCE–8 CE).[6] Ban Gu carried on the bulk of this monumental work for over thirty years. He later died in prison because of political allegation by a corrupt official before he could finish this work. Emperor He of Eastern Han 漢和帝 summoned Ban Zhao to complete it; working tirelessly, she eventually brought the work to fruition with the assistance of Ma Xu 馬續. Her second older brother was a famous general, Ban Chao 班超.

In addition to the *Lessons for Women* and her work on the *Book of Han*, Ban Zhao composed numerous literary works. Her daughter-in-law, Madame Ding, compiled these writings into a book; unfortunately, only some of these writings have survived. Owing to Ban Zhao's broad learning and integrity, Emperor He summoned her multiple times to tutor the empress and royal consorts; she was revered as *Cao Dagu/Taigu* 曹大家, meaning "a great woman-teacher from the Cao family."[7] After Emperor He died, Empress Dowager Deng 鄧太后, mother of the newly crowned infant emperor, was the *de facto* governess for the child, and she often sought advice on government matters from Ban Zhao. Ban Zhao passed away in her seventies. Empress Dowager Deng grieved over Ban's death, don mourning clothes and ordering governmental officials to oversee her funeral.

2. *Cultural and Historical Background*

By the time Ban Zhao had composed the *Lessons for Women* (c. 100 CE), the Han dynasty had already experienced numerous political upheavals, including several incidents of the consort kins' abuse of power,[8] and a fifteen-year interruption in the Han imperial rule by Wang Mang's 王莽 Xin dynasty 新 (9 CE–23 CE), which marked the transition from the Western Han period to the Eastern Han. Confucianism, interfused with the *Yinyang Wuxing* theory 陰陽五行 as expressed by Dong Zhongshu 董仲舒 (c. 179 BCE–104 BCE)—a Western Han philosopher and a chief minister to Emperor Wu—in a work attributed to him, the *Luxuriant Dew of the Spring and Autumn Annals* (*Chunqiu fanlu* 《春秋繁露》), dominated the intellectual atmosphere at the time. This view was later reinforced in an Eastern Han text, the *Comprehensive Discussions in the White Tiger Hall* (*Baihu tongyi* 《白虎通義》, c. 79 CE), allegedly an official transcript of an imperial conference on Confucian classics compiled by Ban Gu.

This school of Confucianism, often called Han Confucianism, departs from the classic reading of the *yin-yang* relation as two co-relative, complementary, interdependent, and mutually generative and transformational paradigms—*yin* (stillness, receptiveness, contraction, rain, etc.) and *yang* (movement, activity, expansion, sun, etc.)[9]—in favor of a bleak hierarchical and oppositional interpretation of the two relations. For example, Dong writes: "When *yang* flourishes, things also flourish. When *yang* declines, things also decline. . . . Based on this, *one should esteem yang and despise yin*."[10] Han Confucianism deploys this recast *yin-yang* theory not merely to organize natural phenomena but, more importantly, to recast three of the five human relationships (ruler–minister, father–son, and husband–wife) and to justify the legitimacy of sociopolitical control of the latter as a law of nature and a mandate from Heaven. By aligning the minister, the son, and the wife with *yin*, the *Luxuriant Dew of the Spring and Autumn Annals*, chapter 43 ("*Yang* the Venerable, *Yin* the Lowly"), states this politicized *yin-yang* metaphysics in the following terms:

> [W]hen counting days, one bases it on day, not on night. When counting years, one bases it on *yang*, not on *yin*. . . . [T]his is using Heaven's way as the measurement. *A husband is yang even if he is base; a wife is yin even if she is noble*. . . . The *Spring and Autumn Annals*, therefore, does not call out rulers' shortcomings nor does it name the ministers-subjects' merits. *All merits belong to the rulers; all shortcomings belong to the minsters-subjects*. . . . Hence, a filial son's conduct and a loyal minister's righteousness all model after Earth. Earth serves Heaven just like how those of the lower position serve those of the higher position. . . . *Everything bad is yin; everything good is yang*. . . . Thus, it is said, *yang* is Heaven's virtue, and *yin* Heaven's punishment.

Chapter 53 ("Basic Meaning") further adds:

> The righteous meaning of the ruler-minister, father-son, husband-wife relations is all taken from the way of *yin* and *yang*. The ruler is *yang* and the minister[-subject] is *yin*; the father is *yang* and the son is *yin*; the husband is *yang* and the wife is *yin*.

In the same vein, the *Comprehensive Discussions in the White Tiger Hall* declares:

> Why is it that a male takes a woman in marriage and a female marries into a man's domicile? *Yin* is lowly, and thus cannot act on its own initiative; one brings it into contact with *yang* in order to perfect it. Thus, the

> commentary says: "*Yang* takes the lead; *yin* acts in concert. The male acts; the female follows."[11]

Furthermore,

> Even if the husband's behavior is evil, the wife may not leave him, because there is no principle whereby Earth can leave Heaven. . . . Perverting human relations, killing the parents of one's wife, and abrogating the bonds [of kinship relations] are the greatest instances of disorder. Only when [a husband] violates [one of these] principles can [a wife] leave him.[12]

The symbolic control of "three bonds" (*sangang* 三綱)—namely "the minister-subject is to serve the ruler, the son is to serve the father, and the wife is to serve the husband"—is fully solidified in Han Confucianism, placing the subject, the son, and the wife in uncompromising subservient roles. Situated in this historical-political-intellectual climate of the Eastern Han, Ban Zhao's *Lessons for Women*, the first of the *Four Books for Women*, strikes quite a conservative tone.

3. *Purpose of Writing, Contents, and Strengths and Weaknesses of the Book*

Ban Zhao stated in her introduction that she wrote this treatise to provide her daughters with marriage advice, since she was quite ill and unsure of life's certainties. Speaking from her personal experience (often humble to a fault), she wrote as a filial daughter, a devoted wife, and a loving mother concerned with the well-being of her daughters. For this reason, the subject matter of this work is limited, primarily focusing on a woman's domestic roles. In Ban's view, a woman's honor and disgrace, thus her happiness, is ultimately determined by whether she can meet the demands of her new roles in her matrimonial family. At times, the author's fear of shame, as well as an unhealthy sense of women as "the weak and the lowly," is overwhelming. And yet as one reads carefully, one finds that even within the utterly feudal-patriarchal ethos of her time, Ban Zhao makes the effort to advocate for women's education (chapter 2), argue against domestic violence (chapter 3), and affirm the supremacy of a woman's virtue over her sexual appeal (chapter 4)—these are things essential for advancing women's causes.

The *Lessons for Women* consists of seven chapters. The force of her argument essentially derives from the authority of canonical texts such as the *Record of Rituals* (*Liji* 《禮記》). To start off, chapter 1 mandates a woman's three principal duties: (1) she should accept her role as the lowly and the weak; (2) she ought to be diligent at her household tasks; and (3) she carries the primary responsibility of continuing the family's ancestral-religious rites.

Chapter 1 lays the theoretical foundation for the remaining six chapters. Chapter 2 applies the Han interpretation of the *yin-yang* binary to the husband–wife relationship. After acknowledging that "the way of the husband and wife is to match *yin* and *yang*" (derivatively, a husband is to manage his wife and a wife is to serve her husband), Ban Zhao nevertheless contends: "If a husband is not virtuous, he will not be able to manage his wife. If a wife is not virtuous, she will not be able to serve her husband." Note how this hypothetical syllogism purposefully places the moral burden on both the male and the female, not just on the woman. Assuming both parties desire to rightfully fulfill their respective obligations, both must cultivate virtue. But to cultivate virtue, she argues, requires both sexes to be properly educated. Yet, this is hardly the case. She thus criticizes existing social biases and makes a strong case for women's education:

> I find that nowadays gentlemen-scholars only know that wives ought to be moderated by their husbands. . . . For this reason, they instruct their sons and teach them canonical classics. . . . Yet only to educate men and not to educate women, are they not being partial (*bi* 蔽) in their treatment of the two sides (*bi ci* 彼此)? According to the *Record of Rituals*, at the age of eight, children should begin receiving instructions on the classics. At the age of fifteen, they should receive adult education. Why is [women's education] alone not following this as a principle?

As conservative as she is, Ban Zhao's argument for women's learning is forcefully made here.

Chapter 3 reaffirms Han Confucians's co-relative *yin-yang* cosmology, physiology, and morality. It states, "Men and women have distinct nature. Firmness is *yang*'s virtue; gentleness is *yin*'s function. A man is honored for his strength; a woman is beautiful in virtue of her weakness," and admonishes how a wife ought to use her gentleness as strength in marital relation lest she brings harm to herself if she were too confrontational. Nonetheless, to prevent potential abuse of power, Ban Zhao warns against domestic violence on the basis of ritual respect and conjugal love, for such acts will irreparably damage the spousal bond.

Chapter 4 discusses the four womanly virtues and conducts (*side* 四德, *sixing* 四行): virtue, speech, bearing, and work. While the *Record of Rituals* and the *Zhou Rituals* (*Zhouli* 《周禮》) only mention the names of *side*,[13] Ban Zhao's chapter for the first time explains concretely what each of these four virtues entails for women. She clarifies that a woman's beauty comes from within, not from her physical attractiveness which inevitably depends on luck and is subject to the passing of time. *Side* expect neither unparalleled brilliance nor exceptional beauty nor unsurpassed skills. If a woman can act morally, speak prudently, attend to clean attire, and work diligently, she has accomplished these four womanly virtues. Every woman can reach this goal. Citing the *Analects* 7.29, she concludes: "Is humaneness really so far away? If I desire humaneness, humaneness will surely come."

The remaining three chapters (chapters 5, 6, and 7) explain how the tenets from the preceding chapters should be carried out in a woman's relationship with her husband and her in-laws. Based on the *Book of Ceremonial Rites* (*Yili* 《儀禮》) and the *Record of Rituals*, as well as the need for continuing ancestral-religious rites, in chapter 5 she advocates a wife's single-minded devotion to her husband and makes the controversial point against women's remarriage. Citing the *Decrees for Women* (*Nüxian* 《女憲》), she further claims that a wife's greatest achievement in life is to win her husband's heart! Nonetheless, as a counterweight, Ban Zhao is careful in insisting that: "[To] seek a husband's heart is not to rely on flattery and charm in a demeaning way in order to gain his affection. Such behavior is not as good as if she is one-minded with solemn appearance."

To build a firm foundation for a woman's relationship with her husband requires a support system. Thus, chapter 6 advises obedience to parents-in-law and chapter 7 counsels women to build friendly relationships with their brothers- and sisters-in-law. It is to be noted that Ban Zhao's emphasis on a woman's total obedience to her parents-in-law (by implication, to one's husband) runs contrary to the advice on admonition, given in the *Analects* (4.18), the *Classic of Filial Piety* (chapter 15), its female counterpart the *Classic of Filial Piety for Women* (chapter 15), and Liu Xiang's *Biographies of Women*. On this point, Ban Zhao's *Lessons for Women* leaves room for reassessment, a task the later three books of the *Four Books for Women* takes up.

The *Lessons for Women* clearly exhibits an ambivalent stand regarding gender dynamics. A contemporary reader, however, should not be too surprised by it, considering that the text was composed two thousand years ago. Furthermore, our contemporary society even today is not immune to similar struggles. On the one hand, Ban Zhao seeks to preserve traditional values; on the other hand, she does not hesitate to question her culture where it is unreasonable. Although she does not see all of the inequity embedded in her society, she nevertheless demonstrates a woman's independent thinking amid the influence of a pervading culture, the importance of which ought not be underestimated.

The chapters that follow are full translations of this text and Wang Xiang's accompanying commentary. To keep the flow of the original text, Wang's commentary in italic and translator's annotations in roman are placed in the "Commentaries and Annotations" section following immediately after the original text.

---

1. Author unknown. This work is now lost.
2. For more on Liu Xiang (c. 77–6 BCE) and his pioneering *Biographies of Women*, see the general introduction to this volume.
3. See Fan Ye 范曄, *Houhanshu* 《後漢書》 (*Book of Later Han*), "Biographies of Women" section, reprinted with modern translation and commentary by Wei Lianke 魏連科 et al., *Xinyi houhanshu* 新譯後漢書 (Taipei: Sanmin, 2013), volume 8, 4663–77, http://ctext.org/hou-han-shu/lie-nv-zhuan/zh.
4. The former two were compiled in the Ming dynasty (1368–1644 CE), and the latter two in the Qing dynasty (1644–1911 CE).
5. Yamazaki Jun'ichi 山崎純一, *Kyōiku kara mita Chūgoku joseishi shiryo no kenkyu: "Onna shisho" to "Shinpufu" sanbusho* 《教育からみた中國女性史資料の研究：「女四書」と「新婦譜」三部書》 (*A View of Education from a Study of Documents on the History of Chinese Women: "Four Books for Women" and "Instructions for New Brides"*) (Tokyo: Meiji shoin 明治書院, 1986), 76–9. See also Huang Liling 黃麗玲, "*Nü sishu* yanjiu《女四書》研究 (Research on *Four Books for Women*)" (MA thesis, Taiwan Nanhua University, 2003), 46–7.
6. The work is also known as *Qianhanshu* 《前漢書》 (*Book of Former Han*).
7. There are multiple ways of pronouncing 大家: *Dagu, Taigu*, or *Dajia*. *Dagu* 大姑 and *Taigu* 太姑 are based on ancient sounds.
8. The clan turmoil of Empress Dowager Lü was the most famous one, historically known as the Lü Clan Disturbance 呂氏之亂.
9. See, for example, the *Daodejing* 《道德經》, the *Zhuangzi* 《莊子》, the *Yijing* 易經 (*Classic of Changes*), the *Huainanzi* 《淮南子》, the *Huangdi neijing* 《黃帝內經》 (*Yellow Emperor's Inner Canon*), and others.
10. Dong Zhongshu, *Chunqiu fanlu* (*Luxuriant Dew of the Spring and Autumn Annals*), chapter 43. All translations are my own unless otherwise noted; emphasis added.
11. Paul R. Goldin, trans., excerpts of "Comprehensive Discussions in the White Tiger Hall," in *Images of Women in Chinese Thought and Culture: Writings from the Pre-Qin Period through the Song dynasty*, ed. Robin R. Wang (Indianapolis: Hackett, 2003), 171.
12. Ibid., 174.
13. See *Liji* (*Record of Rituals*), Hunyi 昏義 chapter; *Zhouli* (*Zhou Rituals*), Jiubin 九嬪 chapter.

Wang Xiang's Biographic Introduction

Cao Dagu/Taigu 曹大家*:* Lessons for Women (Nüjie 《女誡》)

琊琊 王相晉升 箋註
莆陽 鄭漢濯之 校梓

Commentator: Langye Region 瑯琊, *Wang Xiang* 王相
(courtesy name: Jin Sheng 晉升*)*
Proofreader: Fuyang Region 莆陽, *Zheng Han* 鄭漢
(courtesy name: Zhuo Zhi 濯之*)*

曹大家，姓班氏，名昭。後漢平陽曹世叔妻，扶風班彪之女也。世叔早卒，昭守志，教子曹穀成人。長兄班固作《前漢書》，未畢而卒，昭續成之。次兄班超，久鎮西域，未蒙詔還。昭伏闕上書，乞賜兄歸老。和熹鄧太后，嘉其志節，詔入宮，以為女師，賜號大家。皇后及諸貴人，皆師事之。著《女誡》七篇。

Cao Dagu/Taigu's 曹大家 maiden name is Ban 班; her given name is Zhao 昭.[1] She was the wife of Cao Shishu 曹世叔, of the Pingyang 平陽 region, during the Later Han dynasty 後漢,[2] and the daughter of Ban Biao 班彪 of the Fufeng 扶風 area. Her husband Shishu died young. She upheld her vow of chastity and raised their son, Cao Gu 曹穀, to adulthood. Her oldest brother Bao Gu 班固 authored the *Qianhanshu* 《前漢書》 (*Book of Former Han*). But, he passed away before the book could be finished.[3] Ban Zhao continued and completed her brother's work. Her second older brother, Ban Chao 班超 [, an accomplished general,] for decades was stationed on the western border and did not get summoned back by the emperor. Zhao prostrated before the palace to petition the emperor, pleading to permit her brother's return due to his old age. Empress Dowager Hexi

Deng 和熹鄧太后 commended her resolve and integrity, summoned her to the imperial palace, made her a teacher for women (*nü shi* 女師), and bestowed the honorific title *Dagu/Taigu* 大家 on her. Empresses and royal consorts all sought instruction from her as their teacher. She authored the *Nüjie* 《女誡》 (*Lessons for Women*), comprising seven chapters.[4]

Commentaries and Annotations

1. Translator's annotation: *Dagu* (or, *Taigu*) 大家 is an honorary title during the Han dynasty given to a well-respected and learned woman. 家 (*jia*) is pronounced as 姑 (*gu*) in this context. See Huang Yanli 黃嫣梨, ed., *Nü sishu jizhu yizheng* (*Four Books for Women with Selections from Traditional Commentaries*) (Hong Kong: Shangwu, 2008), 6. According to Wang Xiang, 大家 is pronounced as 泰姑 (*Taigu*) or 太姑 (*Taigu*); see his commentary to the Song sisters' preface to the *Nü lunyu* (*Analects for Women*); and chapter 11 of Liu Shi's *Nüfan jielu* (*Short Records of Models for Women*). Cao is Ban Zhao's husband's surname.
2. Translator's annotation: The Later Han dynasty is also known as the Eastern Han dynasty (25–220 CE).
3. Translator's annotation: The *Qianhanshu* 《前漢書》 (*Book of Former Han*) is also known as the *Hanshu* 《漢書》 (*Book of Han*), which recorded the history of the Western Han dynasty (206 BCE–8 CE). Ban Zhao's father started the project. Ban Zhao's old brother carried on the bulk of this work for several decades but died in prison (falsely accused by a corrupt official) before he could finish the work. Later, Emperor He 和帝 of Eastern Han summoned Ban Zhao to complete the project.
4. Translator's annotation: Fan Ye 范曄 (398–445 CE) composed the *Book of Later Han*, recording the history of the Eastern Han dynasty (25–220 CE). He included a biography of Ban Zhao and her work *Nüjie* in the section entitled Lienü zhuan 列女傳 ("Biographies of Women"), under the heading Cao Shishu Qi 曹世叔妻 ("Wife of Cao Shishu").

《女誡》原序

鄙人愚暗，受性不敏。蒙先君之餘寵，賴母師之典訓，年十有四，執箕帚於曹氏，今四十餘載矣。戰戰兢兢，常懼黜辱，以增父母之羞，以益中外之累。是以夙夜劬心，勤不告勞。而今而後，乃知免耳。吾性疏愚，教導無素。恆恐子穀，負辱清朝。聖恩橫加，猥賜金紫，實非鄙人庶幾所望也。男能自謀矣，吾不復以為憂。但傷諸女，方當適人，而不漸加訓誨，不聞婦禮。懼失容他門，取辱宗族。吾今疾在沉滯，性命無常。念汝曹如此，每用惆悵。因作女誡七篇，願諸女各寫一通，庶有補益，俾助汝身。去矣，其勖勉之。

Original Preface to Nüjie *by Ban Zhao*

LOWLY UNREFINED I, am stupid, unenlightened, and by nature dim-witted. Relying on my deceased father's (*xian jun* 先君) love,[1] and my instructress's instruction on canonical classics (*dian xun* 典訓),[2] at the age of fourteen I was in charge of the work of dustpan and broom in the Cao family.[3] Now, more than forty some years have passed; during these years, trembling with fear (*zhanzhan jingjing* 戰戰兢兢), I was constantly afraid that I may be dismissed (*chu* 黜) or humiliated (*ru* 辱).[4] Such an incident, if it happened, would have brought disgrace upon my parents and burdened members of my husband's family (*zhong* 中), as well as my natal family (*wai* 外).[5] Therefore, day (*su* 夙) and night (*ye* 夜) my heart labored in suffering (*qu xin* 劬心); I worked diligently without ever boasting (*gao* 告) my hard work.[6] Nevertheless, henceforth, I know my heart can be freed from such worries.[7]

My innate nature is negligent (*shu* 疏) and stupid (yu 愚). I taught and guided [my children] without regularity (*wu su* 無素). I had oftentimes feared that my son Gu (*zi Gu* 子穀) would bring shame upon our illuminating dynasty (*qing chao* 清朝).[8] The imperial Holy Grace, nonetheless, unexpectedly promoted him and bestowed upon him the honor of carrying gold [seal] with a purple [ribbon], a blessing far beyond what I, a lowly subject, had ever hoped for.[9] Now he can take care of himself; I no longer am worried about him. It, however, grieves me to see you, my daughters, who have just reached the age of marriage, to not have been gradually taught more nor have you learned proper rituals of being a married woman. I fear that you may lose face with other households and bring shame upon your family clan.[10] I am now seriously ill; my life is uncertain. As I think of you in such an [untrained] state, I am distraught by worries and frustration (*chou zhang* 惆悵) whenever this thought comes to my mind.[11] For this reason, I have composed the seven chapters of the *Lessons for Women*. I would like each of you, my daughters, to write out a copy of this book; it may bring remedial benefits that can (*bi* 俾) help your person. Go now (*quyi* 去矣) and do your very best in practicing these lessons![12]

Commentaries and Annotations

1. Wang Xiang's commentary: 先君 (xian jun*) refers to Taigu's/Dagu's father, Biao* 彪. *Biao's courtesy name is Shupi* 叔皮. *During the reign of Emperor Guangwu* 光武帝 *[of Eastern Han (r. 25–57 CE)], Biao held the official rank of* Zhuzuolang 著作郎, *in charge of writing the state history and overseeing the national library. He was a very well-known scholar at the time.* Translator's annotation: *Zhuzuolang* was an imperial title of a high-ranking court historian, a governmental system that began in the Eastern Han dynasty.
2. Translator's annotation: More narrowly, *Dian xun* 典訓 refers to the *Shujing* 《書經》 (*Classic of Documents/History*), also known as *Shangshu* 《尚書》 (*Book of Documents*), comprising speeches given by ancient rulers and officials. It is one of the most revered "five ancient Confucian classics" (*wujing* 五經) and is regarded as a necessary reading for those in charge of government. More broadly, *dian xun* refers to ancient canonical classics in general.
3. Wang Xiang's commentary: 帚 *pronounced as* 肘 (zhou*).* 箕帚 (ji zhou*) are tools used to clean up filth. It is a job for the lowly. Speaking humbly, she [i.e., Ban Zhao] said that she undertook the task of dustpan and broom rather than boasting that she became a daughter-in-law of the Cao family.*
4. Wang Xiang's commentary: Zhan jing 戰兢 *means "fearful, unsettled."* Chu 黜 *means "to dismiss."* Ru 辱 *means "to scold harshly." Her heart was oftentimes fearful, concerned that she may offend her parents-in-law or her husband.*
5. Wang Xiang's commentary: *If she had not cultivated the way of a married woman (*fu dao 婦道*) or if she had been humiliated, it would bring shame to her parents and burden both her husband's family and her natal family.* Zhong 中 *refers to her husband's family and* wai 外 *refers to relatives of her natal family.*

6. Wang Xiang's commentary: Su 夙 *means "daybreak."* Qu 劬 *means "to labor, to suffer."* Gao 告 *means "to boast." It says that she respectfully upheld the way of a married woman, worked laboriously from dawn to dusk with due diligence, but she dared not brag about her work.*
7. Wang Xiang's commentary: *Now in her old age, her offspring were established; she can be freed from such worries and toil.*
8. Wang Xiang's commentary: Shu 疏 *means "broad and omitting."* Wu su 無素 *means "to instruct sometimes but sometimes not."* Zi Gu 子穀 *refers to Taigu's/Dagu's son Cao Gu* 曹穀, *whose courtesy name is Yi Shan* 貽善. Qing chao 清朝 *means "a dynasty of bright sagely governance." She spoke about how she was negligent and inconstant in educating her son. She thus was worried that in Gu's official position, he would bring shame upon the imperial dynasty.*
9. Wang Xiang's commentary: *She said that fortunately her son did not commit any fault, and by the imperial Holy Grace he was promoted in ranks of nobility and salary as well as being bestowed the honor of carrying gold [seal] with a purple [ribbon], a blessing she never dared to hope for.* Translator's annotation: *Jin zi* 金紫 (gold and purple) refers to a gold seal with a purple ribbon (*jin yin zi shou* 金印紫綬). In imperial China, it was a symbol of governmental authority, used as a stamp by high-ranking officials.
10. Wang Xiang's commentary: *This speaks about the fact that men can seek an official position and take care of themselves. Her daughters were at the age of marriage: if they are not taught proper rituals, they could violate ritual propriety and lose face with other families, a disgrace that could be brought upon their fathers, brothers, and family clan.*
11. Wang Xiang's commentary: 惆悵 *pronounced as* chou zhang 紬帳*; it means "worried and frustrated." This passage says that I [Taigu/Dagu] have an illness that cannot be cured for a long time. I am afraid that I may pass away; thereupon, my daughters will have no one to teach them. I am, therefore, worried and frustrated.*
12. Wang Xiang's commentary: Bi 俾 *means "to enable." This passage says that she wrote this book to provide her daughters with guidance. If they can practice these lessons without omission, it will provide remedial help that can benefit their persons and free them from blame.* Quyi 去矣 *speaks of her daughters' departure: they will leave their mother and return to their husbands' homes.*

【卑弱第一】

古者生女三日，臥之床下，弄之瓦塼，而齊告焉。臥之床下，明其卑弱，主下人也。弄之瓦塼，明其習勞，主執勤也。齊告先君，明當主繼祭祀也。三者，蓋女人之常道，禮法之典教矣。謙讓恭敬，先人後己，有善莫名，有惡莫辭，忍辱含垢，常若畏懼，[是謂]卑弱下人也。晚寢早作，不憚夙夜，執務私事，不辭劇易，所作必成，手跡整理，是謂執勤也。正色端操，以事夫主，清靜自守，無好戲笑，潔齊酒食，以供祖宗，是謂繼祭祀也。三者苟備，而患名稱之不聞，黜辱之在身，未之見也。三者苟失之，何名稱之可聞，黜辱之可免哉。

I

The Lowly and the Weak
*(*Beiruo Diyi 卑弱第一*)*[1]

ON THE THIRD day after the birth of a girl, the ancients let her sleep [on the ground] below the bed, let her play with a tile [from a weaving machine] (*wa zhuan* 瓦塼), and after fasting they announced her birth to the ancestors at the ancestral temple (*zhai gao* 齊告).[2] To let her sleep [on the ground] below the bed is to make it clear that she is the lowly and the weak, and that she should place herself beneath others (*xia ren* 下人). To let her play with a tile [from a weaving machine] is to indicate unmistakably that she should be accustomed to labor and be diligent in her work (*zhi qin* 執勤). Fasting and announcing her birth to the ancestors is to convey unambiguously that she is responsible for [preparing ritual offerings and] continuing ancestral religious rites (*ji jisi* 繼祭祀).[3] These three responsibilities depict the constant way of being a woman and the canonical teachings of the ritual law.

A woman should be humble, yielding, reverent, and respectful. She should place others before herself. If she does something good, let her not boast. If she does something bad, let her not deny it. She should endure humiliation and contempt. She should act always as if trembling with fear. This is to act as the lowly, the weak, the one beneath others.[4] A woman should rest late at night and rise (*zuo* 作) early in the morning. Fearing not whether it is morning or night, she should always attend to her household tasks (*si shi* 私事) regardless whether they are difficult or easy. Whatever she does, she will necessarily complete it successfully and attend to it personally. This is being diligent.[5] She should rectify her appearance and her character to serve her husband. She should exhibit tranquility, safeguard her person, and love no silly laughter. She should neatly and orderly prepare wine and food to make offering to the ancestors. This is continuing ancestral religious rites.[6]

There never has been a case of a woman who fulfills all three responsibilities, yet worries about not having a good name or being dismissed in disgrace [by her husband].[7] If, however, she fails to uphold these three responsibilities, how can she have a good name or avoid the disgrace of being dismissed?[8]

Commentaries and Annotations

1. Wang Xiang's commentary: *Heaven is venerable; Earth is lowly.* Yang *is strong;* yin *is gentle. The lowly and the weak is the correct and righteous way of being a woman. If she is unwilling to be the lowly but desires to be the venerable, if she is unwilling to be the gentle but desire to be the strong, then she intrudes upon righteousness and violates rectitude. [If this is the case,] even if she has other talents, what is there in her to be admired?* Translator's annotation: Heaven and Earth, *yin* and *yang,* are conceptual binaries in Chinese consciousness since 600 BCE or earlier. These concepts can be found in the *Yijing* (*Classic of Changes*) . The relative distinction between Heaven and Earth, *yin* (the receptive) and *yang* (the active), was originally an explanation of changes in nature and the framework of space and time. During the Han dynasty (206 BCE–220 CE), Dong Zhongshu's *Chunqiu fanlu* (*Luxuriant Dew of the Spring and Autumn Annals*) accentuated a strict hierarchical nature of the *yin–yang* binary. His interpretation was later codified in a controversial Eastern Han document *Baihu tongyi* (*Comprehensive Discussions in the White Tiger Hall*) by Ban Gu. Dong's teaching ties women to a subservient role, a view that has influenced Chinese culture for millennia. For more on Dong's correlation of *yin–yang* with the female–male binary, see the main introduction to this volume and the translator's introduction to Ban Zhao's *Nüjie* (*Lessons for Women*).
2. Wang Xiang's commentary: 塼 *(*zhuan*) and* 磚 *(*zhuan*) are synonymous.* 齊 *is pronounced as* 齋 *(*zhai*). The* Shijing (Classic of Poetry) *says: "If a boy is born, let him sleep on the bed, dress him up in elaborate clothing (*shang 裳*), and let him play with a jade ritual vessel (*zhang 璋*). If a girl is born, let her sleep on the ground, wrap her up in an infant comforter (*ti 裼*), and let her play with a tile [from a weaving machine]" (*wa 瓦*). "Sleep on bed" symbolizes the venerable. "Sleep on the ground" and lying below the bed symbolize the lowly.* 裳 *(*shang*) means elaborate clothing, a symbol of nobility.*

禓 (ti) *is comforter for infants without further embroidery, a symbol of the lowly.* 璋 (zhang) *denotes half of a jade vessel* (gui 圭), *held in hand by ministers and high-ranking officials at ceremonies, a symbol of esteem and nobility.* 瓦 (wa) *is a ceramic piece, a potsherd from a weaving machine used for weaving; it denotes woman's work, a symbol for the lowly.* 齊告 (zhai gao) *means to announce at the ancestral temple.* 禓 *pronounced as* 替 (ti). Translator's annotation: The verses cited here are from the *Shijing*《詩經》 (*Classic of Poetry*), the Xiaoya 小雅 section, the Sigan 斯干 poem.

3. Wang Xiang's commentary: *This is to make clear the meaning of the foregoing sentence.* Xia ren 下人 *means that one should abide by the rite of being beneath others.* Zhi qin 執勤 *means that a woman should attend in person to the work of weaving and she should work industriously.* Ji jisi 繼祭祀 *means that a wife is primarily responsible for preparing ritual offerings and cleansing wine and food to assist her husband in religious rituals. Mencius's mother says: "Ritual propriety of a married woman is nothing but mastering in cooking, fermenting* (mi 冪) *wine, serving her father- and mother-in-law, and sewing clothes." Thus, a woman should manage the inner quarters (*ku 閫) *but not wish to interfere with affairs outside the inner realm. This is what it means. A girl from birth is expected, and guided, by these guidelines. In fact, the proper way of being a married woman is nothing more than this.* 冪 *is pronounced as* 密 (mi). 閫 *is pronounced as* 困 *in the third tone.*
4. Wang Xiang's commentary: *This again is to explicate the way of these three responsibilities. A woman is to be humble, yielding, reverent, respectful, and dare not neglect others. She is to place others before herself, and dare not be ahead of others. When she does something good and doesn't mention it, it is because she dares not show off. If she does something bad because of upholding a revered person's order, thus what she does is despised by others. She still ought to follow through such an order and dare not decline. She should endure insult and contempt that follows; she dares not explain and defend herself. Always act as if trembling with fear. Dare not enjoy comfort. Humble and weak, she may be said to have fulfilled the way of placing herself below others.* Translator's annotation: Such a subservient attitude to a fault (particularly, doing evil as a consequence of following a revered person's order) is difficult to understand. It is more extreme than some other Confucian classics that admonish against blind obedience: see, for example, Confucius, the *Analects* 4.18; and the *Xiaojing* (*Classic of Filial Piety*), chapter 15. For correlated teaching on a wife's responsibility to rectify her husband, see Zheng Shi, *Nüxiaojing* (*Classic of Filial Piety for Women*), chapter 15; Renxiaowen, *Neixun* (*Teachings for the Inner Court*), chapter 13; and Liu Shi, *Nüfan jielu* (*Short Records of Models for Women*), chapters 6, 9, and 11.
5. Wang Xiang's commentary: 劇 *is pronounced as* 極 (ji). 作 (zuo) *means "to rise."* Si shi 私事 *means "detailed tasks."* 劇 *means "tiresome and heavy." This passage says that a woman should go to bed late, but rise early. She should not fear the late night; rather, she should reverently attend to her woman tasks. Do not ask whether a task is difficult or easy, but only expect herself to work diligently to complete her work. Whatever she writes*

by hand will be done in an orderly manner. Whatever she organizes will necessarily be arranged finely, not coarsely or carelessly. Then, the way of upholding diligence may be said to have been fulfilled.

6. Wang Xiang's commentary: 齊 *retains its original meaning here as* qi 齊. *This passage indicates that a woman should correct her appearance, and rectify her character and conduct, to serve her husband. She should be tranquil, chaste, and quiet. She should be serious in her speech and her laugh. She should cleanse and manage ritual wine and food in an orderly fashion, to assist her husband in carrying out religious rites for the ancestors. In doing so, she may be said to have completed the way of continuing ancestral rites.*
7. Wang Xiang's commentary: *This indicates that a woman should place herself beneath others, work diligently, and continue the ancestral rites. If she can observe all three responsibilities, her reputation will be known both internally and externally. No disgrace of being dismissed by her husband will ever come to her.*
8. Wang Xiang's commentary: *If she does not uphold these three responsibilities, she would not be able to avoid the disgrace of being dismissed by her husband. How can her reputation be honored?*

【夫婦第二】

夫婦之道，參配陰陽，通達神明，信天地之弘義，人倫之大節也。是以禮貴男女之際，詩著關雎之義。由斯言之，不可不重也。夫不賢，則無以御婦；婦不賢，則無以事夫。夫不御婦，則威儀廢缺；婦不事夫，則義理墮闕。方斯二者，其用一也。察今之君子，徒知妻婦之不可不御，威儀之不可不整，故訓其男，檢以書傳。殊不知夫主之不可不事，禮義之不可不存也。但教男而不教女，不亦蔽於彼此之數乎！禮，八歲，始教之書，十五而至於學矣。獨不可依此以為則哉！

2

Husband and Wife (Fufu Dier 夫婦第二)[1]

THE WAY OF husband and wife harmonizes and matches (*can pei* 參配) *yin* and *yang*. It reaches spiritual beings and manifests the great (*hong* 弘) principle of Heaven and Earth and the important morals of human relations.[2] Hence, the *Record of Rituals* honors the essential relation between men and women. The *Classic of Poetry* makes known the meaning of the Guanju 關雎 poem. Based on this, clearly the husband–wife relation ought not to be taken lightly.[3]

If a husband is not virtuous, he will not be able to control (*yu* 御) his wife. If a wife is not virtuous, she will not be able to serve her husband. If a husband cannot moderate his wife, his authority and dignity are abolished and lost. If a wife cannot serve (*shi* 事) her husband, her principle of righteousness has fallen. Although the cases are two, their use is one.[4] I find that nowadays gentlemen-scholars only know that wives ought to be moderated by their husbands, and the authority and dignity of a husband ought to be properly established. For this reason, they instruct their sons and teach them canonical classics.[5] They hardly realize that husbands ought to be served [by their wives], and ritual propriety and righteousness ought to exist.[6] Yet only to educate men and not to educate women—are they not being partial (*bi* 蔽) in their treatment of the two sides?[7] According to the *Record of Rituals*, at the age of eight, children should begin receiving instructions on the classics. At the age of fifteen, they should receive adult education. Why is [women's education] alone not following this as a principle?[8]

Commentaries and Annotations

1. Wang Xiang's commentary: *When a woman can fulfill these three responsibilities, she is fit to be a wife. Nonetheless, the way of husband and wife cannot be ignored. Thus, "husband and wife" follows next as the second chapter.*
2. Wang Xiang's commentary: 參 *(*can*) means "to harmonize."* 弘 *(*hong*) means "great, big." This passage states that the ritual propriety of husband and wife harmonizes and matches* yin *and* yang. *The righteousness of its bond can move spiritual beings. It is the great principle of Heaven and Earth and the great path of human life.* Translator's annotation: For more on *yin* and *yang*, see note 1, chapter 1. For the importance of marriage as a foundation of human relations, see, for example, the *Liji* (*Record of Rituals*), Hunyi 昏義 and Jiaotesheng 郊特牲 chapters.
3. Wang Xiang's commentary: *This speaks about when sagely kings instituted rituals, it began with a careful distinction between men and women. When Confucius edited poems [*Classic of Poetry*], he placed Guanju as the first poem. The poem describes how King Wen [of Zhou] pursued a virtuous lady in order to accomplish the virtuous governance of the imperial inner quarters. The Way of husband and wife is the beginning of human relations; one must not take it lightly.*
4. Wang Xiang's commentary: Yu 御 *means "to control, to moderate."* Shi 事 *means to "respectfully serve." If a husband is unvirtuous, then he has lost his authority and dignity, and is unfit to moderate his wife. If a wife is unchaste and unvirtuous, then her principle of righteousness is abandoned, and she is unfit to serve her husband. Neither can be abandoned.*
5. Wang Xiang's commentary: *It says that gentlemen-scholars of her time all know how to govern a family. They know very well that wives and concubines must be moderated by ritual propriety and husbands' authority and dignity ought to be properly established. Hence, gentlemen-scholars often examine ancient books, canonical classics, histories, and biographies in order to instruct their sons and offspring.*
6. Wang Xiang's commentary: *It is not that these gentlemen-scholars do not understand the teaching [of the classics], but they value the boys and omit the girls. They do not engage in discourse with the girls about the meaning of the* Classic of Poetry, *the* Book of Documents, *and other classics. Thus, at her time [Ban Zhao's time], there were no books designed for women's education. Consequently, women hardly know the*

righteousness of serving their husbands nor do they understand the ritual propriety of the inner quarters.

7. Wang Xiang's commentary: Bi 蔽 *means "partial, partisan." This passage indicates that in instructing men and women, the meaning of righteousness is the same. To know that one [should be instructed] but not the other, is this not being partial?* Translator's annotation: As conservative as she is in upholding Han Confucian values, Ban Zhao's argument for women's learning is forcefully made here. It adeptly rebuts this societal bias.
8. Wang Xiang's commentary: *According to ancient rituals, when boys and girls reach the age of six, they should be taught numbers, and the names of directions. At the age of seven, boys and girls should not eat together or sit together. At the age of eight, boys should attend elementary school and learn from teachers outside the home; at the age of fifteen, they will attend school for adult learning. Girls, at the age of eight, should be instructed by woman teachers; the teachers should teach them ritual propriety and deference, and how to weave silk and make wide and narrow silk belts. At the age of fifteen, girls will pin their hair up. When they turn twenty years old, it is the proper age for marriage. This passage asks that people know they should teach men the classics, why should women alone not be taught [the classics regarding] ritual propriety and deference?* Translator's annotation: The information presented here is taken from the *Liji* (*Record of Rituals*), the Neize 內則 chapter.

【敬順第三】

陰陽殊性，男女異行。陽以剛為德，陰以柔為用，男以強為貴，女以弱為美。故鄙諺有云：「生男如狼，猶恐其尪；生女如鼠，猶恐其虎。」然則修身莫如敬，避強莫如順。故曰敬順之道，為婦之大禮也。夫敬非他，持久之謂也；夫順非他，寬裕之謂也。持久者，知止足也；寬裕者，尚恭下也。夫婦之好，終身不離。房室周旋，遂生媟黷。媟黷既生，語言過矣。語言既過，縱恣必作。縱恣既作，則侮夫之心生矣。此由於不知止足者也。夫事有曲直，言有是非。直者不能不爭，曲者不能不訟。訟爭既施，則有忿怒之事矣。此　出於不尚恭下者也。侮夫不節，譴呵從之；忿怒不止，楚撻從之。夫為夫婦者，義以和親，恩以好合，楚撻既行，何義之存？譴呵既宣，何恩之有？恩義俱廢，夫婦離行。

3

Respect and Compliance
*(*Jingshun Disan 敬順第三*)*[1]

YIN AND *YANG* have diverse essences. Men and women have distinct natures. Firmness is *yang*'s virtue; gentleness is *yin*'s function. A man is honored for his strength; a woman is beautiful in virtue of her weakness.[2] Therefore, a coarse proverb says, "A man is born like a wolf; it is feared that he may develop the illness of having a hunched weak back (*wang* 尪). A woman is born like a mouse; it is feared that she may turn into a tiger."[3]

For self-cultivation, nothing is more essential than developing respect. In avoiding confrontation with the strong, nothing is better than using compliance. Thus, it is said, the way of respect and compliance is women's great ritual principle.[4] Now, respect requires nothing but constancy. Compliance seeks nothing other than leniency and generosity. A person can abide by constancy because she knows when to stop and the benefit of contentment. A person can be lenient and generous toward others because she values reverence and her humble station.[5]

The friendliness and love between a husband and a wife is to be inseparable throughout their lifetimes. They intimately follow each other in their inner rooms. Thereupon, lewdness (*xie* 媟) and indecency (*du* 黷) begin to grow.[6] Once lewdness and indecency grow, speech becomes improper. Once improper speech is used, lack of restraint will necessarily occur. Once lack of restraint occurs, a heart of scorning one's husband will be born. Such a situation is caused by not knowing when to stop and the benefit of contentment.[7]

Affairs are of either crooked or straight nature. Speech may be either right or wrong. Those who are straight will necessarily argue for their case. Those who are crooked will certainly accuse others. Once accusations and arguments come to the fore, angry matters will arise. This is caused by not revering others and one's own humble station.[8]

If a wife does not moderate her affronts to her husband, scolding insults [from him] will ensue. If her husband's anger cannot be stopped, a whipping (*chu ta* 楚撻) will surely follow. To be husband and wife relies on righteousness for harmonious intimacy, loving kindness for friendly union. If beating is enforced, where is righteousness? If scolding (*qian* 譴) and insulting words are spoken, where is loving kindness? When loving kindness and righteousness are both deserted, husband and wife will part their ways (*li hang* 離行).[9]

Commentaries and Annotations

1. Wang Xiang's commentary: *The previous chapter only explained the great beginning of husband and wife. Nonetheless, the way of being a wife must be taught. This chapter thus elaborates on the ritual principles of respect and compliance. Respect and compliance are related to what was discussed in chapter one about the lowly and being diligent in one's work.* Translator's annotation: In two other editions of the *Lessons for Women*, this chapter is entitled Jing Shen 敬慎 ("Respect and Prudence") rather than Jing Shun 敬順 ("Respect and Compliance"). However, the narrative of this chapter uses the phrase *jing shun* 敬順 several times with no mentioning of *shen* 慎. Therefore, the Zhuangyuange 狀元閣 edition (the edition this translation follows) is probably correct in the title of this chapter.
2. Translator's annotation: For more on the *yin–yang* and female–male correlation, see the translator's main introduction to this volume, introduction to Book I, and chapter one, note 1.
3. Wang Xiang's commentary: *This passage explains that* yin *and* yang, *men and women, have diverse natures and distinct actions.* Yang *is firm and* yin *is gentle: this is Heaven's way. Men are strong and women are weak: it is human nature. The coarse proverb says that when a man is born, he is as strong as a wolf. It is feared that he may later*

*develop the illness of having a hunched weak back (*wang lei 尪羸*). When a woman is born, she is as timid as a mouse. It is feared that she may develop the overbearing strength of a fierce tiger. It expresses these ideas in extreme language.* Translator's annotation: *Wang lei* 尪羸 literally refers to a physical defect of a weak and curved spine. It is used as a phrase to describe a man who is thin and weak.

4. Wang Xiang's commentary: *Respect is the foundation for personal cultivation. Compliance is the basis for serving one's husband. Thus, these two are regarded as important ritual principles.* Translator's annotation: For the origin of the teaching on women's obedience—most notably, *sancong* 三從 ("three obediences" or "three followings"), see *Liji* (*Record of Rituals*), Jiaotesheng 郊特牲 chapter, where it says "Men lead (*shuai* 帥) women. Women follow (*cong* 從) men. The way of husband and wife begins from here. Being a woman is to be someone who follows others. When she is young, she follows her father and older brother. When she is married, she follows her husband. When her husband passes away, she follows her son." See also, the *Mencius*, 3B:2, "To regard compliance (*shun* 順) as the correct virtue is the way of a concubine and a wife."
5. Wang Xiang's commentary: 夫 *pronounced as* 扶 *(*fu*). The long-lasting relationship between husband and wife is not a result of exhibiting occasional respect. Only if respect is shown persistently can husband and wife grow old together without a declining relationship. It is also not a result of exhibiting occasional compliance. Only if a wife is lenient, generous, and gentle can she accommodate [her husband] and be weak and compliant. If she knows when to stop, and is content with her role, she will not harbor a heart that demands perfection from her husband. Thus, her respect for him will be sustained. If she is lenient, gentle, reverent, and humble, she will be able to accommodate her husband's shortcomings. Hence, her compliance to him will be long-lasting. When so realized, the way of respect and compliance is complete.*
6. Wang Xiang's commentary: 媟 *pronounced as* 褻 *(*xi*).* 黷 *pronounced as* 讀 (du*).* 媟 *means "lewd, lascivious, lustful."* 黷 *means "impropriety, slight, wantonness." This passage indicates that husband and wife should enjoy a good union throughout their lifetime. In their inner rooms, they live together and are playful with each other intimately. Thereupon, lasciviousness and impropriety grow daily. The way of respect and compliance is thus undermined.* Translator's annotation: 媟 should be pronounced as 謝 (*xie*); it is unclear why Wang Xiang commented that it is pronounced as 褻 (*xi*).
7. Wang Xiang's commentary: *Out of lewdness, disrespect arises. Out of wantonness, noncompliance occurs. Once respect and compliance are undermined, speech becomes arrogant. Thereupon, a wife will indulge herself without restraint, insult her husband, and there is nothing she will not do. Because she does not know contentment, she thus demands perfection from her husband and scolds his imperfection. Because she does not abide her proper wifely role, she thus becomes lawless and self-complacent, not understanding the way of respecting a husband.*

8. Wang Xiang's commentary: 夫 *pronounced as* 扶 *(*fu*). The accusers, whose reasons are crooked, strive to look straight. If husband and wife exchange abusive insulting language, quarrels and accusations will increase daily. They will be angry toward each other and bring instability to their home. If they can be lenient, generous, gentle, reverent, compliant, and humble, whence will they arrive at this stage?* Translator's annotation: 夫 (*fu* in the second tone), not to be confused with *fu* in the first tone, which means "husband," is often used in classic Chinese to start a sentence; it is an adverb with no specific meaning.
9. Wang Xiang's commentary: 夫 *in the* 夫為 *is pronounced as* 扶 *(*fu *in the second tone);* 譴 *pronounced as* 遣 *(*qian*);* 行 *pronounced as* 杭 *(*hang*).* 譴 *means "scolding, insulting."* 楚撻 *(*chu ta*) means "whipping."* 行 *(*hang*) means "array, row."* 離行 *(*li hang*) means "to dismiss, send off, withdraw." This passage makes the point that when a wife does not stop her slights toward her husband, she will necessarily invite the disgrace of being scolded and insulted as well as injuries resulting from being beaten [by her husband]. If this happens, then both loving kindness and righteousness [between husband and wife] are abolished. Thereupon, husband and wife will be separated and never be reunited.* Translator's annotation: Even with her conservative values of wifely compliance, Ban Zhao nonetheless argues here that domestic violence and abuse are detrimental to marriage and should always be avoided.

【婦行第四】

女有四行，一曰婦德，二曰婦言，三曰婦容，四曰婦功。夫云婦德，不必才明絕異也；婦言，不必辯口利辭也；婦容，不必顏色美麗也；婦功，不必技巧過人也。幽閒貞靜，守節整齊，行己有恥，動靜有法，是謂婦德。擇辭而說，不道惡語，時然後言，不厭於人，是謂婦言。盥浣塵穢，服飾鮮潔，沐浴以時，身不垢辱，是謂婦容。專心紡績，不好戲笑，潔齊酒食，以供賓客，是謂婦功。此四者，女人之大節，而不可乏無者也。然為之甚易，唯在存心耳。古人有言：「仁遠乎哉？我欲仁，而仁斯至矣。」此之謂也。

4

Women's Conduct
*(*Fuxing Disi 婦行第四*)*[1]

WOMEN HAVE FOUR [areas of] conduct: first, woman's virtue; second, woman's speech; third, woman's appearance; fourth, woman's work.[2] Speaking about these four, woman's virtue requires neither unparalleled talent nor exceeding brilliance; woman's speech requires neither rhetorical eloquence nor sharp words; woman's appearance requires neither a beautiful nor a splendid look or form; woman's work demands no unsurpassable skills.[3]

Exhibit tranquility (*you* 幽), unhurried composure (*xian* 閒), chastity (*zhen* 貞), and quietude (*jing* 靜). Safeguard the integrity (*jie* 節) of regulations. Keep things in an orderly manner. Guard one's action with a sense of shame. In movement and rest, it is always done in proper measure. This is what is meant by woman's virtue.[4] Choose words [carefully] (*ze ci* 擇辭) in speaking. Never utter slanderous words. Speak only when the time is right; then, others will not dislike one's utterances. This is what is meant by woman's speech.[5] Wash (*guan wan* 盥浣) clothes that are dusty and soiled, and keep one's clothing and accessories always fresh and clean. Bathe regularly, and keep one's body free from filth and disgrace. This is what is meant by woman's bearing.[6] Concentrate on one's weaving and spinning. Love no silly play or laughter. Prepare wine and food neatly and orderly to offer to the guests. This is what is meant by woman's work.[7]

These four areas are matters of great integrity for women. No women should lack them. Yet to do them is quite easy. The key is to always keep them in mind. The ancients [i.e., Confucius] had a saying, "Is humaneness really so far away? If I desire humaneness, humaneness will surely come." This is what it means here.[8]

Commentaries and Annotations

1. Wang Xiang's commentary: 行 (xing) *[in the chapter title] is pronounced in the fourth tone. Respect and compliance [discussed in the previous chapter] mainly reside in the heart, whereas conduct (*xing 行*) manifests in affairs. The four conducts (*sixing 四行*) are the four virtues (*side 四德*).*
2. Wang Xiang's commentary: *The "four conducts" (*sixing 四行*) refer to women's constant conduct. How the heart conducts itself is called virtue. What the mouth articulates is called speech. How the look is decorated is called appearance. What the body does is called work.* Translator's annotation: The concept of the "four [womanly] conducts" (*sixing* 四行) or the "four [womanly] virtues" (*side* 四德) appeared as early as in the *Zhouli* 《周禮》 (*Zhou Rituals*) and the *Liji* 《禮記》 (*Record of Rituals*), for example, the Hunyi chapter. However, the Hunyi chapter only gave the names of the "four conducts." In this chapter, for the first time, Ban Zhao explains what each of these four areas of conduct means to women in their day-to-day routines. Ban Zhao's explanation had a tremendous impact on Chinese women's learning and conduct.
3. Wang Xiang's commentary: 夫 *pronounced as* 扶 *(*fu *in the second tone). For women's four conducts, she only needs to find the middle ground—no need to add anything further. A woman is not expected to significantly surpass others in her talents, eloquence, beauty, or skills.* Translator's annotation: This chapter's emphasis that a woman's beauty rests on internal virtue, rather than outward attractiveness, which is invariably subject to the changes of time and the whims of external conditions, is still an important lesson today. Although Ban Zhao's intent may have been to argue that every woman can cultivate these womanly virtues, her advice that a woman is not expected to be exceptional in her talents and eloquence may also have lowered women's own self-expectations and lent support to society's suppression of women's opportunities.
4. Wang Xiang's commentary: 幽 (you) *means "tranquil."* 閒 (xian) *means "leisurely."* 貞 (zhen) *means "rectitude and firmness."* 靜 (jing) *means "prudence in private space."* 節 (jie) *refers to "integrity of regulations, authority, and rituals"; one should safeguard it with respect and prudence and make no errors. When one acts, one guards one's action with a sense of shame; one's action is in accord with ritual propriety and is nothing to be laughed by others jeeringly. One's movement and rest always follow proper measure; one's action and nonaction are constant and in accordance with the law.*

5. Wang Xiang's commentary: 擇辭 (ze ci) *means before one speaks, one should choose and weigh the appropriateness of one's language so that one does not lose sight of ritual propriety and righteousness. If this is done, one's speech will certainly not contain any slanderous words that may hurt others. Moreover, if one speaks only at the right time, although one's discourse may be filled with details, no one will dislike it.*
6. Wang Xiang's commentary: 盥浣 *pronounced as* 管玩 (guan wan). *Both words mean "to wash." Regardless of whether clothes are new or old, all should be washed, so that they are fresh and clean. Wash one's hair and bath one's body regularly to keep one free from filth so that one does not suffer from disgrace. Thereupon, one's appearance will glow with radiance and health.*
7. Wang Xiang's commentary: *Weaving and spinning are a woman's routine work. She ought to concentrate on learning the work and practice it tirelessly. Silly play and laughter are not suitable for a woman. Thus, she should be prudent in not liking this kind of activities. When guests arrive, she ought to orderly arrange and cleanse wine and food. The* Shijing (Classic of Poetry) *says: "Nothing is done contrary to rituals. Only wine and food are the subject of conversation." This is what it means.* Translator's annotation: The two verses cited here are from the Sigan 斯干 poem in the *Shijing*, Xiaoya section.
8. Wang Xiang's commentary: *This passage states that these four areas (virtue, speech, appearance, and work) are the constants of the way of woman; she should not lack any of the four. Yet to do them is not difficult. Always keep them in mind; then, not one thing will be improper. An ancient sage had a saying: "Is humaneness so far away from humanity? If I single-mindedly desire to practice humaneness, humaneness will surely come." If so, how can one say that a woman's virtue, speech, appearance, and work cannot be accomplished?* Translator's annotation: The sage's saying quoted by Ban Zhao is from Confucius, *Analects* 7.29.

【專心第五】

禮，夫有再娶之義，婦無二適之文，故曰夫者天也。天固不可違，夫固不可離也。行違神祇，天則罰之；禮義有愆，夫則薄之。故《女憲》曰：「得意一人，是謂永畢；失意一人，是謂永訖。」由斯言之，夫不可不求其心。然所求者，亦非謂佞媚苟親也，固莫若專心正色。禮義居絜，耳無塗聽，目無邪視，出無冶容，入無廢飾，無聚會羣輩，無看視門戶，則謂專心正色矣。若夫動靜輕脫，視聽陜輸，入則亂髮壞形，出則窈窕作態，說所不當道，觀所不當視，此謂不能專心正色矣。

5

One-Mindedness (Zhuanxin Diwu 專心第五)[1]

ACCORDING TO THE [*Book of Ceremonial*] *Rituals*, a husband has the ground of righteousness to remarry; however, no existing texts permit a wife to have a second marriage (*er shi* 二適).[2] Therefore, it is said that husbands are like Heaven. Since Heaven should not be disobeyed, a husband must not be deserted.[3] If one's conduct disobeys heavenly and earthly spiritual beings, Heaven will certainly impose punishment. Likewise, if a wife transgresses (*qian* 愆) ritual propriety and righteousness, her husband will treat her with contempt.[4] Thus, the *Decrees for Women* (*Nüxian* 《女憲》) says, "to win the heart of one man (*yi ren* 一人) is the completion of [a woman's] eternal end (*bi* 畢); to lose the heart of one man is to suffer the eternal separation from him" (*qi* 訖). Based on this, a wife must seek to win her husband's heart.[5] Nonetheless, to seek a husband's heart is not to rely on flattery and charm in a demeaning way in order to gain his affection. Such behavior is not as good as if she is one-minded with solemn appearance.

Reside by the measures of ritual propriety and righteousness. Hear no gossip or rumors. Look at nothing wicked. When going out, she does not dress herself in an alluring seductive manner. When at home, she does not therefore neglect her appearance. She does not hold parties or gatherings to entertain her peers. She does not peek outside from inside the house. When these practices are followed, a woman may be called one-minded with solemn appearance.[6]

But if she moves and rests frivolously, her sight and hearing are restless, her hair is messy and appearance sloppy when at home, her mannerisms are alluring and pretentious when outside the home, she speaks about matters that are inappropriate to speak about, and looks at things that are inappropriate to look at, this is called not being one-minded with solemn appearance.[7]

Commentaries and Annotations

1. Wang Xiang's commentary: 專 (zhuan) *means "one." This chapter explains that the way of woman in relation to her husband is to be one-minded without a second intention.*
2. Wang Xiang's commentary: 適 (shi) *means "to marry another person." If a husband has no wife, then no one can oversee the preparation of offerings for ancestral rites; the family lineage is also not established. Hence, he must remarry. The way of woman is to follow her husband from the beginning to the end; therefore, if her husband passes away, it is contrary to ritual propriety for her to remarry.* Translator's annotation: See *Yili* 《儀禮》 (*Book of Ceremonial Rituals*), Sangfu zhuan 喪服傳 chapter; *Liji* 《禮記》 (*Record of Rituals*), Jiaotesheng 郊特牲 and Hunyi 昏義 chapters.
3. Wang Xiang's commentary: *The* [Yili] [Book of Ceremonial] Rituals *says that a husband is his wife's Heaven; since Heaven's mandate should not be violated, the rightness of a husband should not be deserted. If a wife marries someone else after her husband passes away, this is to desert and to betray her husband.*
4. Wang Xiang's commentary: 愆 *pronounced as* 牽 (qian). *If a person's virtue and conduct are deficient, and if he offends and enrages spiritual beings, Heaven will certainly impose calamity and punish that person. Likewise, if a woman repeatedly errs on ritual propriety, her husband will treat her with contempt.*
5. Wang Xiang's commentary: *The* Decrees for Women (Nüxian 《女憲》) *is a book used by ancient worthies to instruct women. Today, it is unclear by whom this work is authored.* 一人 (yi ren) *refers to "a husband."* 畢 (bi) *means "the end, the conclusion."* 訖 (qi) *means "breaking off, separation." This passage makes the point that if a wife can gain her husband's heart, then they can live together peacefully to the end of their lifetimes. However, if she loses her husband's heart, there will be upheaval and separation; as such, the way of husband and wife will end. For these reasons, how can the way of a wife not be to seek her husband's heart, but to lose it?*
6. Wang Xiang's commentary: *This passage says that if a wife wishes to win her husband's heart, she should not rely on flattery and charm to gain his love in a demeaning way; she must concentrate her mind and rectify her appearance. A one-minded person will reside*

in ritual propriety, will use righteousness as her measure, and dare not act immorally. She will neither listen to nor look at anything contrary to ritual propriety. This is called one-mindedness. When going out, she will not dress up in an alluring seductive way. When at home, she will not neglect her appearance because she is now in dark inner rooms. She will not have gatherings with her female companions for silly plays. She will not peek outside from inside the house. This is called correct appearance. Translator's annotation: "[N]either listen to nor look at anything contrary to ritual propriety" echoes Confucius, *Analects* 12.1.

7. Wang Xiang's commentary: 陝 *(*shan*) and* 閃 *(*shan*) are synonymous; they mean "to flicker or to glitter in an indeterminate manner." "Movement and rest are frivolous" means her actions are inconstant and inconsistent. "Her sight and hearing are unsettled" indicates her mind and will are restless. "Her hair is messy and appearance sloppy" conveys that when at home, she neglects her appearance. "Her mannerisms are alluring and pretentious" suggests that when outside the home, she dresses up in a seductive manner. "Speaking about matters that are inappropriate to speak" indicates her utterances are contrary to ritual propriety and righteousness. "Looking at things that are inappropriate to look" reveals that she randomly looks at things that are contrary to ritual propriety. This is called not being one-minded with solemn appearance and not being able to win a husband's heart.*

【曲從第六】

夫「得意一人，是謂永畢；失意一人，是謂永訖。」欲人定志專心之言也。舅姑之心，豈當可失哉？物有以恩自離者，亦有以義自破者也。夫雖云愛，舅姑云非，此所謂以義自破者也。然則舅姑之心奈何？故莫尚于曲從矣。姑云不，爾而是，固宜從令；姑云是，爾而非，猶宜順命。勿得違戾是甚，爭分曲直。此則所謂曲從矣。故《女憲》曰：「婦如影響，焉不可賞！」

6

Conceding Obedience (Qucong Diliu 曲從第六)[1]

IT IS SAID, "to gain one person's heart is the eternal completion of one's end; to lose one person's heart is the eternal break-off [with that person]." This saying advises a woman to have a firm will and one-minded devotion [to her husband]. How can she then afford to lose the hearts of her parents-in-law?[2] Among things, there is self-imposed separation caused by loving kindness; there is also self-inflicted defeat resulted from righteousness.[3] Even though her husband says he loves her, but her parents-in-law say "no," such is a case called "self-inflicted defeat resulted from righteousness."[4]

What can one do with the hearts of one's father- and mother-in-law? Concerning this, nothing is as good as "conceding obedience." When your mother-in-law says, "Do not do this (*fou* 不[=否])," but you believe it is a right thing to do, you should obey your mother-in-law's command. When your mother-in-law says, "Do that," but you believe it is a wrong thing to do, you still should comply with your mother-in-law's command. Do not act contrary to parents-in-law's command regarding right and wrong. Do not argue with them about what is crooked and what is straight. This is called "conceding obedience."[5] Thus, the *Decrees for Women* (*Nüxian*) says, "If a daughter-in-law can act like the shadow and the echo [of her parents-in-law], how can she not be appreciated [by them]?"[6]

Commentaries and Annotations

1. Wang Xiang's commentary: *This chapter illuminates the way of serving parents-in-law. If the parents-in-law's request is right, a daughter-in-law should rightly obey it. If the parents-in-law's command is contrary to what is right, a daughter-in-law should still comply. This is called "conceding obedience." Only "conceding obedience" may be properly called filial piety. Both the Great Shun 大舜 and Min Ziqian 閔子騫 were disliked by their parents but both made concessions in obeying their parents.* Translator's annotation: Min Ziqian 閔子騫 (536–487 BCE) was a prized student of Confucius, well-known for his filial piety. His story was included in the popular "twenty-four exemplars of filial piety" (*ershisi xiao* 二十四孝). Confucius praised Min Ziqian for his filial piety. See Confucus, *Analects* 11.4. The "Great Shun" refers to Yu Shun 虞舜, one of the five legendary sage-kings prior to the ancient Shang 商 and Zhou 周 dynasties. Shun, too, is known for his filial piety. The lesson given in this chapter about "conceding obedience" (and earlier in chapter 1), as well as in *Analects* 13.18, creates a moral tension with other competing Confucian texts (e.g., *Analects* 4.18; the *Classic of Filial Piety*, chapter 15) that repudiate blind obedience. This continues to be a subject of heated debate in contemporary discussions of Chinese ethics.
2. Wang Xiang's commentary: *This passage continues what was stated in the previous chapter. If a wife does not lose the heart of her husband, then they will be forever harmonious to the end of their lifetime. This however only speaks about the husband. If above the husband, there are father- and mother-in-law, how can a wife lose their hearts without culpability?*
3. Wang Xiang's commentary: *This says that in this lifetime, there are cases where one focuses one's loving kindness on one person, but that person despises it; consequently, one is unable to self-defend that loving kindness. Or, one abides with righteousness for one person, but that person brings disorder to it; consequently, one is unable to self-guard that righteousness. This is analogous to the situation where a daughter-in-law cannot win the hearts of her parents-in-law.*
4. Wang Xiang's commentary: *Even though the husband loves his wife dearly, but parents-in-law do not, thereupon loving kindness is separated and righteousness is defeated.* Translator's annotation: In the previous chapter, loving kindness (*en* 恩) and righteousness (*yi* 義) were enumerated as two essential bonds that bind husband and wife together. Here it makes clear that these two essential bonds will be destroyed if a daughter-in-law cannot win the hearts of her parents-in-law. In other words, since a son's filial piety to his parents outweighs his conjugal love to his wife, a daughter-in-law ought to seek to win over her parents-in-law.

5. Wang Xiang's commentary: 不 *pronounced as* 否 (fou). *If one wishes to win the hearts of father- and mother-in-law, nothing is better than obeying their commands. If what a mother-in-law says is incorrect, whereas what a daughter-in-law says is correct, she should obey what her mother-in-law says. If what mother-in-law does is incorrect, and a daughter-in-law knows clearly that it is wrong, still she should obey the command of her mother-in-law in carrying it out. She should not debate with her mother-in-law about right and wrong, the crooked and the straight. This is called "conceding obedience." In doing so, she will certainly win the hearts of her parents-in-law.* Translator's annotation: Again, the lesson here about "conceding obedience" is at odds with competing Confucian texts that advise moral integrity. See note 1, this chapter. Ban Zhao's stand is significantly more conservative than those in Liu Xiang's *Biographies of Women*, Empress Renxiaowen's *Teachings for the Inner Court*, and Madame Liu's *Short Records of Models for Women*.
6. Wang Xiang's commentary: *This passage says if a daughter-in-law's obedience to her father- and mother-in-law is like a shadow following a form, an echo responding to a sound, how can she not win their hearts and not be praised by them?*

【和叔妹第七】

婦人之得意於夫主，由舅姑之愛已也；舅姑之愛已，由叔妹之譽已也。由此言之，我之臧否譽毀，一由叔妹，叔妹之心，不可失也。人皆莫知叔妹之不可失，而不能和之以求親，其蔽也哉！自非聖人，鮮能無過！故顏子貴於能改，仲尼嘉其不貳，而況婦人者也！雖以賢女之行，聰哲之性，其能備乎！故室人和則謗掩，內外離則過揚。此必然之勢也。《易》曰：「二人同心，其利斷金。同心之言，其臭如蘭。」此之謂也。夫叔妹者，體敵而分尊，恩疏而義親。若淑媛謙順之人，則能依義以篤好，崇恩以結援，使徽美顯章，而瑕過隱塞，舅姑矜善，而夫主嘉美，聲譽耀於邑鄰，休光延於父母。若夫愚惷之人，於叔則托名以自高，於妹則因寵以驕盈。驕盈既施，何和之有！恩義既乖，何譽之臻！是以美隱而過宣，姑忿而夫慍，毀訾布於中外，恥辱集於厥身，進增父母之羞，退益君子之累。斯乃榮辱之本，而顯否之基也。可不慎哉！然則求叔妹之心，固莫尚于謙順矣。謙則德之柄，順則婦之行。知斯二者，足以和矣。《詩》曰：「在彼無惡，在此無射。」此之謂也。

女誡終

7

Harmony with Younger Brothers- and Sisters-in-Law (Heshumei Diqi 和叔妹第七)[1]

THE REASON THAT a wife can win the heart of her husband is because her parents-in-law love her. Now, her parents-in-law love her because her younger brothers- and sisters-in-law praise her. For these reasons, whether [her] repute is good or bad, blameworthy, or praiseworthy, all depends on [her] younger brothers- and sisters-in-law. Thus, a wife must not lose the hearts of her younger brothers- and sisters-in-law.[2] People do not know that [the hearts of] their younger brothers- and sisters-in-law must not be lost; consequently, they do not strive to establish harmonious relation with them so as to gain their affections. These people's mistake is evident.[3]

Since one is not a sage, hardly can one be faultless. Therefore, Master Yan (Yanzi 顏子) [Confucius's student] was honored for his ability to rectify his errors. Zhongni 仲尼 [Confucius] praised him for not making the same mistake twice. What more should women be?[4] Even a virtuous woman with right conduct, and endowed with intelligent and wise nature, could she possess all virtues and never commit a fault?[5] Hence, if members of the same household can live in harmony, slanders will be hidden. If the inner realm and the outer realm are alienated from each other, bad things will be known to many. This is naturally the case. The *Classic of Changes* says, "Sharpness/Advantage of two persons with the same mind can cut through gold. Utterances of the same mind emit fragrance like the orchid." This is what it means![6]

Although a daughter-in-law and her younger brothers- and sisters-in-law are equal in rank, the latter is honored for their positions. Furthermore, even though a daughter-in-law is more distant to her brothers- and sisters-in-law in loving kindness, they are close to one another in their righteous relation.

If a woman is virtuous, beautiful, humble, and compliant, she will be able to rely on righteousness to deepen their good wills, and uphold kindness to bind their assistance, which will enable her beautiful virtue to be known while keeping her flaws and mistakes hidden. Thereupon, her father- and mother-in-law will be proud of her goodness; her husband will praise her virtue. Her repute will shine in her district and neighborhood, and the luster of her name will even extend to her own father and mother.[7]

If a woman is stupid and unintelligent (*chun* 惷 = [蠢]), she will rely on her name as an older sister-in-law, acting haughtily toward her younger brothers-in-law; likewise, she will treat her younger sisters-in-law arrogantly because of her husband's favor. Once arrogance is expressed, whence comes harmony? Once kindness and righteousness are violated, whence arrives (*zhen* 臻) good reputation?[8] Consequently, her goodness will be concealed and her faults announced. Her mother-in-law will be angry with her, and her husband irritated. Slanders and criticism will be publicized both inside and outside the household. Disgrace and shame will gather on her person. Moving forward, she will add embarrassment to her parents. Moving backward, she will increase her husband's burden. Hence, a woman's relationship with her younger brothers- and sisters-in-law truly is the basis of honor and shame, the foundation that determines whether one will be noteworthy or insignificant. How could a woman not be prudent in this matter?[9]

Nonetheless, in seeking the hearts of one's young brothers- and sisters-in-law, there is nothing better than humility (*qian* 謙) and compliance (*shun* 順). Humility is the lever of virtue. Compliance is the [right] conduct (*xing* 行) of a married woman. If one knows these two, it will be sufficient to create harmony. The *Classic of Poetry* says, "Over there, no one despises (*wu* 惡) him/her; over here, no one is jealous (*du* 射 [=妬]) of him/her." This is what it means![10]

Lessons for Women ends.

Commentaries and Annotations

1. Wang Xiang's commentary: 叔妹 (shu mei*) refers to younger brothers and sisters of one's husband. Here, the fact that his older brothers or sisters are not mentioned is because his old brothers already have their own families, and his older sisters have married to other households. His younger brothers and sisters, however, are still young; they are often by the side of their parents. One especially should build harmonious friendly relationship with them and make them happy. Thereupon, one will not lose the hearts of one's parents-in-law.* Translator's annotation: The traditional Chinese custom is that older siblings should get married before the younger ones.
2. Wang Xiang's commentary: *To be a wife, one dare not be impolite with one's younger brothers- and sisters-in-law. Only then can one gain the love of one's father- and mother-in-law. Only when one gains the love of one's father- and mother-in-law, can one win the heart of one's husband. Hence, whether a woman's reputation is virtuous, blameworthy, or praiseworthy, all depends on one's younger brothers- and sisters-in-law. One must win their hearts and not be disrespectful to them.*
3. Wang Xiang's commentary: *This passage explains that people do not know that [the hearts of] their younger brothers- and sisters-in-law must not be lost. Thus, these people often offend their parents-in-law.*
4. Wang Xiang's commentary: *This passage states that no one can be faultless. Master Yan was exemplary in virtue. When he had faults, he immediately corrected them; thus, the sage [i.e., Confucius] praised him for not making the same mistake twice. What more are women? Can they be faultless?* Translator's annotation: 顏子 (Yanzi) refers to Yan Hui 顏回 (521–481 BCE); known for his exemplary virtue, he is generally considered Confucius's favorite student. Regarding his virtue, see *Analects* 6.2, 6.5, 6.9, etc. Yan Hui passed away at the age of forty. Confucius wept in deep sorrow for Yan's premature death. See *Analects* 11.8 and 11.9.
5. Wang Xiang's commentary: *Even a virtuous, enlightened, intelligent, and wise woman cannot have all good deeds and be completely faultless.*
6. Wang Xiang's commentary: *This passage states that if people of the same household can live in harmony, even if there are faults, slanders will be concealed. If the inner realm and the outer realm are alienated from each other, even if there is no fault, people will broadcast bad things. Therefore, handling affairs with the same mind has*

the advantage/sharpness of cutting through gold. Utterances of the same mind have fragrance of an orchid. These are the words of the great Yijing (Classic of Changes). *Would they deceive us?* Translator's annotation: These verses are from allegedly Confucius's commentary on the *Yijing*, traditionally called the Xici 繫辭, expounding the meaning of the 64 hexagrams. See the *Yijing*, Xici, part I, chapter 8.

7. Wang Xiang's commentary: *Younger brothers- and sisters-in-law are of equal rank with a daughter-in-law. But a younger brother-in-law is called "uncle"* (shu 叔) *and a younger sister-in-law is called "aunt"* (gu 姑)*; this is because even though they are at the same rank as a daughter-in-law, they are honored for their positions. They have different surnames than oneself; nonetheless they are from the same family lineage as one's husband. Thus, even though a daughter-in-law is more distant to her brothers- and sisters-in-law in loving kindness, they are close to one another in their righteous relation. A virtuous beautiful young woman will be able to extend her husband's righteous relations, as well as her parents-in-law's loving kindness, to deepen friendliness and to assure assistance with her younger brothers- and sisters-in-law. Once younger brothers- and sisters-in-law are in friendly relationship with oneself, one's good name and good deeds will be increasingly known to many as days go on, and one's flaws and mistakes will become hidden. One's parents-in-law and husband will be pleased. One's virtuous and sagely reputation will shine in both neighborhood and district. The luster of one's name will even extend to one's own parents.*

8. Wang Xiang's commentary: 惷 (chun) *and* 蠢 (chun) *are synonymous, meaning "stupid, stupidity."* 臻 (zhen) *means "to arrive, arrival." This passage comments that a stupid and unintelligent person, in treating her younger brothers-in-law, will rely on the fact that she is his older brother's favorite wife, thus acting with a heart of boastfulness and haughtiness; in treating her younger sisters-in-law, she will rely on the fact that she is her husband's helpmate, thus carrying herself in a self-complacent, arrogant manner. Once arrogance and complacency are expressed, naturally the relationship cannot be harmonious. If the relationship become disharmonious, kindness and righteousness will surely be violated and abandoned. If so, whence arrives her good reputation?*

9. Wang Xiang's commentary: *In doing so, one's goodness is hidden day-by-day, and one's fault is announced daily. Parents-in-law are angry. One's husband is infuriated. Slander and criticism will be broadcast inside and outside the household. Disgrace and insults will come to one's person. The embarrassment to one's parents and the burden to one's husband will be significant. Hence, to have a harmonious relation with one's younger brothers- and sisters-in-law is the basis that determines whether one will be honored and noteworthy. Without harmony, the opposite will be the case. Can one not be prudent?*

10. Wang Xiang's commentary: 行 (xing) *and* 惡 (wu) *both pronounced in the fourth tone.* 射 *pronounced as* 妬 (du). *This passage explains that only humility, respect,*

yielding, and compliance can harmonize the hearts of one's younger brothers- and sisters-in-law. Humility is the basis for entering virtue. Compliance is the [right] conduct of a married woman. If a woman does not lose sight of these two, she naturally can establish harmony with her younger brothers- and sisters-in-law, and not lose the hearts of her parents-in-law and her husband. 射 (du) *means "jealousy." Taigu/Dagu* 大家 *[Ban Zhao] cited the* Classic of Poetry *to illuminate this point. If "no one despises her over there, and jealousy does not harm her over here," then wherever she goes, will her goodness not be known to many and her reputation not be noteworthy?* Translator's annotation: These two verses of the *Shijing* are from the Zhousong 周頌 section, the Zhenlu 振鷺 poem.

BOOK II

The Tang Women

The Song Sisters and the *Analects for Women* (*Nü lunyu*): ?–820/825 CE

Translator's Introduction

1. *The Author and the Work*

The *Analects for Women* (*Nü lunyu* 《女論語》), the second of the *Four Books for Women*, was an influential primer for women's education that dates from the Tang dynasty 唐 (618–907 CE). This text was popular not only during the Tang period but also in the subsequent one thousand years. It was included in several important anthologies of later times, such as Tao Zongyi's *Compendium of Famous Writings* (*Shuofu* 《說郛》), Wang Xiang's *Four Books for Women* (*Nü shishu jizhu* 《女四書集註》), Chen Hongmou's *Remaining Instructions for Teaching Women* (*Jiaonü yigui* 《教女遺規》), and Chen Menglei's *Collection of Illustrations and Books from Antiquity to the Present* (*Gujin tushu jicheng* 《古今圖書集成》). The first two were compiled in the Ming dynasty (1368–1644 CE), and the last two in the Qing dynasty (1644–1911 CE).

According to both the *Old Book of Tang* (*Jiutangshu* 《舊唐書》) and the *New Book of Tang* (*Xintangshu* 《新唐書》),[1] Song Ruoxin 宋若莘 (?–820, the older sister, also known as Song Ruohua 宋若華), authored the *Analects for Women*, and her younger sister Song Ruozhao 宋若昭 (?–825) provided the commentary.[2] They came from a family of renowned Confucian scholars. Their father, Song Tingfen 宋廷棻, had five daughters and one son. Since their childhood, he tutored them on the classics and poetry. While the son was quite ordinary, all five daughters were learned and accomplished, capable of composing fine literary works before they reached the age of fifteen. Ruoxin (the oldest) also instructed her four younger sisters, much like a strict teacher. Of the five sisters, Ruoxin and Ruozhao (the second oldest) were the most talented. The sisters preferred a simple and elegant look rather than an embellished appearance, and they wished to remain unmarried and make a name for the family with their scholarship. Their family also did not force them into marriage, instead letting them pursue their study.

In 788, a high-ranking official named Li Baozhen recommended the Song sisters' talents to Emperor Dezong of Tang 唐德宗 (r. 780–805 CE). The five sisters were summoned to the imperial palace and tested for their knowledge of the classics, history, and literary works. Deeply impressed by them, Emperor Dezong did not treat them as female imperial attendants or concubines but, rather, extended them the courtesy due to governmental officials. He addressed them as "*Xueshi*" (學士, "Scholar-Official") or "*Xueshi Xiansheng*" (學士先生, "Sir Scholar-Official"). The five sisters were often invited to participate in various literary gatherings hosted by the emperor, appearing side by side with other officials.

In 791, Ruoxin (a.k.a. Ruohua) was appointed by Emperor Dezong to oversee imperial records, documents, and special collections of books. After Ruoxin passed away in 820, Emperor Muzong 穆宗 (r. 821–824 CE) summoned Ruozhao to fill the position and bestowed on her the official title "*Shanggong*" (尚宫), the highest rank of its kind. Royal consorts, princes, and princesses all received instructions from her and revered her as *Xiansheng* 先生 ("Sir," "Teacher"). Ruozhao passed away in 825.

Of the five sisters, Ruolun and Ruoxun died young. Ruoxian (the second youngest) later served as a secretary to Emperor Jingzong 敬宗 (r. 825–827 CE) and Emperor Wenzong 文宗 (r. 828–840 CE). The five sisters were among the best-known female scholars of the Tang dynasty. Devoting their lives to scholarship and to their work in the Tang imperial court, they collectively served six emperors and participated in governmental affairs for over forty years.

2. *Cultural and Historical Background*

The Tang dynasty was widely regarded as one of the most prosperous periods of imperial China, with a society much more open to gender equality, in contrast with other Chinese dynasties. Not only did Tang women receive increased opportunity of education but also active talented women were well-respected and welcomed by Tang society.[3] Notably, Empress Consort Wu Zetian 武則天 (624–705 CE) was the only empress regnant (equivalent in rank to an emperor) of China in its more than two-millennia history.[4] Like the Song sisters, these talented women wrote books, participated in political affairs, and had opportunities to serve as female officials (*nüguan* 女官) in the imperial palace.

After a long period of stability, however, both imperial families and society had become wasteful and indulged in pleasures. The An-Shi Rebellion 安史之亂 (also known as the An-Lushan Rebellion, 755–763 CE), during Emperor Xuanzong's 唐玄宗 reign, marked a decisive decline of the Tang regime. In addition to blaming the emperor's corruption, many pointed their fingers at his favorite consort, Yang Guifei 楊貴妃, for her sexual allure, nepotism, and interference in political affairs.[5] To complicate the matter further, Consort Yang was originally the wife of Prince Shou 壽王, Emperor Xuanzong's son. It was through much maneuvers that Xuanzong made her his consort, including issuing an imperial edict making her a Daoist priestess Taizhen 太真 for several years and finding a new wife for his son.[6] To regain the culture's footing in the aftermath of the rebellion, reform-minded officials and scholars called for a restoration of Confucian moralism, with special emphasis on ritual propriety and moral behavior. The *Analects for Women* was composed not long after this turbulent time. Its focuses on women's familial roles, the ritual distinction between male and female, the value of diligence and frugality, and the importance of integrity were natural responses to the ethos of the time.

The Song sisters' life and the *Analects for Women* could be read as representing two different social classes during this period. The Song sisters themselves symbolize the paths available to a small group of elite women. Additionally, as stated in its preface, the *Analects for Women* provides practical advice to non-elite women, who likely did not have the freedom to refrain from marriage; the advice covered how they too can secure happiness, cultivate virtue, and exercise relative autonomy under social conditions that would inevitably impact their lives. Before the *Analects for Women*, earlier Confucian texts for women's education—for example, Liu Xiang's *Biographies of Women*, Ban Zhao's *Lessons for Women*, and Madame Zheng's *Classic of Filial Piety for Women*—were addressed mainly to the aristocratic class and required a high degree of literacy. By contrast, the Song sisters' *Analects for Women* sought to instill learning in ordinary women. In Confucius's words, "in education, there should be no class distinction" (*Analects* 15.39).[7] Yet, materialization of such a vision required appropriate textbooks. The *Analects for Women* is written in plain, idiomatic four-word verses, without directly quoting arduous classics, yet paradigmatic Confucian values are embedded in the text.

The Song sisters were contemporaries of the influential Tang literati, notably Han Yu 韓愈 (768–824 CE), Liu Zongyuan 柳宗元 (773–819 CE), Bai Juyi 白居易 (772–846 CE), and Yuan Zhen 元稹 (779–831 CE). The first two were strong advocates for the Classic Prose movement (*Guwen yundong* 古文運動) and the last two initiated the New Music Poetry movement (*Xinyuefu yundong* 新樂府運動).[8] Both movements aimed to reverse the pretentious literary trend of the late Tang, which preferred flowery prose, ornamental words, and citation of difficult and obscure texts, but lacked real content. Leaders in the two movements promulgated writing in plain style and in colloquial language, so that all could understand a work's meaning; also, that the best kind of writing should be relevant to social issues and practical matters. These literary movements possibly had influenced the Song sisters' prose in the *Analects for Women*.

3. *Purpose of Writing, Contents, and Strengths and Weaknesses of the Book*

A word needs to be said about the structural unity of the *Analects for Women*. According to Tang historical records, the work by Song Ruoxin (i.e., Ruohua) comprised ten chapters. It is written in the form of a discourse between Madame Song 宋氏, also known by her honorific title Sir Xuanwen (Xuanwenjun 宣文君),[9] in her role as the female counterpart of Confucius, and Ban Zhao, as well as other women acting as female equivalents of Confucius's students, like Yan Hui 顏回 and Min Ziqian 閔子騫. The question-and-answer style (in ten chapters) differs markedly from the current twelve-chapter version and its straightforward narrative. Some scholars suggest that the original work by Song Ruohua may have been lost and that the current version is Song Ruozhao's commentary—or possibly the original version may have been altered; no consensus has yet been reached. Accordingly, the reader may note that although Wang Xiang named Song Ruozhao as the author of this work, he nonetheless mentions in his biographic introduction of the author(s) of this work that "Ruohua composed the *Analects for Women*; Ruozhao provided the commentary."

As indicated, this work is written for the common people, not for the elite. This is especially obvious in chapter 2 ("Learning Women's Work"), chapter 4 ("Rising Early"), and chapter 9 ("Managing the Household"). These chapters give women detailed advice on how best to rear silkworms, raise farm animals, cook, and manage home economies. These are not tasks that elite women would or could embark on. What is refreshing is that the two sisters make sure the essence of their argument remains in the forefront—namely, that these daily routines ought not rule women out from becoming exemplary models of virtue. Like other women predecessors, these women's good names could be passed down in history for millennia (chapters 1 and 12).

In tandem with Ban Zhao's *Lessons for Women*, the *Analects for Women* stresses the achievability of virtue in daily life. To this aim, it instructs women to first cultivate the self in tranquility (*qing* 清), chastity (*zhen* 貞), and integrity (*jie* 節), and then to sustain and renew these virtues by means of daily practice. The first five chapters address how this can be accomplished by women who live with their maternal families. Chapters 6 to 11 decipher practices appropriate for married women. Chapter 12 concludes and summarizes the main points. These chapters not only commend ritual propriety, diligence and frugality, conjugal love, parental responsibilities, and friendliness but also warn against gossip, wastefulness, laziness, and indecency. In regard to purity, chastity, and integrity, it is noteworthy that the *Analects for Women* (in chapters 1, 7, 12) and the *Lessons for Women* (in chapters 4 and 5) share a more sensible understanding concerning how these virtues manifest themselves in women's bodies. Both works suggest that although a woman's chastity is an important virtue, it does not necessarily supersede other essential virtues (e.g., filial piety or parental duty) or commend self-mutilation or suicide, as was often viewed in later dynasties such as the Ming (1368–1644 CE) and the Qing periods (1644–1911 CE).

The *Analects for Women* (hereafter, *AW*) also differs from the *Lessons for Women* (hereafter, *LW*) in the following ways:

1. *Readership: AW* was written in colloquial language. Consequently, this work reached a broader audience than *LW*.
2. *Rule-based Virtue Ethics*: Although both *LW* and *AW* see virtue as a path to happiness, these two works approach the formation of character very differently. While *LW* offers only broad guidelines about the four womanly virtues (*side* 四德), *AW* codifies every detail of women's behavior. Each chapter stipulates numerous precepts on what to do and what not to do. Even though this extensive set of "dos and don'ts" reduces guesswork, it also contravenes the authors' goal of fostering women's intellectual and moral independence.
3. *Social Life*: While *LW* is centered on the husband–wife relationship, *AW* expands on that. The latter offers advice on other social relationships that shape a woman's experience, including the parent–child relationship, host–guest etiquette, and friendship between neighbors.
4. *The In-laws: LW* advises women to be filial and never offend their in-laws lest it damage the husband–wife relationship, whereas *AW* instructs women to care for their parents-in-law out of genuine concern, just as how they would care for their own parents (chapter 6). Regarding the motive of filialness toward parents-in-laws, *LW* and *AW* diverge on where the force of their arguments lay—the former on utility, the latter duty.
5. *Spousal Relationship: LW* emphasizes spousal respect and marital hierarchy, whereas *AW* stresses conjugal love and mutual dependence. The husband and the wife "should be kind and loving toward one another, and mutually dependent on each other"; "[w]hen dead, buried in the same coffin; when alive, sharing the same bedcover" (chapter 7). Moreover, a wife should be concerned about not only her husband's health and safety but also his morality.
6. *Admonition*: On whether to admonish one's husband, *AW* exhibits a clear departure from *LW*. While Ban Zhao advocates that "the lowly and the weak" (*beiruo* 卑弱) is a woman's proper station and "yielding obedience" (*qucong* 曲從) is an exemplary virtue,[10] the Song sisters steer away from such an injunction. In fact, *AW* never uses words such as "lowly" (*bei* 卑) or "weak" (*ruo* 弱); instead, it uses "gentleness" (*rou* 柔). Even with "gentleness," it is used very sparingly—only once in chapter 7 and once in chapter 11. This choice

of words suggests a more balanced view of the spousal relationship—for a person can certainly be gentle without being weak or lowly. *AW* also advocates for a woman's moral independence from her husband: it says, in serving one's husband, "[s]hould he slide into evil ways, the wife ought to remonstrate with him repeatedly" (chapter 7). On wifely responsibility of admonishing one's husband, *AW* resembles the advice given in the *Classic of Filial Piety for Women* (another text authored by a Tang woman),[11] and influenced two later Ming texts (the *Teachings for the Inner Court* and the *Short Records of Models for Women*, the third and the fourth of these *Four Books for Women*).[12] This departure from Ban Zhao's position is worth noting, since it displays a progression of thought among Chinese woman thinkers.

7. *Religiosity*: The development of Daoism and Buddhism reached its peak in the Tang dynasty—both religions were immensely popular among the aristocrats, the literati, and the commoners. *AW* consequently exhibits a strong presence of religiosity, largely absent in *LW*. For example, the work speaks about prayer to gods and spiritual beings for blessings, healing, and protection when family members are ill (chapters 5 and 7). It invokes karmic retribution for unfilial behavior (chapter 6). It describes marriage in the present life as predestined in a former life (chapter 7).

The translations that follow are full translations of the text along with Wang Xiang's commentary. Again, to keep the flow of the original text, Wang's commentary in italic and the translator's annotations in roman are allocated in the "Commentaries and Annotations" section following immediately after the original text.

---

1. Both are formal accounts of Tang history. Liu Xu et al., *Tangshu* 《唐書》 (*Book of Tang*), also known as the *Jiutangshu* 《舊唐書》 (*Old Book of Tang*), was completed in 945 CE, commissioned by Emperor Gaozu of the Later Jin 後晉 during the Five Dynasties and Ten Kingdoms period. The *Xintangshu* 《新唐書》 (*New Book of Tang*) by Ouyang Xiu, Song Qi, et al., was completed in 1060 CE, commissioned by Emperor Renzong of the Northern Song dynasty 北宋.
2. Liu Xu 劉昫 et al., *Tangshu*, volumes 16 (paragraph 11) and 56 (paragraphs 33–4), http://ctext.org/wiki.pl?if=gb&res=456206&searchu=%E8%8B%A5%E6%98%AD. Ouyang Xiu 歐陽修, Song Qi, et al., *Xintangshu* (*New Book of Tang*), Liezhuan 列傳 ("Biographies"), volume 2 (paragraphs 38–42), http://ctext.org/wiki.pl?if=gb&chapter=114053.

3. Charles Benn, *China's Golden Age: Everyday Life in the Tang Dynasty* (London: Oxford University Press, 2002), 32.
4. Elizabeth Pollard et al., *Worlds Together, Worlds Apart—Volume 1: Beginnings through the 15th Century* (New York: W.W. Norton, 2015), 317–8.
5. Patricia Buckley Ebrey, Anne Walthall, and James B. Palais, *East Asia: A Cultural, Social, and Political History* (Boston: Houghton Mifflin, 2006), 99.
6. Liu Xu et al., *Tangshu*, volume 55 (paragraph 30), http://ctext.org/wiki.pl?if=gb&chapter=80808. Ouyang Xiu, Song Qi, et al., *Xintangshu*, Benji 本紀 ("Basic Records"), volume 5 (paragraphs 38 and 43), http://ctext.org/wiki.pl?if=gb&chapter=566908; and Liezhuan 列傳 ("Biographies"), volume 1 (paragraph 70), http://ctext.org/wiki.pl?if=gb&chapter=506004.
7. In some versions, 15.38.
8. Ebrey et al., *East Asia*, 106.
9. Xuanwenjun 宣文君 (i.e., Song Shi 宋氏, Madame Song) was the mother of Wei Cheng 韋逞, a chief minister of rituals in the Former Qin 前秦 (350–94 CE), a state in the Sixteen Kingdoms (Shiliuguo 十六國) (303–c. 420 CE), a turbulent time in China's history. According to Fang Xuanling et al., *Jinshu* 《晉書》 (*Book of Jin*), Lienü zhuan 列女傳 "Biographies of Women", Madame Song was born into a family of Confucian scholars of the *Zhouli* 《周禮》 (*Zhou Rituals*). Her mother died young. She was raised and educated by her father. At her father's request, she carried on his mission to preserve the *Zhou Rituals*. When Fu Jian 苻堅 (r. 357–85 CE), a king of Former Qin, learned that Madame Song was the only surviving expert on the *Zhou Rituals*, he set up a lecture hall at her residence and appointed her "Sir/Teacher Xuanwen." At the time, she was already eighty years old. Over 120 students received instruction from her. She is often regarded as the first official female grandmaster of the classics. Her story is cited in chapter 11 of Liu Shi, *Nüfan jielu* (*Short Records of Models for Women*), the fourth of the *Four Books for Women*.
10. Ban Zhao, *Lessons for Women*, chapters 1, 3, and 6.
11. Zheng Shi, *Classic of Filial Piety for Women*, chapter 15.
12. Renxiaowen Huanghou, *Teachings for the Inner Court*, chapter 13; Liu Shi, *Short Records of Models for Women*, chapters 6, 9, and 11.

Wang Xiang's Biographic Introduction

Song Ruoxin/Ruohua 宋若莘/若華*, and Song Ruozhao* 宋若昭*:* Analects for Women (Nü lunyu《女論語》)

瑯琊 王相晉升 箋註
莆陽 鄭漢濯之 校梓

Commentator: Langye Region 瑯琊*, Wang Xiang* 王相
(courtesy name: Jin Sheng 晉升 *)*
Proofreader: Fuyang Region 莆陽*, Zheng Han* 鄭漢
(courtesy name: Zhuo Zhi 濯之 *)*

唐書列傳

宋若昭，貝州人，世以儒聞，父棻好學，生五女，若華，若昭，若倫，若憲，若荀，皆慧美能文。若昭文詞高潔，不願歸人，欲以文學名世。若華著《女論語》，若昭申釋之。德宗貞元中，盧龍節度使李抱貞，表其才，詔入禁中，試文章，論經史，俱稱旨。帝每與羣臣賡和，五女皆預焉。屢蒙賞賚，姊妹俱承恩幸。獨若昭願獨居禁院，不希上寵，常以曹大家自許。帝嘉其志，稱為女學士。拜內職，官尚宮，掌六宮文學，職與外尚書等。兼教諸皇子公主，皆事之以師禮，號曰宮師。歷德、順、憲、穆、敬，凡五朝。寶歷中卒，贈梁國夫人。有詩文若干卷，並所訂女論語行世。○棻音焚。

The *Book of Tang*, "Biographies" Section
(*Tangshu:* leizhuan《唐書．列傳》)

Song Ruozhao 宋若昭, a resident of Beizhou, came from a family of well-known scholars.[1] Her father, [Song Ting] Fen ([宋廷] 棻), loved learning and had five daughters: Ruohua 若華, Ruozhao 若昭, Ruolun 若倫, Ruoxian 若憲, and

Rouxun 若荀.[2] All of them were wise, beautiful, and good at literary works. Ruozhao's writings were lofty and pure. She did not want to get married but wished to make a name by her literary work. Ruohua composed the *Analects for Women*; Ruozhao provided the commentary.

During the Zhenyuan 貞元 era of Emperor De 德宗 [of Tang 唐], Li Biaozhen 李抱[真] [733–794 CE],[3] a high-ranking military official of the Lulong area,[4] recommended their talents to the Emperor. Thereupon, the sisters were summoned to the imperial court and tested for their composition skills, as well as their knowledge of the classics and history. They achieved high honors on all subjects. Every time when the Emperor composed and exchanged poetic verses with his ministers and officials at gatherings, the five sisters were invited to participate. Many times, imperial rewards were conferred upon them; all the sisters enjoyed great favors from the Emperor.

Ruozhao alone was willing to reside in the imperial palace. Not because she hoped for special favors from the emperor; rather, she often regarded herself to be like Cao Dagu/Taigu 曹大家.[5] Emperor De commended her aspirations and named her "*Nü Xueshi*" 女學士 ("Woman Scholar-Official"). She was given the official position of *Shanggong* 尚宮 in interior affairs [by Emperor Mu 穆宗], supervising all literary works in the six imperial inner courts (*liugong* 六宮). This was a [high-ranking] position equivalent to *Shangshu* 尚書 [accorded to men] in external affairs. Ruozhao was also asked to instruct princes and princesses; all of them served her with rituals due to a teacher. She was called a "Teacher of the Inner Courts" (*Gongshi* 宮師), and served Emperors De 德 [r. 780–805 CE], Shun 順 [r. 805 CE], Xian 憲 [r. 806–820 CE], Mu 穆 [r. 821–824 CE], and Jing 敬 [r. 825–827 CE]—five regimes in all. She passed away during the Baoli 寶歷 era [825–827 CE] and was given the imperial title "Lady Liangguo" (*Liangguo Furen* 梁國夫人). Several volumes of her poetry and literary work, as well as her commentary on the *Analects for Women* were in circulation. 棻 pronounced as 焚 (*fen*).[6]

Commentaries and Annotations

1. Translator's annotation: Wang Xiang composed this biographic introduction of the author(s) based on materials extracted from Liu Xu et al., *Tangshu* (*Book of Tang*).
2. Translator's annotation: Song Ruoxin 宋若莘 was also known as Song Ruohua 宋若華. See Liu Xu et al., *Tangshu*《唐書》, volume 16, chapter 11.
3. Translator's annotation: According to the *Tangshu*, the Chinese name for Li Biaozhen, the military official who recommended the Song sisters to Emperor De of Tang (mentioned in Wang Xiang's introduction), should be 李抱真, not 李抱貞.
4. Translator's annotation: Based on the *Tangshu*, Li Biaozhen was a high-ranking military official (*Jiedushi* 節度使) in the Zhaoyi area 昭義 (today's southwest region of

the Hebei province and the southeast part of the Shanxi province), not the Lulong area 盧龍 (today's Beijing district).

5. Translator's annotation: Regarding the varied pronunciations of 曹大家, see Ban Zhao, *Lessons for Women*.
6. Translator's annotation: Wang Xiang's text sometimes contains pronouciation notes to teach the readers how to pronounce a less-known word or to alert the readers that a word's pronouciation has changed because of syntax or context. Here is one such example. 棻 is part of Song Ruozhao's father's name and is pronounced as 焚 (*fen*).

【女論語序傳】

大家曰：「妾乃賢人之妻，名家之女，四德粗全，亦通書史。因輟女工，閒觀文字，九烈可嘉，三貞可慕，懼夫後人，不能追步。乃撰一書，名為論語，敬戒相承，教訓女子。若依斯言，是為賢婦，罔俾前人，獨美千古。」

Original Preface to Nü lunyu *by the Song Sisters*

[CAO] DAGU/TAIGU SAID, "I, a lowly woman (*qie* 妾),[1] am the wife of a virtuous man, and a daughter of an eminent family. I am roughly equipped with the four [womanly] virtues[2] and am well-versed in classics and history.[3] For as I stopped my womanly work and took the leisure to read, I found that there were commendable ardent women, who illuminated their nine family clans (*jiulie* 九烈), and admirable females, who were remarkably chaste in three areas (*sanzhen* 三貞). I feared that later generations would not be able to follow in these women's footsteps.[4] Therefore, I wrote this book and titled it the *Analects* in hope that the readers will respectfully observe it, pass it on to others, and use it to instruct young girls.[5] If they can follow these instructions, they will also become virtuous women and will not let (*wangbi* 罔俾) our predecessors alone enjoy splendid reputation through the ages."[6]

Commentaries and Annotations

1. Translator's annotation: Out of politeness, ancient Chinese women often addressed themselves as *qie* 妾 or *qieshen* 妾身.
2. Translator's annotation: For more about the "four womanly virtues" or "four womanly conducts," see chapter 4 of Ban Zhao, *Nüjie* (*Lessons for Women*) and the Hunyi (chapter 44) of the *Liji* (*Record of Rituals*).

3. Wang Xiang's commentary: 大家 *is pronounced as* 泰姑 *(*Taigu*), referring to Cao Taigu of the Han dynasty. This book was Song's work, but Song said that it was by Taigu. This is like the* Classic of Filial Piety for Women, *a work by Madame Zheng of the Tang dynasty, who dare not credit herself, thus attributing the work to Cao Taigu. The preface self-described the purpose of composing this work; it therefore was presented in Taigu's voice: "I am a daughter of an eminent family, the wife of a virtuous scholar, and am roughly equipped with four [womanly] conducts: women's virtue, appearance, speech, and work. I am well-versed in canonical classics, biographies, works by other learned scholars, and books of history."* Translator's annotation: Out of humility, and sometimes to add prestige to one's work, it was common for ancient Chinese authors to attribute their works to another well-respected person. This practice often creates difficulty in identifying who the actual author(s) is. In this case, Song Ruohua (the real author) credited Cao Taigu (Ban Zhao), who authored the *Lessons for Women*, as the alleged author of the *Analects for Women*.
4. Wang Xiang's commentary: 烈 *(*lie*) means "to illuminate, to light up."* 九烈 (jiulie*) describes women who have perfected their chastity and virtue; thus, they bring honor to their husbands and ancestors, pass on blessings to their offspring, and illuminate their nine family clans.* 貞 (zhen*) means "having a pure and one-pointed mind, with unwavering integrity."* 三貞 *(*sanzhen*) refers to the fact that when at home, a young woman is filial toward her parents; when married, she is filial toward her parents-in-law and respectful toward her husband. Of these three relations, she endeavors to attain the virtue of chastity and purity. This is a woman's complete conduct. This is what the ancients often did; the current generation ought to strive to follow their example. She feared that young women of future generations could not follow in their footsteps or emulate their conduct.* Translator's annotation: There are various interpretations about what the "nine family clans" (*jiuzu* 九族) refers to. In one interpretation, it refers to the current generation plus four generations before, and four generations after, along the patrilineal line. Another interpretation refers to four relations on the father's side of the family, three relations on mother's side of family, and two relations on wife's side of the family.
5. Wang Xiang's commentary: *The speaker was worried that women's education is not promulgated. She thus edited and wrote this book, and called it the* Analects for Women. *It is intended to enable women to practice its teachings from childhood. They should respect and take heed of its lessons, comply with its words, and embody its teachings in their conducts. Only then can they become virtuous. Societies should abide by these lessons and use them as women's precepts.*
6. Wang Xiang's commentary: *If young girls and young women can follow and act on these teachings, they will have virtuous names like those virtuous women and chaste ladies from antiquity.* 罔俾 *(*wangbi*) means "to not let it be able to." If young women of future generations can abide these teachings, many will become virtuous. Therefore, they will not let their virtuous predecessors alone have great reputations for millennia with no successors.*

【立身章第一】

凡為女子，先學立身。立身之法，惟務清貞。清則身潔，貞則身榮。行莫回頭，語莫掀唇。坐莫動膝，立莫搖裙。喜莫大笑，怒莫高聲。內外各處，男女異羣。莫窺外壁，莫出外庭。出必掩面，窺必藏形。男非眷屬，莫與通名。女非善淑，莫與相親。立身端正，方可為人。

I

Establishing One's Person (Lishen zhang diyi 立身章第一)

EVERY YOUNG WOMAN should first learn how to establish her person (*lishen* 立身). To establish her person, she must cultivate tranquility and chastity.[1] If she is tranquil, her body will be pure. If she is chaste, her person will be honored.[2]

When walking, she should not turn her head and look back. When speaking, she should not open her lips too wide (*xuan* 掀 [= 軒]). When sitting, she should not shake her knees. When standing, she should not sway her skirt. When happy, she should not laugh aloud. When angry, she should not raise her voice.[3]

[Men and women] should manage the inner sphere and the outer sphere respectively (*gechu* 各處); males and females should be in separate groups. A woman should not peek (*kui* 窺) beyond the outer walls of the residence nor go outside the outer courtyard. [If it is necessary to do so,] she must cover her face when going out and hide her body when peeking [outside].[4] When a woman interacts with a man, if he is not a family member, they should not call each other by name. When interacting with a woman, if that woman is not virtuous, she should avoid becoming too close to her. Only by being established in propriety and rectitude can a woman be [truly] a person.[5]

Commentaries and Annotations

1. Wang Xiang's commentary: 立 (li) *means "to complete, to realize, to establish."* 立身 (lishen) *is to realize the way of "being a person." How to realize the way of being a person? It simply rests on tranquility and chastity. Being proper, clean, peaceful, and undisturbed is called tranquil. Abiding one-minded purity and upholding rectitude are called chastity.*
2. Wang Xiang's commentary: *If a young woman can be tranquil, she will be pure, clean, and without blemish. If she can be chaste, her person will be established and her name honored.*
3. Wang Xiang's commentary: 掀 *pronounced as* 軒 (xuan). *Turning one's head and looking back while walking damages the impression that one leaves to others. Opening one's lips too wide and showing one's teeth [while talking] nullifies [proper] appearance of speech. Shaking one's knees indicates that one cannot sit still. Swaying one's skirt conveys that one cannot stand steadily. All four are signs of debasement; one must take heed and refrain from them. Laughing aloud when rejoicing is to lose one's bearing; raising one's voice when angry is to abandon ritual propriety. How can these two be the proper way of being a woman and a young lady? Both are signs of frivolousness; one must be prudent and not commit such acts.* Translator's annotation: See the *Liji* (*Record of Rituals*), Qulishang 曲禮上 chapter (chapter 1). All these stipulations are cumbersome for women. A more charitable way to look at these strict rules is perhaps to consider them as rules of concentration and stillness, keys to self-cultivation. Swaying skirts, shaking knees, outburst of laughs and anger, etc., are contrary to this goal.
4. Wang Xiang's commentary: 處 *pronounced in the third tone;* 窺 *pronounced as* 虧 (kui). *The* Record of Rituals *says that men should take care of the external realm and women the internal realm. Men walk on the left side of the road and women on the right side. They do not interfere with one another; thus, it is spoken of as "in separate groups." Without legitimate reasons, a woman should neither peek outside the household walls nor go beyond the outer courtyard. If, for unavoidable reasons, a woman must go outside the courtyard, she must cover herself with a handkerchief or a fan so that men cannot see her face. If for some reasons, she must peek outside, she should conceal her figure so that no outsiders can see her body.* Translator's annotation: See *Liji* (*Record of Rituals*), chapters 1 and 12.
5. Wang Xiang's commentary: *A man who is not a woman's brother or close relative, even if there is death in the family, in conversations they should not address each other by name. A woman, who is not virtuous or gentle, even if she is a close relative, one should not interact with her too frequently or intimately, fearing that it may damage one's virtue. In so doing, one will be established in propriety and uprightness. Only then can one [truly] be a person.* Translator's annotation: For more, see *Liji* (*Record of Rituals*), chapter 1.

【學作章第二】

凡為女子，須學女工。紉麻緝苧，粗細不同。車機紡織，切勿匆匆。看蠶煮繭，曉夜相從。採桑摘柘，看雨占風。滓濕即替，寒冷須烘。取葉飼食，必得其中。取絲經緯，丈疋成工。輕紗下軸，細布入筒。綢絹苧葛，織造重重。亦可貨賣，亦可自縫。刺鞋作襪，引線繡絨。縫聯補綴，百事皆通。能依此語，寒冷從容。衣不愁破，家不愁窮。莫學懶婦，積小痴慵。不貪女務，不計春冬。針線粗率，為人所攻。嫁為人婦，恥辱門風。衣裳破損，牽西遮東。遭人指點，恥笑鄉中。奉勸女子，聽取言終。

2

Learning the Work (Xuezuo zhang dier 學作章第二)

ALL YOUNG WOMEN should learn women's work (*nügong* 女工). In braiding (*yin* 紉) hemp (*ma* 麻) and plaiting ramie (*zhu* 苧), note that hemp is coarse and ramie is fine. When using a loom to spin and weave, she must not hasten in this work.[1] In taking care of silkworms and boiling cocoons (*jian* 繭), she must attend to them day and night. She should pick leaves of the mulberry and the zhe 柘 trees [to feed the silkworms] and be watchful of rain and wind. If silkworms' boxes are wet (*zi* 滓), immediately replace them. If the silkworms are cold, warm them up by the fire. In feeding (*si* 飼) the silkworms with leaves, she should observe the moderate amount.

She will reel silk threads from cocoons, use them for the warp and the weft, and complete bolts (*zhang pi* 丈疋)[2] of silk cloth.[3] Store yarns on spools, fabrics in rolls. Weave plenty of silk, ramie, and hemp; these can be used for sale or for one's sewing. Make shoes and socks, stitch, embroider, sew, and mend clothes. A woman should be good at all these tasks. If a woman can follow these lessons, she will be at ease during cold seasons, neither will she have to worry about clothes being torn nor will her household suffer from poverty.[4]

Do not learn from those lazy women. Since childhood (*jixiao* 積小), they were ignorant and indolent, not eager for women's work. They make no plans for spring or winter. Their needlework is rough and careless. Thus, others criticize them. When they get married, they bring shame to both their natal and matrimonial families. When clothes are torn, they use these clothes to repair those clothes (*qianxi zhedong* 牽西遮東).[5] They are pointed to and laughed at by their fellow villagers jeeringly. I respectfully advise all young women to heed my words carefully.[6]

Commentaries and Annotations

1. Wang Xiang's commentary: 紉 *pronounced as* 銀 *(*yin*),* 苧 *pronounced as* 住 *(*zhu*). This chapter talks about the way of women's work. For "work" is one of the four womanly virtues, all women must learn it. Once women know that they ought to learn it, they must be diligent at it.* 紉 *is "to braid, to plait."* 苧 *is ramie (qingma* 檾麻*). A woman needs to braid and plait the threads of these plants, to prepare them to be woven into fabrics. Regarding hemp and ramie, one is coarse and the other is fine. Yet in braiding and plaiting them, she must be one-minded in the required work, not treating them differently because one is coarse and the other is fine. Once braiding is done, she should use a loom to separate the yarns, guide and arrange the yarns in the apparatus, and weave them into fabrics. In weaving, her work should be diligent, prudent, and skillful; the spacing and density of the fabrics should follow what is required. She must not hasten or omit anything.* 檾 *pronounced as* 頃 *(*qing*).* Translator's annotation: 紉 ordinarily should be pronounced as *ren* (in the fourth tone), as in 縫紉 (*feng ren*). It is unclear why Wang Xiang said that it is pronounced as *yin*.
2. Translator's annotation: 丈疋 (*zhang pi*) are ancient Chinese measurements for length of fabrics. One 丈 (*zhang*) is ten feet. Four *zhang* is one 疋 (= 匹 *pi*). For ease of understanding, I have translated the phrase as "bolts."
3. Wang Xiang's commentary: 繭 *pronounced as* 簡 *(*jian*);* 柘 *as* 遮 *(*zhe*) in the fourth tone;* 滓 *pronounced as* 子 *(*zi*);* 飼 *pronounced as* 嗣 *(*si*). This passage speaks about raising silkworms and weaving. Men attend to farming, women to weaving, are two important human affairs. The business of attending to mulberry trees and silkworms is women's specialization. In raising silkworms and reeling silk from cocoons, one should be diligent in taking care of these tasks. Rise early and rest late. Do not be lazy. One should pick the leaves of the mulberry and zhe trees for silkworms' food. Build racks to help feed silkworms and pay attention to wind and rain. If silkworms' boxes are wet, replace them. If silkworms are cold, use coal and fire to keep them warm. In feeding silkworms, the feedings must be done in regular intervals both day and night so that they do not suffer from hunger or over-eating. When silkworms become cocoons, reel the silk threads for the warp and the weft, and weave the threads into bolts of cloth. Then, the work of weaving silk is complete.*

4. Wang Xiang's commentary: *Yarns are raw silk. Whether they are thin or thick, store them on spools. Fine fabrics can be rolled up for ease of storage. Bolts of silk can be stored for sale to help pay for the family's daily expenses. What remains can be used to make clothes in preparation for the cold and hot seasons. If there is spare time, a woman can make shoes and socks. For all women's needlework, there is nothing that she is not good at. If a young woman can follow this lesson, her family will surely have plenty and will have no worries of poverty or deficiency.*
5. Translator's annotation: *Qianxi zhedong* 牽西遮東 literally means "drag the west to cover the east." It is a Chinese expression for a shortsighted and useless attempt to solve a problem.
6. Wang Xiang's commentary: 積小 *(*jixiao*) speaks to the situation that since childhood, a woman has developed a habit of laziness, thus becoming ignorant. Weaving and needlework, which are women's duties, are left behind and not eagerly attended to. Taking care of silkworms in the spring and fermenting wine in the winter, things that young women should know, are abandoned and not properly planned. Even if she reluctantly does needlework, her work is done negligently, roughly, and carelessly. Thus, she is scolded by her parents. When she is married, she is despised by her parents-in-law. She brings disgrace not only to her matrimonial family but also to her parents. Not diligent in her needlework, a woman not only cannot manage her parents-in-law's and husband's clothes, but also cannot mend her own clothes. Using these clothes to patch up those clothes, thus showing collar and elbow, how could she not be pointed to and laughed at by others? Her lazy name will be broadcast among her fellow villagers. A young woman must be prudent about this! She should respectfully listen to these words and not neglect them.*

【學禮章第三】

凡為女子，當知禮數。女客相過，安排坐具。整頓衣裳，輕行緩步。斂手低聲，請過庭戶。問候通時，從頭稱敘。答問殷勤，輕言細語。備辦茶湯，迎來遞去。莫學他人，擡身不顧。接見依稀，有相欺侮。如到人家，當知女務。相見傳茶，即通事故。說罷起身，再三辭去。主若相留，禮筵待遇。酒略沾唇，食無叉箸。退盞辭壺，過承推拒。莫學他人，呼湯呷醋。醉後顛狂，招人所惡。身未回家，已遭點污。當在家庭，少游道路。生面相逢，低頭看顧。莫學他人，不知朝暮。走遍鄉村，說三道四。引惹惡聲，多招罵怒。辱賤門風，連累父母。損破自身，供他笑具。如此之人，有如犬鼠。莫學他人，惶恐羞辱。

3

Learning the Rituals (Xueli zhang disan 學禮章第三)

EVERY YOUNG WOMAN should know proper rituals and etiquette.[1] If female guests are visiting, she should arrange chairs and stools. She should tidy up her clothing, walk lightly, and tread slowly. She should withdraw her hands [to show respect] and speak in a low voice. She should welcome her guests to come inside the courtyard and the inner quarters. She should greet them, inquire about their well-being, and chat with them about the day and the season. From the beginning, she should address them and engage in conversations [properly]. She should reply to her guests' inquiries hospitably and speak in a soft voice. She should prepare tea for the guests, invite them to use it, and offer it to them.[2]

Do not learn from those people, who barely stand up [to welcome their guests]. They neglect their guests, receive them not according to any rituals, and even bully and insult their guests.[3]

If a woman visits someone else's house, she should know women's proper affairs. After the initial meeting and after having tea, she should immediately communicate the reasons for her visit. After she finishes stating her reasons, she should rise, thank the hostess repeatedly, and leave. If the hostess invites her to stay and prepares a banquet to host her, she should only let the wine lightly touch her lips. She should not use her eating utensils to randomly poke at food. [If the hostess offers her more drink,] she should withdraw her cup and send the [wine-] pot away, pass it on, and refuse to have more.[4]

Do not learn from those people, who shout for soup, drink vinegar, and act insanely after getting drunk. They are despised by others. Before they arrive home, their names have already been tarnished.[5]

Women should stay home. Rarely should they wander on the streets. If they encounter strangers on the street, they should lower their heads and only look at themselves.[6]

Do not learn from those people, who do not care to know whether it is day or night, walk all over the village, gossip, and disparage others. They provoke spiteful remarks, and often stir up quarrels and anger. These people bring disgrace to their families, burden their parents, ruin themselves, and become the laughingstock of others. Such people are like dogs and rats. Do not learn from those people [who inflict] fear and shame [upon themselves].[7]

Commentaries and Annotations

1. Translator's annotation: In the Zhuangyuange edition and some other editions, the phrase used here is *lishu* 禮數 (ritual and etiquette), whereas in two other editions the phrase is *nüwu* 女務 (women's affairs).
2. Wang Xiang's commentary: *This chapter addresses the way of receiving [female] guests. Men take charge of the external affairs, women the internal affairs. Men receive their [male] guests and friends in the main hall; women receive their female guests in the inner quarters. This is what ritual propriety mandates. A woman must know proper ritual and etiquette. Before female guests arrive, she should clean and sweep the inner quarters, and arrange the sitting area. Utensils and cups for serving drinks, food, and tea should be prepared in advance. When guests arrive, she should straighten her appearance and tidy up her clothes. Poised and steady, she should tread lightly and speak in a gentle voice. With a pleasant look, she will welcome guests to come inside the courtyard, all in an unhurried and ritually appropriate manner. After everyone sits down, she shall inquire about guests' well-being, wait for them to talk about their hobbies, reciprocate the ritual of gift-giving, and chat with them about daily and seasonal changes of winter and summer at their locality. In speech, everything is done orderly;*

in conversation, she is agreeable, in good pace, and unhurried, and she speaks in a soft, rather than loud, voice. Tea is fragrant and pure; drinks and food are abundant. In welcoming and sending off guests, and in presenting gifts, she always acts in a peaceful and ritually appropriate way. In doing so, the etiquette of receiving guests is certainly fulfilled.

3. Wang Xiang's commentary: *This passage advises all not to learn from arrogant impolite people. When these people see that their guests are coming, they do not bother to stand up. When they reluctantly stand up, they do not pay attention to their guests. They receive the guests neglectfully and arrogantly, hardly according to any etiquette. In conversation, they bully their guests as if the guests are ignorant, or look down on the guests for being poor and lowly. These people are insulting, neglectful, and rude.*
4. Wang Xiang's commentary: *If a woman has reasons to visit a relative, she should act according to rituals appropriate for women, like those prescribed earlier regarding how to receive guests. Once the tea is served, she should inquire about their well-being and explain the reasons for her visit. Once she has finished, she should bid farewell. If the hostess insists that she stays and prepares food and wine, she must not drink to the point that her cheeks turn red. She must also not use her eating utensils to poke food at random. If the hostess refills her wine cup, she should stand up, thank the hostess, and bid farewell. Do not linger, for fear that any delay may result in violation of ritual propriety.*
5. Wang Xiang's commentary: *One must not imitate those women from petty families. They have no table manners; they wolf down food and drink wildly. Even when soups and dishes are gone, they do not know it is time to stop. They become drunk and talk recklessly. On their way home, they walk askew, and their clothes are filthy. Such women are despised by others with contempt.*
6. Wang Xiang's commentary: *This passage conveys that it is better for women not to go beyond the courtyard. They should not wander on the streets. If they must be on the streets for some necessary reason, they should cover their faces so that no strangers can toy with their looks. They must lower their heads, pay attention only to their steps, walk slowly, and not lose their composures.*
7. Wang Xiang's commentary: *Do not learn from those ignorant women, who especially like to wander. They do not care whether it is day or night, walk all over the village, and irresponsibly gossip about others' right and wrong without hesitation. Thus, neighbors from the east and from the west quarrel with one another, yell vicious words, and exchange insults. These conflicts and fights cause one to lose face, bring disgrace to one's family and parents, ruin one's own reputation, and make one become a laughingstock. Such a person does not even measure up to dogs or rats. What use does she have? It cautions young women that they must not learn from this kind of people, who self-inflict fear and shame upon themselves.*

【早起章第四】

凡為女子，習以為常，五更雞唱，起著衣裳。盥漱已了，隨意梳妝。揀柴燒火，早下廚房。摩鍋洗鑊，煮水煎湯。隨家豐儉，蒸煮食嘗。安排蔬菜，炮豉舂薑。隨時下料，甜淡馨香。整齊碗碟，鋪設分張。三飡飯食，朝暮相當，侵晨早起。百事無妨。莫學懶婦，不解思量。黃昏一覺，直到天光。日高三丈，猶未離床。起來已晏，卻是慚惶。未曾梳洗，突入廚房。容顏齷齪，手脚慌忙。煎茶煮飯，不及時常。又有一等，餔餟爭嘗，未曾炮饌，先已偷藏。醜呈鄉里，辱及爺娘。被人傳說，豈不羞惶。

4

Rising Early (Zaoqi zhang disi 早起章第四)

EVERY YOUNG WOMAN should get used to the routine of getting up and putting on clothes at the fifth watch of the night when the roosters are crowing.[1] After she has washed her face and rinsed her mouth, she shall groom and dress herself at will. Thereupon, she will gather firewood to start the fire [for the stove], go to the kitchen early, scrub the pots, wash cooking utensils, boil water, and make tea.[2]

According to the family's condition of having plenty or only simple means, she will steam or boil food, arrange vegetables, quick-fry fermented beans, grind (*chong* 舂) ginger, readily add them to the dishes, and make food suitably sweet, plain, or fragrant. She will also place bowls and plates in an orderly manner and set up the table. All three meals (*can* 飡), whether during the day or at night, should be prepared similarly. Because she rises early at dawn, she can complete all things without problems.[3]

Do not learn from those lazy women, who do not think and measure things [prudently]. They go to bed (*jiao* 覺) at dusk and sleep through the night until daytime. When the Sun has already risen thirty feet high (*san zhang* 三丈), they still have not left their beds.[4] When they get up, it is already late. Feeling ashamed and worried, before washing up they rush into the kitchen. They look ungroomed and dirty (*wo chuo* 齷齪); their hands and feet are in a rush. Even though they make tea and cook meals, still everything gets ready later than the normal hours.[5]

There is also another kind of woman. They compete with others to be the first in eating and drinking (*bu zhuo* 餔餟). Even before the ingredients are quick-fried or prepared, they already steal and hide some food. Their ugly deeds are known to their fellow villagers. They bring disgrace to their parents and are talked about by others. Isn't this something to be ashamed of?[6]

Commentaries and Annotations

1. Translator's annotation: In ancient China, a night is divided into five periods or watches. Each period or watch is about two hours. The first watch begins at approximately 7 P.M. 五更 (*wu geng*), also called 寅時 (*yin shi*), is the fifth watch of the night, about 3 A.M. to 5 A.M., right before dawn.
2. Wang Xiang's commentary: *This chapter speaks about the business of rising early. To rise early in the morning and to rest late at night are the common practice of women. Planning for the day rests in rising early before dawn (*yin 寅*); many things will therefore be properly prepared. The* Record of Rituals *says that the way of a young woman is that at the first crowing of the roosters, she should put on her clothes, wash her face, rinse her mouth, and greet her parents first; then, go to the kitchen, gather firewood, start the fire, wash pots and cooking utensils, cook water, and prepare tea to serve her parents and parents-in-law.* Translator's annotation: 湯 (*tang*) here means 茶湯 (*cha tang*), or tea. 寅 (*yin*) refers to 寅時 (*yin shi*), the fifth watch of the night (3 A.M.–5 A.M.). The *Record of Rituals* cited here by Wang Xiang refers to the Neize chapter (chapter 12).
3. Wang Xiang's commentary: 舂 *pronounced as* 充 (chong). *After tea is finished, breakfast should be served right after. Regarding dishes and vegetables, it depends on the family's finances. If there is plenty, then prepare more; if little, then be frugal. Depending on whether the season is cold or warm, either steam or boil food. Add salt, fermented beans, pepper, or ginger, according to the nature of the dish and prepare the food adequately sweet, plain, or fragrant. Distribute clean bowls and plates evenly according to the number of people. Make sure to only use rich and nutritious ingredient for parents' and parents-in-law's food. As a common practice, all three meals should be prepared similarly. Afterwards, withdraw and do women's work. No work will be abandoned, for rising early can accomplish many things. If one had risen late, one could prepare meals but would not be able to attend to women's work, or one could attend to women's work but would not have time to prepare meals.* Translator's annotation: 飡 (*can*) is synonymous with 餐 (*can*).

4. Translator's annotation: As mentioned earlier, one 丈 (*zhang*) is ten feet. Thus, three *zhang* (*san zhang* 三丈) are thirty feet. The phrase *san zhang* is used metaphorically, expressing that the Sun has risen high.
5. Wang Xiang's commentary: 覺 *pronounced as* 教 *(*jiao*),* 齷齪 *pronounced as* 沃觸 (wo chu*). Lazy women do not think over their daily planning. They only covet more sleep. At dusk, they are already in bed. The Sun has risen high; they still have not gotten up. They are scolded by their parents and parents-in-law. Feeling so ashamed and worried, before washing up they go to the kitchen. Their appearance, hands, and feet are filthy and they are in a hurry. Cooking is not done properly. Tea and meals are not provided in time. A mistake caused by one instance of laziness, nonetheless, destroys hundreds of works.* Translator's annotation: The correct pronunciation for 齪 should be *chuo* 綽, not *chu* 觸 .
6. Wang Xiang's commentary: 餔 *pronounced as* 補 (bu*) in the first tone.* 餟 *pronounced as* 拙 *(*zhuo*). There are also those women who covet food (*haochi 好吃*). Regarding beverage and food, they necessarily taste everything before anyone else. They not only try to eat first but also steal and hide food. They only think about self-enjoyment and do not care about their parents' or parents-in-law' meals at all. When they are found out by their elders, they are shamed and scolded by the elders. They bring disgrace to their parents. That their bad habits of coveting food (*haokou 好口*) cause them to descend to such a state, isn't it (*ke sheng 可勝*) laughable?* 好 *(*hao*) pronounced in the fourth tone.* 勝 *(*sheng*) pronounced in the first tone.*

【事父母章第五】

女子在堂，敬重爹娘。每朝早起，先問安康。寒則烘火，熱則扇涼。饑則進食，渴則進湯。父母檢責，不得慌忙。近前聽取，早夜思量。若有不是，改過從長。父母言語，莫作尋常。遵依教訓，不可強良。若有不諳，借問無妨。父母年老，朝夕憂惶，補聯鞋襪，做造衣裳。四時八節，孝養相當。父母有疾，身莫離床。衣不解帶，湯藥親嘗。禱告神祇，保佑安康。設有不幸，大數身亡。痛入骨髓，哭斷肝腸，劬勞罔極，恩德難忘。衣裳裝檢，持服居喪。安理設祭，禮拜家堂。逢周遇忌，血淚汪汪。莫學忤逆，不敬爹娘。纔出一語，使氣昂昂，需索陪送，爭競衣裝。父母不幸，說短論長，搜求財帛，不顧哀喪。如此婦人，狗彘豺狼。

5

Serving One's Parents (Shifumu zhang diwu 事父母章第五)

ANY YOUNG WOMAN who still stays home ought to revere and value her parents. Every morning when she gets up, she should greet them and inquire about their well-being. If they are cold, warm them up with a fire; if they are hot, cool them down with a fan. If they are hungry, bring them food; if they are thirsty, serve them tea.[1] If parents correct or reprimand one, do not become flustered or act in a hurry. Rather, get closer and listen to them. Day and night, think about what they have said. If one has made mistakes, correct them, and do what is right.[2] Parents' words should not be taken for granted. One should obey their teaching. Do not be defiant (*qiangliang* 強良).[3] If there is anything that one does not understand (*buan* 不諳), it would not hurt to ask for clarification.[4]

When one's parents get old, day and night one is saddened and worried [by their old age]. One ought to patch up and sew their shoes and socks, and make them clothes. During the transition of the four seasons and at the eight major indicators of seasonal changes (*sishi bajie* 四時八節),[5] one should especially be filial and provide them with special nourishment.[6]

If parents become ill, one should not leave their bedside. [In caring for them,] one will not have time to untie the belt of one's clothing.[7] One should personally taste the medicine soup [before offering it to them], and pray to gods and spiritual beings for their safety and health.[8]

If unfortunately, parents pass away, one's pain will be felt as deeply as in the marrow of one's bones. One will wail in sorrow as if one's liver and intestines are about to burst. Parents' labor in caring for one has no limit; their kindness and virtue are unforgettable. Clothe and bury them [in coffins], and make sure everything is done properly. Don mourning clothes and observe the [three-year] mourning rite. Arrange ritual offerings in an orderly manner. Set up the worship site in the family hall. When it is the anniversary of parents' birthday and the date of their death, one will weep as if blood is about to bleed out of one's eyes.[9]

Do not learn from those rebellious women who disrespect their parents. When parents utter only one word, these women are already puffed up with anger. They demand dowry from their parents and compete for clothes and accessories. When parents pass away, they gossip about who is bad and who is good. They search and claim their deceased parents' fortune without showing a sign of sorrow for their death. Such women are like dogs, pigs, jackals, and wolves![10]

Commentaries and Annotations

1. Wang Xiang's commentary: *This chapter speaks about the way of serving one's parents. As a young woman, every morning after she gets up, she should first greet her parents and inquire about their well-being. If they are cold, prepare coal and fire; if they are too warm, fan their bed and sleeping mat. Find a clean and cool place for parents to sit after they get up. If they are hungry, bring them food; if they are thirsty, bring them drinks. Everything will be done appropriately.* Translator's annotation: For more on the prescribed filial acts, see the *Liji* (*Record of Rituals*), Neize 內則 chapter (chapter 12).
2. Wang Xiang's commentary: *If one makes mistakes, parents may be angry and may scold one. When this happens, do not argue with them, but listen to them calmly and respectfully. Do not become flustered and act in a hurry because of it, thus causing further mistakes. Day and night, ponder over what they said: if one indeed made a mistake, think about what one can do so that one does not make the same mistake and how one can be free of parents' rebuke in the future. Only after one's mistakes are corrected can one be relaxed.*
3. Translator's annotation: 強良 (*qiangliang*) is the same as 強梁 (*qiangliang*).
4. Wang Xiang's commentary: 諳 *pronounced as* 安 *(*an*); it means "to understand and practice." Parents' instruction should not be neglected. One should be considerate and*

obey what they said. Do not be defiant or think that one is the smarter person. If there is anything that one does not understand, one can calmly ask parents [for clarification].

5. Translator's annotation: *Sishi* 四時 refers to the four seasons. *Bajie* 八節 refers to the beginning of spring (*lichun* 立春), the spring equinox (*chunfen* 春分), the beginning of summer (*lixia* 立夏), the summer solstice (*xiazhi* 夏至), the beginning of autumn (*liqiu* 立秋), the autumn equinox (*qiufen* 秋分), the beginning of winter (*lidong* 立冬), and the winter solstice (*dongzhi* 冬至). See the *Zhoubi suanjing* 《周髀算經》 (*Classic of Arithmetic from the Gnomon of the Zhou Sundial*); and the *Hanshu* 《漢書》 (*Book of Han*), Lülizhi 律曆志 ("Records of Laws and Calendars"). Traditional Chinese major festivals are often celebrations that coincide with these eight major indicators of seasonal changes.
6. Wang Xiang's commentary: *When parents get old, one is on the one hand delighted to see their longevity, and yet on the other hand one is worried that they may not have many more years to come. One should check parents' clothes and shoes often, and make sure that these items are not torn so that parents do not suffer from cold. Adjust their drinks and food so that they are not overly full or overly hungry. When the eight major pointers of seasonal change during the four seasons take place, make sure that one entertains them with food and activities, and do one's best in being filial and in providing them with [special] nourishment. For when one is young, one is happy whenever a festival approaches. But when one is old, one feels sad when a festival is near. It is because one fears that the good times may not come by again. Thus, when seasonal festivals arrive, make sure that one is not deficient in caring for one's parents. Make them happy so that they forget their old age. This is called filial.* Translator's annotation: Wang Xiang's commentary echoes *Analects* 4.31.
7. Translator's annotation: Ancient Chinese wore a robe tied with a belt at the waistline. "Not having time to untie the belt of one's clothing" (*yibujiedai* 衣不解帶) is an expression conveying that one labors over something attentively without rest.
8. Wang Xiang's commentary: *If parents happen to be ill, day and night she, as a daughter, must not leave their bedside. She will go to bed without undressing herself, sleep lightly with eyelashes barely touching each other, and personally taste the medicine soup before offering it to her parents. Reverently pray to gods and spiritual beings. Supplicate for their safe recovery; only then can she be relaxed.* Translator's note: For more, see the *Liji* (*Record of Rituals*), Qulixia 曲禮下 (chapter 2).
9. Wang Xiang's commentary: *If unfortunately, parents pass away, one must wail in deep sorrow. In thanking those who come to send their condolence, one should kneel, knock one's head on the ground, and weep deeply (*qisang qixue 稽顙泣血*). One should often think about the fact that the kindness of parents' labor is like Heaven without limit. If parents left behind private properties, one should not change one's filial heart simply because their sons and daughters have different opinions on how to handle these properties. One should do one's best to supplement what one's brothers cannot do. Parents' burial clothes, coffins, intimate things to be buried with them*

must be arranged thoroughly with every detail carefully attended to; not one single item should be missing. In observing filial piety and the mourning period, one must be sincere and reverential. In conducting burial and worship rites, one must do one's best. When it is festival time, or the anniversary of their birthday and the date of their death, one necessarily misses parents in sadness and tears. One should not abandon this ritual simply because one is a woman or change one's mind because one has married. Only then can one be called to "do one's best in serving them when parents are alive; miss them to the utmost when they pass away." Translator's annotation: See the *Liji* (*Record of Rituals*), Sangfu sizhi 喪服四制 (chapter 49); Confucius, *Analects* 17.19; and *Xiaojing* (*Classic of Filial Piety*), Sangqin zhang 喪親章 (chapter 18), regarding three-year mourning rite for deceased parents.

10. Wang Xiang's commentary: *Unvirtuous women do not know filialness and reverence. When their parents give them instructions, they do not comply. When their parents reprimand them occasionally, they immediately become enraged. At home, they fight with others for clothing and accessories; they demand dowry from their parents. After they are married, they are close to their husbands but distant from their parents. When their parents pass away, they gossip about others, disparage their sisters-in-law, and search and claim their deceased parents' fortunes without showing any sign of sorrow and mourning for their death. Such women are as evil as jackals and wolves. They do not even measure up to pigs and dogs.*

【事舅姑章第六】

阿翁阿姑，夫家之主。既入他門，合稱新婦。供承看養，如同父母。敬事阿翁，形容不覷，不敢隨行，不敢對語。如有使令，聽其囑咐。姑坐則立，使令便去。早起開門，莫令驚忤。灑掃庭堂，洗濯巾布。齒藥肥皂，溫涼得所，退步［階］前，待其浣洗。萬福一聲，即時退步。整辦茶盤，安排匙筯。香潔茶湯，小心敬遞。飯則軟蒸，肉則熟煮。自古老人，齒牙疏蛀。茶水羹湯，莫教虛度。夜晚更深，將歸睡處。安置相辭，方回房戶。日日一般，朝朝相似。傳教庭幃，人稱賢婦。莫學他人，跳梁可惡。咆哮尊長，說辛道苦。呼喚不來，饑寒不顧。如此之人，號為惡婦。天地不容，雷霆震怒。責罰加身，悔之無路。

6

Serving Parents-in-Law (Shijiugu zhang diliu 事舅姑章第六)

PARENTS-IN-LAW ARE THE head of one's husband's family. Since one has married to another household, and is called a new daughter-in-law, one ought to serve and care for the parents-in-law just like one's own parents.[1] Serve one's father-in-law with respect. [As a daughter-in-law,] one should not look at him directly nor walk or converse with him [as equals]. If he gives an order, one should listen and carry it out.[2] Where one's mother-in-law is sitting, one should stand by her side. If she gives a command, one should immediately follow it through.

Every morning when one opens the door, do not startle the parents-in-law. Sprinkle water and sweep the courtyard and the family hall. Wash linens and towels. [Prepare and bring] dentifrice, soap, and water at the right temperature [to their bedroom]. Withdraw to the outside step. Wait for them to finish washing themselves. When they are done, wish them great happiness (*wanfu* 萬福),[3] and leave immediately.[4]

[In the kitchen,] one should organize tea cups and platters, and arrange spoons and chopsticks. Make sure that the tea and soup are fragrant and clean. Carefully and respectfully offer them to the parents-in-law. Make sure also that rice is steamed soft and meat is fully cooked, because from the ancient times, old people often have sparse and decayed teeth. [Throughout the day,] serve them tea, water, congee, and soup; do not let them spend the day hungry.[5]

When it is late at night and time to go to bed, help parents-in-law get ready for bed and bid them good night before one retreats to one's own room. Day after day one does the same thing. Morning after morning one acts similarly. Then, one's example will be promulgated among the inner quarters and one will be praised for being a virtuous woman.[6]

Do not learn from those women, who are defiant, lawless (*tiaoliang* 跳梁), and despicable. They shout (*paoxiao* 咆哮) at their venerable elders and complain about their hardship and suffering. When their parents-in-law call them, they do not bother to come, nor do they care about whether their in-laws are hungry or cold. Such persons are evil women and will not be tolerated by Heaven or Earth. They provoke the rage of thunder and lightning. Reproach and punishments will surely come to them. There will be no way out even if they regret what they did.[7]

Commentaries and Annotations

1. Wang Xiang's commentary: *This chapter talks about the rituals of serving one's parents-in-law. Parents-in-law are one's husband's parents and they are the head of the household. A young woman follows her husband. In front of her parents-in-law, she ought to strive to carry out the rituals of being a new daughter-in-law. Be respectful in serving them, following the same rituals as how she serves her parents.*
2. Wang Xiang's commentary: *In front of her father-in-law, a new daughter-in-law should be obedient and humble. She dares not to look at him directly nor walk with him in his steps. If a conversation takes place, she should stand on the side while listening, and calmly answer his questions without directly looking at his face. If he gives an order, she should gently obey it, and follow it through without delay.* Translator's annotation: These stipulations can be found in the *Liji* (*Record of Rituals*).
3. Translator's annotation: *Wanfu* 萬福 literally means "ten thousand happinesses."
4. Wang Xiang's commentary: *When a mother-in-law is sitting, a daughter-in-law should stand by her side. If a mother-in-law gives an order, a daughter-in-law should immediately follow it through without disobeying. Every morning when the daughter-in-law gets up, opens the door, and starts the day, she should not make loud noise lest it disrupt parents-in-law's sleep. Use water to sprinkle the floor. Sweep and clean the yard and the halls. Wash towels and linens for later use throughout the day. When parents-in-law get up and it's time for them to wash themselves, warm up the water and arrange*

towels, dentifrice, and soap. The water should be warm, but not too hot or too cold. Send everything to the parents-in-law's room. Withdraw outside to wait for them to finish washing themselves. Once they are finished, inquire about their well-being; then, withdraw to the kitchen, and prepare tea and meals.

5. Wang Xiang's commentary: *Since one is in the kitchen, one should clean up, wash, and wipe. Tea platters, bowls, plates, spoons, chopsticks, tea, and soup must be clean and smell nice. Carefully and respectfully offer them to the parents-in-law. The rice must be steamed soft, not hard. The meat must be fully cooked, not raw. Keep in mind that old people's teeth are sparse, decayed, and infirm. It is better for them to eat food that is soft but not hard. Throughout the day, sometimes abundantly and sometimes less so, one should be diligent in serving them tea, pastry, and fruits. Keep in mind that for older people, the day is long and they may get hungry. Do not let them spend the day in hunger.*
6. Wang Xiang's commentary: *After the dinner is finished, parents-in-law are about to go to bed. A daughter-in-law must help them get ready for bed, bid them good night, and then retreat to her own room. A day's business of serving one's parents-in-law is thus completed. Day after day, morning after morning, she must be tirelessly respectful. Then, she will be a filial daughter-in-law. Everyone knows this is the way of being a daughter-in-law, but they cannot persistently serve their parents-in-law with respect. Doing so for a long time without lessening is what makes it difficult. Once she completes the ritual of serving parents-in-law in its utmost degree, in the inner quarters her sisters-in-law and their children will emulate her deeds and follow her teaching. In the district and neighborhood, married women and young ladies will also respect and revere her actions and praise her filialness. Thus, the saying "if one family is filial, the whole village will be filial."*
7. Wang Xiang's commentary: 跳梁 (tiaoliang) *refers to the situation where a bamboo woven fence was placed in the water to prevent fish from jumping out; yet, a strong fish may still jump over the fence. Here the expression is used to describe women who do not revere the instructions of their parents-in-law and are self-indulgent.* 咆哮 (paoxiao) *means "to yell or shout." It describes women who are impolite and yell in front of their venerable elders. This speaks about unfilial daughters-in-law who are arrogant and self-indulgent, yelling impolitely, bragging about their ability, and complaining about their hardship. In front of their parents-in-law, these women do not listen to their in-laws' instruction, and do not care about whether their in-laws are hungry or cold. These are truly evil women. How is it possible that Heaven and Earth, thunder and lightning, tolerate such unvirtuous and unfilial persons? Thus, the punishment of disasters and illness will surely come to them. Then, they will know the crime of their unfilialness. When this happens, there will be no way out even if they regret what they did.*

【事夫章第七】

女子出嫁，夫主為親。前生緣分，今世婚姻。將夫比天，其義匪輕，夫剛妻柔，恩愛相因。居家相待，敬重如賓。夫有言語，側耳詳聽。夫有惡事，勸諫諄諄。莫學愚婦，惹禍臨身。夫若外出，須記途程。黃昏未返，瞻望思尋。停燈溫飯，等候敲門。莫若懶婦，先自安身。夫如有病，終日勞心。多方問藥，遍處求神。百般治療，願得長生。莫學蠢婦，全不憂心。夫若發怒，不可生嗔。退身相讓，忍氣低聲。莫學潑婦，鬪鬧頻頻。粗絲細葛，熨貼縫紉。莫教寒冷，凍損夫身。家常茶飯，供待殷勤。莫教饑渴，瘦瘠苦辛。同甘同苦，同富同貧。死同棺槨，生共衣衾。能依此語，和樂瑟琴。如此之女，賢德聲聞。

7

Serving One's Husband (Shifu zhang diqi 事夫章第七)

WHEN A YOUNG woman is married, her husband becomes the head of her person and is the closest relation of all. The predestined relationship from a former life results in a marriage in the present life. [The old saying] comparing husband to Heaven, its meaning is not to be taken lightly: the husband ought to be strong and the wife gentle; they should be kind and loving toward one another, and mutually dependent on each other.[1]

When at home, a husband and a wife should treat each other as respectfully as they treat a guest. When the husband is speaking, the wife should listen attentively. Should he slide into evil ways, the wife ought to remonstrate with him repeatedly.[2] Do not learn from those ignorant women, who invite disasters to themselves [by doing evil things].[3]

If the husband goes out, the wife should record his itinerary. If at dusk he still has not returned, she should look outside to search for him or send someone to look for him. Keep the light on and the dishes warm. Wait for him to knock on the door. Do not be like those lazy women, who go to bed themselves [regardless of whether their husbands have returned].[4]

If the husband becomes ill, day and night the wife should be concerned. She should go to as many places as possible to seek a cure, plead to gods everywhere, and find all sorts of treatments, in hope that he can enjoy a long life. Do not learn from those stupid women who are not concerned at all about their husbands' illness.[5]

If the husband gets angry, do not become irritated yourself. Retreat and yield. Suppress your anger and keep your voice low. Do not learn from those loud aggressive women, who fight with their husbands all the time.[6]

Whether clothes are made of rugged silk or fine hemp, one should iron, mend, and sew them. Do not let cold harm the husband's body. Diligently and attentively serve tea and meals. Do not let hunger or thirst cause him to become thin or to suffer. Enjoy happiness and bear suffering together; share wealth and poverty as one. When dead, buried in the same coffin; when alive, sharing the same bedcover.[7]

If a woman can abide by these words, [her relationship with her husband will be] like the harmony produced by the *qin* zither (*qin* 琴) and the *se* zither (*se* 瑟) playing together. Such a woman, her virtuous reputation will be known everywhere.[8]

Commentaries and Annotations

1. Wang Xiang's commentary: *This chapter speaks about the way that a wife should serve her husband. When at home, a young woman is to obey her father; when married, she is to obey her husband. A husband is the leader of his wife. Now a husband and a wife from different surnames are joined together as a married couple, is this simply a coincidence? Because of the predestined relationship from a former life, it brings forth the good marriage of a husband and a wife in the present life. The [*Book of Ceremonial*] *Rituals *says that husbands are the Heaven of their wives.* Yang *is strong and* yin *is gentle; this is the great principle of Heaven and Earth. Husband is kind and wife is loving; this is the great bond of the way of humanity.* Translator's annotation: The proclamation that "husbands are the Heaven of their wives" is from the *Yili* 《儀禮》 (*Book of Ceremonial Rituals*), Sangfu zhuan 喪服傳. It is also cited in chapter 5 of Ban Zhao's *Nüjie* (*Lessons for Women*). The teaching on women's "three obediences" can also be found in the *Liji* 《禮記》 (*Record of Rituals*), Jiaotesheng 郊特牲 chapter, and other Confucian texts.
2. Translator's annotation: On whether to obey or to admonish one's husband, the *Analects for Women* (a Tang text) exhibited a clear departure from the *Lessons for*

Women (a Han text). While Ban Zhao advises absolute obedience (*Nüjie*, chapters 1, 3, and 6), the Song sisters steer away from such an injunction.

3. Wang Xiang's commentary: *That a woman obeys her husband and regards him as the head of her person demonstrates the righteousness between a king and a minister. That she dons mourning clothes for three years [when her husband passes away] exhibits the affection between a father and a son. That a husband and a wife serve his parents together illustrates the friendship between an older brother and a younger brother. That a husband and a wife from different surnames live together harmoniously reveals the way between friends. Therefore, the ritual between a husband and a wife comprises all five human relations. They should be affectionate and loving toward one another and treat each other [respectfully] as they treat their guests. If the husband has something to say, the wife should listen respectfully and obey it. If the husband does something contrary to ritual propriety, the wife should admonish and stop him. Do not imitate those unvirtuous women, who not only do not stop their husbands from doing evil but also help them commit more harm. Or, they themselves do ritually inappropriate things and endanger their husbands. When disasters fall upon them, even if they repent, it is too late.*
4. Wang Xiang's commentary: *When the husband goes out, the wife should inquire about the distance and the direction to his destination. If the place is far away, the information will be helpful for mailing letters. If the place is near, one can keep the lights on and the meals warm in waiting for his return. If for a long time the husband still has not returned, one must send someone to find him to help speed up his return. Do not learn from those unvirtuous lazy women; before their husbands have returned, they already go to bed, neither do they keep the lights on nor do they inquire whether their husbands have eaten.*
5. Wang Xiang's commentary: *If the husband becomes ill, every day the wife should be worried. She should take care her husband attentively, adjust his medicine, plead to gods for guidance, and pray for his well-being. When the husband begins to recover, regarding his drinks, food, and clothes, the wife should especially be careful and prudent to ensure his safety. Do not learn from those unvirtuous women. When their husbands are ill, they do not care at all.*
6. Wang Xiang's commentary: *If the husband gets angry for some reason, the wife should suppress her anger and speak in a pleasant voice. Do not talk back or contradict him. Do not imitate those aggressive angry women, who find faults and fight with their husbands every day.*
7. Wang Xiang's commentary: *The husband's winter and summer clothes should be ironed and mended often, sewed, and organized in an orderly manner. The clothes should be prepared in time lest one is unprepared when the cold weather arrives. As far as tea and meals are concerned, the wife should diligently and attentively serve them lest her husband becomes ill because of hunger and thirst. The way of a husband and a wife is to bear suffering and enjoy happiness together, share poverty and wealth as one. When*

alive, they live together under the same bedcover; when dead, they are buried together in the same coffin. This is what reason stands.

8. Wang Xiang's commentary: *A virtuous woman, who follows these instructions, will bring forth friendly relations between a husband and a wife just like the harmony produced by the* qin *zither* 琴 *and the* se *zither* 瑟 *playing together. Her virtuous name will be well-known in the neighborhood and the district.* Translator's annotation: Both *qin* and *se* are ancient music instruments. *Qin* is a seven-string zither, whereas *se* is either a twenty-five–string or fifty-string zither. These two instruments can be played separately or jointly. "*Qinse hexie*" 琴瑟和諧 ("*qin* and *se* harmonize with one another") is an expression describing a friendly and affectionate relationship between a couple.

【訓男女章第八】

大抵人家，皆有男女。年已長成，教之有序。訓誨之權，實專於母。男入書堂，請延師傅。習學禮儀，吟詩作賦。尊敬師儒，束脩酒脯。女處閨門，少令出戶。喚來便來，喚去便去。稍有不從，當加叱怒。朝暮訓誨，各勤事務。掃地燒香，紉麻緝苧。若在人前，教他禮數。遞獻茶湯，從容退步。莫縱嬌癡，恐他啼怒。莫縱跳梁，恐他輕侮。莫縱歌詞，恐他淫污。莫縱遊行，恐他惡事。堪笑今人，不能為主。男不知書，聽其弄齒。鬬鬧貪杯，謳歌習舞。官府不憂，家鄉不顧。女不知禮，強梁言語。不識尊卑，不能針指。辱及尊親，有沾父母。如此之人，養豬養鼠。

8

Instructing Boys and Girls (Xunnannü zhang diba 訓男女章第八)

GENERALLY, EVERY FAMILY has boys and girls. When children grow older, they should be taught in an orderly manner. The authority to instruct children belongs primarily to the mother.[1]

Boys should be sent to a school and instructed by a teacher. They should learn ritual propriety and etiquette, recite poetry, and compose poems and essays. To show respect to the teacher-scholar, the mother should prepare a bundle of dried meat (*shuxiu* 束脩),[2] and arrange [a banquet with] wine and meat.[3]

Girls should stay in the inner quarters at home; rarely should they go out. They should be taught to come immediately when called, and to leave immediately when dismissed. If they disobey even slightly, they ought to be scolded sternly.[4] Day and night teach the girls that they must be diligent in every task. They should sweep the floors, burn incense [at the family ancestral temple], braid hemp, and plait ramie. If they are in front of guests, the mother should teach them rituals and etiquette. Have them serve the guests tea; and, with good poise, withdraw to the side.[5]

Do not indulge them in pride and foolishness, lest they throw temper tantrums. Do not allow them to be defiant and lawless, lest they become frivolous and shameful. Do not permit them to indulge in singing and lyrics, lest them act lasciviously. Do not let them play and wander on the streets, lest they do evil things.[6]

It is indeed laughable that nowadays people do not take charge of these matters. Boys and young men do not know the classics. They listen to their own empty talk. They love to get into fights, and indulge in drinking. They sing songs and learn dances, but neither fear the law of the government nor care about their obligations to their families. Girls and young women do not know anything about ritual propriety. They use defiant language, do not recognize who is the venerable and who is the lowly, and are incapable of doing needlework. They bring disgrace to their venerable relatives, and tarnish their parents' reputation. To have such children are like raising pigs and rats.[7]

Commentaries and Annotations

1. Wang Xiang's commentary: *This chapter speaks about the way of being a maternal model. A married couple necessarily begets boys and girls. Once boys and girls are born, the precepts of being a maternal model cannot be unknown. Fathers take charge of external affairs, mothers internal affairs. When boys and girls are young, they reside at home. Thus, maternal teachings are the single authority for them.*
2. Translator's annotation: *Shuxiu* 束脩 comprises two words: *shu* means a "bundle of ten," and *xiu* means "dried meat." In ancient China, *shuxiu* was a form of modest honorarium to teachers. See, for example, *Analects* 7.7, where Confucius says that he has never refused to teach anyone who offers a bundle of dried meat.
3. Wang Xiang's commentary: *When boys turn six years old, they can begin to study classics. Their mother ought to find a good teacher to instruct them. In treating venerable teachers, the ceremony of offering a bundle of dried meat as a token of respect and the ritual of a banquet with wine and meat should be planned attentively. One must not omit proper rituals.* Translator's annotation: For more on the Confucian curriculum from early childhood to adulthood, see *Liji* (*Record of Rituals*), chapter 1.
4. Wang Xiang's commentary: *In raising the girls, the mother's instruction is the main authority. Since childhood, girls should not be allowed to go outside the inner chambers. When they are slightly older, they should be taught to obey their mother's instruction. When there is an order, it cannot be disobeyed. If they do not listen or obey, they should be scolded sternly. Do not let them grow a heart of arrogance.*

5. Wang Xiang's commentary: *Day and night, teach the girls the importance of diligence and frugality. In burning incense at the family ancestral temple, reverence is essential. In sweeping floors in the courtyard, cleanness is necessarily expected. Braid hemp to provide threads; plait ramie to complete bolts of fabric. If guests and female relatives are visiting, the mother should teach the girls rituals and etiquette [in hosting guests] thoroughly: offer tea attentively to the guests, then withdraw and stand behind their mother.*
6. Wang Xiang's commentary: *If young women are unvirtuous, it is due to the fault that their mothers pamper and indulge them. If mothers indulge their daughters in conceit and foolishness, these girls will cultivate the habit of throwing temper tantrums for no reason. If mothers allow their daughters to be lawless and to quarrel with their mothers, these young women will develop the errors of being frivolous and neglectful of their parents-in-law, and insult and abuse their husbands. If young women are permitted to hear or sing songs, it is feared that they may become accustomed to lewd lyrics, thus growing hearts of licentiousness. If young women are allowed to wander and play on the streets, it is feared that they may become self-indulgent; therefore, do evil and selfish things. If these cannot be prohibited before they begin to sprout, the habits will have taken root and it will be exceedingly difficult to correct these errors.*
7. Wang Xiang's commentary: *Those unenlightened parents, after they gave birth to their sons, do not know that they ought to teach them the* Classic of Poetry *and the* Book of Documents. *They allow their sons to indulge in disobedience and have clever tongues, get into fights, drink excessively, sing lustful songs, fear no governmental laws, ignore family responsibilities, and do not take care their parents, wives, and children. Eventually, these men become useless people. When these parents raise their daughters, they do not teach them ritual propriety and deference. Instead, they allow their daughters to speak in defiant language, show no respect to venerable elders, know nothing about needlework, and practice no diligence and frugality. Once they are married, they certainly cannot follow the proper way of being a married woman. They become unfilial daughters-in-law and unvirtuous wives. They bring disgrace to their venerable relatives and tarnish their parents' reputation. This all begins with mothers' instruction not being given early enough. Such women, even though they give birth to sons and daughters, are in fact like raising pigs and rats. Alas, the way of being a maternal model cannot be unknown.*

【營家章第九】

營家之女，惟儉惟勤。勤則家起，懶則家傾。儉則家富，奢則家貧。
凡為女子，不可因循。一生之計，惟在於勤。一年之計，惟在於春。
一日之計，惟在於寅。奉箕擁帚，灑掃灰塵。撮除邋遢，潔靜幽清。
眼前爽利，家宅光明。莫教穢汙，有玷門庭。耕田下種，莫怨辛勤。
炊羹造飯，饋送頻頻。莫教遲慢，有誤工程。積糠聚屑，餵養孳牲。
呼歸放去，檢點搜尋。莫教失落，擾亂四鄰。夫有錢米，收拾經營。
夫有酒物，存積留停。迎賓待客，不可偷侵。大富由命，小富由勤。
禾麻菽麥，成棧成囷。油鹽椒鼓，盎甕裝盛。豬雞鵝鴨，成隊成群。
四時八節，免得營營。酒漿食饌，各有餘盈。夫婦享福，懽笑欣欣。

9

Managing the Household (Yingjia zhang dijiu 營家章第九)

WOMEN WHO MANAGE their households should abide by frugality and diligence. If one is diligent, the household will rise; if one is lazy, the household will fall. If one is thrifty, the household will be affluent; if one is extravagant, the household will be poor.[1]

No woman should procrastinate, for the livelihood of a lifetime rests in diligence, the livelihood of a year rests in the springtime, and the livelihood of a day rests at dawn.[2] Carry a dustpan (*ji* 箕) and a broom (*zhou* 帚). Sprinkle water and sweep the floor to remove dust. Get rid of untidiness. Everything will be clean, elegant, and serene. It will please the eyes, and the residence will be bright. Do not let trash and filth spoil the house.[3]

In plowing the fields and plantings seeds, do not complain about the hard work. Make soup and cook meals. Bring them to the fields frequently. Do not let tardiness or slowness delay the work.[4] Collect chaff of grains and crumbs of rice to feed farm animals. Let the animals go out and herd them back [at the right time]. Examine and count them; [if some are lost,] search for them. Do not let lost animals disturb the neighbors.[5]

If the husband has a surplus of money and grains of rice, the wife should collect and manage them properly. If the husband has wine and food, the wife should store and keep them for guests and visitors. Do not secretly consume them.[6]

Grand wealth depends on fate; small riches result from diligence. Store rice grains (*he* 禾), sesame seeds (*ma* 麻), beans (*shu* 菽), and wheat (*mai* 麥) in big or small storage rooms (*zhan jun* 棧囷). Store cooking oil, salt, peppers, and fermented beans in big or small jars. Gather pigs, chickens, geese, and ducks in rows and groups. When the transition of the four seasons and the eight major indicators of seasonal changes arrive, nothing will be rushed: wine, drinks, and food will be plenty. The husband and the wife will enjoy happiness. Smiles and joy will be everywhere.[7]

Commentaries and Annotations

1. Wang Xiang's commentary: *This chapter speaks about the way that a woman should manage and establish her household. To establish a household is not difficult: it simply rests on diligence and frugality. For diligence and frugality mutually depend on one another and they are inseparable, they work in tandem and do not contradict. Diligence enriches frugality, and frugality assists diligence. If one is diligent but unfrugal, one labors in vain. If one is frugal but undiligent, one likes to suffer. Diligence brings prosperity; laziness brings demise. Frugality leads to wealth; extravagance leads to poverty. This is naturally so.* Translator's annotation: Ban Zhao's *Lessons for Women* points out the importance of diligence without referencing frugality. Here, the *Analects for Women* stresses the mutual dependence of the two. That a good life requires both diligence and frugality is also advocated in the *Teachings for the Inner Court* and the *Short Records of Models for Women*.
2. Wang Xiang's commentary: *Those who diligently manage their households must be neither procrastinating nor lax. Delay in affairs may bring liabilities to the person in no small way. For if a young woman is diligent at a young age, she will be skillful in many things, which will provide her a livelihood for her entire lifetime. If she works diligently from the springtime, clothes and food of fine quality will provide her the livelihood of the year. If she works diligently since early morning, all household business will be in order, which will provide her the livelihood of the day.*
3. Wang Xiang's commentary: 箕 (ji) *refers to a container that can hold trash.* 帚 (zhou) *is an instrument used to remove filth. Sprinkling water to sweep the floor is to prevent dust from going everywhere. This speaks about sprinkling water and sweeping the floor in early morning to wash away filth and remove untidiness. This not only creates an elegant and serene environment but also pleases the eyes and makes the house bright.*

4. Wang Xiang's commentary: *As far as farming the fields are concerned, do not fear hard work. When the husband is plowing the fields, the wife will prepare the food. Tea and water should be provided at regular intervals and be taken care of constantly. Do not be tardy, thus causing the husband to be hungry, and delaying agricultural work.*
5. Wang Xiang's commentary: *Save the chaff and crumbs of rice to feed farm animals. Watch over the animals. Let them go out and herd them back at the right time. Examine and count them to make sure none is lost. Do not let them run into people's homes, thus disturbing the neighbors.*
6. Wang Xiang's commentary: *If the husband has a surplus of money and grains, the wife should collect and properly manage them. If there is wine and food left, do not waste them. Store and use them for unexpected guests. Do not secretly consume them.*
7. Wang Xiang's commentary: 棧 *pronounced as* 暫 *(*zhan*);* 囷 *pronounced as* 君 *(*jun*);* 盎 *pronounced as* 昂 *(*ang*) in the fourth tone; and* 盛 (sheng*) pronounced in the first tone here. This passage says that although grand wealth depends on heavenly fate, if there are sufficient clothes and food not exhausted by daily uses, these are small riches accumulated from diligence and frugality.* 禾 *(*he*) is rice,* 麻 (ma*) sesame seeds, and* 菽 *(*shu*) beans.* 棧 *(*zhan*) is a big storage room.* 囷 *(*jun*) is a small storage room for rice, built from branches of brambles and bamboos. The passage says that sesame seeds, beans, rice, and wheat, should be sealed and stored in storage rooms; they should not be discarded, scattered, or neglected. Cooking oil, salt, peppers, and fermented beans, should be stored in jars. Do not expose them [in open air], or their flavors will be spoiled. Chickens, pigs, geese, and ducks, should be raised properly. Gather them into groups so that they can reproduce and propagate. Between seasons and holidays, and on days of hosting guests and banquets, everything will be abundant. There will be no worries of having to run around, or being rushed, to find a solution. Surely, the husband and the wife will have many surpluses!*

【待客章第十】

大抵人家，皆有賓主。洗滌壺缾，抹光橐子。準備人來，點湯遞水。退立堂後，聽夫言語。細語商量，殺雞為黍。五味調和，菜蔬齊楚。茶酒清香，有光門戶。紅日含山，晚留居住。點燭擎燈，安排臥具。枕蓆紗廚，鋪氈疊被。欽敬相承，溫涼得趣。次曉相看，客如辭去，別酒殷勤，十分留意。夫喜能家，客稱曉事。莫學他人，不持家務。客來無湯，慌忙失措。夫若留人，妻懷嗔怒。有筯無匙，有鹽無醋。打男罵女，爭啜爭哺。夫受慚惶，客懷羞懼。有客到門，無人在戶，須遣家童，問其來處。客若殷勤，即通名字。當見則見，不見則避。敬待茶湯，莫缺禮數。記其姓名，詢其事務。等得夫歸，即當說訴。奉勸後人，切依規度。

10

Hosting Guests (Daike zhang dishi 待客章第十)

GENERALLY, EVERY FAMILY will have guests visiting the hosts. Therefore, [the wife should] wash and clean kettles and water bottles, and polish bellows, in preparation for the guests' arrival. Serve guests tea and water. [Once this is done,] withdraw to the back of the hall, and listen for the husband's instruction.[1] [If guests are staying,] discuss quietly with the husband whether to kill a chicken or use millet for the meal. Make sure that five flavors are blended harmoniously, dishes and vegetables are prepared in an orderly manner, and that tea and wine emit a delicate fragrance. It will bring a good name to the household.[2]

If the Sun has set at the mountain ridge and guests are invited to stay overnight, one should light candles and hold lamps, arrange chairs and stools, prepare pillows, mats, and canopy nets, and lay the beddings and fold the comforters. Interact with guests respectfully. Make sure that they are not too warm or too cold. Next morning, check on them. If guests express their thanks and bid farewell, one should attentively prepare a departure drink and pay full attention to them. One's husband will be pleased with one's ability in running the household, and guests will praise one's thoughtfulness.[3]

Do not learn from those women who do not know how to manage a household. When guests arrive, there is no tea to serve. Everything is in a hurry and in disarray. If the husband invites guests to stay, the wife harbors anger. Have chopstick, but no spoons; have salt, but no vinegar. Beat up the boys and scold the girls. Compete with guests for food and drinks (*zhoubu* 啜哺). The husband feels ashamed and unsettled, and guests feel embarrassed and frightened.[4]

If guests are at the door, but the husband is not at home, the wife should send a boy servant to ask where the guests are from. If guests are eager, they will provide their names. If they are people that one should receive, then receive them. If not, then avoid them. Respectfully serve guests tea; do not fall short on ritual propriety and etiquette. Remember their names, and inquire about the business of their visit. Wait for the husband to return home; immediately convey the information to him. I respectfully advise future generations to follow these rules stringently.[5]

Commentaries and Annotations

1. Wang Xiang's commentary: *This chapter addresses the matters of following the husband in hosting guests. Kettles and water bottles should be washed and cleaned with running water. Plates and bellows should be wiped and polished. In case that guests arrive, it will be easier to serve them. If the husband invites guests to stay for drinks and a meal, the wife should stand behind the hall, wait for the husband's instructions, and prepare accordingly.* Translator's annotation: Chapter 3 addresses proper etiquette in receiving female guests, and in visiting women relatives and friends. This chapter discusses how to host guests by following husband's lead.
2. Wang Xiang's commentary: *As guests are outside, discuss in a gentle voice with the husband about what the household has and does not have. Based on what the family has plenty of or has less of, one makes sure that all flavors are blended tastefully; dishes are abundant, clean, and arranged in an orderly manner. Tea bowls and drinking cups are elegant and shine with luster. The taste of tea and wine emit delicate scents and robust fragrances. Thus, guests praise the hosts for their hospitality and virtue, and the family enjoys a good name.*
3. Wang Xiang's commentary: *If it is late at night and it is too far for guests to return home, the wife ought to prepare guest rooms, arrange chairs and stools, and set up their canopy nets. Pillows, mats, beddings, and comforters are laid and folded neatly. Guests are comfortable, neither too cold nor too warm. Next morning, she will prepare wine and food and wait for their itinerary. In so doing, the rituals of hosting guests may be*

called complete. The husband will be happy with her ability in managing the household, and guests will be pleased with her knowledge of ritual propriety.

4. Wang Xiang's commentary: 啜 *pronounced as* 拙 (zhuo). *This speaks about unvirtuous wives. In their leisure, they do not take care of household chores. When guests arrive, they are flustered, not knowing what to do, and tea is not prepared. If the husband invites guests to stay, they become angry and unaccommodating. If they reluctantly let guests stay, spoons and chopsticks are incomplete, and salt and vinegar are not prepared. When guests are in the hall, they beat up their sons, scold their daughters, and fight and quarrel over drinks and food. Their horrible names spread beyond their courtyards. Consequently, their husbands lose face and feel ashamed. Guests are insulted, looking embarrassed and angry.*
5. Wang Xiang's commentary: *If when one's husband goes out, guests arrive, one should send a boy servant to receive them and invite them to sit. Inquire their names and reasons of their visit. If there are elder family members at home, and the guests are people they should receive, then invite them to the back hall and receive them according to rituals. If the guests are people one should not receive, then avoid them. Send a servant to serve guests tea. Record in detail the business of their visit. Wait for one's husband to return home and communicate the information to him clearly without error. Then, one has done one's best in hosting guests.*

【和柔章第十一】

處家之法，婦女須能。以和為貴，孝順為尊。翁姑嗔責，曾如不曾。上房下戶，子侄宜親。是非休習，長短休爭。從來家醜，不可外聞。東鄰西舍，禮數周全。往來動問，款曲盤旋。一茶一水，笑語忻然。當說則說，當行則行。閒是閒非，不入我門。莫學愚婦，不問根深。穢言污語，觸突尊賢。奉勸女子，量後思前。

11

*Harmony and Gentleness (*Herou zhang dishiyi 和柔章第十一*)*

A WOMAN MUST be good at the methods of getting along with others in her household. She should treasure harmony and revere filial piety. If parents-in-law scold her, even if they had already done this before, she should [calmly] accept it as if it never happened before. She should treat nephews and nieces from the upper and the lower households (*shangfang xiahu* 上房下戶) affectionately (*qin* 親).[1] Do not gossip about the right and the wrong [of sisters-in-law] or argue about who is better and who is worse. From the beginning, family scandals should not be leaked to outside the household.[2]

In interacting with neighbors on the east side and on the west side, she should attend to proper etiquette thoroughly. In coming and going, greet the neighbors, and inquire about their well-being. Be good at tactics in social gathering. Offer them a cup of tea or water. Exchange pleasant talks. Say only what should be said. Act only as how one should act. Gossip about others' right and wrong should not enter one's door.[3]

Do not learn from those ignorant women, who do not inquire about what is at the root. They use foul language and offend the venerable and the virtuous. I respectfully advise young women: have foresight about what is to come, and reflect carefully what had happened before.[4]

Commentaries and Annotations

1. Translator's annotation: *Shangfang xiahu* 上房下戶 literally means "upper house and lower house." 房 (*fang*) means "a house, room, branch of a family" or is used as a classifier for wife (*qifang* 妻房, *qishi* 妻室), concubine (*pianfang* 偏房), or daughter-in-law (*yifang xifu* 一房媳婦). In this passage, the phrase *shangfang xiahu* 上房下戶 refers to "sisters-in-laws."
2. Wang Xiang's commentary: *This chapter speaks about the way of harmony and gentleness.* Yang *is firm, and* yin *is gentle; this is the righteous principle between a man and a woman. Therefore, those who manage their households see gentleness and harmony as something precious; those who serve their parents-in-law give priority to gentleness and deference. If parents-in-law scold one, even though they had already done it before, act as if they had not. Keep in mind one's error and correct it; do not harbor resentment in one's heart. Living under the same household and sharing as one family, youngsters, nephews, and nieces should be loved with care and treated with affection. In relation to sisters-in-law, do not discuss who is right and who is wrong, or argue and compete about who is better and who is worse. Even if they have shameful matters, because they are close relatives, their misfortunes are the same as yours. How can one expose them to the public and spread their family scandals?* Translator's annotation: For more on the *yin-yang* binary, its correlation with female and male, gentleness and firmness, and other gendered characteristics, see Ban Zhao, *Nüjie* (*Lessons for Women*), chapters 2 and 3; Renxiaowen Huanghou, *Neixun* (*Teachings for the Inner Court*), chapters 2 and 13; and Liu Shi, *Nüfan jielu* (*Short Records of Models for Women*), chapter 1. Also, the *Liji* (*Record of Rituals*), chapter 11. Moreover, a daughter-in-law's obligations and proper behavior are codified in the *Liji*, chapters 12 and 44.
3. Wang Xiang's commentary: *Regarding neighbors, one should maintain an amicable relationship. Do not lose their friendship. If female members from neighboring households stop by, make sure to inquire whether they are cold or warm, be earnest in socializing, and be thorough in etiquette. Offer them a cup of tea or water; exchange pleasant talk; do not be deficient in rituals. Speak only of matters that can be spoken of; do not talk about anything contrary to ritual propriety. If it is appropriate for one to return a visit, then do so. But do not enter any household contrary to ritual. Regarding the right and the wrong, the strength and the shortcoming, of my neighbors, I will neither interfere nor leak out anything. Then, their right and wrong, fault or guilt, will not involve me.*
4. Wang Xiang's commentary: *Unvirtuous women love to listen to hearsay. Once they hear gossip, without verifying whether it is true or false, they immediately utter foul language. They are headstrong and argumentative. They offend their venerable elders, harm their close relatives, and slander their neighbors; there is nothing that they will not do. That women like these exist is because they were not taught well in their youth. Consequently, they do not understand principles of righteousness. Thus, when in residence, they perform no good deeds; when speaking, they utter no good words. They fail in ritual propriety, desert virtue, and descend to this stage, should one not be cautious?*

【守節章第十二】

古來賢婦，九烈三貞。名標青史，傳到如今。後生宜學，亦匪難行。第一守節，第二清貞。有女在室，莫出閨庭。有客在戶，莫露聲音。不談私語，不聽淫音。黃昏來往，秉燭掌燈，暗中出入，非女之經。一行有失，百行無成。夫妻結髮，義重千金。若有不幸，中路先傾。三年重服，守志堅心。保家持業，整頓墳塋。殷勤訓後，存歿光榮。此篇論語，內範儀刑。後人依此，女德聰明。幼年切記，不可朦朧。若依此言，享福無窮。

12

Guarding One's Integrity (Shoujie zhang dishier 守節章第十二)

SINCE THE ANCIENT times, there were virtuous ardent women who illuminated their nine family clans (*jiulie* 九烈), as well as admirable chaste females who were remarkable in three areas (*sanzhen* 三貞). Their names were recorded in the books of history and passed down to the present day. Students of later times should learn from them and it is not difficult to do so.[1]

The first is to guard one's integrity (*shoujie* 守節). The second is to be serene and chaste (*qingzhen* 清貞).[2] If there are daughters at home, let them not go outside the courtyard of women's quarters. If there are guests at home, let them not make [loud] sounds.[3] Do not speak in indecent language. Do not listen to lewd music. In coming and going at dusk, one should hold a candle or a lamp. Going in and out of dark places [without a candle or a lamp] is not proper for a woman. One flawed act can render hundreds of [good] acts in vain.[4]

The husband and the wife in their first marriage tie their hairs in matrimony (*fuqi jiefa* 夫妻結髮); the righteous meaning of this relationship is as weighty as a thousand pounds of gold. If the husband unfortunately passes away during the middle of this shared life journey, the wife should wear mourning clothes for three years. She should safeguard her will [of chastity], be firm in her heart, protect their family, manage family property, clean her husband's graveside, and earnestly teach their children. Then, both the living and the dead will be honored.[5]

This *Analects* is written to provide norms for the inner quarters as models and principles of conduct. If women [nowadays and] of later times can follow these guidelines, their womanly virtue will be enlightening and luminous. Young women must keep these lessons in mind from childhood; they must not be hazy [on these instructions]. If they can abide by these words, they will enjoy endless happiness.[6]

Commentaries and Annotations

1. Wang Xiang's commentary: *For* jiulie sanzhen 九烈三貞, *see the explanation in a previous chapter* [i.e., Song Sisters' preface and related note]. *This speaks about sagely empresses, noble royal consorts, virtuous women, and ardent ladies. Their names are recorded in the annals of history; their honorable womanly reputations have been passed down through the ages. Women of later times should emulate them and follow their footsteps—it is not something overly lofty or difficult to do.*
2. Translator's annotation: Women's integrity and chastity are a continuing theme in the *Four Books for Women*, though integrity per se is not a gender-specific virtue.
3. Wang Xiang's commentary: *Regarding the way of women, safeguarding one's integrity is the first principle; serenity and chastity come after it. If a woman is serene, she will be like unblemished ice and pure jade. Her will and conduct will be bright and clear. If she is chaste, she will have the integrity of cypress and the perseverance of pine, which will not wither when the year turns cold. If one has daughters, it is best to command them to stay in the inner chambers and not leave the women's quarters. If there are guests, women should talk in a low and gentle voice so that people outside cannot hear them. This is the ultimate key in rectifying the family.* Translator's annotation: Images of evergreens are often used to signify integrity; see, e.g., Confucius, *Analects* 9.28. In Chinese literature and paintings, evergreens, bamboo, orchids, and plum blossom are favorite objects of artistic rendering owing to their symbolic meanings; they are often called "the four friends of a gentleman" (*junzi siyou* 君子四友).
4. Wang Xiang's commentary: *In conversations, a woman should neither speak in indecent language nor listen to wicked lascivious sounds lest they confuse the mind. The* Record of Rituals *says, "When women walk at night, they must light candles. Where there are no candles, they should stop." If a woman walks in darkness without candles, it is feared that she may get involved in matters contrary to rituals, thus incurring slander and gossip. A woman has hundreds of deeds; all of them must be thorough. If one action is flawed, it becomes a burden to her virtue, rendering hundreds of acts in vain.*
5. Wang Xiang's commentary: Jiefa 結髮, *like* zongjiao 總角 *("tying hairs up and making them into two knots on the head"), is done when men and women are in their teens.*

The husband and the wife of their first marriage tie their hairs in matrimony (jiefa fuqi 結髮夫妻)*; it signifies profound kindness and weighty rightness. If unfortunately, the husband passes away, the wife should wail in deep sorrow, and don mourning clothes for three years. She should safeguard her will [of chastity] to the end of her life. Protect her family and family property. Conduct mourning rituals and sweep her husband's tomb. Earnestly teach and raise their sons and daughters to adulthood so as to carry on their deceased father's will. Then, both the living and the dead will be honored.* Translator's annotation: *Zongjiao* is a hairstyle for children in ancient China. In some Chinese paintings, one sees children with their long hair divided in the middle, tied upward to form two knots on the head. The phrase *zongjiao* appears in the *Shijing* (*Classic of Poetry*) and the *Liji* (*Record of Rituals*). *Jiefa fuqi* 結髮夫妻 is an expression referring to the husband and the wife from their first marriage. Generally, there are two interpretations of the origin of *jiefa*: (a) In ancient matrimony, one hair was pulled from the husband's and the wife's heads and tied together to symbolize union, or (b) in ancient China, men at the age of twenty, and women at the age of fifteen, tied their hair upward for capping (for men) or hair pinning (for women), symbolizing the entering of adulthood.

6. Wang Xiang's commentary: *This passage concludes and sums up the meaning of this book. It says that: "I authored twelve chapters of the* Analects for Women. *They are meant to provide norms for women's education as models and principles of conduct: these are what young women should compare themselves to; follow them as models, and act on them as principles. If they can apply these lessons in their conduct, their womanly virtue will be luminous and remarkable. Is this not worthy? Young girls must study this book repeatedly and embody it in their behavior. Accordingly, throughout their lifetime, they will be virtuous daughters, filial daughters-in-law, chaste wives, and caring mothers. How will their enjoyment of happiness and prosperity ever be exhausted?"*

BOOK III

The Ming Imperial Women

Empress Renxiaowen and the *Teachings for the Inner Court* (*Neixun*): 1361–1407 CE

Translator's Introduction

1. *The Author and the Work*

Empress Renxiaowen 仁孝文皇后 (1361–1407 CE) of the Ming dynasty 明 (1368–1644 CE) authored the *Teachings for the Inner Court* (*Neixun* 《內訓》).[1] This work, completed in 1405, is both the longest and the most conceptually sophisticated of the *Four Books for Women* (*Nü shishu* 《女四書》). It not only stresses women's learning but also commends their contributions to the well-being of the state. In terms of subject matter and the impact on women's social standing, this work surpasses both Ban Zhao's *Lessons for Women* and Song Ruoxin's and Song Ruozhao's *Analects for Women*. Even though originally intended mainly for teaching imperial women, this work was promulgated among the common people as a consequence of several emperors' decrees.[2] In addition to Wang Xiang's 王相 *Four Books for Women* (*Nü sishu jizhu* 《女四書集註》), this work is included in Chen Menglei's 陳夢雷 *Collection of Illustrations and Books from Antiquity to the Present* (*Gujin tushu jicheng* 《古今圖書集成》) and is the *only* work of the *Four Books for Women* included in the "masters section" (*zibu* 子部) of Ji Yun's 紀昀 *Complete Library in Four Sections* (*Siku quanshu* 《四庫全書》), the largest Chinese imperial collection of literary works compiled during the Qing dynasty 清 (1644–1911 CE).[3] The *Teachings for the Inner Court* is also well known in Japan and Korea, and was often used to teach empresses.[4]

Empress Renxiaowen (maiden name, Xu) was the oldest daughter of Xu Da 徐達 (1322–1385 CE), a famous Ming general. She loved learning and was known for her virtues. People called her *Nü Zhusheng* 女諸生 ("woman scholar"). Emperor Taizu of Ming 明太祖 (the founding emperor) heard her good name, thereupon asking her father to betroth her to Prince of Yan 燕王 (Zhu Di 朱棣), Taizu's fourth son. In 1376, she became Consort Yan and was known for her exemplary filialness to her mother-in-law and benevolence to others.[5]

In 1399, Emperor Huidi 惠帝 (1377–?; r. 1399–1402 CE), a grandson of Emperor Taizu and a nephew of Prince of Yan, attempted to drastically abolish the princes' and vassal kings' power and territory. The Prince of Yan thereupon initiated the Jingnan Rebellion 靖難之變, a civil war against Emperor Huidi. When he and most of the troops were away to raid the city of Daning, Emperor Huidi's general Li Jinglong seized the opportunity to attack Beijing, Yan's headquarters. When the city was besieged, Consort Yan urged women in the city to defend the capital; she took the lead, gave the women armor, climbed up the city walls, and fought the enemy. The city was thus preserved.

In 1402, the Prince of Yan ascended the throne as Emperor Chengzu 成祖 and installed Consort Yan as his empress. She encouraged her husband to practice humane government: "[I venture to plead with the Emperor:] cherish the people, seek virtuous worthy talents widely, show mercy to family clans, and do not indulge my maternal family." She also summoned wives of high-ranking officials of the imperial court and academy, and advised them:

> A wife, in serving her husband, should not stop at only taking care of his food and clothes. There must be something else that a wife can assist with. One may follow or disobey a friend's advice. Nonetheless, words between a husband and a wife are congenial and easier to keep in mind. Day and night, I serve the Emperor and only think about the people. I urge you too to endeavor to do this.[6]

Empress Renxiaowen, a dedicated Confucian, was also a devout Buddhist and a copious writer. In addition to the *Teachings for the Inner Court* (*Neixun*), she authored several other Confucian and Buddhist texts, as well as a number of poems.[7] In various places in the *Neixun*, albeit a Confucian treatise, she interfused Buddhist karmic law to explain Heaven's distribution of happiness in proportion to a person's deeds. She passed away in 1407, at the age of forty-six. Emperor Chengzu mourned her death and bestowed on her the honorary title of "humaneness" (*ren* 仁) and "filialness" (*xiao* 孝), in addition to her literary achievements (*wen* 文), thus the name Renxiaowen Empress. Later that year, he issued an imperial edict to print and widely circulate two of her works, *Teachings for the Inner Court* and *Exhorting Good* (*Quanshanshu* 《勸善書》).[8] For the rest of his life, he did not install another empress.

2. *Cultural and Historical Background*

Emperor Taizu (r. 1368–1398 CE) of Ming, after defeating the Mongol Yuan Empire 元 (1271–1368 CE), immediately implemented several important policies to restore society from the turmoil caused by famine, corruption, and war at the end of the Yuan regime. These measures included: (1) encouraging agriculture and economic development, (2) lowering taxes (particularly, books and farming instruments were exempt from taxes),[9] (3) promoting education (including women's learning), (4) establishing local schools, (4) observing the ritual distinction between male and female, and (5) promulgating a culture of frugality.[10] Ming emperors and empresses embodied these lessons by example. Ming empresses, far more than any previous dynasties, authored books to teach women of the imperial court.[11]

During the Ming period, the printing system also underwent significant development, partly due to the incentives provided by the government's tax-free policy on books. By the thirteenth century, wooden, ceramic, clay, and metal movable type was invented. By 1600, printing with bronze movable type was nearly perfected, significantly improving the printing process.[12] As a result, in addition to imperial printing facilities, many private print shops also sprung up. The convergence of these factors—the encouragement of learning from above, tax-exempt policy for books, and printing efficiency—greatly contributed to the efficacy of women's education.

Furthermore, to restore moral order and to differentiate Chinese culture from Mongol culture, Ming emperors relied on Confucian teachings, especially Zhu Xi's Neo-Confucianism.[13] Zhu Xi (1130–1200 CE), a noted scholar of the Southern Song dynasty (1127–1279 CE), is best known for his classification and commentary on the *Four Books* (*Sishu* 《四書》), comprising the *Analects*, the *Mencius*, the *Great Learning*, and the *Doctrine of the Mean*—standard textbooks in preparation for imperial civil service examinations from 1313 to 1905. Zhu Xi's Neo-Confucianism focuses particularly on moral cultivation. He regards the three principles (manifesting illuminating virtue, renovating the people, and abiding by the highest good) and the eight steps (investigating things, extending knowledge, making the will sincere, rectifying the mind, cultivating the person, regulating the family, governing the state, and bringing world peace), laid out in the *Great Learning*, as an excellent guide for any person who wishes to establish the self and contribute to the well-being of the family, the state, and the world.

Following Confucius and especially Mencius, Zhu Xi affirms the goodness in innate human nature and the effect of habits. He writes, "[T]he [inborn] nature should necessarily attain the Mean. . . . But the Mean is sometimes not attained because [the person] loses his original nature and beclouds it by habits engendered by [psycho-physical] force [*qi* 氣]."[14] He thus distinguishes "original nature" (endowed good nature) from "physical nature" (nature affected by external conditions):

> [O]riginal nature is perfectly good. This is the nature described by Mencius as "good." . . . However, it will be obstructed if [our] physical nature contains impurity. . . . When we speak of the physical nature, we refer to principle [*li* 理] and [psycho-physical] force [*qi* 氣] combined.[15]

To elucidate the transition between original nature and physical nature, a four-fold distinction of "mind," "nature," "feeling," and "desire" is made:

> [Original] [n]ature is the state before activity begins, the feelings are the state when activity has started, and the mind includes [both] states. For nature is the mind before it is aroused, while feelings are the mind after it is aroused. . . . Desire emanates from feelings. The mind is comparable to water, [original] nature . . . the tranquility of still water, feeling . . . the flow of water, and desire . . . its waves. Just like there are good and bad waves, so there are good desires, such as when "I want humanity," and bad desires which rush out like wild and violent waves.[16]

Thus, the purpose of "learning is to transform this material endowment."[17] For this reason, Zhu Xi also encourages women's learning so that they can become virtuous models for their children, relatives, and villagers. He upholds women's ability to achieve the paramount Confucian virtue of humaneness.[18] The subjects for women's learning, however, were more limited than men's, as Zhu Xi still sees the gendered inner–outer distinction as a ritual mandate and obedience as women's primary virtue.[19] Influenced by earlier Han Confucians' *yin–yang* hierarchy, Zhu Xi's teaching on the *yin–yang* relation was one of inconsistency. On the one hand, following Zhou Dunyi's *Explanations of the Diagram of the Great Ultimate* (*Taijitu shuo* 《太極圖說》), he upholds the complementarity of *yang*/activity/male and *yin*/tranquility/female. On the other hand, women are construed unfairly as the inferior sex because of their *yin* nature. In his *Reflections on Things at Hand* (*Jin silu* 《近思錄》), the inferiority and subordination of *yin*/female/wife to *yang*/male/husband is emphasized: "Between man and woman, there is an order of superiority and inferiority, and between husband and wife, there is the principle of who leads and who follows. This is a constant principle."[20] Zhu Xi's Neo-Confucianism certainly influenced Empress Renxiaowen's *Teachings for the Inner Court*, but not without her own creative invention and female sensibility.[21]

3. *Purpose of Writing, Contents, and Strengths and Weaknesses of the Book*

In her preface to the *Teachings for the Inner Court* (*Neixun*), Empress Renxiaowen explains that her reason for writing this treatise is that no suitable teaching material for educating women is available. In her view, Ban Zhao's *Lessons for Women* is too simple and Zhu Xi's *Elementary Learning* is not written for women. Popular anthologies in the late Yuan dynasty and the early Ming dynasty are too fragmented and superficial—they are simply collections of excerpts from the *Record of Rituals*, a few poems from the *Classic of Poetry*, and a handful of women's biographies, with no explanations. In contrast, the teachings of her mother-in-law (Empress Xiaocigao 孝慈高皇后) are both profound and immediately applicable to women. For these reasons, she wrote the *Neixun*, incorporating her mother-in-law's insights. The twenty chapters of the *Neixun* proceed in a logical order: starting from a discussion of the relation between endowed human nature and its potential for virtue to advice on inner cultivation and external manifestation of these virtues in the web of personal, social, and political relations.

The book has several strengths. First, in making the argument that (a) regardless of their gender or sex, all human beings are endowed with virtuous nature (chapter 1), (b) self-cultivation leads to virtue (chapter 2), and (c) being able to correct one's mistake after knowing it enables sageliness (chapter 9),[22] Empress Renxiaowen opens the door for women's sagehood. In fact, in chapter 10, she explicitly calls her mother-in-law Empress Xiaocigao's teaching "sagely teachings"; and in chapter 11, she firmly states that a woman can become a sage if her deeds equal those of exemplary sage queens. Relatedly, she stresses that women's education should not be delayed: "none [of the exemplary women] could have been so accomplished without being taught first."[23] No previous writers, male or female, ever made this claim as clearly as she does, a remarkable step that has inspired a multitude of later women writers. For instance, Madame Liu (Liu Shi) unapologetically praises exemplary women as "woman sages" in her *Short Records of Models for Women*,[24] the fourth book of the *Four Books for Women*.

Second, she is fully aware of the power of example, as well as the temptations that aristocratic upper-class women face. She therefore especially stresses the timeless beauty of virtue and, by contrast, the fleeting nature of luxuries and physical attractiveness: "fine clothing with five-color embroidery cannot beautify a person. Only . . . [in] following the Way can one advance in women's virtue" (chapter 2); "a woman should not be haughty about her physical beauty; what matters in her is her virtue" (chapter 3); "Pearls and jades are not treasures; virtue and sageliness are" (chapter 11). In the same vein, she exhorts her readers to diligence and frugality, and warns against wastefulness: "It is easy for one who lives in poverty and in an inferior position not to become lazy; it is difficult for one who is affluent to not be lazy" (chapter 5). Furthermore, in considering the labor going into economic production, she adds:

> A single thread of cloth is a result of women's diligent work; a grain of food is a consequence of farmers' hard labor. These things do not come

> by easily. If all use these materials intemperately and waste these materials from Heaven without care—those above lead while those below follow and all walk the same path, who will be able to overturn these corrupt practices? . . . For what is above leads what is below and what is inside manifests in the outside; empresses must observe frugality to lead the six imperial inner quarters. Consorts of marquises and wives of minor officials and the common people all should uphold frugality to lead their households. Accordingly, no citizens will suffer from cold and hunger. (chapter 7)

Third, considering the immense impact of words and actions—especially when they are uttered and carried out by members of royalty, she emphasizes the importance of prudent speech and benevolent conduct (chapters 3 and 4). To prevent cruel treatment and abuse of power that often result from political power struggles, she advises mercy in treating family clans and impartiality in interacting with kings' and consorts' maternal relatives (chapters 17–20).

Fourth, the significance of women's work as inner helpmate—not only to the well-being of a family but also to the flourishing of a society and the stability of a nation—is well articulated in this book. Formerly, neither Ban Zhao's *Lessons for Women* nor the Song sisters' *Analects for Women* made such connections and no other prior authors ever articulated this point with such eloquence. One reads: "Women assist their countries and families from within" (chapter 8); "Since ancient times, the founding of a country has always relied on the virtue of inner helpmates" (chapter 10); "Looking back at ancient times, it had never been the case that the rise and the fall of a nation did not depend on whether women were virtuous" (chapter 13). Moreover, a wife's moral duty requires her to admonish her husband (even if he is an emperor):

> If she cannot mutually rectify her ruler by means of the Way, it must be the case that she has abandoned her own virtue. It is as if a net does not have its principal binding threads; it is difficult for the eyes of the net to open. If a ruler has no one to rely on [for his virtue], those below him will have no one to emulate. Gradually both parties will descend into immorality. (chapter 13)

Fifth, the method of citing former exemplary women as a form of argument begins to emerge in this work. Neither Ban Zhao nor the Song sisters cited any former exemplary women to bolster their arguments. Empress Renxiaowen, to the contrary, presented fourteen examples of virtuous women from history, and four counterexamples, as evidence that reinforces her reasoning. This approach will become a primary form of argument deployed by Madame Liu in her *Short Records of Models for Women*. This method has the benefit of establishing women's tradition enlivened by women—providing a sense of sisterhood with shared purposes—a method that contemporary feminists find so powerful!

This work does have some limitations. Since the intended audience is empresses and imperial consorts, its narrative is quite formal and the selected examples of women are confined to royal women. Although the text mentions the common people several times, its formality and class distinctions make the book less relatable to non-elite women. Moreover, the rules and policies passed down by the founding emperor of Ming propelled Empress Renxiaowen's strict observance of orthodox norms of "three obediences" and "the inner–outer distinction," barring any *direct* involvement in politics by empresses and imperial consorts. These restrictions significantly limited women's *full* political participation.

The translations that follow are full translations of the text and Wang Xiang's commentary. Again, to retain the flow of the original, Wang's commentary in italic and the translator's annotations in roman are placed in the "Commentaries and Annotations" section, following immediately after the original text in each chapter.

---

1. Zhang Tingyu 張廷玉, *Mingshi* 《明史》 (*History of Ming*), volume 113, http://ctext.org/wiki.pl?if=gb&chapter=235681.
2. For example, in 1407 by Emperor Chengzu 成祖, and in 1580 by Emperor Shenzong 神宗, of Ming. See Ji Yun 紀昀 et al., eds., *Siku quanshu* 《四庫全書》 (*Complete Library in Four Sections*) (Beijing, China: Qing Dynasty Imperial Library, 1782; repr., Taipei: Shangwu, 1986), volumes 709, 722; Hu Wenkai 胡文楷, *Lidai funü zhuzuokao* 《歷代婦女著作考》 (*Verified Records of Women's Writings Through the Ages*) (Shanghai: Shanghai Guji, 1985), 138–40; Wang Xiang 王相, *Zhuangyuange nü sishu jizhu* 《狀元閣女四書集註》 (*Zhuangyuange Edition of the Four Books for Women with Commentary*) (Beijing, China: Wenchengtang 文成堂, 1885), 1–2.
3. Ji Yun et al., *Siku quanshu*, volume 709.
4. Yamazaki Jun'ichi 山崎純一, *Kyōiku kara mita Chūgoku joseishi shiryo no kenkyu: "Onna shisho" to "Shinpufu" sanbusho* 《教育からみた中國女性史資料の研究：「女四書」と「新婦譜」三部書》 (*A View of Education from a Study of Documents on the History of Chinese Women: "Four Books for Women" and "Instructions for New Brides"*) (Tokyo: Meiji Shoin 明治書院, 1986), 155; Hye-Kyung Kim, "The Dream of Sagehood: A Re-Examination of Queen Sohae's *Naehoon* and Feminism," in *The Bloomsbury Research Handbook of Chinese*

Philosophy and Gender, ed. Ann A. Pang-White (London: Bloomsbury, 2016), 89–107.

5. Zhang Tingyu, *Mingshi*, volume 113.
6. Ibid.
7. Hu Wenkai, *Lidai funü*, 138–40; Lu Jiaqi 盧嘉琪, "*Siku quanshu* gengxuzhubian suoshou nüxing zhushu" 《四庫全書》賡續諸編所收女性著述 ("Women's Writings Included in Follow-up Volumes and Editions of the *Complete Library in Four Sections*"), *Chengda lishi xuebao* 《成大歷史學報》 32 (2007): 45–7; Huang Yanli 黃嫣梨, *Nü sishu jizhu yizheng* 《女四書集注義證》(*Four Books for Women with Selections from Traditional Commentaries*) (Hong Kong: Shangwu, 2008), 67–8; Lee Hui-shu, "Empress Xu," in *Women Writers of Traditional China: An Anthology of Poetry and Criticism*, ed. Kang-i Sun Chang and Haun Saussy (Stanford, CA: Stanford University Press, 1999), 678–81.
8. Ji Yun et al., *Siku quanshu*, volumes 709, 722; Huang Yanli, *Nü sishu jizhu*, 69.
9. Zhang Tingyu, *Mingshi*, volume 2 ("Basic Annals"), http://ctext.org/wiki.pl?if=gb&chapter=390514; Long Wenbin 龍文彬, *Ming huiyao* 《明會要》 (*Essential Ming Laws and Regulations*), volume 26 ("Schools and Books"), http://ctext.org/library.pl?if=en&file=26765&by_author=%E9%BE%8D%E6%96%87%E5%BD%AC&page=7.
10. Zhang Tingyu, *Mingshi*, volumes 1, 2, and 3 ("Basic Annals").
11. Lu Jiaqi, "*Siku quanshu* gengxuzhubian," 45–8.
12. Tsuen-Hsuin Tsien, "Paper and Printing," in *Science and Civilization in China*, ed. Joseph Needham, volume 5, part I (London: Cambridge University Press, 1985), 201–17.
13. Zhang Tingyu, *Mingshi*, volume 282 ("Biographies of Confucian Scholars"). See also Huang Liling 黃麗玲, "*Nü sishu* yanjiu" 《女四書》研究 ("Research on the *Four Books for Women*") (M.A. thesis, Taiwan Nanhua University, 2003), 37–40.
14. Wing-tsit Chan, *A Source Book in Chinese Philosophy* (Princeton, NJ: Princeton University Press, 1973), 619.
15. Ibid, 624.
16. Ibid, 631.
17. Ibid, 625.
18. Zhu Xi, *Zhuzi yulei* 《朱子語類》 (*Classified Conversations of Zhu Xi*) (Beijing: Zhonghua Shuju, 1986), 57 and 1403. See also Wing-tsit Chan, *Zhuzi xintansuo* 《朱子新探索》 (*New Research on Zhu Xi*) (Taipei: Xuesheng, 1988), 784.
19. This, however, does not mean women cannot influence or reprimand their husbands. The Song sisters, Empress Renxiaowen, and Madame Liu certainly reappropriated this virtue.
20. Wing-tsit Chan, trans., *Reflections on Things at Hand: The Neo-Confucian Anthology Compiled by Chu Hsi and Lu Tsu-Chien* (New York: Columbia University Press, 1967), 272.

21. An important Ming Neo-Confucian is Wang Yangming (1472–1529). But he did not influence Empress Renxiaowen's thought, since he was born after her death.
22. Renxiaowen, *Neixun*, chapter 9, "知而能改，可以跂聖。"
23. Renxiaowen, *Neixun*, preface, "亦未有不由於教而成者。"
24. Liu Shi, *Nüfan jielu*, chapter 2, "可謂女中之堯舜。"

Wang Xiang's Biographic Introduction

Empress Renxiaowen 仁孝文皇后: Teachings for the Inner Court (Neixun 《內訓》)

瑯琊 王相晉升 箋註
莆陽 鄭漢濯之 校梓
Commentator: Langye Region 瑯琊, *Wang Xiang* 王相
(courtesy name: Jin Sheng 晉升*)*
Proofreader: Fuyang Region 莆陽, *Zheng Han* 鄭漢
(courtesy name: Zhuo Zhi 濯之*)*

仁孝文皇后姓余氏，中山武甯王達之女，明成祖文皇帝元配也。博學好文，著《內訓》二十篇，以教宮壼。○壼與閫同。

Empress Renxiaowen 仁孝文皇后, maiden name Xu [徐] 氏,[1] was the daughter of vassal king Zhongshan Wuning 中山武甯王, Da 達,[2] and the principal wife of Emperor Chengzu Wenhuangdi of Ming 明成祖文皇帝 [1360–1424; r. 1402–1424 CE]. She was well-learned and was fond of literature. She authored the *Teachings for the Inner Court* (*Neixun* 《內訓》), a book of twenty chapters to teach women of the imperial palace (*gongkun* 宮壼). 壼 *kun* and 閫 *kun* are synonymous.

Commentaries and Annotations

1. Translator's annotation: The Zhongyuange edition has 余 instead of 徐 in this sentence. Some scholars have argued that 徐 originated from 余 and that the two characters are interchangeable in ancient texts. Most available texts today have 徐 as Empress Renxiaowen's maiden name.
2. Translator's annotation: Xu Da 徐達 (1322–1385 CE) was a founding general of the Ming dynasty (1368–1644 CE).

【御製序】

吾幼承父母之教，誦詩書之典，職謹女事，蒙先人積善餘慶，夙備掖庭之選。事我孝慈高皇后，朝夕侍朝。高皇后教諸子婦，禮法唯謹，吾恭奉儀範，日聆教言，祇敬佩服，不敢有違。肅事今皇帝三十餘年，一遵先志，以行政教。吾思備位中宮，愧德弗似，歉於率下，無以佐皇上內治之美，以忝高皇后之訓。常觀史傳，求古賢婦貞女。雖稱德行之懿，亦未有不由於教而成者。古者教必有方，男子八歲而入小學，女子十年而聽姆教。小學之書無傳，晦庵朱子爰編輯成書，為小學之教者，始有所入。獨女教未有全書，世惟取范曄《後漢書》，曹大家《女誡》為訓。恆病其略。有所謂《女憲》、《女則》，皆徒有其名耳。近世始有女教之書盛行。大要撮曲禮、內則之言，與周南、召南詩之小序，及傳記而為之者。仰惟我高皇后教訓之言，卓越往昔，足以垂法萬世。吾耳熟而心藏之，乃於永樂二年冬，用述高皇后之教以廣之，為《內訓》二十篇，以教宮壼。夫人之所以克聖者，莫嚴於養其德性，以修其身。故首之以德性，次之以修身。修身莫切於謹言行，故次之以慎言謹行。推而至於勤勵節儉，而又次之以警戒。人之所以獲久長之慶者，莫加於積善；所以無過者，莫加於遷善。數者皆修身之要。而所以取法者，則必守我高皇后之教也，故繼之以崇聖訓。遠而取法於古，故次之以景賢範。上而至於事父母、事君、事舅姑、[奉祭祀]。又推而至於母儀、睦親、慈幼、侍下。而終之以待外戚。顧以言辭淺陋，不足以發揚深旨，而其條目亦粗備矣。觀者於此，不必泥於言，而但取於意。其於治內之道，或有裨於萬一云。

永樂[三]年正月望日序。

Original Preface to the Imperial Edition by Empress Renxiaowen

SINCE MY CHILDHOOD I inherited my parents' teaching, read the classics such as the *Classic of Poetry* (*Shijing*《詩經》) and the *Book of Documents* (*Shangshu*《尚書》), and dutifully carried out women's work. Benefiting from the accumulated good merits and the remaining prosperity of my ancestors, I was selected at a young age to be a member of the inner court at the imperial palace (*yeting* 掖庭).[1] I served Empress Xiaocigao 孝慈高皇后,[2] accompanying her day and night (*zhao xi* 朝夕) in the imperial inner court (*shi chao* 侍朝).[3] Empress Gao 高皇后 taught her daughters-in-law that ritual propriety and the law must be carefully observed. I reverently followed her exemplary example.[4] Daily I listened to her teaching; I could only admire her and dare not disobey. I have served our present emperor for thirty some years.[5] During these years, I have one-mindedly followed the lead of our deceased Emperor Gao in carrying out education in governmental affairs.[6] Now I reflect on my position as an empress. I am afraid that my virtue is lacking and I am insufficient in leading those under me. I am incapable of assisting the emperor in governing the inner court so as to add luster to Empress Gao's teachings.[7]

I often consult books of history and biography, seeking examples of virtuous women and chaste ladies. Although they are well-known for their virtuous natures, none of them could have been so accomplished without first being taught.[8] The ancients, in matters of education, necessarily adopted proper methods. Boys entered elementary school when they turned eight years old. Girls received lessons from their female teachers (*mujiao* 姆教) when they were ten years old.[9] However, books for elementary education (*xiaoxue* 小學) were not passed down. Sir Huian (Master Zhu) [of the Song dynasty], thus, edited and compiled materials and published them as a textbook for elementary learning. Only then was there entry to such learning.[10] Still, there was no complete textbook for women's education. People solely relied on Cao Dagu/Taigu's *Lessons for Women* (*Nüjie* 《女誡》) that is included in Fan Ye's *Book of Later Han* (*Houhanshu* 《後漢書》) as the teaching material. The only problem is that *Lessons for Women* is too brief. Even though it mentioned *Nüxian* 《女憲》 and *Nüze* 《女則》, only the titles of these books are in existence today.[11] Only recently textbooks for women's education become popular. Most of them are compilations of selected sayings from the Quli 曲禮 and Neize 內則 chapters of the *Record of Rituals* (*Liji* 《禮記》), poems from the Zhounan 周南 and the Shaonan 召南 sections of the *Classic of Poetry* (*Shijing* 《詩經》), their brief introductions, and some biographies [of women].[12] I recall admiringly the teachings of our deceased Empress Gao. Her words far exceed her predecessors; these words should be passed down to future generations for thousands of millennia. I listened to these words often and have learned them by heart. Therefore, in the winter of the second year of the Yongle era 永樂 [1404], I decided to elucidate and promulgate Empress Gao's teaching. I therefore composed twenty chapters of *Neixun* 《內訓》 as materials for teaching women of the imperial inner court.[13]

Essentially, so that a person can become sagely (*ke sheng* 克聖), nothing is more essential than nourishing one's virtuous nature so as to cultivate one's self.

Hence, the first chapter focuses on virtuous nature, followed by the chapter on self-cultivation.[14] In "cultivating the self," nothing is more pressing than prudent speech and conduct. Therefore, the next two chapters are on prudent speech and careful conduct.[15] These can be further extended to diligence and frugality and followed by watchfulness.[16] Moreover, so that a person can enjoy long-lasting prosperity, nothing is better than accumulating good deeds; so that he or she can be free from fault, nothing is better than [correcting mistakes and] becoming good.[17] The above are all essential items for self-cultivation. To find a norm to emulate, one must abide by the teachings of Empress Gao. Thus, the chapter that follows is named "Revering Sagely/Holy Teachings."[18] One should also look back to the ancient times to find exemplars to emulate. Consequently, the next chapter is entitled "Admiring Wise Role Models."[19] Reaching above, one applies these lessons to serving one's parents, one's ruler, and one's parents-in-law [and to performing religious rites].[20] Next, one applies the lessons to model motherhood, friendly relationship among relatives, caring for the young, and treating imperial concubines. The book ends with the chapter on treating imperial consorts' maternal relatives.[21] My words are shallow and unrefined; they are insufficient in developing Empress Gao's deep teachings. The items and tenets are only roughly prepared. Readers must not overly attach (*ni* 泥) themselves to the words; they should extract their essential meanings. In regard to how to govern the inner realm, it may be beneficial, even if only in one hundredth of a percentage of times.[22]

Preface written on January 15th of the [3rd] year of the Yongle era [1405][23]

Commentaries and Annotations

1. Wang Xiang's commentary: Yeting 掖庭 *refers to the corridor between the two sides of the palace, where the emperor's concubines and maid-attendants lived. Empress Renxiaowen did not want to directly describe herself as being selected as a royal consort; rather, she humbly stated that she was selected as a member of the inner court.* Translator's annotation: Empress Renxiaowen was chosen as the wife of the Prince of Yan 燕王 (later, Emperor Chengzu 成祖) in 1376, when she was only fifteen years old.
2. Wang Xiang's commentary: *Empress Gao* 高皇后, *maiden name Ma* 馬氏, *was the wife of Emperor Taizu Gaohuangdi* 太祖高皇帝. *Emperor Chengzu* 成祖, *the fourth son of Empress Gao, was initially given the title the Prince of Yan* 燕王. *During the Hongwu period* 洪武 *[of Taizu's reign (r. 1368–1398 CE)], Empress Wen* 文皇后 *[then, Lady Xu* 徐氏*] was selected as the Prince of Yan's consort. In the fourth year of the Jianwen period* 建文 *[1402 CE, under the reign of Emperor Hui* 惠帝, *the second emperor of Ming], the Prince of Yan [i.e., Emperor Hui's uncle] usurped the throne, known as the Jingnan Rebellion* 靖難之變. Translator's annotation: Emperor Taizu

Gaohuangdi 太祖高皇帝 was the first emperor of the Ming dynasty. Emperor Hui (1377–?; r. 1399–1402 CE), a grandson of Emperor Taizu and a nephew of the Prince of Yan, was the second emperor of Ming. He initiated many reforms immediately after he ascended the throne, including radically abolishing the power and territory of vassal kings, a contributing cause to his uncle's rebellion, the later Emperor Chengzu. Historical assessments of Emperor Chengzu, also known as Emperor Yongle (Yongledi 永樂帝), was mixed. On the one hand, Chengzu contributed considerably to the cultural, economic, political, and military growth of the Ming dynasty. His reign (r. 1403–1424 CE) was historically called the "Yongle Prosperity" (*Yongle Shengshi* 永樂盛世)—one of the best-known events during his reign was the expansive voyages of exploration to the South Pacific and Indian Oceans led by Zheng He 鄭和. On the other hand, he was criticized for his cruel revenge on his political enemies and his heavy-handed government. For more, see Zhang Tingyu, *Mingshi* 《明史》 (*History of Ming*), volumes 5, 6, and 7 ("Basic Annals").

3. Wang Xiang's commentary: *The first* 朝 *pronounced as* zhao 招*; the second* 朝 *pronounced as* chao 潮.
4. Translator's annotation: Empress Gao 高皇后 is a shortened title for Empress Xiaocigao 孝慈高皇后.
5. Wang Xiang's commentary: *By "the present emperor," she refers to Emperor Chengzu.*
6. Wang Xiang's commentary: *That is, she followed Empress Gao's determination in carrying out education in governmental affairs in the imperial inner court.*
7. Wang Xiang's commentary: *Empress Renxiaowen humbly spoke that she fears that, as an empress, she lacks virtue in leading those under her and in accomplishing the government of the inner court, thus blemishing the deceased Empress Gao's teachings.*
8. Wang Xiang's commentary: *This is speaking about the fact that in historical records, although there were plenty of virtuous women, none of them could have become good without being taught first.*
9. Wang Xiang's commentary: *This is from* Liji 《禮記》 *(*Record of Rituals*)*. Mujiao 姆教 *means "lessons delivered by female teachers."* Translator's annotation: *Liji* (also known as the *Xiaodai liji* 《小戴禮記》) has exercised tremendous influence in Chinese society since its completion, probably in the first century BCE. It codifies proper rituals and appropriate behavior in religious rites, marriage, education, and all areas of private, social, and political realms. Another edition of the *Record of Rituals* is the *Dadai liji* 《大戴禮記》, which contains more chapters and subjects than the *Xiaodai liji*, but most of the contents are now lost. According to these texts, boys and girls before age eight (according to the *Dadai liji*) or age ten (according to the *Xiaodai liji*) are home-schooled by their parents. After this age, boys attend schools outside of the home and girls continue to receive their education at home from female tutors or relatives. The last section of the Neize chapter of the *Liji* outlines a traditional Confucian curriculum plan from early childhood to adulthood (including arithmetic, calendar, social etiquette, moral education, calligraphy, music, poetry,

ritual dance, archery, and more). The curriculum for boys and girls begins to diverge at age ten. Girls' education after age ten focuses mainly on home economics, mannerisms, speech, appearance, cooking, sewing, and religious rites. For adulthood, boys are considered to have reached this stage at the age of twenty; for girls, it is at the age of fifteen. The proper marriage age for men is thirty; for women, twenty.

10. Wang Xiang's commentary: *Books for elementary education (*xiaoxue 小學*) from the ancient times were scattered and lost. Zhu Xi 朱熹 (i.e., Sir Huian 晦庵) of the Song dynasty thus began to edit and compile* Xiaoxue 《小學》 *(*Elementary Learning*) to teach children.* Translator's annotation: Zhu Xi (1130–1200 CE) was an influential Neo-Confucian scholar of the Song dynasty. He is most known for his compilation and commentary of the *Sishu* 《四書》 (*Four Books*) for gentleman learning.
11. Wang Xiang's commentary: *Zhu Xi's* Elementary Learning *is more suitable for teaching young boys. There is no textbook for teaching girls. Only Fan Ye 范曄 (398–445 CE), during the Liu Song period 劉宋 of the Southern dynasty 南朝, authored the* Book of Later Han, *in which it included the seven chapters of Cao Dagu/Taigu's* Lessons for Women. *This is a good thing. However, in Empress Renxiaowen's view, the shortcoming of this work is its brevity. Thus, the development and the explanation of the subject were incomplete. Works that were cited such as* Nüxian *and* Nüze *are lost; only their titles remain.* Translator's annotation: Cai Dagu/Taigu 曹大家 is Ban Zhao 班昭 (c. 45–117 CE). Her *Lessons for Women* is included in the *Four Books for Women* compiled by Wang Xiang.
12. Wang Xiang's commentary: *"Recently" means the later period of the Yuan dynasty and the early period of the Ming dynasty. There were several textbooks for educating women. All of them selected and compiled materials from the* Record of Rituals, *the Mao School's* Classic of Poetry, *and biographies of women from ancient times. None is by a single author.* Translator's annotation: Several versions of the *Classic of Poetry* existed during the Han dynasty (206 BCE–220 CE) and several schools specialized in this classic. However, only the Mao School's edition and commentary survives today.
13. Wang Xiang's commentary: *None of the textbooks for women's learning is sufficiently detailed and complete. She therefore decided to carry on the goal of the deceased [Empress Gao] and adopted [Empress Gao's] lessons and words as the foundation in writing the* Neixun *for teaching women of the imperial inner court.*
14. Wang Xiang's commentary: *This is speaking about how each chapter's name of the* Neixun *is chosen.* Sheng 聖 *means "good." The* Book of Documents *says, "If a person can constantly think about the good, he will become good." If someone wishes to cultivate the self, that person must nourish his virtuous nature first; therefore "Virtuous Nature" is the first chapter and "Self-cultivation" is the second chapter.* Translator's annotation: 克 (*ke*) means "can, be able to."
15. Wang Xiang's commentary: *Prudent speech and careful conduct are the foundation of cultivating the self. Thus, these two subjects are the next two chapters.*

16. Wang Xiang's commentary: *Diligence and frugality are the function of self-cultivation. Watchfulness encourages and reminds us lest our conduct become imprudent and our works in diligence and frugality not at their utmost. Thus, these chapters came after the first four chapters.*
17. Wang Xiang's commentary: *A person who cultivates the self ought to do good when opportunities arise and ought to correct mistakes when they happen. If a person can become good and continue to do good, it may be said that one's path to self-cultivation is completed.*
18. Wang Xiang's commentary: *"Revering Sagely/Holy Teachings" is to not forget Empress Gao's teachings.*
19. Wang Xiang's commentary: *"Admiring Wise Role Models" is to follow the norms of virtuous women of antiquity.*
20. Translator's annotation: The Zhongyuange edition of the *Neixun* inadvertently omitted the title of chapter 15 ("Performing Religious Rites") in the Empress Renxiaowen's preface.
21. Wang Xiang's commentary: *If one can fulfill one's responsibilities toward one's ruler, family members, the elders, and the young to one's best ability, one may be said to have completed the essentials of the human relations. Maternal relatives are members of royal consorts' maternal families; they especially should adhere to ritual propriety, not violating the law. Doing so will ensure long-lasting prosperity. Accordingly, this is how the book* Neixun *ends.*
22. Wang Xiang's commentary: Ni 泥 *here should be pronounced in the fourth tone. Empress Renxiaowen spoke humbly that her book is shallow and inelegant but the tenets are complete. If readers can extract its essential meaning and reflect on it, it can be beneficial in one's governance of the inner court.*
23. Translator's annotation: The Zhongyuange edition of the *Neixun* inadvertently misprinted the completion year as the second year of the Yongle era (1404 CE). In the early part of the preface, however, Empress Renxiaowen stated that she began to compose the *Neixun* in the winter of the second year of the Yongle era. Thus, this writing unlikely had been completed in January 1404 CE. Most other editions of the *Nü sishu* adopted the third year of the Yongle era (1405 CE) as the completion date.

【德性章第一】

貞靜幽閒，端莊誠一，女子之德性也。孝敬[仁]明，慈和柔順，德性備矣。夫德性原於所稟，而化成於習。匪由外至，實本於身。古之貞女，理情性，治心術，崇道德，故能配君子以成其教。是故仁以居之，義以行之，智以燭之，信以守之，禮以體之。匪禮勿履，匪義勿由。動必由道，言必由信。匪言而言，則厲階成焉。匪禮而動，則邪僻形焉。閫以限言，玉以節動，禮以制心，道以制欲。養其德性，所以飭身，可不慎歟。無損於性者，乃可以養德。無累於德者，乃可以成性。積過由小，害德為大。故大廈傾頹，基址弗固也。己身不飭，德性有虧也。美玉無瑕，可為至寶。貞女純德，可配京室。檢身制度，足為母儀。勤儉不妬，足法閨閫。若夫驕盈嫉忌，肆意適情，以病其德性，斯亦無所取矣。古語云：「處身造宅，黼身建德」。詩云：「俾爾彌爾性，純嘏爾常矣」。

I

Virtuous Nature (Dexing zhang diyi 德性章第一)

CHASTITY, TRANQUILITY, SOLITUDE, unhurried elegance, poise, seriousness, sincerity, and one-mindedness, are women's virtuous nature. Filialness, respect, [humaneness,][1] clear-mindedness, benevolence, harmony, gentleness, and compliance, complete their virtuous nature.[2] Virtuous nature is endowed (*bing* 稟) in us originally; change is due to habit (*xi* 習)—it does not come from outside but essentially relies on the person.[3] Chaste women from antiquity managed their emotive nature, governed their thoughts, and held morality in high regard. This is the reason they can become partners of gentlemen in accomplishing their teachings. Hence, one should reside in humaneness, act righteously, illuminate with wisdom, abide in trustworthiness, and guard one's body with ritual propriety.

Do not step on what is contrary to rituals; do not walk on what is contrary to righteousness. Whenever one moves, one necessarily follows the principles of the Way (*dao* 道). Whenever one speaks, one necessarily abides in trustworthiness.[4] Speaking when it is inappropriate to speak creates the staircase (*jie* 階) to disaster (*li* 厲). Making movement contrary to rituals corrupts one's conduct. Use the door's threshold (*yu* 閾) to set limits to one's speech. Use jade to set boundaries on one's movement. Use ritual propriety to control one's mind. Use principles of the Way to regulate one's desires. Cultivate one's virtuous nature to safeguard one's person. Should one not be prudent?[5]

Only things that do not damage one's endowed nature can nourish one's virtue; only things that do not tarnish one's virtue can complete one's endowed nature.[6] Accumulation of small faults will gravely damage one's virtue; the collapse of a large building is caused by its unsound foundation. If one's person is not safeguarded, one's virtuous nature will be deficient.[7] A beautiful jade without blemish can be an ultimate treasure; a chaste woman with pure virtue can become a wife of a great household (*pei jing shi* 配京室). If she can examine herself and keep things in order, she will be a model of motherhood; if she can be diligent and frugal without jealousy, she will be an exemplar of the inner quarters.[8] But if she is arrogant (*jiao* 驕), self-complacent (*ying* 盈), jealous (*ji ji* 嫉忌), unruly in her will (*si yi* 肆意), and unchecked in her emotions (*shi qing* 適情), consequently harming (*bing* 病) her virtuous nature, then nothing in her is worth mentioning.

The old saying goes, "If one wishes to rest one's body, one ought to build a house. If one wishes to embroider (*fu* 黼) one's person, one ought to establish virtue." [In commending King Cheng of Zhou's virtue,] the *Classic of Poetry* says, "Wish you a long life (*bi er mi er xing* 俾爾彌爾性)! Wish you enjoy great happiness in longevity (*chun gu er chang yi* 純嘏爾常矣)!"[9]

Commentaries and Annotations

1. Translator's annotation: Here, I have followed the other editions of *Neixun* in using 仁 (*ren*) instead of 之 (*zhi*) in this sentence. 仁 (*ren*, humaneness) is a virtue, whereas 之 (*zhi*) is a preposition ("of"), a third-person pronoun ("it," "her," "him," "them"), or an adjective ("this"). Because this sentence proclaims essential virtues for women, 仁 makes more contextual sense than 之. Wang Xiang's commentary (see next note) on this clause also mentioned 仁 (humaneness) among the other virtues. Thus, the Zhongyuange edition likely had a misprint.
2. Wang Xiang's commentary: *Chastity, tranquility, solitude, unhurried elegance, poise, seriousness, sincerity, and one-mindedness: the above eight refine women's virtuous nature interiorly. Filial piety, respectfulness, humaneness, clear-mindedness,*

benevolence, harmony, gentleness, and compliance: these eight items manifest women's virtuous nature outwardly. If a woman can do so, her virtue is complete.

3. Wang Xiang's commentary: 夫 *pronounced as* 扶 *(*fu) [, a sentence initial word with no meaning]. Bing 稟 *means "to receive."* Xi 習 *is "what can be moved by being taught." This explains that a person's virtuous nature is endowed at birth. It is originally good without evil. When one becomes older, it changes due to habits and practices. If one's parents teach one to be good, one will become enlightened by means of daily practices. If one is not taught but is influenced by bad habits, one will become ignorant due to daily practice of what is evil.* Translator's annotation: This passage upholds the Mencian teaching on the innate goodness of human nature (contra Xunzi's view). See the *Analects* (17.2), the *Mencius* (2A:6; 6A:1–6), the *Doctrine of the Mean*, among others. Confucian scholars generally agree that practice and habit either transform or corrupt a person, regardless of which theory one holds.
4. Wang Xiang's commentary: *This is speaking about chaste good women from antiquity. Because they can adjust and manage their nature and emotions, they were not in disorder. Because they can rightly govern their thoughts, they were not corrupted. They upheld morality with high regard; they modeled themselves after the virtuous and the enlightened. Consequently, they can become partners of gentlemen in accomplishing education of the inner quarters. Humaneness is mastered in the heart-mind; even when in residence, one would not lose it. Righteousness is tested when affairs happen; in one's conduct, one would not violate it. Use wisdom to illuminate principles. Follow trustworthiness in fulfilling one's words. Carry out ritual propriety in safeguarding oneself. When making movements, one necessarily follows ritual propriety, righteousness, principles of the Way, and trustworthiness. Such a person's virtuous nature is complete.* Translator's annotation: The interworking relations of humaneness, righteousness, ritual propriety, wisdom, modesty, and trustworthiness are upheld in numerous Confucian classics. See, for example, the *Analects* 6.18, 8.2; 12.1; 15.18; the *Mencius* 2A:6; 4A:27; 4B:28; 6A:11; 7A:21; 7A:33; the *Record of Rituals*, chapter 41.
5. Wang Xiang's commentary: 閾 *pronounced as* 鬱 *(*yu*).* Li 厲 *means "calamity, chaos";* jie 階 *means "staircase." The* Shijing《詩經》(Classic of Poetry*) says: "If a woman loves to gossip, it is the staircase to disaster." If a woman speaks when it is inappropriate for her to speak, it necessarily builds a staircase to disaster. When she makes movements contrary to rituals, it invites instances of corruption. Therefore, the door's threshold sets the limit of the inner realm. The* Liji《禮記》*(*Record of Rituals*) says, "The conversations of the inner quarters do not go outside the doorsteps. The words of the outer realm do not enter the inner halls." Thus, the threshold of the inner quarters is the boundary between the inner and the outer realms. Women of antiquity always carried jade on them when they walked; it is to set boundaries to where they go. Jade will make a jingling sound when a woman moves; hence, they dare not go places without a reason. These women feared that their mind may become dogmatic and unruly; they overcome it with ritual propriety. They feared that their desires may become indulgent; they overcome it with principles of the Way. They always safeguarded their persons and*

necessarily carried themselves respectfully and prudently. Therefore, they could nourish their virtuous nature. Translator's annotation: The verses from the *Shijing* cited here are from the Daya 大雅 section, the Zhanyang 瞻卬 poem. The passage on the inner–outer boundary is from the *Liji*, chapter 1 (Qulishang 曲禮上).

6. Wang Xiang's commentary: *Every word and every conduct should not harm the goodness of one's heavenly endowed nature nor blemish the purity of virtue. Virtue nurtures one's endowed nature, and one's endowed nature completes virtue.*
7. Wang Xiang's commentary: *If a small error is not corrected, it will necessarily damage great virtue. If the foundation is unsound, a palace necessarily collapses. If one's virtuous nature is not cultivated, one's person will be in disorder. Then, all conduct will be deficient.*
8. Wang Xiang's commentary: 京 *(*Jing*) means "big, great"; 配京室 (*pei jing shi*) means "becoming a wife of a great household." This explains that the purity and beauty of virtue in a chaste woman is like jade without blemish. She is a match to a great household. Such a woman examines and controls her body and mind. She cultivates and illuminates the order of her household. She is diligent and frugal, neither jealous nor envious. Hence, she can be a model of motherhood, and an exemplar of the inner quarters.*
9. Wang Xiang's commentary: 黼 *pronounced as* 甫 *(*fu*);* 俾 *as* 卑 *(*bi*);* 嘏 *as* 古 *(*gu*).* Jiao 驕 *means "arrogant";* ying 盈 *means "self-complacent";* ji ji 嫉忌 *means "intending to harm out of jealousy";* bing 病 *means "to harm";* fu 黼 *means "silk-embroidered clothing" used as a metaphor for a person's glory. The* Classic of Poetry *here refers to the Daya* 大雅 *section, the Quane* 卷阿 *poem.* Bi 俾 *means "to enable";* mi 彌 *means "long-lasting";* xing 性 *means "life, fate" (*ming 命*);* chun 純 *means "thick, plenty";* gu 嘏 *means "happiness." This statement makes the point that an immoral person will carry herself in an arrogant, self-complacent manner. In treating others, she will intend to harm them out of jealousy; she will be lawless and unruly; and she will indulge her emotions and consequently damage her virtuous nature. Even if she has other talents, nothing there is worth noting. Hence, the old saying goes, "If one desires to comfort one's body, one must build a house. If one desires to embroider one's body, it depends not on the beauty of one's clothes. One must establish virtue; then, one will become glorious." This is like Duke Zhaokang's* 召康公 *following King Cheng of Zhou* 周成王 *and praising the King in the Quane* 卷阿 *poem: The king has virtues. Moreover, the people trust him. A peaceful harmonious follower of the king wishes him a long life, and to constantly enjoy abundant happiness and prosperity. If men and women have such virtues, their happiness and prosperity will be just like this.* Translator's annotation: See *Analects* 8.11, where Confucius comments that even if a person possesses unparalleled talents and skills, if he is arrogant and stingy, there is nothing in him worth seeing. Here, Empress Renxiaowen adapts Confucius's teaching for women's education.

【修身章第二】

或曰：「太任目不視惡色，耳不聽淫聲，口不出傲言。若是者。修身之道乎?」曰：「然。古之道也。夫目視惡色，則中眩焉。耳聽淫聲，則內褫焉。口出傲言，則驕心侈焉。是皆身之害也。故婦人居必以正，所以防慝也。行必無陂，所以成德也。是故五綵盛服，不足以為身華。貞順率道，乃可以進婦德。不修其身，以爽厥德，斯為邪矣。諺有之曰，治穢養苗，無使莠驕，剗荊剪棘，無使塗塞。是以修身，所以成其德也。夫身不修，則德不立。德不立，而能成化於家者，蓋寡矣，而況於天下乎。是故婦人者，從人者也。夫婦之道，剛柔之義也。昔者明王之所以謹婚姻之始者，重似續之道也。家之隆替，國之興廢，於斯係焉。嗚呼，閨門之內，修身之教，其愓慎之哉。」

2

Self-Cultivation (Xiushen zhang dier 修身章第二)

SOMEONE ASKED, "TAIREN 太任 looked at no evil sights, listened to no lewd sound, and uttered no arrogant words. If this is true, is this the way to cultivate the self?"[1] The reply is, "Correct. This is the way of the ancients. When one looks at evil sights, one's center becomes confused (*xuan* 眩). When one listens to licentious sounds, one's interior self is robbed (*chi* 褫). When one utters conceited words, one's heart becomes arrogant and extravagant. These are harmful things to a person. Thus, when a woman is in residence, she necessarily follows principles of rectitude in order to prevent evil thoughts (*te* 慝). When she acts, she is necessarily not partial (*pi* 陂). Hence, she completes her virtue."[2]

Therefore, fine clothing with five-color embroidery cannot beautify a person. Only in cultivating chastity and compliance, and following (*shuai* 率) the Way, can one advance in women's virtue. If one does not cultivate one's person but goes against (*shuang* 爽) virtue, this is heading toward evil.[3] Thus, the proverb (*yan* 諺) says: "Remove debris. Tend to tender seedlings. Do not let weeds (*you* 莠) overgrow. Eradicate (*chan* 剗) wild thorny shrubs; do not let them block the way." Make way for self-cultivation. This is how one attains virtue.[4] For if one's person is not cultivated, one's virtue cannot be established. If one's virtue is not established, it is rarely the case that one can transform one's family—how can one then transform the world?[5]

A woman is to follow others. The way of a husband and a wife is the rightful order of the strong and the gentle. In the former times, illuminating kings were prudent with the inception of a marriage and emphasized the Way of having (*si* 似) continuation (*xu* 續) of family lineage, because the prosperity (*long* 隆) and the decline (*ti* 替) of a family, and the rise and the fall of a country, are closely related. Alas, inside the inner quarters, the teaching on self-cultivation must be prudently observed.[6]

Commentaries and Annotations

1. Wang Xiang's commentary: *The question-and-answer style of writing is used here. Tairen* 太任 *was the wife of King Wangji* 王季 [of Zhou 周] *and mother of King Wen* 文王. *The* Record of Rituals *says, "When she was pregnant with King Wen, she would not look at depraved sights nor listen to lascivious sounds. She would not speak arrogant words. If the seating mate was not straight, she would not sit. This is called prenatal education" (*taijiao 胎教*).* Translator's annotation: For more on Tairen's virtue, consult Liu Xiang's *Lienü zhuan* 《列女傳》 (*Biographies of Women*), volume 1, chapter 6, Zhoushi sanmu 周室三母 ("Three Empresses of the Zhou Dynasty"). Prenatal education was an important element in Confucian philosophy of education, even though the specific phrase "prenatal education" (*taijiao* 胎教) was not found in early Confucian texts. Wang Xiang probably acquired the language from Liu Xiang's *Biographies of Women*, or from Madame Zheng's *Classic of Fililal Piety for Women*. Kinney notes that the desirable attitudes of a pregnant woman mirror those attributed to Confucius in *Analects* 10.6–7. See Anne Behnke Kinney, trans. and ed., *Exemplary Women of Early China: The Lienü Zhuan of Liu Xiang* (New York: Columbia University Press, 2014), 199n49.
2. Wang Xiang's commentary: 褫 *pronounced as* 笞 (chi*);* 慝 *as* 忒 *(*te*);* 陂 *as* 皮 *(*pi*).* 眩 *means "confused";* 褫 *means "being robbed";* 慝 *means "errors";* 陂 *means "partial." This passage replied to the posed question. It is ancient sages' method of self-cultivation. Looking at evil sights confuses a person's emotive nature. Listening to lascivious sounds robs one's virtuous nature. Speaking haughty words gives birth to an arrogant extravagant heart. These three all cause harm to a person. Therefore, when in residence, one necessarily abides by principles of rectitude; when in action, one necessarily is impartial. This is to prevent evil and to accomplish virtue.*

3. Wang Xiang's commentary: Shuang 爽 *means "to go against, to violate"*; shuai 率 *means "to follow." This passage asserts that fine clothing cannot make a person beautiful. Only when one is chaste and compliant and follows right principles can one realize women's virtues. If one does not cultivate one's person but violates virtues, one becomes evil.* Translator's annotation: This is an especially poignant lesson to her intended audience (i.e., court ladies, royal consorts, their relatives, and the affluent class).
4. Wang Xiang's commentary: Yan 諺 *means "proverb"*; you 莠 *means "weeds, unwanted offshoots"*; chan 剗 *means "to cut, to remove." Removing debris and tending to tender seedlings discourage the growth of weeds that would otherwise harm the rice and wheat plants. The metaphor of eliminating weeds so that the pathway is not blocked is analogous to cultivating the self to nurture virtue.*
5. Wang Xiang's commentary: *Without cultivating the self and establishing virtue, rarely can such a person rightly manage a household! Not to mention governing the world!*
6. Wang Xiang's commentary: Si 似 *means "to have"*; xu 續 *"to continue"*; long 隆 *"to prosper, to rise"*; ti 替 *"to abolish, to fall." This passage explains that the righteousness of a woman rests in following others.* Yang *is strong and* yin *is gentle. This is the right order of a husband and a wife. Hence, in ancient times sage emperors and illuminating kings were prudent in the husband–wife relation and valued greatly its responsibility of carrying on their ancestors' surnames and extending the family lineage. The* Classic of Poetry *says, "Continue the lineage of your ancestors." This is what is said here. Whether a woman is virtuous or not directly relates to the prosperity or demise, the rise or fall, of a family and country. Inside the inner quarters, one must not be imprudent!* Translator's annotation: This chapter, on the one hand, asserts the positive teaching of women's ability on self-cultivation and attainment of virtue (equaling their male counterparts). It also teaches the valuable lessons that a woman's inner beauty outweighs her outer appearance, and her virtue contributes to the rise and fall of a family and nation. However, on the other hand, it also restates the extremely conservative value of "three obediences" (*sancong* 三從) as the rightful place for women: obey the father when not yet married, obey the husband when married, and obey the son when widowed. See the *Liji* (*Record of Rituals*), chapter 11 (Jiaotesheng 郊特牲), and *Mencius* 3B:2. For more on the alignment of *yin-yang* with the wife–husband relationship, see chapter 11 of the *Liji*; the beginning chapters of the *Yijing* (*Classic of Changes*); chapter 1 of Liu Shi, *Short Records of Models for Women*; and chapters 2 and 3 of Ban Zhao, *Lessons for Women*. Wang Xiang's citation from the *Shijing* (*Classic of Poetry*) here is from the Xiaoya 小雅 section, the Sigan 斯干 poem.

【慎言章第三】

婦教有四，言居其一。心應萬事，匪言曷宣。言而中節，可以免悔。言不當理，禍必從之。諺曰：「誾誾謇謇，匪石可轉。訿訿譞譞，烈火燎原。」又曰：「口如扃，言有恆。口如注，言無據。」甚矣言之不可不慎也。況婦人德性幽閑，言非所尚，多言多失，不如寡言。故書斥牝雞之晨，詩有厲階之刺，禮嚴出梱之戒。善於自持者，必於此而加慎焉，庶乎其可也。然則慎之有道乎? 曰：「有。學南宮縚可也。」夫緘口內修，重諾無尤，甯其心，定其志，和其氣，守之以仁厚，持之以莊敬，質之以信義，一語一默，從容中道，以合於坤靜之體。則讒慝不作，而家道雍穆矣。故女不矜色，其行在德。無鹽雖陋，言用於齊而國以安。孔子曰：「有德者必有言，有言者不必有德。」

3

Prudent Speech (Shenyan zhang disan 慎言章第三)

WOMEN'S EDUCATION INCLUDES four subjects. [Prudent] speech is one of the four. But a person's heart-mind responds to tens of thousands of things. If one does not speak, how does one communicate? If one's words are temperate, one will have no regrets. If one's words do not meet reason, calamity follows.[1] The proverb says, "Speak in pleasant tones (*yinyin* 誾誾) with words of reason (*qianqian* 謇謇). A person, even as firm as a rock (*feishi* 匪石), can be turned around. Slanderous talks (*zizi* 訿訿) and argumentative words (*xuanxuan* 譞譞) are like rapid fires that can burn down the fields." It also says, "If one's mouth is like a closed door that opens and closes at the right time (*jun/jiong* 扃), one's words will be regarded by others as constant. If one's mouth is like pouring water (*zhu* 注), one's words will be taken by others as baseless." Truly, one's words must not be imprudent.[2]

Furthermore, a woman's virtue comprises solitude and unhurried elegance. Speech is not one of her strengths. The more she speaks, the more she makes mistakes. It is not as good as when she speaks less. Therefore, the *Book of Documents* (*Shangshu*《尚書》) scolds a hen for crowing in the morning (*pinji zhichen* 牝雞之晨). The *Classic of Poetry* (*Shijing* 《詩經》) has the ironic statement about a staircase to disaster. The *Record of Rituals* (*Liji*《禮記》) sternly warns against conversations of the inner quarters going outside the household. Those who are good at self-discipline must especially be prudent on this matter. Then, she has done what she should do.[3]

Is there a proper method of being prudent? Yes, there is. Learn from Nan Gong Tao 南宮縚.[4] If one can close one's mouth (*jian kou* 緘口), focus on inner cultivation, honor one's promises (*nuo* 諾), invite no complaints (*you* 尤), calm one's mind, secure one's will, harmonize one's psycho-physical energy (*qi* 氣), guard them with humaneness, uphold them with seriousness and respect, substantiate them with trustworthiness and righteousness, and in one's speech and silence calmly keep to the middle way so as to match the body of the tranquil *kun* 坤, then slanders and depraved deeds will not arise and the household will be prosperous and harmonious.[5]

Hence, a woman should not be haughty about her physical beauty; what matters is her virtue. Even though Wu Yan 無鹽 [i.e., Zhong Lichun 鍾離春] was physically unattractive, her words when used to govern the State of Qi 齊 brought peace to the country. Confucius said: "One who has virtue will necessarily have words. One who has words may not necessarily have virtue."[6]

Commentaries and Annotations

1. Wang Xiang's commentary: *The four subjects of women's education (*sijiao 四教*) include: virtue, speech, appearance, and work. These are the so-called four virtues (*side 四德*). This passage makes the point that women's speech is one of the four subjects of women's education. A person's heart-mind responds to the tens of thousands of things. If one does not speak, how does one make one's intention known? Certainly, if one's words are temperate, then there will be no regrets. If one's words do not accord with reason, calamity and disgrace will follow.* Translator's annotation: "Three obediences" and "four [womanly] virtues" are often mentioned together as *sancong side* 三從四德, which defines a woman's proper place in life and her moral-social responsibilities in traditional China. For more on the "three obediences," see chapter 2, commentary note 6. For more on the "four [womanly] virtues," see *Liji*, chapter 44 (Hunyi 昏義), and Ban Zhao's *Nüjie*, chapter 4.
2. Wang Xiang's commentary: 誾 *pronounced as* 銀 *(*yin*);* 謇 *as* 遣 *(*qian*);* 訾 *as* 資 *(*zi*);* 譞 *as* 儇 *(*xuan*);* 扃 *as* 君 *(*jun*).* Yinyin 誾誾 *means "pleasant";* qianqian 謇

謇 *means "with right reason and right words"*; feishi 匪石 *"a heart of determination, like a rock"*; zizi 訾訾 *"slander"*; xuanxuan 譞譞 *"overly argumentative, without stillness"*; jun *(or,* jiong) 扃 *means "like a door's opening and closing according to the right time"; and* zhu 注 *"like pouring water without stop once released." This passage speaks about the proverb. If one can be pleasant and speak to others with words of reason, even a person as determined as a rock can be turned around to do what is right. If one utters words of slander and has a nasty mouth that hurts others, the catastrophe would be like rapid fires burning dry grass in an open field. It is beyond rescue! It also says that if one's mouth is like a closed door most of times and it only opens at the right times, then one's words may be valued by others. But if one's mouth, once open, is like pouring water that cannot be stopped, then one's words are arrogant and baseless, hated by others. How can one not be prudent?*

3. Wang Xiang's commentary: Pinji 牝雞 *refers to a hen.* Chen 晨 *means "crowing in the morning." This passage indicates that the proper way of a woman does not include eloquence of speech. The more she speaks, the more she makes mistakes. Hence, the* Book of Documents *says: "When a hen crows in the morning, it begins the decline of a household." This refers to the talkativeness of a woman causing disorder in the governance of the household; like the crowing of a hen in the morning, it is an inauspicious omen and an indicator of the demise of a household. The* Classic of Poetry *says: "If a woman loves to gossip, it is the staircase to calamity," which predicts that disasters will necessarily arise. The* Record of Rituals *says: "The words of the outer world do not enter. The conversations of the inner realm do not exit." It sets the door threshold as the boundary. The warnings given by these sacred classics about women's speech are very prudent. Women who desire to cultivate their persons must be cautious on this matter.* Translator's annotation: The metaphor of a hen crowing in the morning is from the *Shangshu*, Mushi 牧誓 section. The text from the *Shijing* is from the Daya section, Zhanyang 瞻卬 poem. The passage about the inner–outer boundary is from the *Liji*, chapter 1 (Qulishang 曲禮上). Confucian conservatives often used these texts to prohibit women from participating in public affairs or political offices.

4. Wang Xiang's commentary: *This passage returned to the style of question-and-answer. Nan Gong Tao* 南宮縚, *also by the name Kuo* 适, *was Confucius's student. His courtesy name is Zirong* 子容. *Nan Rong* 南容 *[i.e., Nan Gong Tao] was prudent in his speech. He reviewed Duke Weiwu's* 衛武 *poem multiple times daily in order to caution himself. The poem reads: "For blemishes in white jade, one can still polish the stone [to remove them]. For blemishes in one's spoken words, nothing can be done." If white jade has defects, one can still polish the stone to remove them. If spoken words have shortcomings, once they are spoken, it is difficult to take them back—it simply cannot be done! Thus, Confucius commended Nan Rong's prudence in his speech and married his brother's daughter to him. Women who wish to be cautious with their words should follow Nan Rong's example.* Translator's annotation: See *Analects* 11.5 about Nan Rong. Duke

Weiwu's poem, reviewed daily by Nan Rong, is the Yi 抑 poem from the *Shijing*, Daya section.

5. Wang Xiang's commentary: Jian 緘 *means "close"*; nuo 諾 *means "promise"*; you 尤 *means "mistake." If a woman speaks few words, then her inner self will be cultivated and enlightened. If she is prudent in making promises and honor the promises she made, then there will be no complaints. Resolute in her will and psycho-physical energy, pleasant in her words and appearance, humane in her heart-mind, respectful to others far and wide, consistent in regarding trustworthiness and righteousness as the foundation, temperate and proper in speech and silence, and [embodying] the body of the tranquil* kun 坤 *and the way of the Earth* 地: *this is the righteousness of a woman. If a woman can be tranquil and silent, thus matching the body of chaste kun, then slander will not arise and wicked deeds will not occur. Consequently, the household will become prosperous and harmonious.* Translator's annotation: For more on the concept of *kun*, see *Yijing*, hexagram 2 (坤 ䷁); and Liu Shi, *Short Records of Models for Women*, chapter 1.
6. Wang Xiang's commentary: *The passage makes the point that women should not be prideful in their physical appearance. Virtue is of the essence. In the former times, Wu Yan* 無鹽 *was a daughter of the Zhong* 鍾 *household. She was very unattractive physically. King of Qi* 齊 *heard about her virtuous talent, made her queen, and adopted her words in governance. The state of Qi consequently became greatly governed. Hence, Confucius said that a virtuous person is not without words. Rather, it is that what he says is necessarily temperate and proper. If someone speaks only with clever words, this person may not have virtue.* Translator's annotation: For more on Wu Yan, see Liu Xiang's *Biographies of Women*, volume 6, chapter 10; for Confucius's statement on the relation between virtue and weightiness of words, see *Analects* 14.5.

【謹行章第四】

甚哉，婦人之行，不可以不謹也。自是者其行專，自矜者其行危，自欺者其行驕以污。行專則綱常廢，行危則疾戾興，行驕以污，則人道絕。有一於此，鮮克終也。夫干霄之木，本之深也。凌雲之臺，基之厚也。婦有令譽，行之純也。本深在乎栽培，基厚在乎積累，行純在乎自力。不為純行，則戚疏離焉，長幼紊焉，貴賤淆焉。是故欲成其大，當謹其微。縱之毫末，本大不伐。昧於冥冥，神鑒孔明。百行一虧，終累全德。體柔順，率貞潔。服三從之訓，謹內外之別。勉之敬之，始終惟一。由是可以修家政，可以和上下，可以睦親戚，而動無不協矣。易曰：「恆其德，貞，婦人吉。」此之謂也。

4

Careful Conduct (Jinxing zhang disi 謹行章第四)

TRULY, A WOMAN'S conduct must not be careless. A self-righteous person's behavior is autocratic. An arrogant person's action is dangerous. A self-deceiving person's conduct is prideful and indecent. If one's behavior is autocratic, [three] bonds and [five] constants will be abolished. If one's action is dangerous, complaints and disasters will rampage. If one's conduct is prideful and indecent, the way of humanity will be annihilated. Any person, having any of these faults, will rarely (*xian* 鮮) have good endings.[1]

A towering tree that grows as tall as the sky is due to its roots being deeply planted. A soaring terrace that reaches as high as the clouds is due to its foundation being thickly laid. A woman has a good reputation is because her conduct is morally pure. Deep roots depend on cultivation; thick foundations result from accumulation; and, pure conduct rests on self-effort. If one does not endeavor in pure conduct, one's relatives will grow distant; the proper order between the old and young will turn chaotic; and the differentiation between the noble and the ignoble will become confusing (*yao* 淆).[2] Therefore, if a woman wants to accomplish something great, she must be careful with the minute details. If she is careless with a tiny seedling (*haomo* 毫末),[3] once it grows into a big tree, it will be difficult to cut down. If she thinks that one can act unconscionably in dark corners, be aware that gods and spirits can see it very clearly. If one errs once among a hundred deeds, it will damage the whole of one's virtue.[4]

Embody gentleness and compliance. Safeguard chastity and purity. Abide by "three obediences" (*sancong* 三從). Heed the distinction between the inner and the outer realms. Be diligent and be respectful in observing them, one-minded from the beginning to the end.[5] Thereupon, one can cultivate family affairs, harmonize those above and those below, and build friendly relationship among the relatives. Whenever one moves, nothing will be in disharmony (*bu xie* 不協). The *Yijing* 《易經》 (*Classic of Changes*) says, "Constant in her virtue, chastity. It is auspicious for women." This is what it means.[6]

Commentaries and Annotations

1. Wang Xiang's commentary: 鮮 (xian) *pronounced in the third tone. This passage indicates that virtue must be the priority of a woman's conduct. If she does not have virtue and if she is also self-righteous, she will be autocratic, doing things on her own authority without permission. If she is arrogant and self-boasting, her behavior will be dangerous and unsettling. If she is without conscience and self-deceiving, she will carry herself in a prideful lawless manner and do shameful things recklessly. Because a self-righteous woman does not have a ruler or a husband, the great morality of [three] bonds and [five] constants is abolished. A self-endangering woman invites other's complaints and dislikes; hence, disasters arise. A self-arrogant woman who does ignoble things obliterates the way of womanhood, making it inhuman. Rarely can a person, who has one of these three vices, complete her lifetime without blame.* Translator's annotation: The concept of the "three bonds" (*sangang* 三綱) can be traced back to Han Fei 韓非 (281–33 BCE), a scholar of Legalism during the Warring States period. Dong Zhongshu 董仲舒 (179–104 BCE) of the Han dynasty, in his *Chunqiu fanlu* (*Luxuriant Dew of the Spring and Autumn Annals*), stipulated "three bonds and five constants" (*sangang wuchang* 三綱五常) as the orthodox Confucian way of organizing the government and preserving the moral fibers of a society. For more on the "three bonds," see the introduction to this volume and the introduction to the *Nüjie*. "Five constants" refer to five virtues: humanness (*ren* 仁), righteousness (*yi* 義), ritual propriety (*li* 禮), wisdom (*zhi* 智), and good faith (*xin* 信).
2. Wang Xiang's commentary: 淆 *pronounced as* 爻 (yao). *This passage speaks about the fact that a tree that grows as tall as the sky is due to its deep and firm roots. A tower that reaches as high as the clouds depends on its firm and thick foundation. A woman enjoying a virtuous name and a good reputation is due to her pure and complete virtue.*

The depth of the roots relies on the work of cultivating and planting. The thickness and firmness of the foundation come from the effort of accumulation and the increase in height. The purity of a woman's conduct rests on applying her best efforts without lacking even in one single detail. If a woman's conduct is impure, regardless of whether they are relatives or non-relatives they will all leave and keep their distance; the rituals between the old and the young will become disorderly; and the distinction between the honorable and the dishonorable will turn perplexing and unruly.

3. Translator's annotation: *Haomo* 毫末 literally means "the tip of a hair," customarily used to refer to minute things. See, for example, the *Daodejing* 《道德經》, chapter 64; the *Zhuangzi* 《莊子》, chapter 17.
4. Wang Xiang's commentary: *This elucidates that if a person wishes to accomplish great morality, she must carefully observe minuscule details. If she lets go of details as tiny as the tip of a hair (*haomo 毫末*), the problem will begin like the growth of a tiny sprout; its branches and vines will expand so widely that it cannot be cut down. If she thinks that she can act unconscionably in dark corners since no one would know, it shows that she does not understand that gods and spirits can surely see all very clearly. Concerning a woman's conduct, even if it is only one mistake among a hundred acts, the whole of virtue is damaged.*
5. Wang Xiang's commentary: *The way of a woman is to embody the righteousness of gentleness, respect, and compliance, and to uphold the integrity of chastity, tranquility, and purity. If not yet married, she follows her father; if married, she follows her husband; if her husband passes away, she follows her son. If the lesson of the "three obediences" is not abandoned, the rituals of the inner and outer realms will necessarily be observed. Be diligent and self-respectful in guarding one's body and person; be cautious from the beginning to in the end; uphold one-mindedness without wavering. This shall suffice.*
6. Wang Xiang's commentary: Xie 協 *means "harmony, reason." The above are words from the* heng *hexagram (*heng gua 恆掛*) of the* Yijing *(*Classic of Changes*). If a woman's conduct is well-prepared, then family affairs will be cultivated, those above and those below will be harmonized, relatives will be on friendly terms, and the multitude of things will be in accord with reason.* Heng *means "constant and long-lasting." The* Yijing *is commenting on constancy in virtue unchangingly; it is the path to great auspiciousness for women. Therefore, the* Xiangci 象辭 *(*Xiang Commentary*) to hexagram* heng 恆 *states that women's chastity is auspicious; she follows one* [husband] *to the end."* Translator's annotation: For more, see *Yijing*, hexagram 32 (*heng* 恆 ䷟).

【勤勵章第五】

怠惰恣肆，身之災也。勤勵不息，身之德也。是故農勤於耕，士勤於學，女勤於工。農惰則五穀不穫，士惰則學問不成，女惰則機杼空乏。古者后妃親蠶，躬以率下。庶士之妻，皆衣其夫。效績有制，愆則有辟。夫治絲執麻，以供衣服，冪酒漿，具葅醢，以供祭祀，女之職也。不勤其事，以廢其功，何以辭辟。夫早作晚休，可以無憂。縷績不息，可以成匹。戒之哉。毋荒寧，荒寧者，劇身之廉刃也。雖不見其鋒，陰為所戕矣。詩曰：「婦無公事，休其蠶織。」此怠惰之慝也。於乎，貧賤不怠惰者易，富貴不怠惰者難。當勉其難，毋忽其易。

5

Diligence
*(*Qinli zhang diwu 勤勵章第五*)*

LAZINESS AND UNBRIDLED unruliness bring disaster to a person. Untiring diligence is a person's virtue.[1] Therefore, farmers are diligent in farming the field; scholars are diligent in their study; and women are diligent in their work. If farmers are lazy, five grains will not be harvested. If scholars are lazy, learning will not be accomplished. If women are lazy, weaving looms will be empty.[2] In ancient times, queens and royal consorts personally attended to raising silkworms, respectfully acting as role models in leading those under them. Wives of the common people and officials made clothing for their husbands. Orderly policies were put in place to reward good work and to punish errors.[3]

For weaving silk and spinning hemp to provide clothes, and preparing wine (*mi* 冪), pickled vegetables (*zu* 葅), and sauce (*hai* 醢) to make offerings in religious rites are women's vocations. If a woman is not diligent, but instead nullifies previous work, how can she avoid blame or punishment?[4] Rise early to work and rest late: this relieves one from worries. Diligence in weaving without interruption can produce a forty-foot-long (*pi* 匹) fabric.[5] Be warned! Do not abandon work (*huang* 荒) or indulge in leisure (*ning* 甯). Abandoning work and indulging in leisure are like sharp (*lian* 廉) knives that kill (*gui* 劌) a person. Although one may not see the knife's sharpness, one's *yin* has already been harmed (*qiang* 戕).[6]

Thus, the *Classic of Poetry* says, "Women have no obligations of public affairs. Why abandon their work of attending to silkworms and weaving?" This concerns the errors of negligence and laziness. Alas! It is easy for one who lives in poverty and in inferior position not to become lazy; it is difficult for one who is affluent not to be lazy. Be advised to do what is difficult but not omit what is easy.[7]

Commentaries and Annotations

1. Wang Xiang's commentary: *This comments on a person who is negligent and does not respect his or her work, is lazy and not diligent in his or her effort, lacking self-control and not examining oneself, unruly and not observant of ritual propriety. These four are disasters of a lifetime. Diligence and hard work without tiredness are virtues that complete a person.*
2. Wang Xiang's commentary: *Ploughing is the work of farmers. If farmers are lazy in farming, the five grains will be abandoned. Study is the business of scholars. If scholars are lazy in their study, learning will be neglected. Work is women's obligation. If women are not diligent in their work, weaving machines will be empty and the household will become poor.*
3. Wang Xiang's commentary: *In ancient times, queens personally attended to growing mulberry trees and feeding silkworms. They led royal consorts in making clothes for religious rituals. Wives of officials and the common people all respectfully made clothes for their husbands. In the spring, they attended to farming; men plowed and women wove. In the autumn, they calculated merits and rewarded good work. If the harvest was scarce and the woven clothes were few, guilt would be assigned and punishment given. This was the policy of former kings.*
4. Wang Xiang's commentary: 冪 *pronounced as* 密 (mi*);* 菹 *as* 疽 (ju*);* 醢 *as* 海 (hai*).* 冪 *means "to make something by fermentation";* 菹 *means "pickled vegetables";* 醢 *means "sauce." Weaving silk and hemp to make clothes, making wine, pickled vegetables, and sauce to prepare for religious rites and banquets are all women's work. If she is not diligent in attending to her responsibilities but abandons women's work, it would be difficult to exonerate her from blame and punishment.* Translator's annotation: It is unclear why Wang Xiang says that 菹 is pronounced as *ju* 疽. 菹 should be pronounced as *zu* 朱.
5. Translator's annotation: According to the Ming dynasty's measuring system, one *pi* 匹 equals four *zhang* 丈; one *zhang* 丈 equals ten feet (*chi* 尺); one foot equals 34 centimeters (about 1 foot, 1 inch in US measuring system).
6. Wang Xiang's commentary: 劌 *pronounced as* 歲 (sui*);* 戕 *as* 祥 (xiang*).* 荒 (huang*) means "abandon";* 甯 (ning*) means "comfort, leisure";* 劌 (sui*) means "to kill or sever";*

廉 (lian) *means "razor-sharp"*; 戕 (xiang) *means "to kill, to harm." This passage also cites an ancient proverb: If a woman gets up early to work and rests only in the evening, she will not have worries. One silk string, one thread, weaving without rest can produce a forty-foot-long fabric. Do not abandon work and desire comfort and leisure. The harm of comfort and leisure is like a sharp knife that can kill a person. Even though one does not see the knife's sharpness, one's body has already been implicitly injured.* Translator's annotation: It is unclear why Wang Xiang says that 劌 is pronounced as 歲 (*sui*) and 戕 as 祥 (*xiang*). 劌 should be pronounced as *gui* and 戕 as *qiang*.

7. Wang Xiang's commentary: 於 *is pronounced as* 烏 (wu). *The words of the* Classic of Poetry *refer to the Daya section, the Zhanyang* 瞻卬 *poem. This passage cites the* Classic of Poetry *stating that women do not have the responsibility of public affairs. She only needs to attend to feeding silkworms, growing mulberry trees, and weaving. Nowadays, women interfere with governmental business and abandon their work on silkworms and weaving. Their faults of negligence and laziness are severe. Thus, it warns that it is quite easy for women who live in poor families to not be lazy; but for women who live in households of the wealthy and the upper class, it is difficult for them not to become lazy. A person should be advised to do what is difficult, but not to neglect what is easy.* 卬 *is pronounced as* 仰 (yang).

【節儉章第六】

戒奢者，必先於節儉。夫澹素養性，奢靡伐德。人率知之，而取舍不決焉。何也。志不能帥氣，理不足御情，是以覆敗者多矣。傳曰：「儉者，聖人之寶也。」又曰：「儉，德之共也。侈，惡之大也。」若夫一縷之帛，出女工之勤。一粒之食，出農夫之勞，致之不易。而用之不節，暴殄天物，無所顧惜，上率下承，靡然一軌，孰勝其弊哉。夫錦繡華麗，不如布帛之溫也。奇饈美味，不如糲粢之飽也。且五色壞目，五味昏智，飲清茹淡，祛疾延齡。得失損益，判然懸絕矣。古之賢妃哲后，深戒守此。故絺綌無斁，見美於周詩。大練麤疏，垂光於漢史。敦廉儉之風，絕侈麗之質，天下從化。是以海內殷富，閭閻足給焉。蓋上以導下，內以表外，故后必敦節[儉]以率六宮，諸侯之夫人以至士庶之妻，皆敦節儉，以率其家。然後民無凍餒，禮義可興，風化可紀矣。或有問者曰：「節儉有禮乎。」曰：「禮。與其奢也，寧儉。」然有可約者焉，有可腆者焉。是故處己不可不儉，事親不可不豐。

6

Frugality (Jiejian zhang diliu 節儉章第六)

TO GET RID of extravagance, one must start with frugality.[1] Tranquility with few desires and contentment in plainness nourish one's nature. Extravagance and luxury damage virtue. All know this moral; and yet, people are indecisive in choosing what to keep and what to give up. Why so? This is because their will (*zhi* 志) cannot champion their psycho-physical energy (*qi* 氣) and their reason is insufficient in controlling their emotion. Thus, many have failed.[2]

The *Zuo Commentary* (*Zuozhuan* 左傳) says, "Frugality is a treasure of the sages." It also says, "Frugality is what all the virtues have in common (*gong* 共). Wastefulness (*chi* 侈) is the gravest of all vices."[3] A single thread of cloth is a result of women's diligent work; a grain of food is a consequence of farmers' hard labor. These things do not come by easily. If all use these materials intemperately and waste these materials from Heaven without care—those above lead while those below follow and all walk the same path—who will be able to overturn these corrupt practices?[4]

The luxury of embroidered clothing cannot compare to the warmth of cotton clothes. Delicacy and delicious dishes are not as good as the fullness of coarse rice and simple food (*lizi* 糲粢). Furthermore, five colors destroy the eyes; five flavors confuse the mind. Having light drinks and plain dishes drives away (*qu* 袪) illness and extends life. Gain, loss, harm, and advantage can be clearly differentiated![5] Virtuous royal consorts and intelligent queens and empresses during ancient times all seriously took caution. Thus, no dislike (*yi* 斁) of clothes made from either fine or rugged hemp (*chixi* 絺綌) is praised in the Zhou poetry. Plain and rugged white clothes (*cu* 麤) were honored in the history of Han. They upheld the culture of integrity and frugality, and exterminated extravagance and luxury. The world under Heaven was thus transformed. During those times, there was great prosperity within the four seas and all households had plenty.[6]

Because what is above leads what is below and what is inside manifests in the outside, empresses must observe frugality in order to lead the six imperial inner quarters. Consorts of marquises and wives of minor officials and the common people all should uphold frugality to lead their households. Accordingly, no citizens will suffer from cold and hunger. Ritual propriety and righteousness will become prominent. Such transformations of culture will be memorable.[7]

Someone may ask, "Would frugality comply with ritual propriety?" The reply is, "As far as ritual propriety is concerned, it is better to be frugal than extravagant. And yet, there are certain things that one should be frugal about; and there are other things that one should be generous about. Hence, in dealing with the self, one must be frugal; and in serving one's parents one ought to be generous."[8]

Commentaries and Annotations

1. Translator's annotation: The *Siku quanshu* 《四庫全書》 edition, in Ji Yun 紀昀 et al., eds., places the chapter on "frugality" after the chapter on "watchfulness." However, according to Empress Renxiaowen's own preface, the chapter on "frugality" should immediately follow the chapter on "diligence."
2. Wang Xiang's commentary: *The passage conveyed that in stopping extravagance, there is nothing better than frugality. Having few desires and contentment with plainness nurture one's pure nature; extravagance and luxury damage women's virtues. All know this lesson. But many cannot uphold frugality and they prefer extravagance. Why so? It is because their wills are altered by their habits; thus, their wills cannot lead them*

to the right path. Their reason is confused by their emotion and desire; thus, reason is incapable of controlling emotion and desire with ritual propriety. For this reason, many people become morally corrupt.

3. Wang Xiang's commentary: 共 *pronounced as* gong 恭; 侈 *as* chi 恥. Zhuan 傳 *refers to Zuo Qiuming's* 左丘明 Chunqiu zuozhuan 《春秋左傳》 *(*Zuo Commentary to the Spring and Autumn Annals*). This passage explains that the sages enrich all under Heaven by means of frugality. If one would like people to always be respectful and to prevent ritual propriety from decline, nothing is more effective than using frugality. Hence, it says frugality is what all the virtues have in common. For if wastefulness is born of extravagance and arrogance is born of wastefulness, then no cause for trespassing ritual propriety and violating one's role is graver than wastefulness. Thus, wastefulness is described as the gravest of all vices.* Translator's annotation: The *Zuozhuan* is one of the three essential commentaries to the *Spring and Autumn Annals* (*Chunqiu* 《春秋》); it is customarily referred to as *Chunqiu zuozhuan*. The other two commentaries are *Gongyang zhuan* 《公羊傳》 and *Guliang zhuan* 《穀梁傳》. Frugality is a key Confucian and Daoist virtue. See, for example, *Analects* 1.10, 3.4, 7.15, 7.25; *Mencius* 3A:3, 4A:16; *Daodejing*, chapter 67; *Zhuangzi*, chapters 12 and 15.
4. Wang Xiang's commentary: *This passage conveys the lesson that although a thread of cloth is something small, women's work to produce it is not easy. Although coarse grains are not much, they require farmers' hard labor to produce them. If one uses them immoderately, this is wasting materials from Heaven. Nothing is more culpable than this. Unfortunately, the foolish do not understand this lesson; those above lead those below. Do they not know the detriment it causes?*
5. Wang Xiang's commentary: 糲粢 *pronounced as* 勵資 *(*lizi*);* 袪 *as* 驅 *(*qu*).* 糲 *(*li*) means "coarse rice";*粢 *(*zi*) means "plain dishes";* 袪 *(*qu*) means "drive away." The passage teaches that although embroidered clothes are beautiful, they do not compare to the warmth of cotton clothes. While delicacy is delicious, it is not as good as the fullness of coarse rice. Furthermore, five colors blind one's eyes; five flavors harm one's mind. Plain drinks and food, on the contrary, can drive away sickness and extend longevity. Isn't this obvious and easy to see?* Translator's annotation: This passage resembles the *Daodejing*, chapter 12, "Five colors make one's eyes blind. Five sounds make one's ears deaf. Five flavors spoil one's palate."
6. Wang Xiang's commentary: 絺綌 *pronounced as* 笞隙 *(*chixi*);* 斁 *as* 亦 *(*yi*);* 麤 *as* 粗 *(*cu*). Fine hemp is called* chi*; rugged hemp is called* xi. Yi *means "dislike, despise." This passage says that in ancient times, the sagely virtuous queens, empresses, and royal consorts all refrained from extravagance and upheld frugality. The* Getan 葛覃 *poem in the* Shijing *(*Classic of Poetry*) praised the queen and consorts of King Wen* 文王 [of Zhou 周]. *They produced their own fine hemp and rugged hemp to make their clothes and wore these clothes without dislike. The* Houhanshu *(*Book of Later Han*) recorded that Empress Ma* 馬皇后, *consort of Emperor Ming of Han* 漢明帝, *wore white rugged clothes and did not wear any jewelry on her head. The imperial inner quarter was thus*

transformed. All people under Heaven followed her example. Hence during the prosperous times of the Zhou dynasty and the Han empire, all citizens enjoyed wealth and comfort. Every family had plenty to eat, stayed warm, and had sufficient family members. Translator's annotation: For more about these two empresses, see Liu Xiang's *Lienü zhuan*, volume 1 (chapter 6) and volume 8 (chapter 19); Wang Daokun's *Wangshi ji lienü zhuan* (*Wangshi's Biographies of Women*), volumes 1 and 4.

7. Wang Xiang's commentary: *This speaks about the fact that women in the position of queens or empresses must respectfully embody frugality so as to lead royal consorts residing in the six imperial inner quarters. Wives of marquises, high-ranking officials, low-ranking officials, and the common people all should uphold frugality so as to lead members of their households. Thereupon, all citizens will have plenty and will not suffer from cold or hunger. All people will know ritual propriety and righteousness. The beauty of such cultural transformation will be memorable and recorded.*
8. Wang Xiang's commentary: *Someone asked: "Frugality may not comply with ritual propriety. What should one do?" The reply cited Confucius's saying: In observing ritual propriety, rather than being extravagant and immoderate, it is better to be frugal and moderate. And yet, there are things that one can be frugal, for which one must be frugal. And, there are things that one can be generous, for which one must be generous. Thus, be frugal in dealing with the self, and be generous in serving one's parents. This is the ultimate behavior.* Translator's annotation: For Confucius's saying, see *Analects* 3.4.

【警戒章第七】

婦人之德，莫大於端己。端己之要，莫重於警戒。居富貴也，而恆懼乎驕盈。居貧賤也，而恆懼乎敗失。居安甯也，而恆懼乎患難。奉卮在手，若將傾焉。擇地而旋，若將陷焉。故一念之微，獨處之際，不可不慎。謂無有見，能隱於天乎。謂無有知，不欺於心乎。故肅然警惕，恆存乎矩度，湛然純一，不干於非僻。舉動之際，如對舅姑。閨門之間，如臨師保。不惰於冥冥，不驕於昭昭。行之以誠，持之以久，顯隱不貳。由是德宜於家族，行通於神明，而百福咸臻矣。夫念慮有常，動必無過。思患預防，所以免禍。一息不戒，災害攸萃。累德終身，悔何追矣。是故鑒古之失，吾則得焉。惕勵未形，吾何尤焉。詩曰：「相在爾室，尚不愧於屋漏。」禮曰：「戒慎乎其所不覩，恐懼乎其所不聞。」此之謂也。

7

Watchfulness (Jingjie zhang diqi 警戒章第七)

OF WOMEN'S VIRTUES, nothing is greater than rectifying the self. In rectification of the self, nothing is more important than watchfulness. Those who are wealthy and occupy high-ranking positions should be constantly afraid of becoming arrogant and complacent. Those who are poor and lowly should be worried about further failure and loss. Those who are in a state of safety and peace should always be concerned with the possible coming of adversity (*nan* 難).

When holding (*feng* 奉) a wine cup, act as if the cup is about to spill. When choosing a ground to take steps, act as if the ground is about to collapse.[1] Therefore, even as small as a single thought, or when one is alone, one must be prudent. If someone says, "Nobody sees it." Can one hide it from Heaven? If someone says, "Nobody knows." Is one not deceiving one's own conscience?[2]

Hence, be reverent and alert. Always follow the measuring principles. Keep one's mind clear, pure, and one-pointed. Never commit to anything evil. When making movements, act as if one is receiving one's parents-in-law. Even in private inner quarters, act as if one's tutor and attendant-matron are present. Do not be lazy in dark obscure places. Do not act arrogantly in bright public places. Act with sincerity and do so in constancy; whether in public or in private, one does not change. Consequently, one's virtue will transform the family clan. One's conduct will move gods and spirits. Thereupon, all blessings will naturally come.[3]

If one can be watchful about one's thoughts constantly, one will make no errors when making movements. If one can think and prevent potential problems from happening, one can avoid disaster. Not being careful even in the span of one breath, calamity already gathers. Such error harms one's virtue throughout one's lifetime. Although one regrets, nothing can be taken back.[4] Therefore, be able to learn from the mistakes of the ancients is to gain advantage. Being alert about danger before it forms, how then will one be blamed for any wrong-doing?

The *Classic of Poetry* says, "Watching (*xiang* 相) you in your house, [I find that] you do not act dishonorably even in dark corners under a skylight (*wulou* 屋漏)." The *Record of Rituals* says, "[A gentleman] acts prudently even in places where no one sees. He speaks cautiously even in places where no one hears." This is what it means.[5]

Commentaries and Annotations

1. Wang Xiang's commentary: Nan 難 *pronounced in the fourth tone;* feng 奉 *pronounced in the third tone. Of women's virtues, nothing is greater than rectifying one's self. In self-rectification, nothing is more important than watchfulness. Those who are affluent and occupy high-ranking social positions should always be mindful that arrogance and complacency invite reproach. Those who are poor and in lowly positions should always be concerned about failures that leave one no place to live. Those who are in peace and tranquility should worry about the coming of adversity that could endanger their lives. Act as if holding a full wine cup. Be careful so that it does not spill. Walk as if one is in a dangerous terrain. Choose one's steps carefully so that one does not fall. Only in doing so, one may be called as being watchful.*
2. Wang Xiang's commentary: *The smallness of a thought is that which is located in the deepest place of the mind. Aloneness is the most obscure place of all. One must be careful! Anyone who says that nobody sees should know that Heaven is present. Anyone who says that nobody knows should be reminded that one's conscience cannot be deceived.*
3. Wang Xiang's commentary: *One should be reverent, watchful, alert, and always abide by the rules of those who are virtuous. Know how to rectify one's mind; keep it tranquil,*

concentrated, and pure. Never do what is contrary to ritual propriety or anything wicked. Every move one makes should be necessarily respectful and prudent as if one is in front of one's parents-in-law. Although one resides within women's private quarters, always behave seriously and properly as if one's tutor and governess are present. One dares not to be rude. Do not let go one's appearance in a dark or secluded place nor be pretentious about one's look among a large crowd under bright daylight. Handle affairs with honesty. Keep one's mind constant. Whether in public or in private, one's behavior should not change. In doing so, a woman's virtue will transform the family clan, her sincerity and good faith will move gods and spirits, and all good fortune will come to her.

4. Wang Xiang's commentary: *In one's thoughts and deliberations, always keep norms and rules in view. Do not transgress ritual propriety. Accordingly, one's actions will be free from error and blame. For anything with potential problems, before it reaches the person, one should prevent and resolve it. Consequently, disaster will naturally stay away. If it is damage in the size of a breath and one knows its harm but cannot hold it back nor refrain from it, then disaster is already in place. Disaster, then, often gathers in the person and damages the person's virtue. Even if one regrets what happened, it is too late to change it.*
5. Wang Xiang's commentary: Xiang 相 *pronounced in the fourth tone. The verses from the* Shijing *are from the Daya* 大雅 *section, the Yi* 抑 *poem. The two sentences allegedly from the* Liji *are in fact taken from the* Doctrine of the Mean. *This passage says that they are from the* Liji *only because the* Doctrine of the Mean *and the* Great Learning *are both chapters of the* Liji. Xiang 相 *means "to watch, to see";* wulou 屋漏 *means "a corner of a house where there is a skylight." This passage teaches the methods of watchfulness. One should examine the mistakes of the ancients, and take caution not to repeat the same faults. Then, one will be in the advantage of gaining, not losing. One ought to be watchful before disaster takes form; then its injury can be avoided and no fault will occur. The verses from the* Shijing *point out that when one observes someone who stays in a dark room, this person does not act unconscionably in corners with only a skylight. This person is beyond blame. This is because a dark room is a place where nobody sees and hears. A skylight is where only Heaven is present. Can he deceive his own conscience? Hence a gentleman, who remains prudent when alone, acts with a heart of prudence and watchfulness even in places where nobody sees or hears. Being so strict with watchfulness and self-alertness, consequently he has few faults.*

【積善章第八】

吉凶災祥，匪由天作。善惡之應，各以其類。善德攸積，天降陰騭。昔者成周之先，世累忠厚，繼於文武，伐暴救民，又有聖母賢妃，善為內助。故上天陰騭，福慶攸長。我國家世積厚德，天命攸集，我太祖高皇帝，順天應人，除殘削暴，救民水火。孝慈高皇后，好生大德，助勤於內。故上天陰騭，奄有天下，生民用乂。天之陰騭，不爽於德，昭著明鑑。夫享福祿之報者，由積善之慶。婦人內助於國家，豈可以不積善哉。古語云：「積德成王，積怨成亡。」荀子曰：「積土成山，風雨興焉。積水成淵，蛟龍生焉。積善成德，神明自格。」自后妃至於士庶人之妻，其必勉於積善，以成內助之美。婦人善德，柔順貞靜。樂乎和平，無忿戾也。存乎寬洪，無忌嫉也。敦乎仁慈，無殘害也。執禮秉義，無縱越也。祇率先訓，無愆違也。不厲人以適己，不縱欲以戕物。積而不已，福祿萃焉。嘉祥被於夫子，餘慶流於後昆。可謂賢內助矣。易曰：「積善之家，必有餘慶。」書曰：「作善降之百祥。」此之謂也。

8

Accumulating Good Deeds (Jishan zhang diba 積善章第八)

GOOD OR BAD fortunes, disaster or auspiciousness, are not produced by Heaven. Rather, causal responses to good and evil deeds transpire in their own kinds. Accumulate good deeds and virtues. Heaven will bless and grant (*jiang* 降) happiness and prosperity without words (*yinzhi* 陰騭).[1]

In former times, ancestors of Chengzhou 成周 [the capital city of the Zhou 周 dynasty] were loyal and benevolent for generations. Later, King Wen 文王 and King Wu 武王 continued this tradition; they overthrew the tyrannical regime [Shang 商] and rescued the people. Additionally, Zhou had sagely mothers and virtuous royal consorts, who were great inner helpmates. Hence, Heaven from above blessed Zhou with long-lasting happiness and prosperity.[2] Our country for generations had accumulated abundant virtues. When Heaven's mandate coalesced, Emperor Taizu Gaohuangdi 太祖高皇帝, upholding Heaven's mandate and the people's will, overthrew the cruel and violent [Yuan 元] regime and rescued the people from hardship and suffering. Empress Xiaocigao 孝慈高皇后 cared immensely for all living beings. She diligently assisted Emperor Taizu in internal affairs. Accordingly, Heaven blessed them; they established a new kingdom; and the common people enjoyed peace and stability.

Thus, Heaven's blessing will not fail virtuous persons. It is as clear as a bright mirror.[3] For people who enjoyed the reward of happiness and prosperity, it is the celebratory result of their accumulated good deeds. Women assist their countries and families from within. How can they not accumulate good deeds?

The old proverb goes, "Those who accumulate virtues will become king. Those who accumulate complaints will perish." Xunzi says, "Soil piled up inch by inch will eventually become a mountain; [in mountains] wind and rain will naturally emerge. Water accumulated in small portions will eventually turn into a big lake; [in deep lakes] dragons will naturally be born. Accumulate good deeds and realize virtue; gods and spirits (*shenming* 神明) will naturally be moved."[4] From royal consorts to wives of the officials and the common people, all must endeavor in accumulating good deeds to realize the beautiful virtue of inner helpmates.

Women's virtue includes gentleness, compliance, chastity, and quietude. If she delights in peace, there will be no outburst of anger or outrage. If she is generous, there will be no distrust and jealousy. If she is kind-hearted, no harm or injury will come about. If she upholds ritual propriety and abides in righteousness, no transgression will occur. If she respectfully follows past sages' teachings, no fault of the contrary will arise.

Never harm anyone in order to benefit the self. Never indulge in desires thus injuring living beings. Do good deeds without getting tired. Happiness and prosperity will certainly converge in the person. Auspiciousness will also come to one's husband. Remaining merits will benefit later generations. This person is worthy of being called a virtuous inner helpmate.[5] The *Yijing* 《易經》 (*Classic of Changes*) says, "A family that accumulates good deeds will necessarily have merits that benefit later generations" (*yuqing* 餘慶). The *Shangshu* 《尚書》 (*Book of Documents*) says, "Good deeds will bring hundreds of auspiciousness" (*baixiang* 百祥). This is what it means.[6]

Commentaries and Annotations

1. Wang Xiang's commentary: 騭 *pronounced as* 直 (zhi). Jiang 降 *means "to grant, to impart."* Yinzhi 陰騭 *means that Heaven blesses and grants happiness and prosperity without speaking. This chapter elucidates the causal effects of accumulating good deeds. Goodness or badness of a person originates from the heart; good or bad fortunes manifest themselves in affairs. Omens of disaster, abnormality, and auspiciousness come about before good or bad fortunes become obvious. Heaven does not produce these; rather, they are causal responses to a person's goodness and badness. If a person can accumulate good deeds and cultivate virtue in constancy without tiredness, Heaven from above necessarily will bless the person and grant happiness without words. Such is the necessary truth.*
2. Wang Xiang's commentary: *Chengzhou* 成周 *is Luoyi* 洛邑. *Duke Zhou (Zhou Gong* 周公*) built this city for King Cheng of Zhou* 周成王 *to reside in; this capital city of the Zhou dynasty was thus called Chengzhou. This passage explains the former generations of the Zhou dynasty. Hou Yi* 后稷 *[an ancestor of Zhou] taught the common people how to grow trees and five grains as food. He thus accumulated great merits. His sons, grandsons, and offspring of later generations carried on his work for more than one-thousand years. None of them lost the virtue of loyalty and benevolence. This tradition continued with King Tai* 太王, *King Ji* 王季, *and King Wen* 文王; *they all had sagely virtues and cared about the people. Because King Zhou* 紂 *of the Shang dynasty was tyrannical, King Wu* 武王 *drove away this cruel regime, saved the people from turmoil, and established a new dynasty, Zhou. The Zhou dynasty also had Lady Taijiang* 太姜, *consort of King Tai; Lady Tairen* 太任, *consort of King Ji; Lady Taisi* 太姒, *consort of King Wen; and Lady Yijiang* 邑姜, *consort of King Wu. These ladies were all humane, filial, virtuously talented, and enlightened. They were inner helpmates of these sages. It is such a beautiful tradition that their sagely virtues both in the inner quarters and the outer realm continued for generations. Hence, Heaven blessed them. There has never been a dynasty enjoying such longevity of happiness and prosperity like the Zhou dynasty.* Translator's annotation: King Cheng of Zhou, son of King Wu, was the second king of the Zhou dynasty (1046–256 BCE), which is the longest-lasting of China's dynasties. Hou Ji was the son of Di Ku 帝嚳, one of the five legendary emperors (*Wudi* 五帝) of ancient China. Luoyi 洛邑 is today's Luoyang 洛陽. For more on the wise consorts of Zhou, see Liu Xiang's *Biographies of Women*, volume 1, chapters 2 and 6; and Wang Daokun's *Wangshi's Biographies of Women*, volume 1.
3. Wang Xiang's commentary: *This passage says that our Ming Emperor Taizu's* 太祖 *ancestors had accumulated numerous virtues for generations. Hence, Heaven commended Emperor Gao* 高皇帝 *to rise up from the Hao[zhou]* 濠[州] *and Chu[zhou]* 滁[州] *areas, to obey the will of the Heaven and the people, to eliminate cruel robbers, to conquer tyrannical government, and to save people from suffering. Empress Gao* 高皇后, *equipped with the virtues of humaneness and kindness, diligently managed the internal affairs to assist the emperor. They received the silent blessing from Heaven,*

conquered the Yuan dynasty, and established a new kingdom. The people thus enjoyed peace and the later generations enjoyed prosperity. Hence, Heaven's blessing of the virtuous is as clear as a mirror; it will not fail. Translator's annotation: Emperor Taizu Gaohuangdi's original name is Zhu Yuanzhang 朱元章. Zhu was celebrated as a hero of the peasant class, grew up in poverty, and joined the insurgent forces in his teens against the tyrannical reign of the later period of the Yuan dynasty. For more about Emperor Taizu Gaohuangdi and Empress Xiaocigao, see Zhang Tingyu et al., *Mingshi* (*History of Ming*), volume 1; and Wang Daokun's *Wangshi's Biographies of Women*, volume 14. Their story is also cited in chapter 2 of Liu Shi, *Short Records of Models for Women*.

4. Wang Xiang's commentary: *The fact that people can enjoy happiness and prosperity is all due to accumulation of good deeds. Women assist their husbands in the inner realm and thus make their families and countries prosper. How can women not accumulate good deeds? The old proverb says: "If a marquise accumulates virtues, he will accomplish kingly affairs. If he lacks virtues, amasses complaints, and is hated by the people, he will self-destruct and perish." Xunzi stated that if mountains are tall, clouds and fog will gather, and wind and rain will occur. If water is deep, it will generate spiritual animals and dragons will emerge. If a person can accumulate good deeds and accomplish virtue, gods and spirits will be moved and the person will be comforted by happiness and prosperity.*
5. Wang Xiang's commentary: *Royal consorts and wives of the officials and the common people all have the vocation to help their husbands from within. Since they have been diligent and frugal to benefit their households, they must also accumulate virtue and humaneness in order to extend their household's happiness. What is a good deed? It is accommodating gentleness, respectful compliance, chastity, and quietude. If her mind is peaceful, there will not be deception and outrage. If she is broad-minded and accommodating, her heart will not be suspicious or jealous. If she is humane, kind, and loving, she will have no thoughts of injuring or harming others. If she upholds ritual propriety and righteousness, she will not behave presumptuously. If she respectfully follows the teaching of past sages, she will not have errors of not obeying. Do not harm others in order to benefit one's wishes. Do not indulge one's wishes, thus injuring living beings. Continue to do good untiringly. Then, happiness and prosperity will gather in her person. Celebratory auspiciousness will come to her husband and children and the good will continue to later generations. Is this not the ultimate way of being an inner helpmate?*
6. Wang Xiang's commentary: Yuqing 餘慶 *means happiness is unceasingly abundant and will extend to one's offspring.* Baixiang 百祥 *means auspiciousness gathers and all things are successful. The* Yijing *(*Classic of Changes*) says: "A family that accumulates good deeds will necessarily have merits that benefit later generations. A family that accumulates evils will necessarily pass on demerits to later generations." The* Shangshu *(*Book of Documents*) says: "Doing good will bring innumerable auspiciousness. Doing evil will bring innumerable disasters." Sages' words are so clear and evident.*

【遷善章第九】

人非上智，其孰無過。過而能知，可以為明。知而能改，可以跂聖。小過不改，大惡形焉。小善能遷，大德成焉。夫婦人之過，無他，惰慢也，嫉妬也，邪僻也。惰慢則驕，孝敬衰焉。嫉妬則刻，菑害興焉。邪僻則佚，節義頹焉。是數者，皆德之弊而身之殃。或有一焉，必去之如蟊螣，遠之如蜂蠆。蜂蠆不遠，則螫身。蟊螣不去，則傷稼。已過不改，則累德。若夫以惡小而為之無恤，則必敗。以善小而忽之不為，則必覆。能行小善，大善攸基。戒於小惡，終無大戾。故諺有之曰：「屋漏遷居。路紆改塗。」傳曰：「人孰無過。過而能改。善莫大焉。」

9

Becoming Good (Qianshan zhang dijiu 遷善章第九)

NO HUMAN BEING is exceedingly wise. Who does not make mistakes? If one can understand what mistakes one has made, one can surely be enlightened. If one can correct one's mistakes after knowing them, one can certainly be like (*qi* 跂) the sages.[1] If one does not correct small faults, great evil will take form. [Contrarily,] if one can engage in small good deeds, great virtue can be attained.

Of women's faults, there is nothing worse than laziness, jealousy, and depravity. Laziness gives rise to arrogance. Consequently, filial piety and reverence will decline. Jealousy engenders cruelty. Thereupon, disasters (*zai* 菑) will rise. Depravity results in lasciviousness. Accordingly, temperance and righteousness will be abandoned.[2] All of these will disadvantage virtue and bring calamity to the person. If she has any of these vices, she must eliminate it like getting rid of root-eating leaf-eating insects (*mao te* 蟊螣). She must distant herself from it as if she is facing bees (*feng* 蜂) and scorpions (*chuai* 蠆). If one does not keep away bees and scorpions, they will sting (*zhe* 螫) one's body. If pests and insects are not eliminated, they will damage the crops. If one does not correct one's mistakes, it will impede one's virtue.[3]

If one thinks that an evil is very small and acts on it carelessly (*wuxu* 無恤), one will necessarily fail. If one believes that a good is very little and neglects it, one will necessarily collapse (*fu* 覆). Contrarily, if she can do small good deeds, she has begun to build a foundation for great good. If one can refrain from small evils, she will avoid serious disasters.[4] Therefore, the proverb says, "If the roof is leaking, move to a different house. If the road is winding (*yu* 紆), take an alternative route." The *Zuo Commentary* says, "Who can be without fault? If one can correct one's fault when one has it, there is no greater good than this."[5]

Commentaries and Annotations

1. Wang Xiang's commentary: 跂 (qi) *means "to hope, or to expect, to be at the same level." The chapter explains the method of correcting mistakes and becoming good. It says since human beings are not sages, no one can be free from mistakes. However, only enlightened persons can immediately know their mistakes after they are made. Only virtuous persons can correct their mistakes after knowing them. If a person can correct her mistakes, she will become more enlightened daily and eventually become like the sages. If she thinks that it is only a small mistake and is unwilling to correct it, she will in the end become a heinous person. If she believes that it is only a small good and is unwilling to complete the good, then she does not have any virtue worth-mentioning. Only if she can do small good deeds to realize virtue and continue to do them untiringly, will she be able to realize great virtue.* Translator's annotation: This passage opens the door of sagehood for women. Although classic Confucian texts often used gender-neutral language in their discussion of virtue and sagehood (e.g., *Mencius* 2A:6, 6A:6, 6A:7), they never clearly asserted that women can become sages. Some Confucians disputed this possibility. Here, Empress Renxiaowen advocated for the potential of woman sagehood, so did Madame Liu in her *Short Records of Models for Women*, a pivotal point for the debate on the potential of Confucian feminist philosophy.
2. Wang Xiang's commentary: 菑 *is same as* 災 zai *(disaster). Three kinds of faults concern women. The first is laziness, which gives rise to arrogance. Consequently, filial piety and reverence decline. The second is jealousy, which causes cruelty to prevail. Thereupon, disasters rise. The third is depravity and selfishness, which bring out lustfulness. As a result, moderation and righteousness are lost. These three are the gravest vices for women.*
3. Wang Xiang's commentary: 蟊螣 *pronounced as* 矛特 (mao te); 蠆 *as* 揣 (chuai) *in the fourth tone;* 螫 *as* 哲 (zhe). Mao te *are insects that injure the crops. Those that eat the roots are called* mao; *those that feed on leaves are called* te. Feng 蜂 *refers to bees.* Chuai *refers to scorpions. Both are insects that sting human bodies. It takes a while for such pain to subdue. These metaphors allude to laziness, jealousy, and lasciviousness.*

Any one of them is a serious evil that damages a person. Just as mao te *feed on the seedlings of the crops and* feng chuai *sting the human body—if one has any of these evils, one must readily remove it—so too, one must endeavor to correct mistakes and do the good so as to not hinder women's virtues.*

4. Wang Xiang's commentary: Wuxu 無恤 *means to take something lightly.* Fu 覆 *means to collapse or to be toppled. Emperor Zhaolie* 昭烈 *of [Shu* 蜀*] Han* 漢 *[i.e., Liu Bei* 劉備*, during the Three Kingdoms period] issued an imperial order to his successor Hou Zhu* 後主 *[Liu Shan* 劉禪*], stating that "Do not refrain from good because it is small. Do not act on evil because it is minute." This is because if one is accustomed to do small good deeds, one will achieve great good. If one is habituated in doing evil, one will necessarily commit serious evil eventually. Hence, if one does not desist in doing small evil deeds, rarely can one accomplish virtue and avoid disasters.*
5. Wang Xiang's commentary: 紆 *(*yu*) means "meandering, zigzag." This proverb is saying that one cannot reside in a house with a leaky roof. One must quickly move to another place. If a road is meandering and difficult to travel, one should seek a straight path to go forth. Thus, if a person can correct his faults when he has them, he is good.*

【崇聖訓章第十】

自古國家肇基，皆有內助之德，垂範後世。夏商之初，塗山有莘，皆明教訓之功。成周之興，文王后妃，克廣關雎之化。我太祖高皇帝，受命而興，孝慈高皇后，內助之功，至隆至盛。蓋以明聖之資，秉貞仁之德，博古今之務。艱難之初，則同勤開創。平治之際，則弘基風化。表壼範於六宮，著母儀於天下。驗之往哲，莫之與京。譬之日月，天下仰其高明。譬之滄海，江河趍其浩溥。然史傳所載，什裁一二。而微言奧義，若南金焉，銖兩可寶也。若穀粟焉，一日不可無也。貫徹上下，包括鉅細。誠道德之至要，而福慶之大本也。后妃遵之，則可以配至尊，奉宗廟，化天下，衍慶源。諸侯大夫之夫人，與士庶人之妻遵之，則可以內佐君子，長保富貴，利安家室，而垂慶後人矣。詩曰：「姒嗣徽音，則百斯男。」敬之哉。敬之哉。

10

Revering Sagely Teachings (Chongshengxun zhang dishi 崇聖訓章第十)

SINCE ANCIENT TIMES, the founding of a country has always relied on the virtue of inner helpmates. They set exemplary norms for later generations to follow. At the inception of the Xia 夏 and the Shang 商 dynasties, there were Tu Shan 塗山 and You Shen 有莘; both had the merits of teaching essential lessons to the inner courts. The rise of Chengzhou 成周 was due to the Guanju 關雎 cultural transformation promulgated by the royal consorts of King Wen 文王 [of Zhou 周].[1] Our founding Emperor Taizugao 太祖高皇帝 inherited the mandate of Heaven and rose [from the peasant class]. Empress Xiaocigao's 孝慈高皇后 work as his inner helpmate was immense. She used her inborn illuminating sagely nature to uphold chastity and humaneness and to acquire broad knowledge in ancient and contemporary affairs. At the beginning, in adversity she toiled diligently with the emperor to found this nation. During times of peace, she strengthened the foundation to transform culture. She is an exemplar to the six imperial inner courts and a remarkable maternal model to the world.[2]

I have inspected the records of intelligent (*zhe* 哲) royal consorts from former times and found that none of them is comparable (*jing* 京) to Empress Gao. Her virtue is like the Sun and the Moon; all under Heaven admire their loftiness and brightness. Her virtue is like an immense ocean; all rivers converge (*qu* 趍) to its vastness (*hao pu* 浩溥).[3] Yet what is recorded in books of history only gets (*cai* 裁) one- to two-tenths of her teachings. The subtlety of her words and the depth of their meanings are like precious gold produced in the south—only a miniature amount is regarded as treasure, and like grain—one cannot survive a day without them. Her teachings penetrate matters both above and below, comprise both grand ideas and minute details, and elucidate the essentials of morality and the important foundation for happiness and prosperity.[4] If empresses and royal consorts can follow Empress Gao's teachings, they will be able to match their emperors, serve ancestral temples, transform the world, and extend the source of prosperity. If consorts of marquises and high-ranking officials and wives of minor officials and the common people can follow her teachings, they will be able to assist their husband from within, enjoy long-lasting wealth and nobility, bring benefits and peace to their families, and create prosperity for their offspring.[5] The *Shijing* (*Classic of Poetry*) says, "[Tai]si [太] 姒 continued [her mother-in-law's] fine (*hui* 徽) reputation. She thus had one hundred sons." Revere it! Revere it![6]

Commentaries and Annotations

1. Wang Xiang's commentary: *Since the time of antiquity, every founding ruler of a country necessarily had virtuously talented consorts as his inner helpmates. Tu Shan* 塗山氏, *Queen of King Yu of Xia* 夏禹, *and You Shen* 有莘氏, *Queen of King Tang of Shang* 商湯, *both assisted illuminating virtuous kings, transformed the palatial court, and completed the governance of the inner realm. King Wen of Zhou* 周文王 *married sagely lady Taisi* 太姒: *this completed the good match of a gentleman. The imperial inner court admired their virtuous cultural transformation and thus composed the Guanju poem.* Translator's annotation: Chengzhou (today's Luoyang) was the capital city the Zhou dynasty. Guanju is the first poem in the *Shijing*, Zhounan 周南 section. *Guan* describes the sound of bird's singing. *Ju* refers to the osprey, or fish hawk. This poem describes the courtship between a gentleman and a virtuous lady.
2. Wang Xiang's commentary: *This passage says that Emperor Taizu founded the Ming dynasty. Although he inherited the mandate of Heaven in doing so, Empress Gao's work as his inner helpmate is significant. She had the illuminating sagely virtue of chastity*

and humaneness and penetrated the knowledge from antiquity to the present on governance in times of chaos. She assisted Emperor Taizu and they rose from adversity together. She toiled with him in founding this nation and brought forth peace. She taught the imperial inner court, commemorated virtuous ladies, and praised their good deeds. She is a paradigm for the six imperial inner courts and an exemplar maternal model for hundreds of thousands of nations.

3. Wang Xiang's commentary: 趍 *pronounced as* 趨 (qu)*;* 溥 *as* 普 (pu)*.* 京 (jing) *means "comparable." This passage states that although there were virtuous (*xian 賢*) and intelligent wise (*zhe 哲*) empresses and royal consorts in the past, none of them matched or was comparable to our Empress Gao's sageliness. Her virtue is like the loftiness and brightness of the Sun and the Moon; all benefited from their rays. Her virtue is like the immenseness of an ocean; all rivers flow toward it.* Translator's annotation: 哲 (*zhe*) means "intelligent, wise; intelligence, wisdom." This is the word used to translate "philosophy" (*philosophía*) in Chinese. The earliest uses of the word *zhe* are found in the *Classic of Poetry* and the *Book of Documents*. From the perspective of women's studies, the use of *zhe* here in describing past women role models by Empress Renxiaowen is significant, in that it recognizes women's equal ability in intelligence and wisdom.

4. Wang Xiang's commentary: 裁 *(*cai*) is the same as* 纔 (cai)*. This passage states that Empress Gao's compassionate words and esteemed lessons can be found in the* Huanghou shixun 《皇后實訓》, *the* Gaodi shilu 《高帝實錄》, *and the* Xiaocilu 《孝慈錄》, *among others. Yet these are all selected and edited words by court historians based on hearsay. They only catch one- to two-tenths of her complete lessons. Even though the subtlety of her words and the depth of their meaning are not passed down today, I [i.e., Empress Renxiaowen] have heard some of them. Her words are worthy of being a norm for the world; they are like gold that have been smelt a hundred times in the Jingyang region* 荊楊 *of the south. Just a small amount is regarded as treasure by the world. Her words are also like five grains that sustain a person daily; one cannot do without them even for a day. Her words are suitable for people above and below and are inclusive of both grand ideas and small details. I therefore follow her teaching and compose this book, making the essentials of women's virtue known to the people. If a person can comprehend these lessons and put them into action, it will truly be the foundation for happiness and prosperity.*

5. Wang Xiang's commentary: *This speaks about Empress Gao's teaching that if empresses and royal consorts can abide by it, they will be able to match their emperors, inherit ancestral temples, transform the world, and prolong the source of happiness and prosperity for their offspring. If the wives of marquises, high-ranking officials, minor officials, and the common people can follow it, they will be able to aid their husbands, protect their families, enjoy long-last wealth and nobility, and bring prosperity to their offspring.*

6. Wang Xiang's commentary: *These verses of the* Shijing *are from the Daya section, Sizhai* 斯齊 *poem. Taisi* 太姒 *is the queen of King Wen [of Zhou].* 徽 *(*hui*) means "beautiful." The verses describe Taisi's sincerity, respect, virtue, and filial piety. She continued the fine reputation of her mother-in-law, Tairen* 太任. *She was not jealous or suspicious. She had many offspring and the celebratory happiness of one hundred sons. Empresses and royal consorts of later times should abide by Empress Gao's* 高皇后 *teaching so as to equal the consorts of Zhou.* 齊 *pronounced as* 齋 *(*zhai*).* Translator's annotation: For more on Taisi, see Liu Xiang's *Biographies of Women*, volume 1, chapter 6. The poem's title is misprinted in Wang Xiang's commentary; it should be 思齊, not 斯齊.

【景賢範章第十一】

詩書所載，賢妃貞女，德懿行備，師表後世，皆可法也。夫女無姆教，則婉娩何從。不親書史，則往行奚考。稽往行，質前言，模而則之，則德行成焉。夫明鏡可以鑑妍媸，權衡可以擬輕重，尺度可以測長短，往轍可以軌新跡。希聖者昌，踵弊者亡。是故修恭儉，莫盛於皇英。求誠莊，莫隆於太任。孝敬。莫純於太姒。儀式刑之，齊之則聖，下之則賢，否亦不失於從善。夫珠玉非寶，淑聖為寶。令德不虧，室家是宜。詩曰：「高山仰止，景行行止。」其謂是與。

11

Admiring Wise Role Models (Jingxianfan zhang dishiyi 景賢範章第十一)

VIRTUOUS ROYAL CONSORTS and chaste ladies, recorded in the *Shijing* (*Classic of Poetry*) and the *Shangshu* (*Book of Documents*), possessed splendid virtues and all-encompassing good deeds. They were exemplary models for later generations. All of them are examples that we can follow.[1] If a girl does not have a woman teacher to teach her (*mujiao* 姆教), whence can she learn the lessons of respect, compliance, pleasantness, and understanding (*wan mian* 婉娩)? If she does not study the classics and histories, how does she examine past conducts? Study former virtuous ladies' conduct, verify their words, and imitate their exemplary behavior. Consequently, one's virtue will be complete.[2]

A clear mirror can reflect (*jian* 鑑) whether a person is beautiful or ugly (*yan chi* 妍媸). A weight (*quan* 權) and a scale (*heng* 衡) can differentiate whether something is light or heavy. A ruler can measure whether an object is long or short. A previous cart track (*gui* 軌) can be followed by a new cart. Those who emulate the sages will prosper; those who repeat predecessors' faults will perish.[3]

In cultivating reverence and frugality, no model can surpass [Er] Huang [娥]皇 and [Nü] Ying [女]英. In pursuing sincerity and dignified deportment, no other is greater than Tairen 太任. In filial piety and respect, nobody is purer than Taisi 太姒. Following their examples, one may become a sage if one's deeds equal theirs. If one falls short, one can at least be a virtuous person. If one can hardly measure up, still one would not go wrong in adhering to the good.[4]

Pearls and jades are not treasures; virtue and sageliness are. If a woman does not lack virtue, she will be able to put her household in order. The *Classic of Poetry* says, "A lofty mountain, its height I look up to. A wide road, its path I shall follow." This is what it means.[5]

Commentaries and Annotations

1. Wang Xiang's commentary: *This passage states that the* Shijing *and the* Shangshu *recorded virtuous royal consorts and chaste women from antiquity. Their virtues are abundant and their deeds are all-encompassing. They are recorded in books of history and are role models that can teach later generations. One can read about them and follow their examples.*
2. Wang Xiang's commentary: 婉娩 *pronounced as* 晚免 *(*wan mian*).* Wan 婉 *means "courteous and compliant";* mian 娩 *means "pleasant and understanding." The Neize chapter [of the* Liji*] says, "When a girl reaches age ten, she does not go outside the household. A woman teacher/tutor will teach her respect, compliance, pleasantness and understanding." This is correct.* Mu 姆 *means "a girl's woman teacher/tutor." This passage says if a girl does not have a woman tutor to teach her, she would not hear virtuous words. If she does not attend to ancient histories, she will not know what good deeds are. Therefore, she must examine previous virtuous women's moral conduct, verify their fine words, and emulate their exemplary behavior. Only then can she complete her virtue.*
3. Wang Xiang's commentary: 妍媸 *pronounced as* 嚴蚩 *(*yan chi*).* Jian 鑑 *means "to reflect."* Yan 妍 *means "beautiful";* chi 媸 *means "ugly."* Quan 權 *refers to weights used by a scale;* heng 衡, *to a scale.* Gui 軌 *means "cart track, to follow the track in proceeding." This is saying that a mirror can reflect a person's appearance. A scale can distinguish whether something is light or heavy. A ruler can measure the length of an object. When proceeding, if one follows existing cart tracks, one will not go off the track. By analogy, if a person admires the sages and follows their examples, she will prosper and enjoy happiness. But if she imitates predecessors' unwise errors and repeats them, she will necessarily perish.*
4. Wang Xiang's commentary: *Huang Ying* 皇英 *are [King] Yao's daughters and [King] Shun's wives, Er Huang and Nü Ying. This passage states that if one desires to follow the sagely virtues of reverence and frugality of the ancients, there is none other than Er Huang and Nü Ying. As princesses, they married a commoner Shun; reverently and prudently they served him and assisted him in sagely transformation of the people. If one*

*wishes to abide by the norms of sincerity, humanness, and dignified deportment, none is better than Tairen, the mother of King Wen [of Zhou]. She was prudent in prenatal education. Thus, she gave birth to a sage and began the reign of Chengzhou. If one is to model herself after exemplars of filial piety and respect, none is greater than King Wen's consort, Taisi. She manifested the virtues of ease, chastity, and quietude; she served the empress dowager filially and treated royal consorts kindly; she thus enjoyed the celebratory happiness of having one-hundred sons. These are all sagely queens and virtuous royal consorts. If one can imitate them and follow them as norms and standards, one can become a sage if one equals them. Next best, one can be a virtuous person. If one falls short and only resembles them distantly (*fangfu 彷彿*), still one has the virtue of doing good.* 彷彿 *pronounced as* 倣弗 *(*fangfu*), meaning "resembling in broad strokes."* Translator's annotation: According to Chinese legends, the "Yao Shun Abdication" (*Yao Shun chanrang* 堯舜禪讓) represented a virtuous peaceful power transition from one sagely monarch to another. According to these legends, Shun was a commoner and King Yao married his two daughters to Shun owing to Shun's virtue. Later, King Yao abdicated his reign to Shun. For more about these sage queens, see Liu Xiang's *Biographies of Women*, volume 1, chapters 1 and 6; and Wang Daokun's *Wangshi's Biographies of Women*, volume 1.

5. Wang Xiang's commentary: *This passage conveys that pearls and jades are not women's treasures. Rather, graciousness and sageliness are the treasures of women's virtues. If a woman does not lack virtue, she can put her household in order. The Chexia poem* 車舝 *from the Xiaoya section* 小雅 *makes the point that a high mountain, whether it is far or near, everyone looks up to see it. All must climb up the mountain to reach its peak. If a person is virtuous, all will admire and aspire to be like her. They ought to emulate her so that their personal virtue may be realized. If one only admires the mountain's loftiness but does not climb up to reach its peak, or if one sees others' virtues but does not consider equaling them, what does one benefit from such admiration?* 舝 *pronounced as* 轄 *(*xia*).* Translator's annotation: Literally, the Chexia 車舝 poem describes the excitement and longing of a young man on his way to marry a virtuous young lady, whom he deeply admires. Here the two verses are interpreted figuratively.

【事父母章第十二】

孝敬者，事親之本也。養非難也，敬為難。以飲食供奉為孝，斯末矣。孔子曰，孝者，人道之至德。夫通於神明，感於四海。孝之至也，昔者虞舜善事其親，終身而慕。文王善事其親，色憂滿容。或曰：「此聖人之孝，非婦人之所宜也。」是不然。孝悌，天性也，豈有間於男女乎。事親者，以聖人為至。若夫以聲音笑貌為樂者，不善事其親者也。誠孝愛敬，無所違者，斯善事其親者也。縣衾斂簟，節文之末。紉箴補綴，帥事之微。必也恪勤朝夕，無怠逆於所命。祇敬尤嚴於杖履，旨甘必謹於餕餘，而況大於此者乎。是故不辱其身，不違其親，斯事親之大者也。夫自幼而笄，既笄而有室家之望焉。推事父母之道於舅姑，無以復加損矣。故仁人之事親也，不以既貴而移其孝，不以既富而改其心。故曰：「事親如事天。」又曰：「孝莫大於甯親。可不敬乎。」詩曰：「害澣害否。歸寧父母。」此后妃之謂也。

12

Serving One's Parents (Shifumu zhang dishier 事父母章第十二)

FILIAL PIETY AND respect are the fundamentals in serving one's parents. It is not difficult to provide them with material sustenance; what is difficult is to demonstrate proper respect. To regard offering parents with drinks and food as filial is to attend to the least important part of the matter.[1] Confucius says that filial piety is the ultimate virtue of the way of humanity. For filial piety can reach spiritual beings and transform people within the four seas.[2] Ultimate examples of filial piety include: in former times, [King] Shun of Yu, who was great at serving his parents—he adored them throughout his whole lifetime [although they abused him], and King Wen [of Zhou], who was also excellent in serving his parents—he was full of worries [when he heard his father's health was not optimal.][3]

If someone says, "This is the sages' way of exhibiting filial piety. It is not suitable for women." I say: "This is incorrect. Filial piety and fraternal affection are part of heavenly endowed nature. How can there be a difference (*jian* 間) here between a man and a woman? In serving one's parents, one ought to follow the supreme models of the sages."[4]

If someone merely takes pleasure in uttering obedient words and putting on pleasant appearances, this person is not doing one's best in serving one's parents. If he or she demonstrates sincerity, filialness, love, respect, and does not disobey parents' wishes, this person truly knows how to serve his or her parents. To hang up (*xuan* 縣) parents' comforter and to fold up their bamboo sleeping mats (*dian* 簟) are only minor details; to use thread and needle (*zhen* 箴) to sew (*ren* 紉) and patch (*zhui* 綴) parents' clothes are only the minutest of all conduct (*shuai* 帥 [= 率]). Still, one respectfully and diligently works at it day and night and does not neglect or disobey parents' instructions (*dai ni suo ming* 怠逆所命). One's sincerity (*zhi* 祇) and reverence even manifest themselves in taking care of parents' canes and shoes. In preparing delicacies (*zhigan* 旨甘) for them, care is even extended to their leftovers (*jun* 餕). How could one not act accordingly on matters of greater importance?[5] Therefore, "do not disgrace one's body" and "do not disobey one's parents" are two important matters in serving parents.

A woman grows from childhood to the age of hair pinning. At the time when a woman pins her hair, she begins to have the prospect of starting her own family. If she can extend the way she serves her father and mother to her in-laws, there is nothing she needs to add or subtract.[6] Hence, a humane person, in serving her parents, does not act contrary to filial piety after she attains a high social rank nor does she change her heart after she becomes affluent. Thus, the old saying goes, "Serve one's parents as how one serves Heaven." It also says, "In filial piety, nothing is greater than comforting one's parents. Can one not be reverent?" The *Classic of Poetry* says, "Which (*he* 害) clothes should I wash (*han* 澣) and which one should I not? I am returning to my maternal family to see my father and mother (*guining* 歸寧)." This speaks about royal consorts' filialness.[7]

Commentaries and Annotations

1. Wang Xiang's commentary: *This chapter emphasizes that respect is the foremost essential element in filial piety. To provide parents with material sustenance is not difficult; what is difficult is to demonstrate proper respect. Offering parents drinks and food is of the least important matters in filial piety.* Translator's annotation: Confucianism places a strong emphasis on filial piety. When expanded, filialness becomes a social virtue in caring for other elders, or even a political virtue to one's rulers. Demeanor

and reverence are essential to genuine filial piety. For more, see *Analects* 1.2, 2.5–8, 4.18–21, 17.19; and *Xiaojing* 《孝經》 (*Classic of Filial Piety*).

2. See *Xiaojing*, chapters 1 and 16.
3. Wang Xiang's commentary: *The* Classic of Filial Piety *says, "Filial piety is the root of all virtues." Filial piety can reach spiritual beings and transform all people within the four seas. [King] Shun of Yu epitomized filial piety. Mencius complimented him, saying "great filial piety adores one's parents throughout one's whole lifetime." The* Record of Rituals *says, "King Ji did not feel well. [Crowned Prince] King Wen was full of anxiety. He can't even walk straight."* Translator's annotation: The *Mencius*, 5A:1–3, elucidates at length Shun's exemplary filial acts and his love toward his abusive parents and step-brother even after Shun became a king. The sentence cited here is from *Mencius* 5A:1. Also, see the preceding chapter (chapter 11) and related note regarding Er Huang and Nü Ying (Shun's wives). Additionally, King Wen's filialness is praised in the opening paragraph of chapter 8 of the *Liji* (*Record of Rituals*).
4. Wang Xiang's commentary: 間 (jian*) pronounced in the fourth tone. Someone asks, "Filial piety of a sage is the utmost. It is not something that a woman can achieve. The author answers that filial piety and fraternal affection originate from our endowed nature—how can there be difference between a man and a woman about this? In serving one's parents, one ought to follow the sages as the norm.*
5. Wang Xiang's commentary: 縣 *pronounced as* 懸 *(*xuan*);* 簟 *as* 玷 *(*dian*);* 紉 *as* 寅 *(*yin*).* 箴 *is synonymous with* 針 *(*zhen*),* 綴 *pronounced as* 墜 *(*zhui*),* 帥 *same as* 率 *(*shuai*),* 餕 *pronounced as* 俊 *(*jun*). In serving parents and parents-in-law according to the rituals, as a young lady not yet married and as a married woman, one necessarily hangs their quilt after they get up, folds up their pillow and bamboo sleeping mat, and sets it up again when it is bedtime. If one sees that parts of their clothes are torn, one necessarily picks up needle and thread to repair them.* Shuai 帥 *means "conduct";* dai ni suo ming 怠逆所命 *means "neglecting and disobeying parents' orders";* zhi 祗 *means "sincerity." Where parents' canes and shoes are, one necessarily protects them sincerely and respectfully so as not to damage them.* Zhigan 旨甘 *means "delicious food."* Jun 餕 *means "leftover." The* Record of Rituals *says that one dares not to use parents' eating and drinking vessels, unless they are leftovers; so too, one dares not to eat parents' food, unless they are leftovers. If there are leftovers in parents' plates, sons and daughters-in-laws will necessarily finish the food. It is to avoid the suspicious that one despises parents' food, and fearing that the practice may develop into disrespect over time. The* Teachings for the Inner Court *elucidates that if sons and daughters do not have a sincere and respectful heart but only entertain their parents with pleasant appearances and words, this is not sufficient for a filial heart. Filialness is derived from ultimate sincerity; respect originates from ultimate love. Not going against parents' instructions is called good conduct. Hanging up parents' quilts, folding up their bamboo sleeping mats, and sewing and patching their clothes: these are but details of this matter. Only be respectful and reverent day and night and do not disobey their teachings and instructions. Even parents' canes and shoes should be respectfully protected. What parents eat, one must*

make sure that its taste is delicious. Even with their leftovers, one necessarily handles their eating utensils and the food prudently. One attends to minute details like these! How can one not act respectfully when situations involve matters of greater importance than these? 敦 *pronounced as* 對 (dui*) is a food vessel.* 牟 *pronounced as* 模 *(*mo*) is a vessel used during a mealtime.* 卮 *pronounced as* 支 *(*zhi*) is a wine vessel* 酒器. 匜 *pronounced as* 移 *(*yi*) is a vessel for water and liquid.* Translator's annotation: 紉 should be pronounced as *ren*, as in *feng ren* 縫紉; it is unclear why Wang Xiang says that it is pronounced as 寅 (*yin*). So too, 牟 should be pronounced as 謀 (*mou*) rather than 模 (*mo*). The text from the *Liji* (*Record of Rituals*) referred here is from the Neize chapter (chapter 12).

6. Wang Xiang's commentary: Ji 笄 *is a hairpin a woman wears when she is promised to a marriage prospect. The way of a woman is to safeguard her body lest she disgrace her person; she is to serve her parents and does not disobey them. A woman is raised by her parents and she depends on them since childhood. Now she is promised to someone, pins her hair, is about to marry into another household, and begins the way between a husband and a wife. Soon she will leave her parents. If she is filial at home and is able to serve her parents-in-law in the same manner, what is there for her to lose?*
7. Wang Xiang's commentary: 害 *pronounced as* 曷 *(*he*);* 澣 *pronounced as* 翰 *(*han*). This passage speaks about royal consorts, who left their natal parents and enjoyed the prosperity and high social rank of their matrimonial households, and yet, neither do they forget filial piety because of their high social rank nor do they change their hearts because of prosperity. Thus, it is said: "Serve one's parents as how one serves Heaven." Heaven is something that cannot be moved.* Ning 寧 *means "guining"* 歸寧*—that is, "returning home and inquiring whether parents are doing well."* He 害 *means "how, which."* Han 澣 *means "to wash." The Getan* 葛覃 *poem [from the* Classic of Poetry, *Guofeng section] speaks about Taisi's desire to return to her maternal family to see whether her parents are doing well. She is to wear washed clothes made of hemp. She thus asks her female tutor about which clothes to wash and which one not to wash. She will wear these clothes and return to her natal family to see how her parents are doing. This speaks about royal consorts' filialness.*

【事君章第十三】

婦人之事君，比昵左右，難制而易惑，難抑而易驕。然則有道乎？曰：「有。」忠誠以為本，禮義以為防，勤儉以率下，慈和以處眾。誦詩讀書，不忘規諫。寢興夙夜，惟職愛君。居處有常，服食有節。言語有章，戒謹讒慝。中饋是專，外事不涉，教令不出。遠離邪僻，威儀是力。毋擅寵而怙恩，毋干政而撓法。擅寵則驕，怙恩則妬，干政則乖，撓法則亂。諺云：「汨水淖泥，破家妬妻。」不驕不妬，身之福也。詩曰：「樂只君子，福履綏之。」夫受命守分，僭黷不生。詩曰：「夙夜在公，寔命不同。」是故姜后脫簪，載籍攸賢。班姬辭輦，古今稱譽。我國家隆盛，孝慈高皇后，事我太祖高皇帝，輔成鴻業。居富貴而不驕，職內道而益謹。兢兢業業，不忘夙夜。德蓋前古，垂訓萬世，化行天下。詩曰：「思齊太任，文王之母。思媚周姜，京室之婦。」此之謂也。縱觀往古，國家廢興，未有不由於婦之賢否。事君者不可以不慎。詩曰：「夙夜匪懈，以事一人。」苟不能胥匡以道，則必自荒厥德。若網之無綱，眾目難舉。上無所毗，下無所法，則胥淪之漸矣。夫木瘁者，內蠹攻之。政荒者，內嬖蠱之。女寵之戒，甚於防敵。詩曰：「赫赫宗周，褒姒滅之。」可不鑒哉。夫上下之分，尊卑之等也。夫婦之道，陰陽之義也。諸侯大夫士庶人之妻，能推是道，以事其君子，則家道鮮有不盛矣。

13

Serving One's Ruler (Shijun zhang dishisan 事君章第十三)

FOR WOMEN WHO serve their ruler, because they are intimate (*ni* 昵) with him and constantly at his side, it is difficult for them to control themselves, but easy for them to bewilder their ruler. It is also difficult for them to humble themselves, but easy for them to become arrogant.[1] If someone asks, "Are there methods to correct this?" "Yes, there is." One should regard loyalty and sincerity as the roots, use ritual propriety and righteousness to prevent wrongdoing, cultivate diligence and frugality to lead those below, and be kind and harmonious in interacting with the multitude. Read the *Shijing* (*Classic of Poetry*) and study the classics. Do not forget the corrections and admonitions offered by others.[2] Rising early in the morning and resting late at night, one's only vocation is to love one's ruler. Keep to a constant living place. Be temperate in one's clothing and food. Be proper in one's speech. Be cautious about slander and wickedness. Concentrate one's attention on preparing drinks and food. Do not meddle with external affairs. Do not let one's teachings and orders go outside the inner court. Steer away from evil. Endeavor in dignified deportment.[3] Do not monopolize the ruler's love, thus relying on (*hu* 怙) his special favor. Do not interfere with governmental affairs, therefore bending (*nao* 撓) the law. Monopolizing the ruler's love makes one haughty; relying on his special favor makes one jealous. Interfering with governmental affairs creates perverseness and bending the law generates chaos.

The proverb says, "Turbid (*mi* 汨) water, deep mud (*nao* 淖), a jealous wife destroys the household." Thus, being able to refrain from arrogance and jealousy is a woman's happiness. The *Shijing* says, "Joyful (*luozhi* 樂只) is the gentleman! May happiness and prosperity (*lu* 履) keep you safe (*sui* 綏)."[4] Accept [the ruler's] commands (*shouming* 受命) and abide by one's duties (*shoufen* 守分). Then, transgression and adulteration will not occur. The *Shijing* says, "From early in the morning till late at night I am busy with official business; truly (*shi* 寔) my fate (*ming* 命) is different from others." Thus, Queen Jiang 姜后 took off her hairpin [to wait for her punishment]; her virtue was recorded in numerous books. Royal Consort Ban 班姬 declined to ride the carriage [with the emperor]; many from antiquity to the present time praised her example.[5] Our nation is prosperous and great. This is due to Empress Xiaocigao, who served our Emperor Taizugao and assisted him in accomplishing kingly affairs. She occupied a position of wealth and high social rank and yet she was not arrogant. She upheld the proper way of the inner realm and was extremely prudent. Careful and hard-working, neither during the day nor at night did she ever neglect it. Her virtue surpassed her predecessors, her teachings will be passed down to hundreds of thousands of future generations, and her work has transformed all under Heaven. The *Shijing* says, "How dignified and respectful (*zhai* 齊) is Tairen 太任, the mother of King Wen. She loved (*mei* 媚) [her mother-in-law] Zhou Jiang 周姜. She is a daughter-in-law of the royal household (*jingshi* 京室)." This is what it means.[6]

Looking back at ancient times, it had never been the case that the rise and the fall of a nation did not depend on whether women were virtuous. Those who serve their rulers must be prudent about this. The *Shijing* says, "Day and night do not be lax in serving one person."[7] If she cannot mutually (*xu* 胥) rectify (*kuang* 匡) her ruler by means of the Way, it must be the case that she has abandoned her own virtue. It is as if a net does not have principal binding threads (*gang* 綱); it is difficult for the eyes of the net to open. If a ruler has no one to rely on (*pi* 毗) [for his virtue], those below him will have no one to emulate. Gradually both parties will descend (*lun* 淪) into immorality.[8] For if a tree is withering and sick (*cui* 瘁), it is because insects (*du* 蠹) are attacking it from within. If government is neglected, it is due to a king's favorite women (*bi* 嬖) in the inner court confusing (*gu* 蠱) him. Caution against spoiled women is even more critical than guarding against enemies. The *Shijing* says, "The great glorious Zhou dynasty is destroyed by Baosi 褒姒." How can one not take a lesson from it?[9] The distinction between the above and the below indicates the differentiation between the venerable and the lowly. The way between a husband and a wife is the righteousness of *yin* and *yang*: If wives of marquises, high-ranking officials, low-ranking officials, and the common folk can infer its meaning in serving their rulers and husbands, rarely (*xian* 鮮) would their families not become prosperous.[10]

Commentaries and Annotations

1. Wang Xiang's commentary: 昵 *pronounced as* 溺 (ni*); it means "close, dear, intimate."* Yi 抑 *means "humble, obedient"; it states that for women who enter the imperial inner court to serve their kings, because they are so intimate with their rulers, it is hard for them to control their hearts and easy for them to bewilder their rulers; it is hard for them to humble themselves, and easy for them to become conceited toward those under them.*
2. Wang Xiang's commentary: *Someone asks: "Is there a way to handle this problem?" The reply is: "Yes, there is." One should regard loyalty, good faith, and honesty as the roots. Abide by ritual propriety and uphold righteousness to prevent laxness. Be diligent and frugal in leading royal consorts. Be benevolent and friendly in interacting with the common folk. Read and study poetry and classics and adopt predecessors' words and deeds to complete one's virtue. When one hears advice and criticism, one should listen respectfully and not forget.*
3. Wang Xiang's commentary: *This passage states that a woman ought to rise early and rest late. She should take her respect and love for her ruler-husband as her vocation. Reside in a constant place. Observe temperance and frugality. Avoid extravagance in one's clothing and food. Be pleasant and moderate in one's speech. Be careful and do not listen to slanderous words. Be prudent and refrain from evil deeds. Concentrate on preparing drinks and food to serve the rulers and the ancestral rites. Do not interfere with external political affairs. Do not let one's teachings and commands go outside the confines of the inner court. Stay away from lewdness and licentiousness. Endeavor,*

without tiredness, with dignified bearing. Translator's annotation: See chapters 1 and 12 of the *Liji* (*Record of Rituals*) regarding women's work and the normative separation of the inner and outer realms.

4. Wang Xiang's commentary: 怙 *pronounced as* 戶 *(*hu*),* 汨 *as* 密 *(*mi*),* 淖 *as* 鬧 *(*nao*),* 樂只 *as* 洛只 *(*luozhi*),* 綏 *as* 雖 *(*sui*).* Hu 怙 *means "to rely on something";* nao 撓 *means "to bend"*; mi 汨 *means "to sink, to get stuck"*; nao 淖 *means "deep and widespread mud." This passage speaks about the proper way of being a royal consort. She should not monopolize the ruler's love or rely on his favor. She should not interfere with state affairs or bend the country's law. If she monopolizes the rule's love and relies on his favor, the harm of arrogance and jealousy arises. If she interferes with politics and bending the country's law, then the disaster of perversity and chaos will arrive. The proverb says that if a person is stuck in turbid waters and cannot get out, it is due to the deep mud in the waters. If someone destroys a household (thus, it can no longer prosper), it is due to the damage done by a jealous wife. Thus, if a woman is neither arrogant nor jealous, it brings happiness to her and her household.* Luoshi 樂只 *means "to be pleased with"*; junzi 君子 *[here] means "concubines," referring to royal consorts.* Lu 履 *means "prosperity"*; sui 綏 *means "safe, safety." This poem speaks about Taisi, who is not jealous but was gracious in treating those under her. Hence, all royal consorts were delighted with her virtue and they praised her, "There is a Jiu tree in the south. It is intertwined with vines. Joyful is the gentleman! May happiness and prosperity keep you safe."* 樛 *pronounced as* 鳩 (jiu*);* 藟 *as* 壘 lei*;* 纍 *as* 雷 lei. *This poem is from the Zhounan* 周南 *section, the Jiumu* 樛木 *poem.* Translator's annotation: Due to royal consorts' influence on the emperor, Empress Renxiaowen again is extremely concerned with spoiled jealous consorts and the harm they could do to the country.

5. Wang Xiang's commentary: Shouming 受命 *here means "to receive or to accept the ruler's command."* Shoufen 守分 *means "to abide by a royal consort's duties." The* Shijing *refers to the Zhaonan* 召南 *section, Xiaoxing* 小星 *poem.* Shi 寔 *is the same as* shi 實. Ming 命 *means "destiny bestowed by Heaven." Queen Jiang* 姜后 *is King Xuan of Zhou's* 周宣王 *wife. Lady Ban* 班姬 *is Emperor Cheng of Han's* 漢成帝 *royal consort. This passage speaks about the fact that queens and royal consorts all follow the king's order in serving him. They should adhere to their respective duties without any intention of transgression. Thus, the Xiaoxing poem describes that when an imperial concubine serves her king at night, she carries her bed cover with her. She enters the king's chamber when the stars already rise and she leaves the room before the stars recede. She dares not to monopolize the king's favor throughout the night. She thus walks in only during late night and walks out by early morning. It is her official duty in following her endowed destiny, which differs from the queens and higher-ranking royal consorts. In former times, King Xuan of Zhou stayed overnight with an imperial concubine and rose late. Queen Jiang took off her hairpins and earrings to wait for her punishment in the imperial inner court. She blamed herself for not teaching royal consorts and imperial concubines well, and caused the king's error in rising late and neglecting governmental affairs. King Xuan bowed and thanked her.*

He dared not become lazy and negligent again. Thus, many books of history praise her virtue. One day, Emperor Cheng of Han finished having an audience with governmental officials at the imperial court. He invited Lady Ban Jieyu 班婕妤 *to ride in the carriage with him. Lady Ban prostrated herself before the emperor and said, "I have heard that when the Son of Heaven goes out or comes in, he always has virtuous men at his side to assist him. I have never heard that he rides in his carriage with his favorite concubine." The emperor felt ashamed and thanked her. Both Queen Jiang and Lady Ban understood the proper way to serve their rulers and abide by their respective duties.* 婕妤, *pronounced as* 捷予 *(*Jieyu*), is a woman's name.* Translator's annotation: The anecdotes about Queen Jiang and Lady Ban in this chapter (as well as the one on Wu Yan 無鹽 in chapter 3) clearly teach that, at right times for right reasons, women ought to admonish their husbands' errors. It should be read as a counterweight to chapter 2's lesson on "three obediences" and chapter 3's teaching on "having few words." Lady Ban Jieyu is the grand-aunt of Ban Zhao. Ban Zhao is the author of *Lessons for Women*, the first book of the *Four Books for Women*.

6. Wang Xiang's commentary: 齊 *pronounced as* 齋 *(*zhai*). This passage expresses that Empress Gao loyally served Emperor Gao and assisted him in accomplishing great affairs. Yet, she still could act respectfully and prudently. Day and night, she was diligent in her work. Her virtue exceeded her predecessors. Her cultural transformation benefited all under Heaven. Her benevolent lessons would be passed down through many future generations!* Mei 媚 *means "love."* Jing 京 *means "the Zhou dynasty." The Sizhai* 思齊 *poem in the Daya section of the* Shijing *depicts respectful and dignified Tairen, the mother of King Wen. She loved her mother-in-law Taijing, and was very filial in serving her. She was a filial daughter-in-law of the Zhou dynasty. That her offspring could establish a kingdom under Heaven really relied on the foundation she first laid.* Translator's annotation: For more about Tairen, see Liu Xiang's *Biographies of Women*, volume 1, chapter 6; and Wang Daokun's *Wangshi's Biographies of Women*, volume 1. A minor misprint is found in the first line of Wang Xiang's commentary: it should be 齊音齋, not 齊音齊.
7. Wang Xiang's commentary: *It explains that Empress Renxiaowen observed the histories of ancient times. She found that when a nation was about to flourish, there were necessarily virtuous queens and royal consorts who assisted from within. When a nation was about to perish, licentious confusion and chaos of the inner court were always the cause. A family's rise and fall is also like this. How can one not be careful? Therefore, the Zhengmin* 蒸民 *poem in the Daya section says that as a minister, one ought to be alert and diligent day and night without negligence or laziness in serving one's ruler. For queens and royal consorts, their happiness and misfortune are closely related to their rulers. How can they not reflect on the lessons of "not being lax" in serving their rulers?*
8. Wang Xiang's commentary: 毗 *pronounced as* 皮 *(*pi*).* Xu 胥 *means "mutually";* kuang 匡 *"to rectify";* gang 綱 *"main threads of fishing net";* pi 毗 *"to rely on";* lun 淪 *"to sink, to indulge." This conveys the message that if a wife cannot rectify and assist her*

husband by means of the right Way, she must have neglected her own virtue. This is as if a fishing net does not have essential threads, all the eyes of the net can hardly open. The above and the below cover up each other's faults with no principles to follow. Then, both will indulge in immorality and eventually arrive at danger and destruction.

9. Wang Xiang's commentary: 瘁 *pronounced as* 翠 (cui*),* 蠹 *as* 妬 (du*),* 嬖 *as* 僻 *(*bi*),* 蠱 *as* 古 (gu*), and* 褒 *as* 包 *(*bao*). It is due to insects attacking and consuming its insides that a tree withers and shrivels. That government and political affairs are abandoned is caused by spoiled and lustful women who confused their rulers. Our ancestors called beautiful women "an army of women"; they must be guarded against like enemy troops. The Zhengyue* 正月 *poem describes that King You* 幽王 *spoiled Baosi* 褒姒 *and lost his life; the Western Zhou dynasty perished afterwards. Hence, the glorious Zhou dynasty is destroyed by one person, Baosi.* Translator's annotation: The Zhengyue poem is from the Xiaoya section of the *Shijing*. For more about Baosi, see Liu Xiang's *Biographies of Women*, volume 7, chapter 3. Obviously, this anecdote oversimplistically places the blame solely on women regarding the demise of a nation. Kings and emperors, as moral agents, surely bear culpability for succumbing to their own inordinate desires.
10. Wang Xiang's commentary: 鮮 *(*xian*) pronounced in the third tone. Heaven is above and Earth below. Heaven is the venerable and Earth the lowly. If a woman can serve her husband like how she serves Heaven, then the distinction between the venerable and the lowly is made clear. Husband is* yang, *and wife is* yin. *The essential nature of* yang *is movement; thus,* yang *is strong and authoritarian. The essential nature of* yin *is quietness; hence,* yin *is gentle, compliant, and obedient. If, from empresses and royal consorts to the wives of officials and the common people, all can follow this principle in serving their husbands, nothing will be disadvantageous.* Translator's annotation: The conceptual binaries of *yin–yang* 陰陽 and *qian–kun* 乾坤 have been present in Chinese consciousness since 600 BCE or even earlier. Chapter 1 of the "Appendix Remarks" (Xici 繫辭) to the *Yijing* 《易經》 *(Classic of Changes)* states that "Heaven is the venerable and Earth the lowly. . . . The way of *qian* generates male; the way of *kun* generates female; *qian* is the great beginning of time, and *kun* the space that completes all things." The differentiation between Heaven and Earth, *qian* and *kun*, was originally more an explanation of complementary cosmic changes and the framework of time and space. Dong Zhongshu 董仲舒's *Chunqiu fanlu* (*Luxuriant Dew of the Spring and Autumn Annals*) in the second century BCE nonetheless essentialized these prototypes and accentuated the strict hierarchical nature of *yin* and *yang*: "*yang* is venerable and *yin* is lowly" (chapter 43); "the husband is *yang*, the wife *yin*" (chapter 53). Dong's teaching tied women to a subservient role and has exercised its influence in Chinese culture since then. For more on Dong's Han Confucianism, see the main introduction to this volume and the translator's introduction to Ban Zhao's *Nüjie* (*Lessons for Women*).

【事舅姑章第十四】

婦人既嫁，致孝於舅姑。舅姑者，親同於父母，尊擬於天地。善事者在致敬，致敬則嚴在致愛，致愛則順，專心竭誠，毋敢有怠。此孝之大節也，衣服飲食其次矣。故極甘旨之奉，而毫髮有不盡焉，猶未嘗養也。盡勞勩之力，而頃刻有不恭焉，猶未嘗事也。舅姑所愛，婦亦愛之。舅姑所敬，婦亦敬之。樂其心，順其志。有所行不敢專，有所命不敢緩。此孝事舅姑之要也。昔太任思媚，周室以隆。長孫盡孝，唐祚以固。甚哉，孝事舅姑之大也。夫不得於舅姑，不可以事君子。而況於動天地，通神明，集嘉禎乎。故自后妃以下，至卿大夫及士庶人之妻，壹是皆以孝事舅姑為重。詩曰：「夙興夜寐，無忝爾所生。」

14

Serving Parents-in-Law (Shijiugu zhang dishisi 事舅姑章第十四)

AFTER A WOMAN has married, she should be filial toward her father- and mother-in-law. Parents-in-law are to be treated with affection as one treats one's own parents; they are to be revered as Heaven and Earth.[1] Respect is the key in serving one's parents-in-law. If one is respectful toward them, one will be solemn in demonstrating one's love for them. If one loves them, one will be compliant, one-minded, sincere, and dare not be negligent. This is the most essential element of filial piety. Clothing and food are secondary.[2]

Therefore, in providing them with delicious food and drink, if there is a small detail where one did not do one's best, it is as if one has not provided them with any nourishment. In bearing the weight of their labors tirelessly (*yi* 勩), if one is disrespectful even for one single moment, it is as if one has not labored for them.[3] What parents-in-law love, daughter-in-law also loves. What parents-in-law respect, daughter-in-law also respects. Make their hearts joyful. Obey their wills. In whatever one does, one dares not insist on one's own way. When parents-in-law issue commands, one dares not put them off. These are the essentials in serving parents-in-law.[4]

In former times, Tairen 太任 loved and respected [her mother-in-law]. The Zhou 周 dynasty thus became prosperous. Zhangsun 長孫 was very filial [toward her parents-in-law]. The blessing of the Tang 唐 dynasty was thus secured. Hence, it is clear how important it is to serve one's parents-in-law filially.[5] If a woman cannot serve her parents-in-law well, she will not be able to serve her husband—not even to mention moving Heaven and Earth, understanding spiritual beings, or gathering auspiciousness. Therefore, from empresses and royal consorts to the wives of high-ranking officials, minor officials, and the common people, all should regard serving parents-in-law filially a serious matter. The *Classic of Poetry* says, "Rise early in the morning and rest late at night. Do not bring shame to your parents."[6]

Commentaries and Annotations

1. Wang Xiang's commentary: *This speaks about how a woman should treat her father- and mother-in-law. Love them affectionately in the same way as she loves her natal parents. Revere them in the same way as she reveres Heaven and Earth.* Translator's annotation: The lesson on treating and serving parents-in-law as one treats one's natal parents can be found in the *Analects for Women* (*Nü lunyu*), the *Classic of Filial Piety for Women* (*Nü xiaojing*), and the *Record of Rituals* (*Liji*).
2. Wang Xiang's commentary: *The principle of serving one's parents-in-law rests on respect and love. If one is respectful, one will be solemn and reverent, single-minded, loving, gentle, compliant, and sincere. This is what is meant by filial piety. Providing them with food and drink, and cleaning their clothes, are secondary.* Translator's annotation: See Confucius, *Analects* 2.7 and 2.8 in regard to the importance of intention and reverence in filial piety.
3. Wang Xiang's commentary: 勩 *pronounced as* 異 (yi)*; it means "to bear the brunt of labor tirelessly." It speaks about when providing sustenance to one's parents-in-law, one prepares the best delicacies; however, if one small detail is not attended to, it is just like one has not provided them with sustenance. In bearing the weight of their labors, one works diligently with utmost effort. Nonetheless, if a single thought becomes disrespectful, it is just like one has not born their labors. This passage reminds one to do one's best throughout lifetime, not being lax even for a single day.* Translator's annotation: For more on how to serve parents-in-law food and drink, see the *Liji* (*Record of Rituals*), the Neize chapter; and the Song sisters' *Nü lunyu* (*Analects for Women*), chapter 6.
4. Wang Xiang's commentary: *Persons whom parents-in-law respect and love, daughter-in-law also respects and loves. Please their hearts. Respect and obey their wills. Whatever*

one does, one should necessarily consult with them and not act willfully. If one receives an order from them, one respectfully carries it out without delay. These are the essentials of filial piety.

5. Wang Xiang's commentary: *Empress Zhangsu Wende* 長孫文德皇后 *was the principal wife of Emperor Taizong of Tang* 唐太宗. *This passage conveys that because Tairen* 太任 *loved Taijiang* 太姜, *she thus gave birth to King Wen and made the Zhou dynasty prosper. Zhangsu was filial and respectful toward her parents-in-law; she thus married Taizong and extended the blessing of the Tang dynasty. Both are virtuous empresses who helped found a nation.* Translator's annotation: For more about Tairen, see previous chapters. For more about Empress Zhangsu Wende, see Liu Xu, *Tangshu* 《唐書》 (*Book of Tang*), the section entitled Houfei zhuan 后妃傳 ("Biographies of Empresses and Royal Consorts").
6. Wang Xiang's commentary: *A woman who cannot serve her parents-in-law well will not be able to serve her husband. If she desires to be comparable to filial daughters-in-law and chaste wives of antiquity, in moving Heaven and Earth, illuminating spiritual beings, gathering auspiciousness, and making her honorable name for future generations to see, how can she achieve it? Therefore, from empresses and royal consorts to the wives of officials and the common people, all should regard serving their parents-in-law well as a serious matter. The Xiaoya section in the* Classic of Poetry *says: rise early and rest late, do one's best, and do not bring shame to one's parents. If a daughter-in-law can serve her parents-in-law well, then she does not bring shame to her parents.* Translator's annotation: The verses referred here are from the Xiaowan 小宛 poem in the Xiaoya section of the *Shijing* (*Classic of Poetry*).

【奉祭祀章第十五】

人道重夫昏禮者，以其承先祖，共祭祀而已。故父醮子，命之曰：「往迎爾相，承我宗祀。」母送女，命之曰：「往之女家，必敬必戒，無違夫子。」國君取夫人，辭曰：「共有敝邑，事宗廟社稷。」分雖不同，求助一也。蓋夫婦視祭，所以備外內之官也。若夫后妃奉神靈之統，為邦家之基。蠲潔烝嘗，以佐其事。必本之以仁孝，將之以誠敬。躬蠶桑以為玄紞，備儀物以共豆籩。夙夜在公，不以為勞。詩曰：「君婦莫莫，為豆孔庶。」夫相禮罔愆，威儀孔時，宗廟享之，子孫順之。故曰：「祭者，教之本也。」苟不盡道，而忘孝敬，神斯弗享矣。神弗享而能保躬裕後者，未之有也。凡內助於君子者，其尚勖之。

15

Performing Religious Rites (Fengjisi zhang dishiwu 奉祭祀章第十五)

THE WAY OF humanity emphasizes the importance of the marriage rite (*hunli* 昏禮). This is because [husband and wife] continue the lineage of ancestors and jointly carry out religious [ancestral] rites.[1] Hence, [in preparation for an upcoming wedding,] a father offers a drink to his son (*jiao* 醮) and says, "Go and welcome your helpmate. Together you will continue the family ancestral rituals." So, too, a mother bids farewell to her daughter with a drink and says, "Go to your family (*rujia* 女家). Always act with respect and caution. Do not disobey your husband." When a king marries a wife, he addresses [his bride's family] saying, "She and I will govern our state together and preside over the rituals at our ancestral temples and to the gods of Earth and grain" (*sheji* 社稷). Although these people's positions and duties are different, their desire to seek a helpmate is the same.[2]

Since both husband and wife will preside over the ancestral rite, external and internal responsibilities (*guan* 官) are delegated. This is comparable to empresses and royal consorts, who perform principal rites to spiritual beings and lay the foundation for the nation. They fast and purify their body and mind (*juan* 蠲) for the winter rite (*zheng* 蒸) and the autumn rite (*chang* 嘗) so as to assist [the Son of Heaven] in officiating these rites.

Rituals must be rooted in humaneness and filialness, and complemented by sincerity and reverence. Hence, an empress should personally attend to silk worms and care for mulberry trees in order to make ritual clothing with black silk ribbons (*dan* 紞). She should prepare ritual items to fill up ritual vessels made of wood and bamboo. She should attend to official business day and night, without seeing it as a burden. The *Classic of Poetry* says, "The king's spouse is serene and reverent. How abundant are the goods in the ritual vessels!"[3] In assisting [her husband] in performing religious rites, nothing is amiss. Her appearance is dignified and all rituals are carried out properly at the best time. When doing so, all spiritual beings memorialized in ancestral temples will enjoy the rituals. One's offspring will reverently follow suit. Therefore, it is said, "ancestral rites are the foundation of teaching."

If one does not exert one's best effort, and if filialness and reverence are forgotten, then spiritual beings will not enjoy the rituals. When spiritual beings do not enjoy the rituals, it has never been the case that one will be able to protect one's person and bring prosperity to the future generations. All inner helpmates who assist their rulers and husbands must take heed of this.[4]

Commentaries and Annotations

1. Wang Xiang's commentary: 昏 *is the same as* 婚 (hun). *This passage makes it clear the importance of religious rites. It says that the way of human moral relations sees marriage rite as an essential ritual. The righteous union of husband and wife begets children, continues the lineage of ancestors, and prepares offerings for ancestral rites. Thus, the marriage rite must not be overlooked.* Translator's annotation: In the Confucian family tradition, religious rites mainly refer to ancestral rites. The Hunyi 昏義 chapter of the *Liji* (*Record of Rituals*) proclaims the importance of the marriage rite as such:

   > The marriage rite brings forth the blessings of two surnames. It serves the ancestral temples above and it continues future offspring. Thus, gentlemen stress the marriage rite.... Reverence, prudence, solemnity, and correctness come first, and affection follows. This is the essential of ritual propriety.... Only after the distinction between man and woman is established, can the righteousness of husband

and wife be accomplished. Only after the righteousness of husband and wife is established, can the affection between father and son be accomplished. Only after the affection between father and son is established, can the rectitude between ruler and minister be accomplished. Thus, it is said that the marriage rite is the root of all rituals.

2. Wang Xiang's commentary: 女 *pronounced as* 汝 *(*ru*).* Jiao 醮 *refers to the departure drink that parents offer to their sons and daughters before the wedding. Here, the distinction between the venerable and the lowly is not observed. There is a toast of wine offered by one party (*zuo 酢*) but no toast is returned by the other party (*chou 酬*). Like the blessings that one receives from Heaven and Earth and the spiritual beings, a toast is given but no toast is returned. Thus, it is called* jiao 醮. *When a son is about to personally welcome and receive his bride to his household, his father will toast him with a drink saying: "Go and welcome your inner helpmate to your household. Together you will continue rites at our ancestral temple." A daughter is about to marry to another household, in sending her off her mother will offer a toast of wine saying: "You are going to your household. You must always uphold respect, caution, and prudence. Do not disobey your husband." When a king is about to marry a wife, he addresses his wife's household: "She will assist me in safeguarding our country and preside over official rites at our ancestral temples and to the gods of Earth and grain" (*sheji 社稷*). From this, one sees that although the social positions of those above and those below differ, their desires in seeking inner helpmates are the same.* Translator's annotation: *She* 社 originally means the god of Earth and *Ji* 稷 refers to the god of grain. Later, the two words together (*sheji* 社稷) covey the meaning of a country or a nation. According to the Hunyi chapter of the *Liji* (*Record of Rituals*), the marriage rite involves six steps: (1) making a marriage proposal (*nacai* 納采), (2) asking the bride's name and date of birth (*wenming* 問名), (3) presenting divination results and betrothal gifts (*naji* 納吉), (4) sending wedding gifts to the bride's home (*nazheng* 納徵), (5) requesting a wedding date (*qingqi* 請期), and (6) welcoming the bride in person (*qinying* 親迎). English translation of the six steps of the marriage rite is adopted from Paul R. Goldin's presentation at the University of Scranton on September 30, 2016, with slight modification. For proper procedures in conducting the ancestral rites, see the Jitong 祭統 chapter of the *Liji* (*Record of Rituals*).

3. Wang Xiang's commentary: 蠲 *pronounced as* 涓 *(*juan*);* 紞 *as* 坦 *(*tan*).* 官 *(*guan*) means "responsibility." For religious ritual, both husband and wife must be present to attend to their respective external and internal responsibilities. Just as empress and royal consorts in their physical presence are comparable to that of the Son of Heaven, they are officiators of the rituals toward Heaven, Earth, and spiritual beings, and they lay the foundation for the blessings of the nation. They fast and purify their body and mind (*juan 蠲*) for the winter and the autumn rites so as to assist [the Son of Heaven] in officiating these rites. These rituals are extremely important; they must be preceded with humaneness, filial piety, sincerity, and reverence. The empress ought to personally care for silkworms and mulberry trees to make ritual clothing with black silk ribbons. She*

should prepare ceremonial texts and ritual vessels, and have ritual instruments made of wood and bamboo ready for use at the ancestral temple. Day and night, she must be reverent, hard-working, and tireless. The Chuci 楚茨 poem [from the Shijing*] portrays the principal wife of a king being serene, sincere, reverential, and solemn in assisting him in officiating the rites. She cleaned and prepared wood and bamboo ritual instruments and had them all filled with abundant goods.* Translator's annotation: For more on proper preparation of rituals, consult the Jiyi 祭義 and the Jitong 祭統 chapters of the *Liji* (*Record of Rituals*). The proper pronunciation of 統 should be *dan* 膽, not *tan* 坦.

4. Wang Xiang's commentary: *Empresses, royal consorts, and wives of marquises and high-ranking officials—all have the duty of assisting their husbands in completing religious rites. When assisting in performing the rite, she should ensure that nothing is contrary to proper ritual, that her appearance is dignified, and everything is performed at the right time; then, all spiritual beings of the ancestral temples will enjoy the rite. Children and offspring who participate in the rite will reverently emulate the process. Therefore, the* Record of Rituals *says that in religious rites, one leads one's offspring in serving the ancestors. One guides, and the other follows. The rituals are thereupon passed down to future generations. Thus, the rites are the foundation of teaching. If one is irreverent in offering the rites, then one lacks a filial and reverent heart. If so, the spiritual beings from above will not enjoy the rite. If spiritual beings do not enjoy the rite, how can one protect one's person or pass down prosperity to one's offspring? All who have the virtue of being inner helpmates must be advised on this: show respect on these matters without negligence.* Translator's annotation: See *Liji* (*Record of Rituals*), the Jitong chapter.

【母儀章第十六】

孔子曰：「女子者，順男子之教，而長其理者也，是故無專制之義。」所以為教，不出閨門，以訓其子者也。教之者，導之以德義，養之以廉遜，率之以勤儉，本之以慈愛，臨之以嚴恪，以立其身，以成其德。慈愛不至於姑息，嚴恪不至於傷恩。傷恩則離，姑息則縱，而教不行矣。詩曰：「載色載笑，匪怒伊教。」夫教之有道矣，而在己者，亦不可不慎。是故，女德有常，不踰貞信。婦德有常，不踰孝敬。貞信孝敬，而人則之。詩曰：「其儀不忒，正是四國。」此之謂也。

16

Model Motherhood
(Muyi zhang dishiliu 母儀章第十六)

CONFUCIUS SAYS, "WOMEN, as a consequence of following men's education, thereby increase (*zhang* 長) their reason. Therefore, they must not be autocratic." The reason that a women receives education is not to go outside the inner quarter; rather, it is to teach her children.[1] When teaching them, she should guide them with virtue and righteousness, cultivate them with honesty and humility, lead them with diligence and frugality, plant their root in benevolence and love, and top off her teaching with strictness and respect so as to establish their persons and complete their virtue.[2] She ought to be benevolent and loving without being lax, strict and respectful without damaging kindness. Damaging kindness in relationship will cause children to become distant. Being overly permissive will spoil a child.

The *Shijing* (*Classic of Poetry*) says, "He is always pleasant with a smile, never angry in teaching."[3] Thus, there is a right method in teaching; it rests on the self. One cannot be imprudent concerning this. Constant virtues for young women do not go beyond chastity and trustworthiness. Constant virtues for married women are nothing more than filial piety and respect. If a woman is chaste, trustworthy, filial, and respectful, people will surely emulate her. The *Shijing* says, "His behavior does not err. It can rectify neighboring countries from all four sides." This is what it means.[4]

Commentaries and Annotations

1. Wang Xiang's commentary: *This is to illuminates the nature of the mother's teaching. It first speaks about the origin of knowledge. Originally, daughters do not have any knowledge. Sons are educated first. Out of convenience, parents also teach their daughters and their daughters follow their teaching. This is done in hope to open their daughters' minds and to increase their understanding of the moral principles of human relations. Therefore, at home a daughter obeys her father; after she has married, she obeys her husband. She ought not to be domineering. Her orders and commands are not to go outside the inner quarters. Teaching her sons and daughters is her maternal duty.* Translator's annotation: The saying attributed to Confucius is from the *Dadai liji* 《大戴禮記》 (*Dadai Record of Rituals*), Benming 本命 chapter; and Wang Shu, *Kongzi jiayu* 《孔子家語》 (*Family Discourse of Confucius*), Benmingjie 本命解 chapter. For women's "three obediences," see the *Liji* (*Record of Rituals*), Jiaotesheng chapter; the *Dadai liji* (*Dadai Record of Rituals*), Beiming chapter; and Wang Shu, *Kongzi jiayu* (*Family Discourse of Confucius*), Beimingjie chapter.
2. Wang Xiang's commentary: *The right method of teaching sons and daughters is to guide them with the correctness of virtue and righteousness, cultivate them with the temperance of integrity and humility, lead them with the way of diligence and frugality, plant their roots with a heart of benevolence and love, and top it off with the weightiness of seriousness and reverence. Only so can their persons be established and their virtue complete.*
3. Wang Xiang's commentary: *Benevolence and love ought to originate from the heart without pampering. Seriousness and reverence should manifest themselves in one's appearance without damaging kindness. If one is overly strict thus damaging kindness, children will leave without any affection. If one loves but pampers them, children will become spoiled and they will abandon ritual propriety. Therefore, the Panshui 泮水 poem in the Lusong 魯頌 section of the* Shijing *describes how a person, good at teaching others, never loses his pleasantness and smile. Thus, his students are joyful in following his teaching.*
4. Wang Xiang's commentary: *The right method of teaching is nothing else than this. It rests on one's self-cultivation. If a woman can be virtuous without deficiency, she is fit to be a maternal model. One cannot be imprudent concerning this. Women's virtues are nothing else than chastity and good faith; wives' virtues are no more than filialness and respect. Be chaste, trustworthy, filial, respectful, and not corrupted by indecency! Consequently, one's offspring and daughters-in-law will emulate one's example. As such, one does not bring disgrace to the motherly model. The meaning of the poem from the Caofeng 曹風 section of the* Shijing *is that a gentleman carries himself in a dignified solemn manner. His conduct does not err. Thus, neighboring countries from all four sides follow him as their norm. This can be the way of the motherly model as well.* Translator's annotation: The poem referred here is the Shijiu 鳲鳩 from the *Shijing* (*Classic of Poetry*).

【睦宗章第十七】

仁者，無不愛也。親疏內外，有本末焉。一家之親，近之為兄弟，遠之為宗族，則同乎一源矣。若夫娣姒姑姊妹，親之至近者矣，宜無所不用其情。夫木不榮於幹，不能以達支。火不灼於中，不能以照外。是以施仁，必先睦親。睦親之務，必有內助。一源之出，本無異情，間以異姓，乃生乖別。書云：「惇睦九族。」詩云：「宜其家人。」主乎內者，體君子之心，重源本之義，敦頍弁之德，廣行葦之風。仁恕寬厚，敷洽惠施，不忘小善，不記小過。錄小善則大義明，略小過則讒慝息，讒慝息則親愛全，親愛全則恩義備矣。疎戚之際，藹然和樂。由是推之，內和而外和，一家和而一國和，一國和而天下和矣。可不重哉。

17

*Friendly Relationship with Family Clans (*Muzong zhang dishiqi 睦宗章第十七*)*

A HUMANE PERSON has no one whom she does not love.[1] Nonetheless, between close relationships and distant ones, and between those who are members of the household and those outside the household, there is certainly a distinction between the roots [i.e., the fundamental] and the branches [i.e., the secondary].[2] When speaking about affectionate relationships in a family, they can be as close as between brothers and as distant as between relatives with the same surname. All come from the same origin.[3] Wives of one's husband's younger brothers and older brothers, his older and younger sisters, are all members of very close relations; one should express utmost affection toward them.[4]

A tree that does not have a strong trunk cannot generate lush branches. Fire that does not burn in the center cannot illuminate its surroundings. Hence in practicing humaneness, one must begin with cultivating friendly relationships with relatives. To cultivate friendly relationships with relatives, one necessarily relies on one's inner helpmate.[5]

Originating from the same one source, essentially there is no difference in affection. Nevertheless, when someone begins to disparage differences in the surnames, disharmony and separation arise. The *Shangshu* (*Book of Documents*) says, "Promote (*dun* 惇) amicable relations among the nine family clans." The *Shijing* (*Classic of Poetry*) says, "Cultivate friendly relationships with one's relatives." One who oversees inner affairs should understand her husband's mind, take seriously the righteousness of originating from the same origin, nourish virtue as advocated in the Kuibian 頍弁 poem, and expand cultural transformation as taught in the Xingwei 行葦 poem.[6]

Be humane, altruistic, broad-minded, and generous. Apply kindness and do favors. Do not forget small good deeds that others did. Do not remember small mistakes that others made. Record others' small good deeds; thereupon, great righteousness will be illuminated. Omit others' small mistakes; then, gossip and slander will stop. If gossip and slander are stopped, affection will be complete. If affection is complete, feelings of gratitude will be in place.[7] Between the distant relations and the close ones, all relations will be amicable, harmonious, and pleasant.

From this, one can infer that the harmony of the inner realm leads to the harmony of the outer realm. The harmony of a family leads to the harmony of a nation; the harmony of a nation leads to the harmony of the world. How can one not weigh it heavily?[8]

Commentaries and Annotations

1. Translator's annotation: Only the Zhuangyuange edition has Muzong zhang 睦宗章 as this chapter's title. All other editions have it as Muqin zhang 睦親章. According to Empress Renxiaowen's preface to the *Neixun* and the frequent use of the phrase *muqin* 睦親 in this chapter, the correct chapter title probably contains Mu*qin* rather than Mu*zong*. *Qin* 親 means "relatives"; *zong* 宗 means "family clans."
2. Wang Xiang's commentary: *This chapter elucidates the way of cultivating friendly relations among relatives. It says that even though it is in the nature of a humane person to love all people, he still makes a distinction between close relations and distant ones, the inner and outer spheres, the roots and the branches. One should use this as a guide to differentiate what is less important and what is more important, what is secondary and what is fundamental. Only then can one be on the right path of cultivating friendly relations among relatives.* Translator's annotation: Humaneness (*ren* 仁) is regarded as the paramount virtue in Confucian thought, and it manifests itself as

a love for humanity (*Analects* 4.1, 6.30, 12.22). This chapter derives its inspiration from Mencius's theory on the "gradation of love" (*tuiai* 推愛), as opposed to the competing Mohist philosophy of "love without distinction" (*jianai* 兼愛). For more on Mencius's teaching on the gradation of love, see *Mencius* 7A:45, 7A:46, 7B:1. For his critique of Modi's 墨翟 Mohism and Yangzhu's 楊朱 Egoism, see *Mencius* 3B:9, 7A:26, 7B:26.

3. Wang Xiang's commentary: *Within a family, the relationship between brothers is the closest, whereas other family relatives are of a more distant relation. Even though there is a distinction between close relations and distant ones, all can be traced back to the same lineage of ancestors just as diverse rivers come from the same origin. Nonetheless, from the perspective of a wife, even though my natal brothers and relatives are from the same origin as I, but since I have followed my husband, these close relations are also distant. My husband's brothers and relatives though have a different surname from mine, and yet because a wife should regard her husband's family as the weightier one, these relations though distant are also close.*
4. Wang Xiang's commentary: *One's husband's younger brother's wife is called* di 娣, *his older brother's wife is called* si 姒, *and his older and younger sisters are all persons of close relations. There is the comradeship in serving parents-in-law together. Thus, one should love them to the utmost degree.*
5. Wang Xiang's commentary: *When a tree grows its foundation, it is called a trunk. When a tree trunk generates outgrowth, it is called branches. When a trunk is not strong, its branches cannot flourish; when a fire does not burn vibrantly, it cannot illuminate its surroundings. Therefore, when a gentleman orders a family, he necessarily attends to the cultivation of friendly relations among relatives. If he desires to cultivate friendly relations among relatives, he necessarily has a virtuous inner helpmate who masters it.*
6. Wang Xiang's commentary: 惇 *(*dun*) and* 敦 *(*dun*) are synonymous.* 頍弁 *is pronounced as* 跬卞 *(*kuibian*). Kuibian* 頍弁 *is a poem from the Xiaoya section; Xingwei* 行葦 *is a poem in the Daya section. Both are from the* Shijing *(*Classic of Poetry*); they depict brothers and relatives who enjoy a good time together in banquets hosted by the other. The poems describe that a gentleman regards his brothers, sisters, and family relatives as persons of the same origin and he desires to build friendly relationships among them. Nevertheless, a depraved wife sees these relatives of different surnames from hers as distant strangers. She disparages them. Consequently, disharmony and differentiation arise. Few gentlemen were not confused by their wives. The* Shangshu *(*Book of Documents*) says that Emperor Yao was enlightened and exceedingly virtuous; he cultivated friendly relationship among the nine family clans. The* Shijing *praises empresses' and royal consorts' transformation of culture. Both Nan sections [i.e., Zhounan and Zhaonan sections] have many examples of virtuous ladies who rightly order their families. If a virtuous inner helpmate can experience the heart of her husband, take the meaning of originating from one source weightily, promote the culture*

of the Kuibian and Xingwei poems, no family clans will be unfriendly. Translator's annotation: The sentence from the *Shangshu* is from the Gaoyaomo 皋陶謨 chapter. 陶 is pronounced as *yao* (not *tao*) in this title. Gaoyao 皋陶 was a well-known virtuous minister, who assisted the legendary sage king Shun 舜. The sentence from the *Shijing* comes from the Zhounan section, the Taoyao 桃夭 poem.

7. Wang Xiang's commentary: *The way to cultivate friendly relations among relatives is to begin with humaneness, treat relatives altruistically, lead them with broad-mindedness, and cultivate them with generosity. Apply kindness widely. Do them favors. Although they only do some small good, one will remember and not forget it. Although they commit a small fault, one will forget and not remember it. If one can remember others' good deeds, feelings of gratitude will grow daily. If one can forget others' faults, gossip and slander will not arise. Affection will be complete and feelings of gratitude will be in place.*
8. Wang Xiang's commentary: *If inner helpmates are virtuous, relatives will be friendly to one another. All will be gracious and joyful. One should follow this path and promulgate it. If wives of marquises, ministers, low-ranking officials, and the common people can all assist their husbands in cultivating friendly relations among relatives, thus accomplishing the beautiful virtue of inner helpmates, then both the inner and the outer realms will be agreeable and friendly, the household and the state will be in harmony, and the world will be in peace. How can one not be serious about this?* Translator's annotation: For a succinct description of the progression from self-cultivation to world peace, and from world peace back to self-cultivation, see the *Daxue* 《大學》 (*Great Learning*). In contemporary terms, these Confucian texts essentially argue for the nonseparateness of the personal, the social, and the political, while affirming normative priority of the familial relations.

【慈幼章第十八】

慈者，上之所以撫下也。上慈而不懈，則下順而益親。故喬木竦而枝不附焉，淵水清而魚不藏焉。甘瓠藟於樛木，庶草繁於深澤。則子婦順於慈仁，理也。若夫待之以不慈，而欲責之以孝，則下必不安。下不安則心離，心離則忮，忮則不祥莫大焉。為人父母者，其慈乎！其慈乎！然有姑息以為慈，溺愛以為德，是自蔽其下也。故慈者非違理之謂也，必也盡教訓之道乎。亦有不慈者，則下不可以不孝，必也勇於順令，如伯奇者乎。

18

Benevolent Love for the Young (Ciyou zhang dishiba 慈幼章第十八)

BENEVOLENT LOVE IS love expressed by persons in the higher positions to comfort those who are in the lower positions. If those in the higher positions are tirelessly benevolent, those in the lower positions will be compliant and affectionate. Hence, Qiao trees stand tall rigidly; consequently, no branches are attached to them. When gorge waters are too clear, fish will not hide under them.[1] Contrarily, sweet melons that grow on vines attach themselves to [winding] Jiu trees; grasses propagate in deep marshes. That sons and daughters-in-law naturally comply with benevolence and humaneness is where the principle of reason stands.[2]

If those in the higher positions do not treat those in the lower positions lovingly, but scold them for lack of filial piety, those in the lower positions will feel unsettled. Once they feel unsettled, their hearts will depart. If their hearts depart, thoughts of doing harm will arise. If thoughts of doing harm arise, there is nothing more inauspicious than this.[3] Those who are parents must practice benevolence! They must practice benevolence!

Certainly, there are parents who are lax with their children and mistake it for benevolence; they spoil their children and mistake it for virtue. This is nothing but covering up for their children. Accordingly, benevolent love is not synonymous with violation of principles. Parents ought to rectify their children.[4] There are also parents who are unloving. Even so, children ought not to be unfilial; they must be courageous in complying with parents' wishes, like Boqi 伯奇.[5]

Commentaries and Annotations

1. Translator's annotation: In several other editions of the *Neixun* (*Teachings for the Inner Court*), gorge waters that fish avoid were described as 涸 (*hao*), "drained, dried up," rather than 清 (*qing*), "clear, clean." 清 (*qing*) is used in the Zhuangyuange edition.
2. Wang Xiang's commentary: *This chapter explains the way to love the young benevolently. When those above comfort those below, this is called benevolent love. If those above are benevolent without neglect, then the lowly and the young will surely comply and stay close. Qiao trees have leaves on the top but have no branches at the lower bottom. Gorge waters that are overly clear are avoided by fish. Contrarily, sweet melons that grow on vines attach themselves to winding Jiu trees; diverse grasses propagate in deep marshes where water plants flourish (*yi yi 蓊翳*). This is because these things and places are accommodating. If those above are benevolent and accommodating, then their offspring and daughters-in-laws will be compliant and affectionate. The reason behind it is easy to see. 蓊翳 pronounced as 醫義 (*yiyi*) is where water plants and vines grow luxuriantly.* Translator's annotation: The Jiu tree metaphor is from the Jiumu 樛木 poem in the Zhounan section of the *Shijing* (*Classic of Poetry*); the fish metaphor is from the Nanyoujiayu 南有嘉魚 poem in the Xiaoya section.
3. Wang Xiang's commentary: *If those above are not benevolent, but scolding and demanding filial piety from those in the lower position, those in the lower position will abandon them and feel unsettled. Once they feel unsettled, thoughts of harm arise. This is the worst kind of inauspiciousness.*
4. Wang Xiang's commentary: *It says that as parents, they must use benevolent love as the foundation. This is said two times for emphasis. Nevertheless, if parents mistake being lax with their children, indulging them, and covering up for them to be caring love, this is self-deceiving and will do harm to their offspring. It is not benevolence. If parents do not violate moral principles, teach children to be persons of rectitude, and develop their hearts and minds of humaneness and righteousness, then it can be called benevolence.*
5. Wang Xiang's commentary: *Benevolent love is really a favor done by those who are in the higher positions to those who are under them. This is something one must understand. Those above may not be benevolent, but those below cannot be unfilial. In former times, Yi Jipu 尹吉甫 of the Zhou dynasty was bewildered by his second wife; he planned to kill his son Boqi [born by Jipu's first wife]. Boqi 伯奇 dared not argue with*

his father; he followed his father's command to die. This is an example of the utmost filialness. Nonetheless, Boqi's filialness is used to explain those situations where parents lack benevolence. Still, parents should place emphasis on benevolence. Translator's annotation: Accounts of what happened to Boqi varied. Some said that Boqi was banished by his father; others said that he committed suicide; some others said that Boqi's father eventually discovered the truth and mended fences with Boqi. For more, see Liu Xiang, *Shuoyuan* 《說苑》 (*Garden of Stories*); and Yanli Huang, *Nü sishu jizhu yizheng* (*Four Books for Women with Selections from Traditional Commentaries*), 152. Praise for Boqi's choice to die seems extreme; it is at odds with equally weighty Confucian advice against blind obedience to authority, especially immoral parental demands, so as not to trap parents in immorality. See, for example, Confucius, *Analects* 4.18; and the *Xiaojing* (*Classic of Filial Piety*), chapter 15. This exhibits a perennial tension in Confucian ethics.

【逮下章第十九】

君子為宗廟之主，奉神靈之統，宜蕃衍嗣續，傳序無窮。故夫婦之道，世祀為大。古之哲后賢妃，皆推德逮下。薦達貞淑，不獨任己。是以茂衍來裔，長流慶澤。周之太姒，有逮下之德，故樛木形福履之詠，螽斯揚振振之美。終能昌大本枝，綿固宗社。三王之隆，莫此為盛。故婦人之行，貴於寬惠，惡於妬忌。月星並麗，豈掩於末光。松蘭同畝，不嫌於並秀。自后妃以至士庶人之妻，誠能貞靜寬和，明大孝之端，廣至人之意，不專一己之欲，不蔽眾下之美，務廣君子之澤。斯上安下順，和氣烝融，善慶源源，肇於此矣。

19

Treating Imperial Concubines (Daixia zhang dishijiu 逮下章第十九)

GENTLEMEN ARE THE heads of their ancestral temples. They carry on the orthodox system of spiritual beings. It is fitting for them to propagate offspring and to pass down the family lineage through innumerable generations.[1] Therefore, of the way between a husband and a wife, having offspring is the most important responsibility of all.

In ancient times, virtuous empresses and royal consorts all extended their virtues in reaching out to imperial concubines under them. They recommended chaste and virtuous women to their husbands rather than monopolizing their husbands' love for themselves. Consequently, they had abundant offspring. Happiness for their families continued extensively.[2] Taisi of the Zhou dynasty treated imperial concubines with virtue. Hence, the Jiu Tree (Jiumu 樛木) poem wished her happiness and auspiciousness and the Locust (Zhongsi 螽斯) poem praised her for the prosperity and uprightness (*zhenzhen* 振振) of her offspring.[3]

She had made the [Zhou] family lineage great and had fortified the ancestral temple of the [Zhou] ruling house. Of the flourishing periods of the Three Kings (*sanwang* 三王) [i.e., the Xia 夏, Yin 殷, and Zhou 周 dynasties], none is more prosperous than the Zhou dynasty.[4] Therefore, of women's conduct (*xing* 行), the most precious virtues are generosity and kindness; the worst vice (*wu* 惡) is jealousy.

The Moon and the stars shine beautifully in the sky together; there is no need to block the light of a star. Cypress and orchids grow in the same field; the cypress does not hold the orchids in disdain for sharing (*bing* 並) the limelight.[5] From empresses and royal consorts to the wives of the officials and the common people, if all can sincerely cultivate chastity, quietude, generosity, and friendliness; understand the inception of great filialness; promulgate the meaning of ultimate [humaneness];[6] refrain from acting on selfish desires; abstain from hiding the virtues of those under them; and endeavor to propagate their husbands' offspring, then those who are in the higher positions will be peaceful and those who are in the lower positions will be compliant. Harmony and peace will be widespread. Goodness and auspiciousness will be unstoppable. These all begin here![7]

Commentaries and Annotations

1. Wang Xiang's commentary: *Here, the writer uses the phrase* junzi 君子 *(gentleman) instead of* tianzi 天子 *(emperor, Son of Heaven) in order to include marquises, ministers, and officials.* Dai 逮 *[in this chapter's title] means "reaching down from above." This chapter elucidates the way to reach down from above with grace and kindness. It speaks about the facts that since gentlemen provide care for the ancestral temples, make sacrifice to spiritual beings, and carry on the orthodox family succession, it is fitting for them to propagate offspring and to pass on ministerial order so as to extend auspiciousness endlessly.*
2. Wang Xiang's commentary: *This passage explains that a husband and a wife must regard carrying on the family succession and lineage as their most important responsibility. Virtuous empresses and royal consorts of ancient times all could extend their grace and virtue to those under them. They selected concubines of chastity and fine virtue, and recommended them to their husbands. These empresses and royal consorts did not monopolize their husbands' love for themselves. Consequently, they had many sons and grandchildren. Happiness for their families continued for hundreds of generations.*
3. Wang Xiang's commentary: 螽 *pronounced as* 中 (zhong)*;* 振 *(*zhen*) pronounced in the second tone. For the meaning of the Jiumu* 樛木 *poem, see the previous chapter. Zhongsi* 螽斯 *is a species of locust; a locust can procreate ninety-nine offspring at one time.* Zhenzhen 振振 *means "prosperous." The* Classic of Poetry *says, "Locusts are flapping their wings. They are making loud sounds. Your offspring will be prosperous!"*

This is a metaphor for empresses and royal consorts who are unjealous; thus, they have abundant offspring and all of them will be prosperous, just as locusts have abundant offspring and they all live harmoniously and happily together, and fly together. Taisi's virtue is as such. Thus, poets sang her praises, comparing her to Jiu trees and locusts—each kind is virtuous and beautiful in its own way and each is sufficiently so.

4. Wang Xiang's commentary: Sanwang 三王 *refers to the three dynasties, Xia, Yin [i.e., Shang], and Zhou. This passage speaks about the facts that if empresses and royal consorts are virtuous, their offspring will be abundant, their family lineages will be great, and their ancestral temples and their states will be peaceful. During the Xia and the Yin dynasties, even though there were virtuous royal consorts, there were neither as many of them nor were they as great as those of the Zhou dynasty.*
5. Wang Xiang's commentary: 行 *(*xing*),* 惡 *(*wu*), and* 並 *(*bing*) are pronounced in the fourth tone. This chapter explains that a women's virtue is to value generosity and to despise jealousy. The Moon is big and the stars are small. Both shine beautifully in the same sky. A cypress tree is tall and an orchid is short. Both grow in the same earth. The Moon will not hide a star's light; a cypress will not hinder an orchid's beauty. These are analogies for the virtue and beauty of a principal wife, who can accommodate her husband's concubines without jealousy.*
6. Translator's annotation: 廣至人之意 is used in the Zhongyuange edition; but 廣至仁之意 were used in other editions. The difference rests in one word: 人 (*ren*, person) or 仁 (*ren*, humaneness). Since this sentence enumerates a list of virtues, 仁 fits better than 人.
7. Wang Xiang's commentary: *This passage explains that if empresses, royal consorts, and the principal wives of the officials and the common people can all sincerely promulgate the virtue of virtuous empresses and royal consorts from ancient times, refrain from selfish desires or concealing the virtue of those under them, and be generous and friendly in propagating the family lineage, then both the above and the below will be peaceful and compliant. Harmony and peace will gather in the inner quarters. The origin of blessings and auspiciousness certainly begins from here.*

【待外戚章第二十】

知幾者，見於未萌。禁微者，謹於抑末。自昔之待外戚，鮮不由始縱而終難制也。雖曰外戚之過，亦係乎后德之賢否耳。漢明德皇后，修飾內政，患外家以驕肆取敗，未嘗加以封爵。唐長孫皇后，慮外家以富貴招禍，請無屬以樞柄。故能使之保全。其餘若呂霍楊氏之流，僭踰奢靡，氣燄熏灼，無所顧忌，遂致傾覆。良由內政偏陂，養成禍根，非一日矣。易曰：「馴致其道，至堅冰也。」夫欲保全之者，擇師傅以教之，隆之以恩，而不使撓法。優之以祿，而不使預政。杜私謁之門，絕請求之路，謹奢侈之戒，長謙遜之風。則其患自弭矣。若夫恃恩姑息，非保全之道。恃恩則侈心生焉，姑息則禍機蓄焉。蓄禍召亂，其患無斷。盈滿招辱，守正獲福。慎之哉。

內訓終

20

Treating Imperial Consorts' Maternal Relatives (Daiwaiqi zhang diershi 待外戚章第二十)

ONE WHO KNOWS subtle signals at the onset of a movement can see the signs before it emerges. One who wishes to prohibit small matters [of destruction] from happening must carefully take preventive measures in guarding the minutest parts.

Since former times, regarding treating imperial consorts' maternal relatives, these relatives became difficult to control in the end often because they were spoiled in the beginning. Although these were the maternal relatives' faults, it was also related to whether empresses were virtuous or not.[1] Empress Mingde 明德皇后 of the [Eastern] Han 漢 well governed the affairs of the inner court. Concerned with the potential demise of her maternal family if it were to become arrogant and unruly, she ensured that it was never bestowed with aristocratic titles. Empress Zhangsu 長孫皇后 of Tang 唐 was worried that her maternal family would invite calamity upon itself owing to wealth and high-ranking social status. She asked the emperor not to appoint any of her maternal relatives to powerful positions. The two empresses were thus able to preserve their maternal families.[2] The rest, such as Empress Lü 呂, Empress Huo 霍, Empress Yang 楊, and their kind, transgressed the law and lived extravagantly. Their arrogance resembled a raging flame (*yan* 燄). They had neither hesitation nor any fear whatsoever, which resulted in their demise. This was due to favoritism and partiality in internal affairs that nourished the roots of disaster. It was not an outcome of a single day. The *Classic of Changes* says, "Following the way [of frost], it will naturally arrive at the season of hard ice."[3]

If one wishes to preserve one's maternal relatives, one should select a good teacher to teach them. Treat them with kindness and grace, but do not allow them to obstruct the law. Reward them with generous revenues, but do not permit them to interfere with state affairs. Block the door that allows them to come to the imperial court for self-benefiting private matters. Terminate their path for asking for special favors. Keep them away from extravagant life styles. Help them develop a demeanor of humility and obedience. Then, disaster will dissolve (*mi* 弭) on its own.[4] If one relies on special favors [from the emperor] and is lax with maternal relatives, this would hardly be the way to protect them. Relying on special favors breeds the heart of extravagance; being lax accumulates the chances of disaster. Accumulated chances of disaster will lead to chaos; their troubles will have no end. Fullness and complacency attract disgrace; abiding in rectitude brings happiness. Be vigilant on this matter![5]

The *Teachings for the Inner Court* ends.

Commentaries and Annotations

1. Wang Xiang's commentary: *This passage explains how empresses and royal consorts should treat their maternal relatives. They should see subtle signs before they take form, thus preventing [harmful] affairs before they take place. They should be careful in keeping small matters in check. They should warn [their maternal relatives] when minor faults were committed. This will make maternal relatives take caution and dare not to do wrong. In ancient times, the fact that maternal relatives monopolized power and harmed the country was all because kings and empresses spoiled them. Thus, these relatives became arrogant and fearless. Later, even though the imperial court desired to restrain them, it was instead being controlled by them and the country was in chaos. When the chaos was grave, the state would be in ruin. When the chaos was less severe, persons and the family lineage would be destroyed. Although these are the faults of maternal relatives, it is also a result of kings' and empresses' ignorance.*

2. Wang Xiang's commentary: *Empress Ma* 馬后, *wife of Emperor Ming of [Eastern] Han* 漢明帝 *[r. 58–75], was concerned that her maternal relatives would become arrogant and oppressive because of the emperor's favors. Thus, she ensured that members of the Ma family were never bestowed with aristocratic titles. Empress Zhangsun* 長孫后, *wife of Emperor Taizong of Tang* 唐太宗 *[r. 627–649], often advised the emperor not to place her maternal relatives in powerful positions. These two empresses thoroughly understood what the overall situation called for. Thus, the two families were preserved.* Translator's annotation: For more about Empress Ma of Eastern Han (i.e., Empress Mingde, which means "bright virtue"), see Liu Xiang's *Biographies of Women*, volume 8, chapter 19; and Wang Daokun's *Wangshi's Biographies of Women*, volume 4. For more about Empress Zhangsun of Tang, see Liu Xu, *Tangshu* (*Book of Tang*).
3. Wang Xiang's commentary: 餤 *pronounced as* 晏 (yan). *All three families of Empress Lü* 呂氏, *wife of Emperor Gao of Han [r. 206 –195 BCE]* 漢高帝, *Empress Huo* 霍氏, *wife of Emperor Xuan of Han [r. 73–49 BCE]* 漢宣帝, *and Empress Yang* 楊氏, *wife of Emperor Wu of Jin [r. 265–290 CE]* 晉武帝, *transgressed the law, counting on special imperial favors. They dictatorially interfered with state affairs, unbridled and with no fear. They invited their own extinction. This is due to empresses and royal consorts engaging in nepotism in interior affairs; they, thus, nourished the roots of disaster. They were unable to even preserve their own lives. Therefore, hardened ice is not the result of one cold day. Calamity is not the result of one morning's accumulation. In the* Yijing *(*Classic of Changes*), the line script of the first six of the* kun *hexagram (*chuliu 初六*) reads, "Walking on frost-covered ground, one knows that [the season of] hard ice is about to arrive." The Xiang Commentary says, "The first six [of the kun hexagram]: Walking on frost-covered ground [, one knows that the season of hard ice is about to arrive.] This is because the* yin *energy begins to condense. Following the way [of frost], it will naturally arrive at [the season of] hardened ice." It is to make it clear that if one walks on frost-covered ground at first instance, one knows that the* yin *energy is condensing and [the season of] hard ice will soon arrive. If one does not from the beginning refrain from unruliness and from reliance on special favors, one knows that the temperament of arrogance will grow rapidly and calamity will come soon.* Translator's annotation: For more about Empress Huo, see Liu Xiang's *Biographies of Women*, volume 8, chapter 10. For Empress Lü, see the "Biography of Empress Lü" in Ban Gu et al., *Hanshu* (*Book of Han*). For Empress Yang, see Fang Xuanling et al., *Jinshu* (*Book of Jin*). The symbol for the hexagram *kun* 坤 is ☷. The first line of a hexagram refers to its bottom line. The first line of the *kun* hexagram is called *chuliu* 初六, or the "first six" because 6 is the number representing *yin*, symbolized by a divided line. For more on the *Yijing* (*Classic of Changes*) and the concepts of *yin, yang, qian, kun*, eight trigrams, and sixty-four hexagrams, see Madame Liu, *Nüfan jielu* (*Short Records of Models for Women*), chapter 1 and related note. Wang Xiang inserted the words 初六 and omitted the words 堅冰 in his quotation of the Xiang Commentary 象辭; the essential meaning remains intact.

4. Wang Xiang's commentary: 弭 *is pronounced as* 米 *(*mi*); it means "to dissolve." This passage advises that if empresses and royal consorts wish to protect their maternal families, they should model themselves after Empress Deng* 鄧皇后, *consort of Emperor He of [Eastern] Han* 漢和帝 *[r. 89–105], in selecting well-learned scholars of fairness, loyalty, and integrity to teach children of their maternal families. Set up schools to educate maternal relatives and make them discuss and study the lessons. This will teach them the proper way. Additionally, treat them with kindness and grace, but do not allow them to obstruct the law. Reward them with generous income, but do not permit them to interfere with state affairs. Block the door that allows them to come to the imperial court for self-benefiting private matters. Terminate their path for asking for special favors. Teach them humility and deference. Caution them to refrain from extravagance. Then, wealth and nobility will be long-preserved and disaster will dissolve on its own.* Translator's annotation: For more about Empress Deng, see Wang Daokun's *Wangshi's Biographies of Women*, volume 4; and Fan Ye, *Houhanshu* (*Book of Later Han*). Deng was the empress dowager who commended and consulted state affairs with Ban Zhao.
5. Wang Xiang's commentary: *Neither is maternal relatives' reliance on the emperor's special favors nor is the empress's and a royal consort's permissiveness the way to preserve one's person or the maternal family. For relying on special favors breeds arrogance and extravagance; permissiveness leads to calamity. Maternal relatives then harbor the thought of troubles, eventually leading to disaster and extinction. Their trouble is that from the beginning there is no stopping it. If empresses and royal consorts are enlightened in ending it and they can stop signs of disaster before chaos breaks out, then the destruction that would have toppled the maternal family lineage will not occur. Therefore, fullness and complacency are ways to failure and disgrace; abiding by rectitude is the origin of happiness and blessing. Should one not be careful?*

BOOK IV

The Ming Women

Madame Liu and the *Short Records of Models for Women* (*Nüfan jielu*): c. 16th century CE

Translator's Introduction

1. *The Author and The Work*

Madame Liu (Liu Shi 劉氏) of the Ming dynasty 明 (1368–1644 CE), also known by her honorific title Chaste Widow Wang (Wang Jiefu 王節婦), was the author of *Nüfan jielu* 《女範捷錄》 (*Short Records of Models for Women*). She was the mother of Wang Xiang 王相, a Ming scholar and the compiler and annotator of the *Four Books for Women* (*Nü shishu* 《女四書》). Very little historical material is available about her (except for Wang Xiang's introduction), possibly in part because she was not from a prominent elite family. According to Wang Xiang's introduction, one learns that Madame Liu was a resident of Jiangning (today's Nanjing City, in China) and was talented in literary works. She married Wang Jijing 王集敬, Wang Xiang's father, and became a widow when she was thirty years old. She endured hardships, single-handedly raised Wang Xiang, and safeguarded her chastity for sixty years. She passed away at the age of ninety. Imperial officers Wang Guongfu 王光復, from the Ministry of Rituals, and Zheng Qianan 鄭潛庵, from the Ministry of Justice, publicly commended her virtue of chastity on behalf of the imperial court. She authored two books: the *Lessons for Women from the Ancient Times to the Present* (*Gujin nüjian* 《古今女鑑》) and the *Short Records of Models for Women* (*Nüfan jielu* 《女範捷錄》).

The exact dates of Madame Liu's life are unclear. However, based on the evidence that the 1624 Duowentang 多文堂 edition is the earliest print version of the *Four Books for Women* known today—and that Hu Wenkai, a contemporary scholar, dates the collection to around 1580, according to Emperor Ming Shenzong's 明神宗 imperial edict—one may infer that Liu lived during the sixteenth century.[1] Her *Short Records of Models for Women* was probably composed sometime during the mid- to the late sixteenth century, one to two hundred years after Empress Renxiaowen's *Teachings for the Inner Court*. In addition to Wang Xiang's *Four Books for Women with Commentary*, this work is included in Chen

Menglei's *Collection of Illustrations and Books from Antiquity to the Present* (*Gujin tushu jicheng* 《古今圖書集成》), and has been in circulation in Japan and Korea.[2]

2. *Cultural and Historical Background*

Both Madame Liu and Empress Renxiaowen lived during the Ming dynasty. Accordingly, they shared a relatively similar cultural, historical, philosophical, and political climate. To avoid redundancy, those contents will not be repeated here. Readers may refer to the translator's introduction to Empress Renxiaowen's *Teachings for the Inner Court* (Book III, this volume) for more information.

3. *Purpose of Writing, Contents, and Strengths and Weaknesses of the Book*

Madame Liu explains in the opening chapter that children grow up to be men and women, and husbands and wives; consequently, education for both boys and girls is essential for a rightly ordered family life. The inner–outer distinction (*neiwai zhibie* 內外之別), she quickly points out, places women in a disadvantaged position because, unlike men, women are not allowed to attend schools outside the household. However, this does not mean that women have absolutely no recourse. She wrote the work to encourage women not to despair but, rather, to draw inspiring lessons from historically exemplary women: for "[a] person who uses a bronze as mirror can straighten clothes and cap; a woman who uses history as her teacher can surely find worthy role models. If she can take the ancients as her teachers, there is no reason she should be worried that her virtue is not cultivated" (chapter 1). In doing so, women could also become like the sage kings of Yao 堯 and Shun 舜 (chapter 2).

As a form of argument, the *Short Records of Models for Women* cites more than one hundred and fifty examples of real women from history—far surpassing the examples mentioned in the earlier three books of the *Four Books for Women*, both singularly and collectively. Madame Liu pays tribute to these women and their contributions, each by name. In addition to using ample examples from formal dynastic histories, she frequently consulted Liu Xiang's 劉向 *Biographies of Women* (*Lienü zhuan* 《列女傳》 from Han 漢); Guo Jujing's 郭居敬 *Twenty-Four Exemplars of Filial Piety* (*Ershisi xiao* 《二十四孝》 from Yuan 元); and Wang Daokun's 汪道昆 *Wangshi's Biographies of Women* (*Wangshi ji lienü zhuan* 《汪氏輯列女傳》 from Ming 明), also known as *Qiu Shizou's Illustrated Biographies of Women* (*Qiu Shizhou xiu xiang lienü zhuan* 《仇十洲綉像列女傳》). She also synthesized ideas originating from previous women authors into a consistent whole, including Ban Zhao's *Lessons for Women* (*Nüjie* 《女誡》), the Song sisters' *Analects for Women* (*Nü lunyu* 《女論語》), Empress Renxiaowen's *Teachings for the Inner Court* (*Neixun* 《內訓》), and Madame Zheng's *Classic of Filial Piety for Women* (*Nü xiaojing* 《女孝經》), among others.

The book consists of eleven chapters. Although the author still subscribes to gendered norms such as the "three bonds" (*sangang* 三綱), *qian* 乾 (male) and *kun* 坤 (female), and the inner–outer female–male distinction, she provides *innovative* interpretations and often breaks *new* ground. The *Short Records of Models for Women* is easily the most outspoken of the *Four Books for Women*, making numerous unorthodox statements that directly challenge the tradition. For instance, the opening chapter immediately argues for a bold thesis that women's education is even more important than men's, owing to the inaccessibility of external schooling for women at the time (chapter 1) and the significance of a mother's influence on prenatal, as well as childhood education (chapter 3). Thus, she says that "the model of the correct inner realm should come before that of the external realm" (chapter 1) and "model motherhood is prior to the teaching of a father" (chapter 3).

Chapter 3 ("Loyalty and Righteousness") cites twenty-four wide-ranging examples, from aristocratic women to maids, from elite women to courtesan-prostitutes, from martial heroines to peasants. This chapter redefines what courage means for women, challenges the stereotypical view of women as "the weak and vulnerable," and recognizes their immense contributions to the society and the state:

> The old saying goes, "All under Heaven are the ministers of the emperor." How could it be that in the inner quarters of women there is no loyalty and righteousness? . . . Madame Liang climbed up the Jin Mountain to beat the martial drums for the troop, thus defeating the invading Jin soldiers. . . . Guier [an imperial servant] sacrificed her life in scolding the traitors. . . . Mao Xixi, a courtesan-prostitute, would rather be killed than to sing for the defector-general. . . . It is not that Madame Zhang [a general's mother] does not want to protect her own family—rather, that she wished for the safety of the whole city. These are the resounding examples of women's ardency, their remarkable expressions of the principle of *kun*. Their exemplary loyalty and righteous courage is sufficient to inspire hundreds of generations and revive the bonds and constants of morals.

Chapter 8 ("Upholding Ritual Propriety") makes the case for equal application of ritual propriety to both sexes, and the necessary circumstances in which women must use ritual propriety creatively as an instrument (rather than as a fetter) to defend their rights and to reprimand their male counterparts:

> Just like virtue, appearance, speech, and work are four principal conducts of a woman, ritual propriety, righteousness, honesty, and a sense of shame, are the four pillars of a country. . . . Mencius intended to divorce his wife. His mother reproached him for violating ritual propriety. A man in the region of Shen wanted to marry a woman [without following proper marriage rites]. The woman shamed him for abandoning rituals. . . . Yangzi brought home some gold [that he picked up from the streets]. His wife and children ridiculed him for being unrighteous. . . . These women admonished their husbands so as to rectify their mistakes. They disciplined their own persons to make good the Way.

Chapter 9 ("Wisdom") further contends that, in handling contingencies and emergencies, women are better than men, owing to their sensitivity to context and their ability to observe minute details.[3] Moreover, women's wisdom is beneficial not only in household management but also in state affairs; note how the message crosses the inner–outer boundary between the private and the public:

> Although the great way of governing in peace rests on men, yet a wise woman surpasses a man. Grand long-term planning can be premeditated and predicted. Changes due to sudden emergencies, nonetheless, are vastly varied and infinite. . . . [Zhao Kuo] studied his father's books [of military strategy] only superficially; his mother knew that he should not be deployed as a general. . . . Yue Yangzi could listen to his wife's admonition; he thus became accomplished. Ning Chenhao brought his state to destruction because he did not listen to a woman's warning. . . . These were all examples of women's great strategies and plans in governance and their keen understanding. . . . These women were the protectors of their countries and families and the helpmates of their husbands!

Chapter 11 ("Talent and Virtue") rebukes a commonly held sexist belief that "without talent is a woman's virtue"—often used by societies to deprive women of access to learning and opportunities, and to keep them in subservient roles. Madame Liu debunks this myth by three powerful reproofs: First, the "setting the right priority" argument. She elucidates that virtue is the foundation, talents the end result. If a person does evil, it is not the fault of her or his talent but, rather, it is due to a lack of virtue. Thus, "talents and skills in economics, governance, and salvation of the people, even women's advice ought to be used and taken seriously.

Crafty skills in erroneous evil matters, even for men, these are inappropriate." Second, there is the *reductio ad absurdum* argument. She argues that if "without talent" were indeed "a woman's virtue," four absurd conclusions would follow: (a) all women without talent are all virtuous; (b) all virtuous women are all talentless; (c) all women without virtue are all talented; and (d) all women with talent must all lack virtue. Surely, none of these is true. Third, to drive her point home, she further pressed an argument "by historical examples." She recounts that, of the three hundred plus poems in the *Classic of Poetry* (a revered Confucian text), most were composed by women—these talented women surely did not lack virtue. In addition, there were a multitude of women throughout history who were both talented and exemplary in their virtues—just look at Ban Zhao, the Song sisters, and Empress Renxiaowen, among many others. In contrast, many licentious women were illiterate, having neither talent nor virtue. Accordingly, talent does not contradict virtue, nor would getting rid of one necessarily guarantee the other.

Another way of assessing the extent to which the *Short Records of Models for Women* differs from its predecessors is to look at the subject matter of each chapter, the length allocated to each, and the number of exemplary women cited in each. A glance at table IV.1 finds that women's wisdom, talents, and courage, which had been neglected in the first two books of the *Four Books for Women*,

Table IV.1 Number of Words and Examples Used in Each Chapter of the *Short Records of Models for Women*

Chapter #	Title	Word Count (Chinese Characters)	Examples Cited
1	Unifying Thesis 統論	174	0
2.	Queenly Virtues 后德	170	21
3	Model Motherhood 母儀	227	14
4	Filial Conduct 孝行	244	15
5	Chastity and Ardency 貞烈	349	23
6	Loyalty and Righteousness 忠義	306	24
7	Benevolent Love 慈愛	155	13
8	Upholding Ritual Propriety 秉禮	186	11
9	Wisdom 智慧	341	20
10	Diligence and Frugality 勤儉	180	10
11	Talent and Virtue 才德	407	14
Total		2,739	165

were not only included in this work but also occupied a central place. For example, the chapter on "Talent and Virtue" is the longest based on word count (407 words with 14 examples), next comes the chapter on "Wisdom" (341 words with 20 examples—comparable to the chapter on "Chastity and Ardency"), followed by the chapter on "Loyalty and Righteousness" (306 words with 24 examples). From this, Madame Liu emphasizes not merely women's *moral education* but also their *intellectual development*, not simply women's *chastity* but also their *courage*. Some of these subjects were covered in Liu Xiang's *Biographies of Women*, but they were swiftly dropped after the Western Han dynasty (206 BCE–8 CE) for various historical and political reasons. It is encouraging to see that these subjects were brought back into the spotlight fifteen hundred years later, albeit long overdue, with new insights and vigor.

Like previous writers, Madame Liu stresses filial conduct and chastity as integral parts of women's virtue (but with greater fervor). The Ming laws, beginning with its first emperor, Ming Taizu 明太祖, stipulated an honor-commending system (*jingbiao* 旌表) that welcomed local boroughs to nominate persons of exemplary filial piety, chastity, and integrity for special commendation by the government.[4] Thus, with both the encouragement of the imperial authority and the influence of Neo-Confucian values,[5] Ming citizens were especially mindful of cultivating filialness and integrity. This phenomenon also appears in the *Short Records of Models for Women*—two chapters are devoted to filial piety and chastity. The examples cited in these two chapters present a fascinating portrait of popular beliefs held by the populace during this period. Several examples also exhibit strong Buddhist and Daoist religious and folk beliefs on merits and punishment imposed by supernatural powers. At times, an overreaching zeal for filialness and chastity is also evident in these chapters. Some extreme cases that involved mutilating one's body or harming one's life for filialness and chastity are praised, even though the Ming laws prohibited such practices. For example, the following imperial edict was issued in 1394:

> Anyone who severs their body thus harming their lives, or lies on ice thus frozen to death, was never regarded as filial since the ancient times. If such acts were commended, it is feared that others will imitate. Thus, a prohibition is issued: such deeds are not permitted for commendation.[6]

In sum, Madame Liu and the *Short Records of Models for Women* broke new ground in several important ways for women's learning. In comparison to the other women authors of the *Four Books for Women*, Liu's style is freer, more straightforward, less confined, and less ornamental. Her arguments and positions are bolder, especially regarding women's wisdom, talent, and courage; on more than one occasion, she challenges head-on the patriarchal tradition of feudal China and renegotiates new spaces for women's intellectual development. Furthermore, she wrote for a broad audience, tapping a wide range of real-life examples, including not only aristocratic elite women but also courtesans, servants, lower-class women, and peasants. In doing so, she adeptly dismantles the rigidity of the social hierarchy and creates a sense of shared destiny and a kindred spirit open to all women from every social class.

The translations that follow are full translations of the book and Wang Xiang's commentary. Again, to keep the flow of the original text, Wang's commentary is placed in the "Commentaries and Annotations" section in italic and the translator's annotations are set in roman.

---

1. Hu Wenkai 胡文楷, *Lidai funü zhuzuokao* 《歷代婦女著作考》 (*Verified Records of Women's Writings Through the Ages*) (Shanghai: Shanghai guji chubanshe, 1985), 4 and 843.
2. Huang Liling 黃麗玲, "*Nü sishu* yanjiu" 《女四書》研究 ("Research on *Four Books for Women*,") M.A. thesis, Taiwan Nanhua University, 2003, 52–4.
3. To some degree, this resonates with contemporary ethics of care's concerns, albeit anachronistically.
4. Shen Shixing 申時行 et al., *Daming huidian* 《大明會典》 (*Great Ming Laws*) (1587; reprint, Taipei: Xinwenfeng chubangongsi, 1976), volume 79, 1254; also known as *Ming huidian* 《明會典》 (*Ming Laws*) (Beijing: Zhonghua shuju, 2007), 457. Also http://ctext.org/wiki.pl?if=gb&chapter=644358. See also Huang Liling, "*Nü sishu* yanjiu," 30.
5. See the translator's introduction to Book III, Empress Renxiaowen's *Teachings for the Inner Court*, regarding the Ming imperial endorsement of Zhu Xi's Neo-Confucian teachings.
6. Shen Shixing et al., *Ming huidian*, 457.

Wang Xiang's Biographic Introduction

Chaste Widow Wang 王節婦*:* Short Records of Models for Women *(*Nüfan jielu 《女範捷錄》*)*

男 王相 晉升 訂註

Proofreader and Commentator: Son Wang Xiang 王相 *(courtesy name: Jin Sheng* 晉升*)*[1]

先慈劉氏，江寧人，幼善屬文，先嚴集敬公之元配也。三十而先嚴卒，苦節六十年，壽九十歲。南宗伯王光復，大中丞鄭潛庵兩先生，皆旌其門。所著有《古今女鑑》，及《女範捷錄》行世。

My deceased mother Madame Liu 劉氏 was from Jiangning 江寧.[2] She had been talented in literary writing since she was quite young. She was the principal wife of my deceased father, Sir [Wang] Jijing 集敬公. When she was thirty years old, my father passed away. She safeguarded her chastity for sixty years. My mother enjoyed a long life of ninety years. Imperial officers, Sir Wang Guongfu 王光復, from the Ministry of Rituals,[3] and Sir Zheng Qianan 鄭潛庵, from the Ministry of Justice,[4] publicly commended her [on behalf of the imperial court].[5] She authored the *Gujin nü jian* 《古今女鑑》 (*Lessons for Women from the Ancient Times to the Present*) and *Nüfan jielu* 《女範捷錄》 (*Short Records of Models for Women*). Both are in circulation.

Commentaries and Annotations

1. Translator's annotation: Wang Xiang was the compiler of the *Four Books for Women*. He provided the first systematic commentary on these four books. Chaste Widow

Wang was Wang Xiang's mother. The exact dates of Chaste Widow Wang, also known as Liu Shi 劉氏 (Madame Liu), are unclear, but she lived in the sixteenth century during the Ming dynasty.

2. Translator's annotation: Jiangning is a town located in today's Nanjing 南京, in Jiangsu 江蘇 province of China.
3. Translator's annotation: *Nanzongbo* 南宗伯 (imperial officer of religious rites and ceremony) was a high-ranking official position in the Ming dynasty (1368–1644 CE). The person holding the position oversaw all the imperial court's religious rites, as well as the imperial family temple. The title of this position can be traced back to the Zhou dynasty (ca. 1046–256 BCE). See the *Zhouli* 《周禮》 (*Zhou Rituals*).
4. Translator's annotation: *Dazhongcheng* 大中丞 (imperial officer of inspection) was a high-ranking position in the Ming dynasty. The person holding this position served a monitoring function similar to that of the Department of Justice nowadays. The position reported directly to the emperor, oversaw reports from officials, and made recommendations for the promotion, censure, and firing of governmental officials. This system began in the Qin 秦 (221–206 BCE) and Han 漢 dynasties (206 BCE–220 CE), and the position was called *yushidafu* 御史大夫 during the Qin–Han periods. See Sima Qian, *Shiji* 《史記》 (*Historical Records*); and Ban Gu et al., *Hanshu* 《漢書》 (*Book of Han*).
5. Translator's annotation: In the Ming 明 (1368–1644 CE) and Qing 清 dynasties (1644–1911 CE), it was a common practice that widows known for their virtues and contributions to the public received imperial commendation. The recognized family would receive a decorated banner or plate engraved with the emperor's congratulatory words. Or, a pair of stone pillars and a gate engraved with the emperor's sayings would be erected at the family residence. The family was often exempt from taxes and labor.

【統論篇】

乾象乎陽，坤象乎陰，日月普兩儀之照。男正乎外，女正乎內，夫婦造萬化之端。五常之德著，而大本以敦，三綱之義明，而人倫以正。故修身者，齊家之要也，而立教者，明倫之本也。正家之道，禮謹於男女，養蒙之節，教始於飲食，幼而不教，長而失禮。在男猶可以尊師取友，以成其德。在女又何從擇善誠身，而格其非耶？是以教女之道，猶甚於男，而正內之儀，宜先乎外也。以銅為鑒，可正衣冠；以古為師，可端模範；能師古人，又何患德之不修，而家之不正哉！

I

Unifying Thesis (Tonglun pian 統論篇)

THE SIGN OF *qian* 乾 [☰] is *yang*; the sign of *kun* 坤 [☷] is *yin*. The Sun and the Moon are the universal reflections of the two signs.[1] Men's correct place is to govern the outer realm; women's correct place is to manage the inner realm. The relationship between a husband and a wife is the beginning of myriad transformations.[2]

When the five constant virtues (*wuchang* 五常) are established, the great foundation will flourish.[3] When the right meaning of the three bonds (*sangang* 三綱) is clearly understood, the human relations will be made correct.[4] Therefore, cultivating the person is essential to the right ordering of the family.[5] Establishing education is the very foundation of making human relations illuminating.[6]

The Dao/Way to rectify a family begins with prudently following the right rituals between men and women. Childhood education for boys and girls begins with teaching proper rituals of drinking and eating at mealtimes.[7] If children are not educated when they are young, they will be disrespectful and neglect rituals when they become adults. Men still can benefit from revering [good] teachers and selecting [good] friends to complete their virtues. Whence can women select good role models to make their persons sincere and to correct their mistakes?[8] Therefore, the way of educating women is even more important than the way of teaching men. The model of the correct inner realm should come before that of the external realm.[9]

A person who uses a bronze as a mirror can straighten her clothes and cap; a woman who uses history as her teacher can surely find worthy role models.[10] If she can take the ancients as her teachers, there is no reason she should be worried that her virtue is not cultivated or her household is not put in order!

Commentaries and Annotations

1. Wang Xiang's commentary: Qian *and* kun *are the forms of Heaven and Earth. The Sun and the Moon are the bodies of* yin *and* yang. *In between Heaven and Earth, wherever there is* yin, *there is* yang*; therefore, male and female are generated. Wherever there is a Sun, there is also a Moon; thus, day and night there are separated.* Yin *and* yang, *Sun and Moon, are the two modes of being.* Translator's annotation: *Qian, kun, yin*, and *yang* have been conceptual paradigms in Chinese consciousness since 600 BCE, or even earlier. Symbolically, *yin* (the yielding receptive paradigm or force) is represented by one divided line, whereas *yang* (the assertive active paradigm or force) is represented by one solid line. When the lines are tripled in various forms, we have the eight trigrams: *qian* 乾 (☰, Heaven), *kun* 坤 (☷, Earth), *li* 離 (☲, fire), *kan* 坎 (☵, water), *zhen* 震 (☳, thunder), *xun* 巽 (☴, wind), *dui* 兌 (☱, marsh), and *gen* 艮 (☶, mountain). The eight trigrams multiplied by eight generates the sixty-four hexagrams and forms the basis of the *Yijing* 《易經》 (*Classic of Changes*). Each hexagram is formed by six lines. The most fundamental hexagrams are *qian* (乾 ䷀) and *kun* (坤 ䷁); the rest are derived from these two. The opening sentence of the *Yijing*, part A, chapter 1, states: "The hexagram of *qian* symbolizes the origination of all things—it is everywhere without limit, beneficial to all beings, pure and without any blemish." Chapter 2 states: "the hexagram of *kun* represents the origin of all things and is present everywhere without limit. It benefits all things like the female horse with its virtue of purity.... It assists [*yang*] to accomplish kingly affairs but does not intend to claim credit for itself. It is the way of the Earth, of a wife, and of a minister." In addition, chapter 1 of the Xici 繫辭 ("Appendix Remarks") to *the Yijing* (*Classic of Changes*), a work traditionally attributed to Confucius, reads: "The Moon and the Sun rotate unceasingly.... The way of *qian* generates male; the way of *kun* generates female; *qian* is the great beginning of time, and *kun* the space that completes all things." Chapter 6 of the "Appendix Remarks" records: "*Qian* symbolizes things of *yang* nature; and *kun* symbolizes things of *yin* nature. When *yin* and *yang* embody the unifying virtue, the soft and the hard will manifest their orderly principles. When one relies on these principles, one will be able to understand the operation of Heaven and Earth and penetrate the bright virtue of spiritual transformation."

2. Wang Xiang's commentary: *Wherever there is male and female, the relation of husband and wife necessarily follows. If the way of the husband and the wife is cultivated, the ritual propriety of the inner and the outer realms will be rectified. Zisi* 子思 *says: "The way of a gentleman begins in the way of husband and wife." Cultivating the self and regulating the family are the foundation of education.* Translator's annotation: Zisi was a student of Confucius. The passage cited by Wang Xiang is from chapter 12 of the *Zhongyong* 《中庸》 (*Doctrine of the Mean*).
3. Wang Xiang's commentary: *Humaneness, righteousness, ritual propriety, wisdom, and trustworthiness are the five constant virtues (*wuchang 五常*). The virtue of the five constant virtues always resides in human hearts. If a person can cultivate and expand it, surely this is the basis of becoming a sage.* Translator's annotation: The phrase *wuchang* (five constant virtues) was coined by Dong Zhongshu 董仲舒 (c. 179–104 BCE), an influential Han Confucian scholar and a prime minister to Emperor Wu of Han 漢武帝 (r. 140–87 BCE). *Wuchang* is a part of Dong's cosmic *yinyang wuxing* 陰陽五行 topology that correlates the five elements with the order of the three realms (Heaven, Earth, and human). *Wuchang* corresponds, for instance, to the five classics (*wujing* 五經), five elements (*wuxing* 五行), and five human relations (*wulun* 五倫). *Wuchang* was discussed multiple times in Ban Gu's *Baihu tongyi* 《白虎通義》 (*Comprehensive Discussions in the White Tiger Hall*), allegedly the official record of an imperial conference on the Confucian classics convened in the first century.
4. Wang Xiang's commentary: *The ruler is the principle of the minister, the father is principle of the son, and the husband is the principle of the wife. If the ruler is righteous and the minister loyal, the father is caring and the son filial, and the relationship between husband and wife is harmonious and smooth, human relations will be correct.* Translator's annotation: The terms and the concepts of the "three bonds" (*sangang*) and the "five constant virtues" (*wuchang*) come from Dong Zhongshu's *Chunqiu fanlu* 《春秋繁露》 (*Luxuriant Dew of the Spring and Autumn Annals*).
5. *Xiu shen* 修身 is here translated as "cultivating the person" rather than "cultivating the body." In Chinese, *shen* 身 can be understood as simply referring to "the body," as in *shen xin* 身心 or as referring to the whole person as in *shen fen* 身分. Because this passage refers to *Daxue* (*Great Learning*), it is more appropriate to render *shen* as "person."
6. Wang Xiang's commentary: *The* Classic of Poetry *states: "If one desires to put family in order, one must cultivate one's person first." If the personal life is not cultivated, one cannot teach one's family. The relations between the ruler and the minister, the father and the son, the husband and the wife, the older brother and the younger brother, and a friend to a friend are the five human relations (*wulun 五倫*). The sage king Yao* 堯 *employed Qi* 契 *as the minister of education (*situ 司徒*) so that moral human relations could be taught: affection between the father and the son, righteousness between the ruler and the minister, distinct functions between husband and wife, proper order between the older and the younger, trustworthiness*

between friends and friends. If moral human relations are made clear to all, then all under Heaven will be in order. Therefore, promulgating education is the very foundation of making moral principles known to all. Translator's annotation: See the *Mencius* 3A:4 for the five human relations, and the *Daxue* (*Great Learning*) for the concentric eight-step process that stems from the personal to the familial, the social, and the political.

7. Wang Xiang's commentary: *The* Liji *(*Record of Rituals*) states that after boys and girls turn six years old, they should not sit together or eat together. Boys should have teachers from outside and girls should obey and respect women teachers' teaching. It also states that when the boys and girls begin to feed themselves, they should be taught to use their right hands. And, they should drink and eat only after the adults and the elderly have done so. Women teachers will teach them to be docile and diligent, to listen attentively, and be obedient. [When they begin to learn how to speak,] boys will reply with the word* wei *and the girls will reply with the word* yu. *Men will not talk to others about the affairs of the inner quarters. Women will not comment on the affairs of the external realm. Men walk on the left side of the road, and women walk on the right side.* Translator's annotation: The *Liji* exercised tremendous influence in Chinese society since its composition in probably the first century BCE. The book contains a total of forty-nine chapters. It codifies proper rituals in religious rites, marriage, education, and all aspects of proper behavior in the private, social, and political realms. The quotation cited by Wang Xiang is loosely adapted from the Neize 內則 chapter.
8. Wang Xiang's commentary: *The proper way to educate males and females should begin in childhood. If children are not properly taught, then they will grow up without knowing proper civil decorum. Males can still benefit from teachers and friends [outside the home] in correcting their mistakes. Females, however, live within the inner quarters. If they are not educated early on, when they grow up but do not have teachers for them to model after, they will be unable to differential what is morally good.* Translator's annotation: This is because children under age ten are taught by mothers or women relatives. After age ten, boys go to school outside of the household, whereas girls stay home and can continue their education only through the instruction of their mothers or women relatives. If their mothers pass away or if they do not have proper women teachers, it is very difficult for girls to receive further education.
9. Wang Xiang's commentary: *This passage says that teaching women is even more important than teaching men.*
10. Wang Xiang's commentary: *This passage explains the meaning of authoring this book for instructing women. If one uses a mirror to check one's appearance, one ensures that one's appearance and deportment are proper. If one uses histories as models, the sages and the worthy can certainly be one's teachers. Thus, the* Short Records of Models for Women *was composed.*

【后德篇】

鳳儀龍馬，聖帝之祥；麟趾關睢，后妃之德。是故帝嚳三妃，生稷契唐堯之聖。文王百子，紹姜任太姒之徽。溈汭二女，紹際唐虞之盛。塗莘雙后，肇開夏商之祥。宣王晚朝，姜后有待罪之諫。楚昭宴駕，越姬踐心許之言。明和嗣漢，史稱馬鄧之賢。高文興唐，內有竇孫之助。曁夫宋室之宣仁，可謂女中之堯舜。烏林盡節於世宗，弘吉加恩於宋后。高帝創洪基於草莽，實藉孝慈。文皇肅內治於宮闈，爰資仁孝。稽古興王之君，必有賢明之后，不亦信哉。

2

Queenly Virtues (Houde pian 后德篇)

THE APPEARANCE OF an elegant phoenix and the emergence of a dragon-like horse are the auspicious signs of sage-kings.[1] Linzhi 麟趾 and Guanju 關睢 speak about the virtues of empresses and royal consorts.[2]

Consequently, one notes that Emperor Ku's 帝嚳 three consorts gave birth to three sages: Ji 稷 [ancestor of Zhou dynasty], Xie 契 [ancestor of Shang dynasty], and Tang Yao 唐堯 [founder of Tang dynasty].[3] King Wen 文王 [of Zhou 周] had a hundred sons. This is due to the merits (*hui* 徽) of [Tai]jiang [太]姜 [King Wen's grandmother], Tairen [太]任 [King Wen's mother], and Taisi 太姒 [King Wen's wife].[4] Two ladies who lived where the rivers Gui and Rui merged continued the glorious reign of the Tang 唐–Yu 虞 periods.[5] Queen Tu 塗 and Queen Shen 莘 inaugurated the good fortune of the Xia 夏–Shang 商 dynasties.[6] King Xuan 宣王 [of Zhou] was often late for morning meetings with his ministers and officials. Queen Jiang 姜后 blamed herself [even though it is not her fault] and awaited her punishment, thus [indirectly] admonishing the king [and making him change his ways].[7] [King] Zhao of Chu 楚昭[王] passed away. Lady Yue 越姬 fulfilled the promise in her heart [following the king unto death].[8] Emperors

Ming 明 and He 和 [of Eastern/Later Han] were able to successfully carry on the Han lineage; historical records attributed this fact to Empresses Ma's 馬 and Deng's 鄧 virtues and abilities.[9] Emperors Gao[zu] 高[祖] and Wen [Huangdi] 文[皇帝] founded the prosperous Tang 唐 dynasty. Their accomplishments were due to the assistance of Empresses Dou 竇 and [Zhang]sun [長]孫 from within.[10] Similarly, Empress Xuanren 宣仁 of the Song 宋 dynasty was regarded as the female equivalent of sage-kings Yao 堯 and Shun 舜.[11] Lady Wulin 烏林 committed suicide to preserve her chastity for Emperor Shizong 世宗 [of Jin].[12] Empress Hongji 弘吉 [of Yuan] treated the Empress Dowager [of the defeated Southern Song] with grace and care.[13] Emperor Gao 高帝 founded the [Ming] empire following a peasant revolution. The credit should be attributed to Empress Xiaoci 孝慈.[14] Emperor Wen 文皇 [of Ming] rectified internal state matters by means of straightening affairs inside the palace. He relied on the help of Empress Renxiao[wen] 仁孝[文].[15]

Therefore, is it not simply true that since the ancient times all accomplished great emperors must have had wise empresses?[16]

Commentaries and Annotations

1. Wang Xiang's commentary: *When Shun 舜 was the king, the phoenix (*feng 鳳*) appeared in elegant deportment. During the period of legendary sage-king Fuxi 伏羲, the dragon-like horse (*longma 龍馬*) carried the diagram on its back. These are all auspicious signs of a sage-king's reign. This sentence reveals the meaning of texts that follow.* Translator's annotation: Both are mystical animals. The appearance of a phoenix and a dragon-like horse carrying a diagram (*tu* 圖) on its back in the [Yellow] River (*he* 河) were regarded as auspicious omens foretelling the coming of the sage-kings. Both images were mentioned in multiple Chinese ancient texts. For instance, in *Analects* 9.9, Confucius laments: "The phoenix has not come and the River has not issued its diagram. I am finished, am I not?" See also the *Shangshu* 《尚書》 (*Book of Documents*) and the *Liji* 《禮記》 (*Record of Rituals*). The diagram revealed on the back of a dragon-like horse was often interpreted as a symbol that inspired Fuxi's 伏羲 invention of the *Bagua* diagram 八卦圖. For an excellent in-depth discussion of the origin(s) of the river diagram (*hetu* 河圖) and its connection to the *Bagua* diagram and the *yin–yang* symbol, see Robin R. Wang, *Yinyang: The Way of Heaven and Earth in Chinese Thought and Culture* (New York: Cambridge University Press, 2012), 205–6.
2. Wang Xiang's commentary: *Linzhi 麟趾 and Guanju 關雎 are two poems in the* Shijing 《詩經》*) (*Classic of Poetry*), which praise the virtues of Taisi 太姒, queen-consort of King Wen of Zhou 文王. These poems speak about qilin 麒麟 [a mystical animal] whose feet will not step on fresh grass or live insects, an analogy for the benevolence of empresses and royal consorts. Jujiu 雎鳩 [i.e., ospreys] at birth already have*

their spouses selected. The two birds [throughout their lifetime] accompany each other intimately but not licentiously, a metaphor for the virtues of empresses and royal consorts. Translator's annotation: For more on Taisi's virtues, consult Liu Xiang's *Lienü zhuan* 《列女傳》 (*Biographies of Women*), volume 1, chapter 6; Wang Daokun's 汪道昆 *Wangshi ji lienü zhuan* 《汪氏輯列女傳》 (*Wangshi's Biographies of Women*), volume 1

3. Wang Xiang's commentary: 嚳 *pronounced as* 酷 (ku*);* 契 *as* 屑 *(*xie*). Emperor Ku's* 帝嚳 *first royal consort, Jiang Yuan* 姜嫄, *performed a ritual prayer to the god Mei* 禖 *for an offspring. She then gave birth to Ji* 稷. *Emperor Ku's second consort, Jian Di* 簡狄, *consumed an egg laid by a black swallow from the sky and gave birth to Xie* 契. *Emperor Ku's third consort, Qing Du* 慶都, *gave birth to Tang Yao* 唐堯 *after she carried him in the womb for fourteen months. All three ladies were courteous, frugal, compassionate, and good-natured. Therefore, their sons were also wise, illuminating, benevolent, and sagely.* 嫄 *pronounced as* 原 (yuan*);* 禖 *as* 梅 *(*mei*).* Translator's annotation: According to the Wudi Benji 五帝本紀 ("Annals of the Five Emperors"), in Sima Qian's 司馬遷 *Shiji* (*Historical Records*), Emperor Ku was the great grandson of the Yellow Emperor (Huangdi 黃帝). The Yellow Emperor and Emperors Ku, Ji, Xie, Yao, Shun 舜, and Yu 禹 were all legendary sage-rulers of ancient China. According to the *Liji*, chapter 6 (Yueling 月令), Mei was a god in charge of marriage and offspring. In the springtime, as a matter of state affairs, emperors and their spouses prepared sacrificial items and performed proper rituals to Mei for blessings to the royal family and continuation of their lineage.
4. Wang Xiang's commentary: 紹 (shao*) means "to continue";* 徽 *(*hui*) means "beauty or merits." The* Shijing *says: "Taisi carried on the good family name. She had a hundred sons." This is speaking about King Tai's wife Taijiang* 太姜, *King Wangji's wife Tairen* 太任, *and King Wen's wife Taisi* 太姒. *They were all humane, generous, compassionate, and filial. They inherited and built on the previous royal consorts' merits and each in turn gave birth to King Wangji* 王季, *King Wen* 文王, *and King Wu* 武王. *They embodied the [Zhou* 周 *] kingdom and extended the joy of a hundred sons.* Translator's annotation: For more information, consult Liu Xiang's *Biographies of Women*, volume 1, chapter 6; and Wang Daokun's *Wangshi's Biographies of Women*, volume 1.
5. Wang Xiang's commentary: 溈汭 *pronounced as* 圭芮 *(*gui rui*). Emperor Tang Yao knew that [Yu] Shun [a commoner known for his filial piety] possessed sagely virtues and therefore married his two daughters to Shun. Yao's two daughters lived with Shun at his humble residence where the rivers Gui and Rui convened. Erhuang* 娥皇 *and Nüying* 女英, *two princesses, were filial in serving their in-laws and conciliatory toward Shun in their wifely duties. Although they were the daughters of the emperor, the two princesses never acted arrogantly toward Shun or Shun's family. They were the daughters of Yao and wives of Shun; their father and husband were both sages. Thus, this is described as "the continuation of the glorious reign of the Tang-Yu periods."* Translator's annotation: Both Yao 堯 and Shun 舜 were legendary sage-rulers of ancient China.

They are two of the five emperors recorded in Sima Qian's *Shiji* (*Historical Records*), "Annals of the Five Emperors." Their stories are well known to the Chinese. Shun is often regarded as the paradigm of filial piety. Although he was severely abused by his father, stepmother, and stepbrother, he always acted filially toward his parents and respectfully toward his stepbrother. Yao married his two daughters to Shun to observe Shun's virtues and to determine Shun's suitability in running the state. For Shun's virtuous wives, Erhuang and Nüying, see Liu Xiang's *Biographies of Women*, volume 1, chapter 1; and Wang Daokun's *Wangshi's Biographies of Women*, volume 1.

6. Wang Xiang's commentary: *Royal consort Tushanshi* 塗山氏 *was married to Emperor Yu of Xia* 夏禹 *for only four days when Yu needed to attend to the state affairs in managing the flood. Yu did not return home for eight years. Lady Tushanshi was skilled in raising and teaching their son Qi* 啟. *Qi was a wise ruler, who governed the country with sincerity and respect. Royal consort Youshenshi* 有莘氏 *of Emperor Tang* 湯 *[of Shang* 商 *] was prudent, courteous, sincere, conciliatory, composed, reverential, and wise. Both were adept in founding the countries and in managing the households so as to inaugurate the reigns of the Xia and Shang dynasties.* Translator's annotation: For more information, see Liu Xiang's *Biographies of Women*, volume 1, chapters 4 and 5; and Wang Daokun's *Wangshi's Biographies of Women*, volume 1.
7. Wang Xiang's commentary: *King Xuan of Zhou* 周宣王 *was often late in holding the morning court with his ministers and governmental officials. Queen Jiang* 姜后 *took off her hairpins, earrings, and accessories, and awaited punishment at the inner quarters of the imperial palace (*yong xiang 永巷*). Because of her admonition, King Xuan became diligent in state affairs.* Translator's annotation: Queen Jiang's approach is the *yin* strategy in advising the emperor—an indirect and less confrontational way to express the disapproval of someone who is higher in rank and position. For more information, see Liu Xiang's *Biographies of Women*, volume 2, chapter 1; and Wang Daokun's *Wangshi's Biographies of Women*, volume 1. *Yong xiang* was the imperial residence quarters in feudal China, strictly reserved for the consorts of kings and emperors and their servants. A separate group of administrators, a court, and a prison were set up for residents of *yong xiang*.
8. Wang Xiang's commentary: Yanjia 晏駕 *means "passing away of an emperor" (*hong 薨*). King Zhao [of Chu]* 楚昭王 *was on an outing with his royal consorts. When they were enjoying their time together, Emperor Zhao asked: "If I died, would any of you follow me to the underworld?" All the consorts said that they would, except Lady Yue, who was silent. Later, Emperor Zhao died in a military expedition, but while none of the consorts would follow, Lady Yue said: "In the past, I did not verbally consent only because I did not wish to die with the emperor for his fondness of pleasure. But in my heart, I had nonetheless given my promise. Nowadays the emperor died in the army in serving his country, how could I not keep my promise?" Thereupon, she died with the emperor.* Translator's annotation: See Liu Xiang's *Biographies of Women*, volume 5, chapter. 4; and Wang Daokun's *Wangshi's Biographies of Women*, volume 3.

9. Wang Xiang's commentary: *Empress Ma* 馬皇后, *consort of Emperor Ming of Han* 漢明帝, *and Empress Deng* 鄧皇后, *consort of Emperor He* 和帝, *were virtuous, bright, courteous, frugal, benevolent, generous, and loved the people. Therefore, the Eastern Han dynasty* 東漢 *became well governed.* Translator's annotation: Both empresses were also known for their love of learning, knowledge of the classics, and dislike of extravagance. Empress Ma was also known by her posthumous title, Empress Mingde 明德皇后, meaning "bright virtue". She was unable to bear a son, but encouraged without jealousy other royal consorts to bear children to extend the royal lineage. She was also known for her integrity. She advised her husband against nepotism, especially rejecting any special treatment for her maternal relatives. Empress Deng 鄧皇后 (also known as Empress Hexi 和熹皇后, meaning "harmonious happiness") also did not bear any children. Known for her frugality, intelligence, skills in government, and advocacy of education and scholarship, she summoned many intellectuals including Ban Zhao (the author of *Lessons for Women*) to the imperial court to give lessons to governmental officials and members of the royal family. After her husband passed away, she became the regent of China as the empress dowager of the newly enthroned Emperor An 安帝, who was only thirteen years old at the time. In a traditional patriarchal society, Deng's regency was quite controversial. It is interesting that Madame Liu still cited her here as a role model for women. For more about Empress Ma, see Liu Xiang's *Biographies of Women*, volume 8, chapter 19. For more about both empresses, see Fan Ye's *Houhanshu* 《後漢書》 (*Book of Later Han*), Houji 后紀 ("Biographies of Empresses"); and Wang Daokun's *Wangshi's Biographies of Women*, volume 4.
10. Wang Xiang's commentary: *Empress Dou* 竇皇后, *consort of Emperor Gaozu* 唐高祖 *of Tang, and Empress Zhangsun* 長孫皇后, *consort of Emperor Taizong* 太宗, *gave good advice to the two emperors and assisted them in establishing the Tang empire. Empress Zhangsun was especially virtuous. She provided Taizong with good recommendations and admonitions. Emperor Taizong was always pleased to accept them.* Translator's annotation: Emperor Taizong was also known as Wen Huangdi 文皇帝. His wife, Zhangsun, authored *Nüze* 《女則》 (*Regulations for Women*). For more on these two empresses, see volume 51 of Liu Xu's *Jiutangshu* 《舊唐書》 (*Old Book of Tang*).
11. Wang Xiang's commentary: *Empress Dowager Xuanren Gao Taihou* 宣仁高太后, *consort of Emperor Yingzong of Song* 宋英宗, *supported her grandson Child-Emperor Zhezong* 哲宗. *She held court alongside him by sitting behind a lowered screen (*chui lian ting zheng 垂簾聽政*). She employed only the virtuous and the worthy. She warded off the flatterers and trusted men with integrity. Political corruption and crooked policies were eradicated. She was regarded by history as a female sage-ruler like Yao and Shun (*nü zhong Yao Shun 女中堯舜*).* Translator's annotation: Empress Xuanren 宣仁皇后 (also known with her maiden name as Empress Gao 高皇后 of the Northern Song dynasty 北宋) was the wife of Emperor Yingzong 英宗 and

the mother of Emperor Shenzong 神宗. When Emperor Shenzong passed away, his son (Emperor Zhezong 哲宗) was only ten years old. Before his death, Emperor Shenzong issued an imperial edict appointing his mother as the regent in order to assist the underage Emperor Zhezong. For more information, see Tuo Tuo et al.'s *Songshi* 《宋史》 (*History of Song*).

12. Wang Xiang's commentary: *Lord Liang of the Jin dynasty* 金主亮 *[also known as King Hailinyang* 海陵煬王 *] was a depraved man who forced sexual intercourse on many women of his clan. Lady Wulin* 鳥林, *queen-consort of King Ge* 葛王, *would not yield. She hung herself inside the carriage sent by Liang. King Ge later became Emperor Shizong* 世宗. *In honoring her, he never appointed another woman as his empress.* Translator's annotation: *Lady Wulin* was bestowed the title Empress Zhaode 昭德皇后 posthumously. For more information, consult Tuo Tuo et al.'s *Jinshi* 《金史》 (*History of Jin*).
13. Wang Xiang's commentary: *The Southern Song dynasty* 南宋 *surrendered to the Yuan dynasty* 元. *Empress Dowager Xie* 太后謝氏 *[of Southern Song] went to Yuan [as a political prisoner]. Empress Hongji* 弘吉氏, *consort of Emperor Shizu of Yuan* 元世祖, *treated Empress Dowager Xie like a sister, with great kindness and respect.* Translator's annotation: Emperor Shizu of Yuan (r. 1271–1294 CE) is also known as Kublai Khan, or Qubilai Qaγan, the fifth ruler of the Mongol empire, who also founded the Yuan dynasty in China. The Yuan dynasty (1271–1368 CE) is the only Chinese dynasty established by the Mongols. For more information, see Song Lian's *Yuanshi* 《元史》 (*History of Yuan*).
14. Wang Xiang's commentary: *Empress Xiaoci* 孝慈皇后 *(Madame Ma* 馬氏*), consort of Emperor Gao of the Ming dynasty, rose from the peasant class. She knew first hand the hardships faced by the citizens. She advised Taizu* 太祖 *[Emperor Gao] to be frugal and to love the people—to be generous, humane, and caring. Taizu had twenty-some sons borne by his other consorts; Empress Xaoci treated them as her own sons.* Translator's annotation: Emperor Gao [Gaodi 高帝] of Ming refers to Zhu Yuanzhang 朱元璋, also known as the Hongwu Emperor 洪武皇帝 or Ming Taizu 明太祖, who founded the Ming empire. Zhu was born and raised in a poor farming family. In his teens, his family died as a result of severe famine. In destitution, Zhu became a Buddhist novice monk and even a beggar. Later he joined an insurgent force against the Mongol-led Yuan dynasty's rule. He rose to power as a leader of the insurgent forces during the late period of Yuan (c. mid-fourteenth century), when the dynasty suffered political and social turmoil that resulted from famines, plaques, and peasant revolts. Empress Xiaoci, also known as Empress Ma (not to be confused with Empress Ma of Eastern Han), was known for her frugality and virtue. For more information, see Zhang Tingyu, *Mingshi* 《明史》 (*History of Ming*), volume 1; and Empress Renxiaowen's description of her mother-in-law (Empress Xiaoci) in her preface to *Neixun* (*Teaching for the Inner Court*), included in this volume.

15. Wang Xiang's commentary: *Empress Renxiaowen* 仁孝文皇后 *(Madame Xu* 徐氏*), consort of Emperor Chengzu* 成祖, *was the daughter of Vassal King Zhongshan, Xuda* 徐達. *Her temperament was humane, empathetic, filial, and respectful. She authored the* Neixun 《內訓》 *(*Teachings for the Inner Court*), which consisted of twenty chapters designed to teach princesses and daughters of both officers and the populace.* Translator's annotation: Emperor Wen (r. 1402–1424), also known as Emperor Chengzu of Ming (Ming Chengzu 明成祖) or Emperor Yongle (Yongle Di 永樂帝), was the third emperor of the Ming dynasty. His reign was historically called the "Yongle Prosperity" (Yongle shengshi 永樂盛世). The *Neixun* authored by his consort, Empress Renxiaowen, was one of the *Four Books for Women*. For more information, see the translator's introduction to *Neixun* in book III, this volume.
16. Wang Xiang's commentary: *This sentence is stating that any emperor who had founded a country necessarily had a virtuous wise empress who completed the governance of internal affairs.*

【母儀篇】

父天母地，天施地生。骨氣像父，性氣像母。上古賢明之女有娠，胎教之方必慎。故母儀先於父訓，慈教嚴於義方。是以孟母買肉以明信，陶母封鮓以教廉。和熊知苦，柳氏以興。畫荻為書，歐陽以顯。子發為將，自奉厚而卹下薄，母拒戶而責其無恩。王孫從君，主失亡而已獨歸，母倚閭而言其不義。不疑尹京，寬刑活眾，賢哉慈母之仁。田稷為相，反金待罪，卓矣孀親之訓。景讓失士心，母撻之而部下安。延年多殺戮，母惡之而終不免。柴繼母舍己子而代前兒，程祿妻甘己罪而免孤女。程母之教，恕於僕妾，而嚴於諸子。尹母之訓，樂於菽水，而忘於祿養。是皆秉坤儀之淑訓者，母德之徽音者也。

3

Model Motherhood (Muyi pian 母儀篇)

FATHER IS LIKE Heaven; mother is like Earth.[1] Heaven blesses and Earth begets.[2] The physical-psycho energy of one's bones (*guqi* 骨氣) resembles the father; the physical-psycho energy of one's nature (*xingqi* 性氣) resembles the mother.[3] Since antiquity, it was always the case that when virtuous wise women were expecting a child, prenatal education was carefully considered and executed.[4] Therefore, a mother's virtuous models precede a father's instructions. The teaching of a mother should be even stricter than [a father's lessons on] moral rightness.[5]

Therefore, [in the Warring States period,] Mencius's mother 孟母 purchased meat to teach Mencius trustworthiness.[6] Tao [Kan]'s mother 陶[侃]母 [of the Jin 晉 dynasty] sealed and returned the fish to teach her son incorruption.[7] Madame Liu 柳氏 [of the Tang 唐 dynasty] blended ground powder from a bear's bile into pills to teach hardship; the Liu family thus became prosperous.[8] Madame Ouyang 歐陽 [of the Song 宋 dynasty] used giant reeds to write book lessons [on the ground to educate her son]; her son later became accomplished.[9] Zifa 子發 was a general. He treated himself generously but was stingy toward his subordinates. His mother refused to let him come into the house and scolded him for being an uncaring leader.[10] Wang Sun [Jia] 王孫 [賈] followed King [Min of Qi 齊湣王]. The king was killed during his exile. Wang Sun [Jia] returned home by himself. His mother, waiting for him at the village gate, reproached him for being unrighteous.[11] [Han 漢] Official [Juan] Buyi [雋] 不疑 was the governor of the capital city. Lenient in punishment, he released many prisoners. Wise was his compassionate mother's humaneness![12] Tian Ji 田稷 was a prime minister [of Qi]. He returned the bribery of gold and beseeched his punishment. Remarkable was his mother's teaching.[13] [Li] Jingrang 李景讓 [of the Tang dynasty] lost his repute with his soldiers. Li's mother punished him in court with a beating. Her action calmed Li's subordinates.[14] [Yan] Yannian [嚴] 延年 [of Han] executed many people. His mother was appalled by his cruelty. She predicted that his end was inevitable.[15] A stepmother Cai 柴繼母 was willing to sacrifice the life of her natural son in order to save her stepson's life.[16] Cheng Lu's wife 程祿妻 was willing to take the blame and receive punishment in order to save the life of her orphaned stepdaughter.[17] The teaching of Cheng brothers' mother 程母 was to be kind with servants and concubines but strict with sons.[18] Yin [Tun]'s mother 尹[焞]母 taught a lesson about being content with simple fare, like beans and water, and forgetting about lavish lodging.[19]

These are women who upheld the virtuous lessons of the *kun* 坤 model and promulgated the beautiful sounds of motherly virtues!

Commentaries and Annotations

1. Wang Xiang's commentary: Qian 乾 *is the Way of father.* Kun 坤 *is the Way of mother.* Translator's annotation: For more on the meaning of *qian* and *kun* in Chinese cosmology and hexagrams, see chapter 1, "Unifying Thesis."
2. Wang Xiang's commentary: *Heaven blesses with rain and dew. Earth begets myriad things.*
3. Wang Xiang's commentary: *The physical-psycho energy of the bones controls one's will; the physical-psycho energy of one's nature controls one's emotions. The will is the* yang *energy and emotions are the* yin *energy. Each follows the essence of its kind.* Translator's annotation: *Qi* 氣 is translated here as physical-psycho energy. To preserve the texture of the original phrases, I have opted to translate *guqi* (骨氣) literally as physical-psycho energy of the bones, rather than as one's willpower, and *xingqi* (性氣) as physical-psycho energy of one's nature, rather than as one's emotive energy.
4. Wang Xiang's commentary: *The* Liji *(*Record of Rituals*) says: "In ancient times when women were expecting a child, they necessarily attended to prenatal education.*

*They would not lean on one foot when standing. They walked with composure. They would not sit if the seating mats were not positioned straight, nor eat any meat not cut straight, nor look at any immoral sights, nor listen to any wicked sounds, nor eat anything with a strange taste. At night, they requested blind musician(s) (*guzhe 瞽者*) to cite the* Shijing *(*Classic of Poetry*) and the* Shangshu *(*Book of Documents*) and to discuss rituals and music with them. As a result, when these women gave birth, the forms and appearances of their sons and daughters were in harmonious proportions and their ability and intelligence surpassed others."* Translator's annotation: Prenatal education was essential in Confucian philosophy of education. However, no direct discussion of prenatal education (*tai jiao* 胎教) was found in the *Liji* (i.e., *Xiaodai liji* 《小戴禮記》). Nonetheless, the volume named Baofu 保傅 ("Female Caregiver and Governess") in the *Dadai liji* 《大戴禮記》 did present a preliminary concept and used the phrase "prenatal education" (*tai jiao* 胎教). The closest resembling texts to Wang Xiang's commentary are from Liu Xiang's *Biographies of Women* (c. 100 BCE), volume 1, chapter 6; and Madame Zheng's *Fililal Piety for Women* (c. 700 CE). In several medical texts, including the *Huangdi neijing* 《黃帝內經》 (*Yellow Emperor's Inner Canon*), dated two millennia ago, there were careful instructions on how an expecting mother should take care of her body during each month of the gestational period to ensure a healthy pregnancy.

5. Wang Xiang's commentary: *In educating children, if mothers' teaching by examples is understood, children will then be able to abide by the moral principles taught by their fathers.*
6. Wang Xiang's commentary: *When Mencius was young, he lived near a slaughterhouse. He asked his mother: "Why are they killing the pigs?" Mencius's mother jokingly replied: "They want to give you pork to eat." Afterwards, Mencius's mother regretted what she said: "To joke with a child like this is to teach him untrustworthiness." Thereupon, she pawned her hairpin and earrings to buy pork to illustrate good faith.* Translator's annotation: See Han Ying's *Hanshi waizhuan* 《韓詩外傳》 (*Outer Commentary to the* Classic of Poetry *by Master Han*), volume 9, chapter 1.
7. Wang Xiang's commentary: *Tao Kan* 陶侃 *of the Jin* 晉 *dynasty was a state inspector of fisheries. He sent a fish to his mother as a gift. His mother sealed the package and sent it back to him with a note: "You are a state inspector. You however used this governmental good as a private gift to your relative. This is a violation of integrity and the law." Kan was moved by his mother's reproof. He later became a renowned official.* Translator's annotation: See Wang Daokun, *Wangshi's Biographies of Women*, volume 6; and Fang Xuanling, *Jinshu* 《晉書》 (*Book of Jin*).
8. Wang Xiang's commentary: *Lady Han* 韓夫人, *wife of Liu Gongchuo* 柳公綽 *[of the Tang dynasty], blended ground power made from a bear's bile into pills. She commanded her son and nephew to hold the pills in their mouths during their study to develop their will and perseverance in hardship.* Translator's annotation: This anecdote plays on the meaning of the word *ku* 苦, which means "bitter taste"

or "hardship." According to ancient Chinese texts such as Li Shizhen's *Bencao gangmu* 《本草綱目》 (*Compendium of Materia Medica*), bear's bile tastes bitter. Lady Han utilized the physical taste of bitterness to induce the mental readiness for hardship in her son and nephew.

9. Wang Xiang's commentary: *Ouyang Xiu* 歐陽修 *[of the Song dynasty] grew up in poverty when he was young. His mother used a giant reed to write lessons on the ground to teach him how to read.*

10. Wang Xiang's commentary: *Zifa* 子發 *was a general of the Chu state during the Warring States period. He came home to see his mother. His mother locked the door and would not let him come in the house. She scolded him: "You are a grand general of an army. You fed yourself with delicious meat but starved your lieutenants and soldiers with beans. This is acting like a tyrant without showing care for those who are under you. This kind of behavior will necessarily bring defeat in battles and shame to your country. I do not have a son like you." Zifa repented his faults. Since then, he was one with his troops in both good times and hardship. His lieutenants and soldiers were very pleased with him.* Translator's annotation: See Liu Xiang's *Biographies of Women*, volume 1, chapter 10; and Wang Daokun's *Wangshi's Biographies of Women*, volume 4.

11. Wang Xiang's commentary: *Wang Sunjia* 王孫賈 *followed King Min of Qi* 齊湣王 *into exile. He lost the king and returned home by himself. His mother said: "When you left home in the morning but did not return home, I waited and looked for you at the front door. When you left home in the evening but did not return home, I waited for you at the village gate. Today you followed the king into his exile but now you do not know his whereabouts. How can this behavior be called righteous?" Thereupon, Wang Sunjia left the house [to look for the king]. Knowing that the king was murdered, he went to the city and organized the people into an army. They killed the traitor who murdered the king and enthroned the king's son as King Xiang* 襄王. Translator's annotation: See Liu Xiang's *Biographies of Women*, volume 8, chapter 4; and Wang Daokun's *Wangshi's Biographies of Women*, volume 1.

12. Wang Xiang's commentary: *Han official Juan Buyi* 雋不疑 *was the governor of the capital city [Changan]. When he gave sentences for punishment, if many were punished, his mother would be angry and would abstain from food. If many were alive, she would be full of joy. Therefore, when Buyi was the governor, he was humane and not cruel. He respectfully obeyed his mother's teaching.* Translator's annotation: See Liu Xiang's *Biographies of Women*, volume 8, chapter 8; and Wang Daokun's *Wangshi's Biographies of Women*, volume 5.

13. Wang Xiang's commentary: *Tian Ji* 田稷 *was the prime minister of Qi. He accepted a bribe of gold from his subordinates and gave the gold to his mother. His mother returned the gold to him and chastised him for being greedy. Tian Ji thereupon went to see the king and asked for punishment. King [Xuan of Qi] forgave him. Tian Ji later became a virtuous wise minister.* Translator's annotation: See Liu Xiang's *Biographies of

Women, volume 1, chapter 14; and Wang Daokun's *Wangshi's Biographies of Women*, volume 1.

14. Wang Xiang's commentary: *Li Jingrang* 李景讓 *of the Tang dynasty was a high-ranking military official at the border (jiedushi* 節度使*). He had a very strict temperament. A plan of revolt was simmering among his lieutenants and officers. His mother Madame Zheng* 鄭氏 *held court and punished him with a beating. His lieutenants and officers pleaded with Madame Zheng to spare him. The frontier thus gained peace and Li later became a wise general.* Translator's annotation: For more information, see Ouyang Xiu, *Xintangshu* 《新唐書》 (*New Book of Tang*).
15. Wang Xiang's commentary: *Yan Yannian* 嚴延年 *was a prefect of the Henan province during the Han dynasty. His mother had five sons; all of them held prefect positions. People called her Madame Wanshi* 萬石夫人. *When she traveled by the Henan province, it happened to be the time that Yannian was giving sentences for punishment. Many people were executed. It formed pools of blood. Yannian's mother was infuriated: "People's lives are serious matters. Why do you act with such cruelty? Danger is imminent." Thereupon, she refused to enter the city. Yannian was later indeed executed.* Translator's annotation: See Ban Gu et al., *Hanshu* 《漢書》 (*Book of Han*); Liu Xiang's *Biographies of Women*, volume 8, chapter 11; and Wang Daokun's *Wangshi's Biographies of Women*, volume 5.
16. Wang Xiang's commentary: *During the reign of King Xuan of Qi* 齊宣王, *a man was killed. Two brothers were next to the dead man. The older brother said: "I killed the man." The younger brother said: "I killed the man." King Xuan was unable to determine who was telling the truth. He asked their mother. Their mother said: "Punish the younger man." King Xuan asked: "Isn't the younger man your son?" The mother replied: "The younger man is my biological son. The older one is my stepson from my husband's former wife. I really do not know who killed the man. But if the older son died, I would be forsaking the promise I made to my husband and abandoning the orphaned son from his former wife." The king valued her integrity and forgave the punishment.* Translator's annotation: See Liu Xiang's *Biographies of Women*, volume 5, chapter 8; and Wang Daokun's *Wangshi's Biographies of Women*, volume 2.
17. Wang Xiang's commentary: *Madame Wang* 王氏 *was the second wife of a military official of Yazhou* 崖州 *in Nanqi* 南齊. *Her husband passed away. She was returning home with her young son and stepdaughter to arrange the funeral. Madame Wang made a bracelet with big pearls for her stepdaughter to wear. At the time, the law against smuggling pearls was very strict. If a person did not pay taxes and smuggled pearls across the border, the person would be punished by death. Her stepdaughter thus threw away the pearls. But her young son unknowingly picked up the pearls and put them inside the cosmetic case. Neither the stepmother nor the stepdaughter knew about this. When they were crossing the border, the inspector found the hidden pearls. According to the law, the death penalty should be applied. The inspector asked: "Who should receive the punishment?" The stepmother replied: "I love the pearls. Punish*

me." The stepdaughter said: "My stepmother already threw away the pearls. It is I who secretly took them back. Punish me." Both the stepmother and stepdaughter wailed at the court, fighting to die. The inspector investigated the reasons and spoke in awe: "Wise is the stepmother! Filial is the daughter!" Thereupon, he released them. Translator's annotation: This story is based on Liu Xiang's *Biographies of Women*, volume 5, chapter 13; and Wang Daokun's *Wangshi's Biographies of Women*, volume 5.

18. Wang Xiang's commentary: *Madame Hou* 侯氏 *was the mother of two Song scholars, the Cheng* 程 *brothers. She was stern in teaching them. Even when small faults were committed, she made sure to have their father correct them. She often said: "If a father does not know the faults of his sons, it is because their mother spoils her sons and conceals their faults." Therefore, in teaching her sons she was strict, while following ritual propriety. In treating servants and concubines, she was always kind and gracious and never used any corporeal punishment on them. Her two sons, Sir Mingdao* 明道 *and Sir Yichuan* 伊川, *following their mother's teaching, later all became great Confucian scholars.* Translator's annotation: See Wang Daokun's *Wangshi's Biographies of Women*, volume 11. The two "Cheng brothers" refers to Cheng Hao 程顥 (Sir Mingdao 明道先生, 1032–1085), and Cheng Yi 程頤 (Sir Yichuan 伊川先生, 1033–1107). Both were renowned Song Neo-Confucian philosophers and educators.

19. Wang Xiang's commentary: *Madame Chen* 陳氏, *mother of Sir He Jing* 和靖先生 *(i.e., Yin Tun* 尹焞*) of the Song dynasty, taught him that "In learning, if one does not strive to reach the highest point, it is as if one toils in plowing the field but does not persist to the harvest time. Thus, a person should not quit in the middle of the process." In the beginning of the Shaosheng* 紹聖 *period, Yin Tun took the national magistrates' examination. At the time, the two Cheng brothers' teachings were banned. Tun left without finishing his test. When he returned home, he told his mother what he did. His mother responded: "I prefer being provided with beans and water* (shushui zhiyang 菽水之養*) to being supported by you with an officer's position." Sir Yichuan sighed in admiration and said: "Only a mother like this can give birth to a son of such caliber!"* Translator's annotation: The two Cheng brothers were renowned Neo-Confucian scholars, as stated in the previous note. Yin Tun 尹焞 (1071–1142) was a prized student of Cheng Yi (i.e., Sir Yichuan). Tun's act of not finishing the test was a gesture of respect to his teacher. Because of his knowledge and talents, later in his life Yin Tun was called to serve at various governmental posts. *Shushui zhiyang* 菽水之養 ("providing parents with only beans and water") is a phrase often used to describe filial acts of sons and daughters in poor families. Confucius used this phrase in his discussion of filial piety with his student Zilu. Zilu felt sad for the poor, saying "While [their parents] are alive, they have no means to nourish them; and when they are dead, they have no means to carry out the mourning rites for their parents." Confucius replied, "Providing bean soup for them to sip and water

to drink while the parents are made happy may be called filial piety. If one could only wrap the body of deceased parents from head to foot and bury it immediately without a [coffin], that being all what one's means can allow, one may be said to have fulfilled the rites of mourning." Confucius's emphasis is that sincerity is more important than providing material comfort in filial acts. See the *Liji* (*Record of Rituals*), Tangongxia 檀弓下 chapter.

【孝行篇】

男女雖異，劬勞則均。子媳雖殊，孝敬則一。夫孝者，百行之源，而猶為女德之首也。是故楊香搤虎，知有父而不知有身。緹縈贖親，則生男而不如生女。張婦蒙冤，三年不雨。姜妻至孝，雙鯉湧泉。唐氏乳姑，而毓山南之貴胤。盧氏冒刃，而全垂白之孀慈。劉氏醫姑之蛆，刺臂斬指，和血以丸藥。聞氏舐姑之目，斷髮矢志，負土以成墳。陳氏方於于歸，而夫卒於戍，力養其姑五十年。張氏當雷擊，而恐驚其姑，更延厥壽三十載。趙氏手戮讐於都亭以報父，娟女躬操舟於晉水以活親。曹娥抱父屍於盱江，木蘭代父征於絕塞。張女割肝，以蘇祖母之命。陳氏斷首，兩全夫父之生。是皆感天地，動神明，著孝烈於一時，播芳名於千載者也，可不勉歟。

4

Filial Conduct *(*Xiaoxing pian 孝行篇*)*

ALTHOUGH THERE IS a distinction between males and females, there is no difference in the amount of labor that parents have taken in raising them.[1] Although there are differences between a son and a daughter-in-law, the way they should care for, and revere, their parents and parents-in-law should be the same.[2] Filialness is the life-spring of all good deeds and it is the head of all womanly virtues.[3]

Therefore, Yang Xiang 楊香 choked a tiger—she knew only to save her father but forgot about her own safety.[4] Tiying 緹縈 offered to become a slave-servant in exchange for the release of her father from debilitating corporeal punishment. Thus, it is said: having a son is not as good as having a daughter.[5] Madame Zhang 張婦 was wrongly executed. In the town where the execution took place, it did not rain for three years.[6] Jiang [Shi]'s wife 姜 [詩] 妻 [i.e., Madame Pang 龐氏]

was exemplarily filial toward her mother-in-law, who liked the taste of freshwater fish. Pang labored to catch fish at the local river. One day, two carp suddenly emerged from a spring in their yard [and continued to appear each day].[7] Madame Tang 唐氏 breastfed her aging mother-in-law [who had no teeth for food]. Tang's action instilled filial piety in her grandson [Cui] Shannan [崔]山南, which later enabled him to earn a prestigious official position.[8] Madame Lu 盧氏 courageously risked her own life to protect her mother-in-law's life.[9] [To cure the infection,] Madame Liu 劉氏 gnawed on the maggots that grew out of her mother-in-law's wounds. [To make the medicine more potent,] she pierced her arms and cut her fingers to blend her blood with the medicine to cure her mother-in-law.[10] Madame Wen 聞氏 licked the eyes of her mother-in-law [to treat her eye illness], cut her hair to uphold her will [of chastity], and dug a burial site to bury her mother-in-law [because they were poor and could not afford to hire a worker].[11] Madame Chen 陳氏 was just married to her husband (*yugui* 于歸).[12] Shortly, he died during a military expedition. Without hesitation, Chen cared for her mother-in-law for fifty years.[13] Madame Zhang 張氏 was to be struck [to death] by lightning. She was worried that the thunder and the lightning would startle her mother-in-law. [Knowing her impending death was inevitable, she went outside to wait for the lightning to strike.] Because of her filial deeds, her life was extended for another thirty years.[14] Madame Zhao 趙氏 killed the murderer at Duting to revenge her father's death.[15] Young girl Juan 娟女 operated the boat on the River Jin [in her father's stead], thus saving his life.[16] Caoe 曹娥 held tight to her deceased father's body in the Gan River.[17] Mulan 木蘭 took her father's place in a military expedition to the northern borders.[18] Young woman Zhang 張女 severed part of her liver in order to save her grandmother from grave illness.[19] Madame Chen 陳氏 was beheaded to save the lives of her husband and father.[20]

These are all examples that moved Heaven and Earth, gods and spirits. These women's filial acts were well known at their time; their names were passed on for thousands of years in history. How can one not be motivated by them?

Commentaries and Annotations

1. Wang Xiang's commentary: *This comments on the fact that although people are born with the distinction of [being] a male or a female, the loving care that parents give in raising and educating their children is the same.*
2. Wang Xiang's commentary: *Sons and daughters are biological children. Daughters-in-laws are results of marriage unions. Even though they are from different origins, the way to serve one's parents and parents-in-law and the rituals of showing filial piety and reverence to them are the same.*

3. Wang Xiang's commentary: *Speaking about the beginning of all that is good, there is nothing prior to filial piety. For this reason, filial piety is regarded as the life-spring of all good deeds. Among women's obligations, there is nothing more important than filial piety. Thus, filial piety is the foremost of all womanly virtues.* Translator's annotation: The importance of filial piety is a constant theme in Confucian classics; for example, *Analects* 1.2 states "Filial piety and fraternal duty—surely they are the roots of humaneness," and the *Xiaojing* (*Classic of Filial Piety*), chapter 1, reads "Filial piety is the foundation of all virtues." Female virtues (*nüde* 女德) and women's virtue (*fude* 婦德) are used interchangeably: it is one of the four areas of the "four [womanly] virtues" (*side* 四德).
4. Wang Xiang's commentary: *Yang Xiang* 楊香 *was the daughter of Yang Feng* 楊豐, *a farmer during the Jin dynasty. She was only fourteen years old when a tiger attacked her father while he was farming the field. Xiang jumped forward, choking the tiger by the neck. The tiger was startled and ran away. Her father's life was spared. How is it possible for a young girl to overcome a tiger? It is only because she was desperate in saving her father's life. She only thought about her father and forgot about her own life.* Translator's annotation: For more information, see Wang Daokun's *Wangshi's Biographies of Women*, volume 6. The story about Yang Xiang is also included in Guo Jujing's *Ershisi Xiao* 《二十四孝》 (*Twenty-Four Exemplars of Filial Piety*), a popular work produced during the Yuan dynasty (1271–1368 CE).
5. Wang Xiang's commentary: *Chun Yuyi* 淳于意 *was the head of the state granary (*taichanglin 太倉令*) in the Han dynasty. He was accused of crimes and was to receive severe punishment. He had five daughters but had no son. When he was about to depart, he lamented: "Having daughters, but no sons, is no help when emergency strikes." His youngest daughter, Tiying* 緹縈, *was saddened by what she heard. She accompanied her father to the capital city and wrote a letter to the emperor stating that she was willing to be a slave-servant at an aristocratic household in exchange for her father's release. Emperor Wendi* 文帝 *[of Han] commended her filial piety, and forgave the sentence. He also consequently abolished corporeal punishment (*rouxing 肉刑*).* Translator's annotation: For more information, see Liu Xiang's *Biographies of Women*, volume 6, chapter 15.
6. Wang Xiang's commentary: *During the Han dynasty, Madame Zhang* 張氏 *was a widow at Tunghai* 東海. *Zhang was very filial in caring for her mother-in-law. Her mother-in-law sympathized with Zhang's young age and did not want to become a burden that would hinder her from getting remarried. The mother-in-law thereupon killed herself. Zhang's sister-in-law went to the court, accusing Zhang of murder. The local official did not investigate the matter carefully. The court sentenced Zhang to death. The region of Tunghai suffered from three years of severe drought. Later, a new governor arrived and learned that Zhang was very filial and her death was unjust. The new official personally went to Zhang's burial site and performed proper rites to memorialize her. Before the rituals were completed, heavy rain poured down and the drought was relieved.* Translator's annotation: See Wang Daokun's *Wangshi's Biographies of*

Women, volume 5; and Ban Gu et al., *Hanshu* (*Book of Han*), "Biography of Yu Dingguo 于定國."

7. Wang Xiang's commentary: *Madame Pang* 龐氏, *wife of Jiang Shi* 姜詩 *of Han, was exemplarily filial. Her mother-in-law loved to drink river water. Pang traveled far daily to fetch the water for her. Her mother-in-law liked river fish. Pang never minded getting messy to catch it. She did this frequently without tiredness. One day a spring suddenly emerged from the ground in their yard. The taste of the spring water is even better than the river water. Two carp jumped out of the spring daily. Pang offered the fish to her mother-in-law. All this was because her filial piety moved Heaven.* Translator's annotation: This anecdote is included in Fan Ye, *Houhanshu* (*Book of Later Han*); Wang Daokun, *Wangshi's Biographies of Women*, volume 5; and Guo Jujing, *Twenty-Four Exemplars of Filial Piety.*
8. Wang Xiang's commentary: *Madame Zhangsun* 長孫氏 *was the great-grandmother of Cui Shannan* 崔山南 *of Tang. Because of her old age, she had no teeth. Cui's grandmother (Madame Tang* 唐氏*) breastfed her mother-in-law. Madame Zhangsun thus enjoyed longevity before she passed away. Later, Cui became a high-ranking military officer (*jiedushi 節度史*). He displayed great filial piety toward his grandmother. It was the effect of Madame Tang's filial care for her mother-in-law!* Translator's annotation: See Wang Daokun's *Wangshi's Biographies of Women*, volume 8; and Guo Jujing's *Twenty-Four Exemplars of Filial Piety*. According to the *Bencao gangmu* (*Compendium of Materia Medica*), compiled by Li Shizhen 李時珍 (a renowned Ming Confucian physician and pharmacologist, 1518–1593), human breast milk has more nutrients and medicinal effects than animal milk, especially for the elderly. The use of breast milk as medicine can be traced back to the Han dynasty (206 BCE–220 CE). Induced lactation is possible for women after menopause.
9. Wang Xiang's commentary: *Madame Lu* 盧氏 *was the wife of Zheng Yizong* 鄭義宗 *of Tang. One night, robbers ransacked their household. Everyone was running to escape. Only Madame Lu's mother-in-law was still in her room. Lu used her body to shield her mother-in-law from the attackers' knives. She was almost beaten to death by the robbers. After the robbers left, people asked her: "Why didn't you escape?" She replied: "When our neighbors encounter difficulties, it is our duty to come to their rescue. Today my aging mother-in-law was still in her room. If I did not come to her rescue because I feared death, it would be behaving like an animal."* Translator's annotation: See Liu Xu, *Tangshu* (*Book of Tang*); and Wang Daokun, *Wangshi's Biographies of Women*, volume 9.
10. Wang Xiang's commentary: *When her mother-in-law was quite ill, Madame Liu* 劉氏 *(wife of Han Taichu* 韓太初 *of Ming) attended to her bedside throughout the night, driving away mosquitoes. When her mother-in-law suffered from bedsores, she gnawed on the maggots that grew out of the wounds. She pierced her arms, cut her fingers, and blended her blood with medicine [to increase its potency]. Her mother-in-law gradually recovered from the illness.* Translator's annotation: For more information,

see Zhang Tingyu et al., *Mingshi* (*History of Ming*); and Wang Daokun, *Wangshi's Biographies of Women*, volume 15. Moreover, according to Li Shizen's *Compendium of Materia Medica*, saliva is the result of *qi* energy via meridians from the heart and the kidney. When a person is healthy, the saliva is clear and abundant. When a person is ill, saliva dries up. Consequently, in traditional Chinese medicine (TCM), saliva can be used as external medicine for cleansing and healing, particularly in treating skin disease and eye illness, as illustrated in Madame Liu's case here and Madame Wen's case later in this chapter.

A word about cultural sensibility is in order. Some practices of TCM may seem unintelligible to modern audiences. However, if one situates TCM in Chinese cosmology, *yin–yang* theory, and the oneness of human–nature relation, the logic of using herbal medicine and animal materials is internally coherent. It, however, should be noted that using materials from the human body for healing is a morally contentious topic in TCM. Li Shizhen, for example, saw medicine as an art of humaneness, and argued that the practice of medicine must abide by the highest Confucian moral principles of humaneness and righteousness. Anything that harms the human body or human life is immoral. Thus, using saliva, nails, breast milk, and the like is morally permissible, but using blood and human flesh is morally abhorrent. Even though folk beliefs consider the use of human flesh by children to be a potent filial act to cure parents or grandparents, Li strongly opposed such practice. Since one's body is a gift from one's parents, a filial son and daughter must not harm his or her body. Therefore, in Li's view, Madame Liu's action of piercing arms and blending blood with medicine to treat her mother-in-law's illness, and Madame Zhang's cutting off a part of her liver when alive as medicine to bring her grandmother back to health (later in this chapter), seriously violate Confucian moral values. For an informative discussion on the Confucian view of human drugs, consult Ruiping Fan, ed., *Confucian Bioethics* (Dordrecht: Kluwer, 1999), 14–7; and Jing-Bao Nie, "'Human Drugs' in Chinese Medicine and the Confucian View: An Interpretive Study," in Ruiping Fan, ed., *Confucian Bioethics*, 167–206.

11. Wang Xiang's commentary: *Madame Wen* 聞氏 *was the wife of Yu Xin* 俞新 *in Huijun* 徽郡 *during the Ming dynasty. Xin passed away. Wen cut her hair to observe the vow of chastity and to care for her mother-in-law. When her mother-in-law suffered from eye illness, Wen washed her mouth frequently and licked her mother-in-law's eyes, who regained her eyesight. When her mother-in-law passed away, Wen personally dug the tomb to bury her [because they were so poor and could not afford to hire a worker]. Local officials officially commemorated Wen's filial piety.* Translator's annotation: See Wang Daokun, *Wangshi's Biographies of Women*, volume 13. For more on the medicinal effect of saliva, see commentary and annotation in note 10. It is worth noting that these female examples of filial piety broke down the body dichotomy of clean versus unclean, as well as exhibited the "emotional engrossment" and "motivational displacement" much discussed in the contemporary ethics of care.

12. Translator's annotation: The phrase *yugui* 于歸 (literally, "returning home") is used here. It first appeared in the *Shijing*: "The daughter is about to get married [= "to return home"] (*zhiziyugui* 之子于歸). She will bring good order to her husband's household (*yiqishijia* 宜其室家)." In traditional Chinese culture, the husband's home is considered the real home for a woman. Thus, when a woman is getting married, it is described as "returning home." The phrase is still used today as a greeting to a woman who just become engaged, about to get married, or has just married (*yugui zhixi* 于歸之喜).
13. Wang Xiang's commentary: *Madame Chen* 陳氏 *of the Song dynasty was just married to her husband. In less than ten days after their wedding, her husband suddenly needed to join a military expedition to the border. He asked his wife Madame Chen to care for his mother. Later, her husband died; thus, he did not return home. Her father advised her to remarry. She responded: "How can I, who have already promised my husband to care for his mother, break my promise now?" She intended to commit suicide. Fearing this possibility, her father stopped pushing her. Chen cared for her mother-in-law for over fifty years and later buried her according to proper rituals. The imperial court honored her with gold and banners, declaring her a "filial woman."*
14. Wang Xiang's commentary: *Madame Zhang* 張氏, *wife of Gu Deqian* 顧德謙 *of the Song dynasty, had a dream in which a deity revealed to her that she would be struck to death by lightning the next day [due to demerits from her previous life]. Next morning, she heard loud thunder. She was concerned that her mother-in-law would be startled by the loud sounds. She went outside and kneeled under a mulberry tree to await her death. A god, appearing in the air, pronounced: "This is a filial woman. Her life shall be extended for another thirty years."* Translator's annotation: This story is found in the *Yijian zhi* 《夷堅志》 (also known as the *Yijian jiazhi* 《夷堅甲志》), volume 20, probably influenced by Buddhist teachings on karma and reincarnation. Hong Mai's 洪邁 *Yijian zhi* is a collection of Song urban legends, folk tales, news, essays, and literary works. The original collection was 420 volumes; over half the contents are now lost.
15. Wang Xiang's commentary: *Madame Zhao [i.e., Zhao E* 趙娥*] was the wife of Pang Yu* 龐淯 *of the Han dynasty. Her father was murdered by Zhao Shou* 趙壽*. Madame Zhao had three brothers, who all desired to revenge their father's death. Unfortunately, all three brothers died before they could do so. Zhao Shou laughed and said: "Now I have no more worries." Madame Zhao sent a messenger to tell Zhao Shou: "I am still alive. Don't be overjoyed." One year after she gave birth to her son, she happened to find Shou drunk and rode a horse passing by the place called Duting. Madame Zhao made him fall off the horse and killed him. Afterwards, she brought Shou's head, turned herself in at the local judicial court, and asked for the death penalty. The local official Yinjia* 尹嘉 *disagreed with her and pled [to the higher courts] to forgive the death penalty.* Translator's annotation: For more information, see Wang Daokun, *Wangshi's Biographies of Women*, volume 5; Li Fang et al., *Taipin yulan*《太平御覽》;

Fan Ye, *Houhanshu* 《後漢書》; and Chen Shou, *Sanguozhi* 《三國志》. Rarely, Wang Xiang presented erroneous information in his commentary. Here is one such rare occasion. According to *Taipin Yulan*, *Houhanshu*, and *Sanguozhi*, Madame Zhao's husband is Pang Zixia, not Pang Yu. She is Pang Yu's mother, not his wife. In addition, her father was killed by Li Shou, not Zhao Shou.

16. Wang Xiang's commentary: *Zhao Jianzi* 趙簡子 *[?–476 BCE] was going to cross the river [during a military expedition]. But when he was at the pier, the local pier official was intoxicated and passed out. Jianzi intended to execute the local official. The official's daughter Juan made a plea to speak with Jianzi: "My father was concerned that you, sir, were going to cross the treacherous river today. He thus prepared the rituals praying to gods for your safety. He became drunk because of that. If you kill him now, he will be so intoxicated that he will not know why he is guilty. Please let me operate the boat in my father's stead." She sang while she was rowing. The wind was pleasant and the waves were calm. Jianzi was very pleased. He later married her as his royal consort.* Translator's annotation: See Liu Xiang's *Biographies of Women*, volume 6, chapter 7; and Wang Daokun's *Wangshi's Biographies of Women*, volume 4.
17. Wang Xiang's commentary: *In the Han dynasty, after a ritual prayer service to gods, Caoe's* 曹娥 *father was drunk and drowned in the Gan River. Caoe jumped into the river to search for her father for two days. She died holding tight to her father's body when they emerged from the Gan River.* Translator's annotation: See Fan Ye, *Houhanshu*; and Wang Daokun, *Wangshi's Biographies of Women*, volume 6.
18. Wang Xiang's commentary: *During the early Tang dynasty, Mulan's* 木蘭 *father was required to join the military expedition. Being old and sick, he was unable to do so. Mulan's younger brother was still young and not strong enough. Therefore, she disguised herself as a man and joined the army in his father's stead. She was in the military for ten years. After many accomplishments at the border, she returned home. No one knew that she was a woman.* Translator's annotation: See Wang Daokun, *Wangshi's Biographies of Women*, volume 9. Historical records were unclear about Mulan's dates, last name, and birthplace. She was said to be a person during the Wei, Sui, or early Tang dynasties. Among her many possible last names, Hua 花 was the most popular one.
19. Wang Xiang's commentary: *Madame Zhang Erniang* 張二娘, a resident *of Huaian, her grandmother was very ill. The doctor indicated that the grandmother might recover by eating liver. Erniang could not get liver from other places after many tries. She then cut herself to acquire the liver. She first made a horizontal cut, but could not reach her liver. She then made a vertical cut and succeeded. She prepared a soup with the severed part of her liver for her grandmother. Her grandmother indeed recovered from the illness. Erniang often woke up from her sleep because of the severe pain. Gradually her wound healed. The red scar looked like a cross.* Translator's annotation: For moral problems of using the human body in traditional Chinese medicine, see note 10.

20. Wang Xiang's commentary: *Madame Chen* 陳氏 *was a resident of Changan during the Tang dynasty. A rival wanted to kill her husband. The rival kidnapped her father and forced her to open the door in order to kill her husband. She thought that if she followed the order, her husband would be harmed; but if she did not obey, her father would be killed. She therefore said to the rival: "When my husband takes a bath, he always let his hair down and sleeps in the main room. I will ask him to take a bath. I will open the door to wait for you then." She returned home, intoxicated her husband, and made him sleep upstairs. She then took a bath and slept in the main hall with the door open for the rival. The rival came, killed her by mistake, and left. The lives of her husband and her father were saved.* Translation's annotation: For more information, see Wang Daokun's *Wangshi's Biographies of Women*, volume 5. Liu Xiang's *Biographies of Women*, volume 5, chapter 15, provides a slightly different version about the ending. According to Liu's account, the rival later realized that he killed the wife instead of the husband. In admiration of her character, the rival decided not to kill the husband.

【貞烈篇】

忠臣不事兩國，烈女不更二夫。故一與之醮，終身不移。男可重婚，女無再適。是故艱難苦節謂之貞，慷慨捐生謂之烈。令女截耳劓鼻以持身，凝妻牽臂劈掌以明志。共姜髡髦之詩，之死靡他。史氏刺面之文，中心不改。皇甫夫人，直斥逆臣，膏斧鉞而罵不絕口。竇家二女，不從亂賊，投危崖而憤不顧身。董氏封髮以待夫歸，二十年不施膏沐。妙慧題詩以明己節，三千里複見生逢。桓夫人義不同庖，而吟匪石之詩。平夫人持兵閭巷，而卻闔閭之犯。夫之不幸，妾之不幸，宋女以言哀。使君有婦，羅敷有夫，趙王之章止。梁節婦之卻魏王，斷鼻存孤。余鄭氏之責唐帥，嚴詞保節。代夫人深怨其弟，千秋表磨笄之山。杞良妻遠訪其夫，萬里哭築城之骨。唐貴梅自縊於樹以全貞，不彰其姑之惡。潘妙圓從夫於火以殉節，而活其舅之生。譚貞婦廟中流血，雨漬猶存。王烈女崖上題詩，石刊尚在。崔氏甘亂箭以全節，劉氏代鼎烹而活夫。是皆貞心貫乎日月，烈志塞乎兩儀，正氣凜於丈夫，節操播乎青史者也，可不勉歟。

5

Chastity and Ardency (Zhenlie pian 貞烈篇)

A LOYAL MINISTER will not serve two nations. An ardent, chaste woman will not marry two husbands.[1] Therefore, once the wedding banquet is set for a woman to marry a man, her mind should not change throughout her lifetime.[2] A man may remarry, but a woman should not.[3] Therefore, to go through hardship but retain her integrity is called being "chaste." Generously sacrificing her life for her spouse is called being "ardent."[4]

[Hence,] Lady Lingnü 令女 cut off her ears and nose to protect her person.[5] Official [Wang] Ning's wife 凝妻 cut off her hand to express her will after a man [other than her deceased husband] touched her hand.[6] Madame

Gongjiang 共姜 stated in her Tanmao 髧髦 poem, "Till death I will not have any other man."[7] Madame Shi 史氏 tattooed her face with these words: "I will never change my mind."[8] Lady Huangfu 皇甫夫人 forthrightly scolded a treacherous minister; even when she was beaten to death, she did not stop.[9] The two daughters of the Dou family 竇家二女 would not yield to bandits; they unhesitantly jumped over a cliff [to protect their chastity].[10] Madame Dong 董氏 sealed her hair [with her husband's ink writing] to wait for his return; for twenty years, she did not untie it even when taking a bath.[11] Miaohui 妙慧 composed a poem to make her principles known; after being separated by three thousand miles, she finally was reunited with her husband.[12] Lady Huan 桓夫人 would not remarry because of the principle of righteousness, citing the Feishi poem [to make it known].[13] [Lady Boying 伯嬴], wife of King Ping 平夫人, held weapons in her hands inside the imperial inner court; she thus warded off King Helu's 闔閭 impeding harassment.[14] "A husband's misfortune is also a wife's misfortune," a lady from the state of Song 宋女 said in lament.[15] [Luofu wrote the poem,] "The Governor has a wife. Luofu 羅敷 has a husband." Thereupon, King Zhao stopped his pursuit of her.[16] Chaste Widow Liang 梁節婦 refused King Wei's pursuit; she cut off her nose and only stayed alive to raise her orphaned son.[17] Madame Yu-Zheng 余鄭氏 scolded the Superior General of [Southern-] Tang with stern words and preserved her chastity.[18] Lady Dai 代夫人 deeply resented her brother [for killing her husband]. Histories through the millennia commemorated [her at] Mountain Mo Ji [, where she was buried].[19] Qiliang's wife 杞良妻 visited her husband from afar [to send him winter clothes]; traveling thousands of miles, [when she arrived,] she could only weep over the bones [of her deceased husband who was drafted to] build the Great Wall.[20] Tang Guimei 唐貴梅 hanged herself on a tree in order to preserve her chastity and avoid revealing her mother-in-law's evil deeds.[21] Pan Miaoyuan 潘妙圓 followed her husband and jumped into the fire to die for her integrity; her action saved her father-in-law's life.[22] Chaste Woman Tan 譚貞婦 [was killed at a temple by the invading Yuan soldiers]; her blood stains [on the temple stones] still seem fresh when it rains.[23] Ardent Chaste Woman Wang 王烈女 wrote a poem on the cliff; the poem, later engraved on a rock, is still there.[24] Madame Cui 崔氏 was willing to be shot to death by flying arrows to preserve her chastity.[25] Madame Liu 劉氏 willingly took her husband's place to be cooked [by the soldiers]; her husband's life was spared because of her.[26]

These are the chaste hearts that reached above to the Sun and the Moon, the ardent wills that embraced the two exemplary modes [of *qian* and *kun*],[27] the righteous *qi* that equals great men,[28] and the virtuous characters known through history without blemish. Should we not be encouraged and learn from them?

Commentaries and Annotations

1. Wang Xiang's commentary: *King Zhu of Qi* 齊王蠋 *said: "A loyal minister will not serve two kings [with different surnames]. An ardent chaste woman will not marry two husbands." This speaks about how a wife serving her husband is like a minister serving his king. A minister, who serves two surnames, is disloyal. A woman, who serves two husbands, loses her integrity.* Translator's annotation: This well-known saying appeared in texts as early as the Han dynasty—for example, in the "Biography of Tian Dan," in Sima Qian's *Shiji* (*Historical Records*); and Liu Xiang's *Shuoyuan* 《說苑》(*Garden of Stories*), chapter 4. It was emphasized in Ming–Qing Neo-Confucian ethics. Popular literature further engrained these values.
2. Wang Xiang's commentary: Jiao 醮 *means "banquet." When men and women are getting married, their fathers and mothers set a farewell banquet. Before a woman is married, she follows her father. To have a second farewell banquet is against ritual propriety.*
3. Wang Xiang's commentary: *Men have the principal responsibility of carrying on the family lineage with offspring and of performing religious rites. Therefore, if their wives pass away, they can remarry. But for women, to remain chaste is the correct act.* Translator's annotation: According to some Confucian scholars (e.g., Chang Yi and Zhu Xi), it's best for both husband and wife to remain chaste if family lineage is not a problem.
4. Wang Xiang's commentary: *When a woman loses her husband, but remains one-minded in hardship, this is called chaste and principled. If she will not yield when facing adversity, will not comply when forced and threatened, and will rather die than being humiliated, such a person is called an ardent woman if married and an ardent lady if not yet married.*
5. Wang Xiang's commentary: *Lingnü* 令女 *of the Xiahou* 夏侯 *family was the wife of Cao Wenshu* 曹文叔 *of Wei* 魏. *When Wenshu died, Lingnu's parents intended to remarry her. Lingnu said: "A humane person will not give up his principles due to prosperity and misfortune. A righteous person will not change his heart because of life and death." She then cut off her ears to swear by her principles. When her husband's entire family died out [because of political power struggles], her parents again wanted to remarry her, and she cut off her nose to preserve her chastity.* Translator's annotation: For more, see Chen Shou, *Sanguozhi* (*History of the Three Kingdoms*), "Biography of Cao Suang" 曹爽傳; and Wang Daokun, *Wangshi's Biographies of Women*, volume 6.
6. Wang Xiang's commentary: *Madame Li* 李氏 *was the wife of Huzhou official Wang Ning* 王凝 *during the Five Dynasties period. Her husband passed away. She was to return home with her young son to arrange the funeral. They stopped at an inn, but the owner would not let them come in because they were dressed in mourning clothes. Madame Li pled repeatedly. The inn owner grabbed her hand and drove her out. Madame Li wept and said: "Heaven above! I am already unfortunate in losing my*

husband, how could my hand be allowed to be held by another man?" She picked up a knife and cut off her hand. Local officials heard this, honored Madame Li, and reprimanded the inn owner. Translator's annotation: For more information, see Wang Daokun, *Wangshi's Biographies of Women*, volume 9.

7. Wang Xiang's commentary: 髧髦 *pronounced as* 坦毛 (tan mao). *Gongbo* 共伯, *prince of Wei* 衛, *died young. His wife Gongjiang* 共姜 *kept to the principle of righteousness. [Her parents wanted her to remarry.] She would not yield. Instead, she wrote a poem named Bozhou* 柏舟 *to express her feeling: "I cut and clipped my hair on the top of the head, and let it fall on the sides of my ears. This is my way of proceeding. Till death I will not change my mind for another man."* Tan 髧 *means "to drape down."* Mao 髦 *means "to cut one's hair and clip it on the top of the head, while letting it fall on the sides of the two ears." This is the principled action showing that a son serves his parents. Here, it refers to one's husband. It means that Gongjiang tied her hair with her husband in becoming a husband and a wife. Today, her husband passed away. It describes her determination in remaining chaste, to have no other man till death.* 顖 *is pronounced as* 信 *(*xin*).* Translator's annotation: The story is from the *Shijing* (*Classic of Poetry*), Yongfeng 鄘風 section, Bozhou 柏舟 poem.
8. Wang Xiang's commentary: *During the Ming dynasty, Madame Shi* 史氏, a resident *of Liyang, was to marry Shao Yilong* 邵一龍. *Before their wedding day, Shao passed away. Her parents planned to select another son-in-law. Shi tattooed her face with the words: "My mind will never change." She fainted due to the extreme pain. After regaining her consciousness, she used black ink to color the words. If a stroke was not deep enough, she would retattoo it. When the news spread, the government commemorated her integrity. She lived a long life.*
9. Wang Xiang's commentary: *Sir Huangfu Gui's wife* 皇甫規夫人 *was very talented in writing and calligraphy. When Gui died, Dong Zuo* 董卓 *[the minister at the time] heard about her beauty and desired to marry her. She knew that she could not avoid it. She thus went to Zuo's residence and knelt at the front gate. She tried to persuade him with the lesson of righteousness. But Zuo would not bend. Thereupon, she scolded him: "I am the wife of a grand official. My principles will not be insulted. You are but an uncultured barbarian who worked under my husband in the past. How dare you to be disrespectful to your superior's wife?" Upon hearing this, Zuo was furious. He tied her head to the pole of a carriage, and ordered his staff to beat her. She cursed him unceasingly. Eventually she was beaten to death.* Translator's annotation: See Fan Ye, *Houhanshu* (*Book of Later Han*), "Biographies of Women."
10. Wang Xiang's commentary: *During the reign of Emperor Dezong of Tang* 唐德宗, *there was the Zhuzi Revolt* 朱泚之亂. *Robbers and bandits were everywhere. Two daughters of the Dou family* 竇氏二女 *in the Fengtian region were about to be raped by bandits. The older sister jumped off the cliff first. The young sister followed. The older sister died. The younger sister was severely injured from broken bones, but survived. When the emperor learned about this, he issued an imperial edict to honor them.*

Translator's note: See Wang Daokun, *Wangshi's Biographies of Women*, volume 9; and Liu Xu et al., *Tangshu* (*Book of Tang*), "Biographies of Women."

11. Wang Xiang's commentary: *Jia Zhiyan* 賈直言 *of Tang was demoted to [the remote] Lingnan area. He spoke with his wife Madame Dong* 董氏: *"In my post there, life and death are unknown matters. You are young and should not live alone. You should make plans." Dong used a cotton cloth tying her hair up and asked her husband to seal it with his ink writing. She swore: "It will not be untied until my husband returns." Twenty years later her husband returned. He personally untied her hair.* Translator's annotation: see Ouyang Xiu, Song Qi, et al., *Xintangshu* (*New Book of Tang*), "Biographies of Women."
12. Wang Xiang's commentary: *Madame Li Miaohui* 李妙慧 *was the wife of Scholar Lu* 盧進士 *of Yangzhou during the Ming dynasty. Her husband passed the imperial magistrates' examination but did not return home. Rumors said that he had died. Her parents pitied her conditions of poverty and widowhood. They intended to remarry her. At the time, Xie Tang* 謝唐 *was a very wealthy businessman of Nanchang. He had no son. His mother Madame Li* 李氏 *lived in Yangzhou. Madame Li was a distant aunt from Miaohui's family clan (zugu* 族姑*); she wanted to have Miaohui as her son's concubine. Miaohui's father took her to the Xie family's boat and left. She found out the reasons behind her father's act, attempted suicide several times, and was rescued by her maids. When Madame Li heard about this, she adopted Miaohui as her daughter and took her aboard the returning boat. When their boat was passing the Jinshan Temple* 金山寺, *Miaohui wrote a poem at the Temple and signed it as "a poem composed by the wife of Scholar Lu of Yangzhou, Li Miaohui." The poem contained the following verses: "Even when coffined, I will not be a woman with unrighteous gold. Entering this land, I only look for the man who picked the cinnamon tree branch. Hereby a new poem is composed at the Jinshan Temple. Aboard a boat with tall sails, of Yuzhang, I journey." Later, Scholar Lu was given an official position and returned home. But he could not find any traces of his wife. By chance, he passed the Jinshan Temple. Upon seeing this poem, he resigned from his official position and went looking for the commercial boat with tall sails with Yuzhang signs. But there were too many boats to find the right boat. Lu decided to be at the pier at night circling around the commercial boats, singing Miaohui's poem. Miaohui's aunt, mother of Xie, heard it and called Lu to the boat. Lu finally saw his wife but she had already become a nun. They reunited. The government heard this news and reinstated Lu's official position.* Translator's annotation: See Wang Daokun, *Wangshi's Biographies of Women*, volume 14.
13. Wang Xiang's commentary: *Madame Jiang* 姜氏 *was the wife of Duke Huan of Wei* 衛桓公. *She was on her way from the state of Qi to the state of Wei [to marry him]. Before she arrived at the border of Wei, Duke Huan was killed. Citizens of Wei enthroned Huan's brother Duke Xuan as the new leader. Her attendants advised her to return to the state of Qi. She would not yield. She built a room, lived in the state of Wei alone, and observed the three-year mourning rite for her husband. When the*

mourning rite was over, Duke Xuan proposed to marry her. She declined. She cited the Feishi 匪石 *poem as her oath. She passed away in the state of Wei. The poem can be found in the* Classic of Poetry, *Beifeng volume, Bozhou chapter*. Translator's annotation: See Liu Xiang's *Biographies of Women*, volume 4, chapter 3; and Wang Daokun's *Wangshi's Biographies of Women,* volume 1. The identity of Madame Jiang is unclear. In some accounts, she was identified as the wife of Duke Xuan (not Huan). In other accounts, she was recorded as a widow of a Duke of Wei. Names were not mentioned. See, for example, Li Fang, *Taiping yulan* (*Taiping Imperial Record and Collection of Books*).

14. Wang Xiang's commentary: *King Helu* 闔閭 *of the state of Wu* 吳 *conquered the state of Chu* 楚. *King Zhao* 昭王 *[of Chu] went into exile. The king of Wu heard that King Zhao's mother, Boying* 伯嬴 *[King Ping's wife], was beautiful and wished to be intimate with her. Boying held weapons in her hands guarding the inner court. She said to the king of Wu: "Great King, you initiated a military conquest to rectify the State of Chu. If you act in an unrighteous way, how can you govern the world? The righteous duty of a woman is to never have intimacy with two men even when facing death. If you come near me, I will definitely kill myself. Then, where is the pleasure for you? But if you kill me, you will earn the reputation of killing the mother of a defeated king and being lascivious. What would the benefits be for you?" The king of Wu felt ashamed and stopped. Boying resisted in the inner court for thirty days. The rescue troops from the state of Qin finally arrived. King Zhao of Chu also returned from exile.* Translator's annotation: See Liu Xiang's *Biographies of Women*, volume 4, chapter 9; and Wang Daokun's *Wangshi's Biographies of Women,* volume 3.
15. Wang Xiang's commentary: *The wife of a man in the state of Cai* 蔡 *was a woman from the state of Song* 宋. *She was just married when her husband suddenly developed a terrible disease. She served her husband diligently without tiredness. Her parents were saddened by her condition, planning to remarry her. She said to them: "My husband has a terrible disease. A husband's misfortune is also a wife's misfortune. If I abandon my husband when he has an illness, it is inhumane. If I marry another man and betray my husband, it is unrighteous. Being inhumane and unrighteous, why live at all?" She tried to commit suicide. Thereupon, her parents gave up the idea. She continued to serve her husband. He was able to complete his natural span of life.* Translator's annotation: For more information, see Liu Xiang's *Biographies of Women*, volume 4, chapter 4.
16. Wang Xiang's commentary: *Qin Luofu* 秦羅敷, *wife of King Zhao of Han's* 漢趙王 *head housekeeper, was very beautiful. The king wanted to have her. Luofu wrote a poem [to quell his interest]: "The governor came from the south. [When the governor saw Luofu,] the five horses [pulling the carriage] stopped and hesitated. The governor asked Luofu: "Would you like to ride with me?" Luofu came forward and replied: "Why does the governor speak so foolishly? The governor has a wife and Luofu has a husband." Upon hearing this, the king ended his pursuit.* Translator's annotation: See Wang Daokun, *Wangshi's Biographies of Women*, volume 5.

17. Wang Xiang's commentary: *Chaste Widow Liang's 梁節婦 husband passed away. She was very attractive. King Wei 魏 wanted to marry her. She cut off her nose and said: "The reason that the lord desires me is due to my look. Today I have disfigured my face. Would the lord still desire me? The reason that I did not kill myself is because I have a young son. I would like to raise him until he reaches adulthood." King Wei felt ashamed when he heard this. He bestowed on her the honorary title of "A Principled Widow with Exemplary Virtue."* Translator's annotation: See Liu Xiang's *Biographies of Women*, volume 4, chapter 14; and Wang Daokun's *Wangshi's Biographies of Women*, volume 5.
18. Wang Xiang's commentary: *The state of Southern Tang* 南唐 (937–975) *waged a war with the state of Min* 閩. *Madame Zheng* 鄭氏, *wife of General Yuhong* 余洪 *of Min, was captured by a Southern-Tang general, Wang Jianfeng* 王建封. *Wang offered Madame Zheng to the Superior General Cha Wenzheng* 查文徽. *Cha was enticed by Zheng's beauty and wanted to have her as a concubine. Zheng reprimanded him: "When you, the Superior General, are conquering different countries, it is always the case that you reward loyal men and praise principled women. Your purpose is to promote the transformation of culture. Today [Wang] Jianfeng, who is but a military man, even knows not to soil principled righteousness. You are the Superior General. Why do you want to risk becoming the leader of a catastrophe?" Cha was ashamed. Thereupon, he helped find her husband and sent her home.*
19. Wang Xiang's commentary: *Lady Dai* 代夫人 *was the daughter of [the former minister of Jin], Zhao Jianzi* 趙簡子. *Her brother Xiangzi* 襄子 *hosted a banquet for her husband, King Dai, but ordered his servant(s) to strike King Dai with bronze wine vessels to kill him. Her brother then waged a war and eliminated the Dai kingdom. Afterwards, he welcomed his sister to return home. His sister looked up to Heaven and wailed. She sharpened her hairpin and killed herself by piercing her throat. The people of Dai grieved over her death, and they named the place where she was buried the Moji Mountain* 磨笄山. Translator's annotation: *Mo* 磨 means "to grind or sharpen" and *ji* 笄 means "a hairpin." For more, see Liu Xiang's *Biographies of Women*, volume 5, chapter 7; and Wang Daokun's *Wangshi's Biographies of Women*, volume 4.
20. Wang Xiang's commentary: *Fan Qiliang* 范杞良 *of the Qin dynasty* 秦 *only married his wife for three days when the government drafted him to build the Great Wall. Because the weather would soon change into the winter, his wife Madame Jiang* 姜氏 *made winter clothing for him and went on a long journey to find him. When she heard that her husband was dead, she went through piles of corpses and picked through bones to test them with her blood to distinguish which bones were her husband's. But none of the tested bones would absorb her blood. Jiang wailed for three days and three nights. The Great Wall suddenly collapsed; it revealed several skeletons. Jiang again did the test with blood. This time her blood saturated the bones and could not be wiped off. She knew these were her husband's remains. She then carried her husband's remains and exited the Tong Gate. Exhausted and incapable of going any farther, she placed*

his remains at a temple, sitting next to them, and passed away. The people at the Tong Gate commiserated with these two. They buried the couple and erected a commemorative temple to make an offering to them. The Mencius *said: "The wives of Huazhou 華周 and Qiliang 杞梁 were good at weeping and mourning for their husbands. The customs of the country were thus transformed by them." Here, it talked about the wives of the two generals of the Qi 齊 state. Two generals died in a battle. Their wives cried for three days and [their eyes] bled. The city wall collapsed because of it. They were also two ardently chaste women.* Translator's annotation: In both Liu Xiang's *Biographies of Women*, volume 4, chapter 8, and Wang Daokun's *Wangshi's Biographies of Women*, volume 1, the event took place during the Spring and Autumn period (771–476 BCE), not the Qin dynasty (221–206 BCE). In neither was building the Great Wall mentioned.

21. Wang Xiang's commentary: *During the Ming dynasty, Tang Guimei 唐貴梅 of the Guichi region became a widow and kept her chastity when she was seventeen years old. Her mother-in-law had an adulterous relationship with a businessman. That man also wanted Guimei, but she would not yield even after her mother-in-law had scolded her. Her mother-in-law went to the court to sue her for being unfilial. The local official reprimanded Guimei. Even being blamed [unjustly], Guimei did not argue. After returning home, she hanged herself on a tree, thereby avoiding speaking about her mother-in-law's fault.* Translator's annotation: See Zhang Tingyu, *Mingshi* (*History of Ming*), "Biographies of Women."
22. Wang Xiang's commentary: *During the Yuan dynasty, Xu Yunrang's 徐允讓 wife (Pan Miaoyuan 潘妙圓) accompanied her husband [to the mountain area] to hide from the war. The bandits captured her father-in-law, killed her husband, and wanted to rape Pan. Pan said: "If you would let my father-in-law go and cremate my husband's body, I will certainly yield to your request." The bandits freed her father-in-law and were cremating her husband's corpse. Pan jumped into the burning flame and died.* Translator's annotation: See Song Lian, *Yuanshi* (*History of Yuan*), "Biographies of Women."
23. Wang Xiang's commentary: *Madame Tan 譚氏 of the Zhao 趙 family during the Song dynasty was a resident of Jian. The Yuan army [invaded the Song territory and] occupied Jian. The Zhao family escaped. Madame Tan, carrying her son, hid from the soldiers in the Temple of Letters (*wenmiao 文廟*). The soldiers [found them and] wanted to rape her. Madame Tan scolded the soldiers. They killed both the mother and the son. Their blood stained the stones of the temple. People were unable to wash the stains off. Even nowadays, when it is cloudy or raining, the blood stains seem still fresh.* Translator's annotation: See Tuo Tuo, *Songshi* (*History of Song*), "Biographies of Women."
24. Wang Xiang's commentary: *Woman Wang 王氏, a resident of Linhai during the late period of the Yuan dynasty, was very attractive. In the havoc of war, soldiers killed her husband. The soldiers drove Wang, passing through the Sheng borough where the*

Clear Wind Mountain was. Wang wrote a poem on the top of the mountain, which read: "The emperor lost the Way; I therefore suffer from this calamity. Leaving behind my daughters and sons, I came on the back of a horse. Knowing not which day I will see my husband's face again, my wifely soul knows not when to return. Two streams of bitter tears drop down on my cheeks. A pair of sorrowful eyebrows cannot be unlocked. Searching for my hometown from afar, I know not where it is. To live, or to die, are but two words of sorrow." Thereupon, she jumped off the cliff and died. People of later times mourned her death and carved her poem on the wall of the mountain. Translator's annotation: A similar version of the story can be found in the *Shinü shizuan* 《詩女史纂》 (*Compiled History of Women Poets*), volume 12, by Ming scholar Chunangzhai Zhuren 處囊齋主人. A slightly different version of the story is found in Wang Daokun, *Wangshi's Biographies of Women*, volume 11; and Ke Shaomin et al., *Xinyuanshi* (*New History of Yuan*), volume 244.

25. Wang Xiang's commentary: *Madame Cui* 崔氏 *was the wife of Zhao Yuankai* 趙元楷 *of the Tang dynasty. At the time, the Hebei province was in grave chaos. She and her husband hid from the war. Later, Cui was captured and her husband was let go. The bandits wanted to rape her. Cui held up a knife and resisted the bandits. The bandits were furious; they killed her with flying arrows.* Translator's annotation: See Li Yanshou, *Beishi* (*History of the Northern Dynasties*) and Wang Daokun, *Wangshi's Biographies of Women*, volume 7.
26. Wang Xiang's commentary: *Toward the end of the Yuan dynasty, the middle region of the country suffered from severe famine. The soldiers kidnapped and ate humans. They captured a man named Li Zhongyi* 李仲義 *and planned to cook and eat him. Zhongyi's wife, Madame Liu* 劉氏, *rushed to see the soldiers and pleaded with them: "My husband has been starved for a long time; he is too thin to eat. I have heard that the meat of a plump dark-skinned woman tastes the best. I am willing to take my husband's place." Thereupon, the soldiers released her husband and cooked her. People from both afar and near all felt saddened by what happened.* Translator's annotation: For more, see the Song Lian et al., *Yuanshi* (*History of Yuan*).
27. Translator's annotation: *Liangyi* 兩儀 (literally, "two modes of being") refers to *qian* 乾 and *kun* 坤, the Sun and the Moon, and Heaven and Earth, which in turn connote the exemplary ways of being a man and a woman. The concept is from the *Yijing* (*Classic of Changes*). For more information, see chapter 1 of Madame Liu, *Nüfan jielu* (*Short Records of Models for Women*).
28. Translator's annotation: *Zheng qi* 正氣 is translated here as "righteous *qi*." *Qi* is physical-psycho energy or force. The concept can be traced back to *Mencius*, 2A:2, where Mencius said, "I am skilled in nurturing my vast flowing [righteous] *qi* (*haoran zhiqi* 浩然之氣)."

【忠義篇】

君親雖曰不同，忠孝本無二致。古云：「率土莫非王臣」，豈謂閨中遂無忠義。詠小戎之駟，勉良人以君國同讎。伐汝墳之枚，慰君子以父母孔邇。美范滂之母，千秋尚有同心。封卞壼之墳，九泉猶有喜色。江油降魏，妻不與夫同生。蓋國淪戎，婦恥其夫不死。陵母對使而伏劍，經母含笑以同刑。池州被圍，趙昂發節義成雙。金川失守，黃侍中妻女同盡。朱夫人守襄陽而築城，以卻秦寇。梁夫人登金山而擊鼓，以破金兵。虞夫人勉子孫力勤王事，謝夫人甘俘虜以救民生。齊桓尸蟲出戶，晏娥逾垣以殉君。宇文白刃犯宮，貴兒捐生以罵賊，魯義保以子代先公之子，魏節乳以身蔽幼主之身。孫姬婢也，匍伏湖濱，以保忠臣血胤。毛惜妓也，身甘刀斧，恥為叛帥謳歌。劉母非不愛子，知軍令之不可干。章母非不保家，願闔城之俱獲免。是皆女烈之錚錚，坤維之表表。其忠肝義膽，足以風百世，而振綱常者也。

6

Loyalty and Righteousness (Zhongyi pian 忠義篇)

EVEN THOUGH THE ruler of one's state differs from one's parents, there is no difference in one's loyalty toward one's ruler and one's filialness toward one's parents.[1] The old saying goes, "All under Heaven are the ministers of the emperor."[2] How could it be that in the inner quarters of women there is no loyalty and righteousness?[3]

The people [of Qin] in the Xiaorong 小戎 poem praised four-horse drawn military carriages, and their wives encouraged their husbands to see the emperor's enemies as their own enemies.[4] The women in the Rufen 汝墳 poem picked up tree branches [for firewood] along the banks (*fen* 墳) of the Ru 汝 River; they comforted their husbands [to keep up their duties to the state] as if their parents were nearby.[5] [Madame Cheng 程氏, mother of Su Zizhan 蘇子瞻 of Song] praised the virtue of Fan Pan's mother 范滂之母 [of Han]. Virtuous minds think alike even across the millennia.[6] The tome of Bian Kun 卞壼 was sealed [by Emperor Taizu of Ming because of Bian's wife]. There was a smile even in the underworld.[7] [During the period of the Three Kingdoms,] when the city of Jiang You 江油 surrendered to the [enemy] state of Wei, the [defense general's] wife refused to survive [in shame] with her husband.[8] [Toward the end of the Western Zhou dynasty,] the vassal state Ge 蓋 was defeated by the tribe of [Quan]rong [犬] 戎. The wife [of Ge general, Qiu Zi 丘子,] was ashamed that her husband did not make himself a martyr for Ge.[9] [When the state of Chu and the state of Han were fighting for its sovereignty,] [Wang] Ling's mother [王] 陵母 [, refusing to be used as a hostage to threaten her son's loyalty,] killed herself with a sword after speaking to the messenger.[10] [During the period of the Three Kingdoms,] [Wang] Jing's mother [王] 經母 smiled at the execution site, willingly being executed with her son.[11] Chizhou 池州 was surrounded [by the invading Yuan army]. Zhao Maofa 趙昴發 [and his wife, Madame Yong 雍氏] accomplished both chastity and righteousness together.[12] When the Jinchuan [Gate] 金川 [門] was lost to the enemy forces, [Ming] imperial official Huang [Guan] 黃 [觀], his wife, and his daughter committed suicide [to preserve their loyalty and chastity].[13] Lady Zhu 朱夫人 helped build the city wall to defend the city of Xiangyang 襄陽 and warded off the Qin 秦 soldiers.[14] Lady Liang 梁夫人 climbed the Jin Mountain 金山 to beat the martial drums [to encourage the troop] and thus helped defeat the invading Jin 金 soldiers.[15] Lady Yu 虞夫人 encouraged her son and grandson [, not to worry about her old age, but] to be diligent in state affairs.[16] Lady Xie 謝夫人 was willing to be captured by enemies in order to save the lives of local residents.[17] Flies generated from King Huan of Qi's 齊桓公 corpse were coming out the palace's doors. Yan E 晏娥 [, a maid, who could not bear to see such unfilial neglect,] jumped over the wall to die for her king.[18] Yuwen [Huaji] 宇文 [化及] trespassed against the [Sui] palace with force. Guier 貴兒 [, an imperial servant,] sacrificed her life in scolding the traitors.[19] A righteous nanny from the state of Lu 魯義保 substituted her former king's son with her son [in order to save her prince's life,].[20] A principled nursing nanny from the state of Wei 魏節乳 used her body as shield to protect her young master's life.[21] Madame Sun 孫氏, a servant, hid near a lake in order to preserve a patriotic official's offspring.[22] Mao Xixi 毛惜惜, a courtesan-prostitute, would rather be killed than to sing for the traitor-general.[23] It is not that Madame Liu 劉母 did not love her son; rather, it is only because she knew that she should not interfere with military orders.[24] It is not that Madame Zhang 章母 did not want to protect her own family; rather, only that she wished for the safety of the whole city.[25]

These are the resounding examples of women's ardency, their remarkable expressions of the principle of *kun* 坤. Their exemplary loyalty and righteous courage are sufficient to inspire hundreds of generations and revive the bonds and constants of morals.[26]

Commentaries and Annotations

1. Wang Xiang's commentary: *This saying is from Scholar Yangjie Pan* 陽節潘. *It speaks about if one can be filial to one's parents, one will be loyal to one's rulers. This is the righteousness of human moral relations.* Translator's annotation: Yangjie Pan is also known as Pan Rong 潘榮; he authored *Gangjian zonglun* 《綱鑑總論》(*General Discussion of the Main Points and Reflection*), which provides a critical assessment of Chinese history, https://babel.hathitrust.org/cgi/pt?id=hvd.32044068371640;view=1up;seq=11;size=125. See also Nicolas Standaert, *The Intercultural Weaving of Historical Texts: Chinese and European Stories* (Leiden: Brill, 2016), 48.
2. See the *Shijing* (*Classic of Poetry*), Xiaoya section, Beishan 北山 poem.
3. Wang Xiang's commentary: *All under Heaven are the emperor's ministers. Both men and women are the emperor's citizens. How could it be that among women, there is no loyalty and righteousness?*
4. Wang Xiang's commentary: *Official Qin Zhong* 秦仲 *died in a state battle against the invading tribe, Quanrong* 犬戎. *His king, Duke Xiang of Qin* 秦襄公 *[?–766 BCE], thereupon diligently trained the soldiers and fed the horses well. The Duke swore that he would not give up until he eliminated Quanrong. The Qin people all regarded the duke as their own family member and were willing to die for their country. Their wives all encouraged their husbands to act with loyalty and righteousness. This illustrates the meaning that the king and his people have the same enemy. Read the [*Shijing,*] Qinfeng* 秦風 *section, Xiaorong* 小戎 *poem, and one will understand the meaning.* Translator's annotation: Quanrong was a powerful tribal state in the west of the Zhou territory. Thus, Quanrong is oftentimes called Xirong 西戎, meaning "Rong from the West." Quanrong's invasion caused the collapse of the Western Zhou (c. 1046–771 BCE) and the beginning of the Eastern Zhou (c. 771–256 BCE), which consisted of the Spring and Autumn period and the Warring States period. Duke Xiang of Qin lived during the very end of the Western Zhou period and the beginning of the Spring and Autumn period.
5. Wang Xiang's commentary: *King Wen* 文王 *[of Zhou* 周*] led the peoples of six states; his people were bound to serve the [tyrannical] King Zhou* 紂王 *[of Shang* 商*] by labor and military obligations. Therefore, women described in the Rufen* 汝墳 *poem picked up tree branches [for firewood, along the banks of the River Ru], and missed their husbands [who were drafted by King Zhou]. These women praised the fish for their tails turning red [because they have worked hard] to commend their husbands [for their hard work]. They encouraged their husbands to remember King Wen's virtues as if their parents were close by. They advised their husbands to fulfill their state duties and to return home soon. See [the* Shijing,*] Zhounan section, Rufen chapter.*

6. Wang Xiang's commentary: *Han Official Fan Pang 范滂 died of integrity. His mother said to him: "You are a loyal minister. I am a loyal minister's mother. What regrets do I have?" Madame Cheng 程氏, mother of Su Zizhan 蘇子瞻 of the Song dynasty, read the biography of Fan Pang and was in awe. Zizhan said to his mother: "I desire to become like Fan Pang; would my mother permit it?" His mother replied: "If you can be like Fan Pang, would I not be able to be like Pang's mother?"* Translator's annotation: For more on Fan Pang, see Fan Ye, *Houhanshu* (*Book of Later Han*). Su Zizhan is Su Shi 蘇軾 (1037-1101 CE), a famous Song poet, literati, and scholar-official, best known by his literary name, Su Dongpo 蘇東坡.
7. Wang Xiang's commentary: 壼 *pronounced as* 閫 *(*kun*). Official Bian Kun* 卞壼 *of the Jin* 晉 *dynasty and his son both died in battles. They were buried in Zhicheng* 治城. *When Emperor Taizu of Ming* 明太祖 *was building the Chaotian Temple* 朝天宮, *he planned to flatten the site. One day, he saw a woman dressed in mourning clothes, laughing aloud. He was puzzled by the sight and inquired about the reasons. The woman replied: "My husband died for his loyalty to the state. My son died for filial piety. I am the wife of a loyal minister and the mother of a filial son. What else should I feel sorrowful about?" She disappeared as soon as she finished her sentences. Bewildered, Taizu asked around about who that woman was. He discovered that the site was Bian Kun's tomb and the woman was Bian Ku's wife. Taizu thereupon built a memorial shrine at the site and sealed the tomb.* Translator's note: See Fang Xuanling et al., *Jinshu* (*Book of Jin*) about Bian Kun.
8. Wang Xiang's commentary: *The state of Wei* 魏 *initiated a war with the state of Shu* 蜀. *Shu's defense general of Jiang You, Ma Miao* 馬邈, *surrendered to Wei. His wife, Madame Li* 李氏, *spit in his face and said: "You are a state official charged with the duty to protect its territory. You did not fight to death to defend it; on the contrary, you surrendered to the enemies. You are not my husband." Thereupon she hanged herself.* Translator's annotation: See Chen Shou, *Sanguozhi* 《三國志》 (*History of the Three Kingdoms*); and Luo Guanzhong, *Sanguo yanyi* 《三國演義》 (*The Three Kingdoms*).
9. Wang Xiang's commentary: 蓋 *is pronounced as* 閣 *(*ge*). [Toward the end of the Western Zhou dynasty,] [Quan]rong attacked the vassal state of Ge. Ge's king was killed. The ruler of [Quan]rong issued a command: "If any Ge general dares not surrender but commits suicide, execute his wife and children." Ge general Qiu Zi* 丘子, *attempted to kill himself, but was rescued by his attendants. He returned home. His wife asked him: "Our country is abolished and our king is killed. Why are you still alive?" The general replied: "I desired to die but was rescued by others. That's why I am still alive." His wife then said: "You are alive because you were rescued then. Why don't you die [for your country] now?" Qiu Zi replied: "I am afraid that you and children will be executed." His wife responded: "Being a general but not fighting with your utmost strength is disloyalty to your country. Without making yourself a martyr when your king was killed is inhumane. Attachment to your wife and children but forgetting to revenge your king's death is unrighteousness. I cannot bear to survive*

like this with you." Thereupon, she hanged herself. The king of [Quan]rong was moved by her virtue, held a funeral for her according to proper rituals, and let the state of Ge continue to exist. Translator's annotation: See Liu Xiang's *Biographies of Women*, volume 5, chapter 5; and Wang Daokun's *Wangshi's Biographies of Women*, volume 4. For more on Quanrong 犬戎, see note 4.

10. Wang Xiang's commentary: *[At the end of the Qin 秦 dynasty, the state of Chu 楚 and the state of Han 漢 fought for their sovereignty]. While Wang Ling 王陵 served Han, his mother lived in Chu. King Xiang [of Chu] 項王 held Wang Lin's mother hostage and told the Han messenger to send the message to Wang Ling: "If Lin does not come, I will kill his mother." Wang Lin's mother said to the messenger: "Tell my son to serve the Han King well. Do not worry about his mother." Thereupon, she killed herself with a sword.* Translator's annotation: See Liu Xiang's *Biographies of Women*, volume 8, chapter 6; and Wang Daokun's *Wangshi's Biographies of Women*, volume 5.
11. Wang Xiang's commentary: *[During the period of the Three Kingdoms,] Wang Jing* 王經 *of Wei* 魏 *pledged allegiance to the young Emperor Mao* 帝髦 *and initiated a coup against [the powerful unruly General] Shima Zhao* 司馬昭. *Shima Zhao killed Emperor Mao. Wang Jing and his mother were to be executed at the city center. Right before the execution, Wang Jing wept and said to his mother: "I have burdened you." His mother responded: "You are a loyal minister. I will smile in my grave. What regrets do I have?" They died together.* Translator's annotation: See Wang Daokun, *Wangshi's Biographies of Women*, volume 6.
12. Wang Xiang's commentary: *[Toward the end of the Song dynasty,] Zhao Maofa* 趙昴發 *was the deputy magistrate (*tong pan 通判*) of Chizhou* 池州. *When the Yuan army surrounded the city, the magistrate (*tai shou 太守*) abandoned the city and escaped. The defense commander (*du tong 都統*) surrendered. Zhao Maofa said to his wife Madame Yong* 雍氏: *"I am a deputy magistrate of the City. I should die with this place. You should leave now." His wife replied: "You are a governmental official and I am an official's wife. You can be a loyal minister. Why cannot I be a loyal minister's wife? I would like to die before you." Maofa followed. When the Yuan army entered the city, the couple wore formal clothes with formal hats. These sentences were written on the desk: "Neither should the country be betrayed nor should the city be surrendered. The husband and the wife shall die together, thus accomplishing both integrity and righteousness." They hanged themselves in the Calmness Hall (*Congrong Tang 從容堂). Translator's annotation: See Chen Menglei, *Gujin tushu jicheng* 《古今圖書集成》 (*Collection of Illustrations and Books from Antiquity to the Present*), volume 398, Guiyuan dian 閨媛典 ("Biographies of Ladies"), under Guiyi bu 閨義部 ("Righteous Women"), the entry for "Zhao Maofa's wife, Madame Yong." Volumes 395–422 of the *Gujin tushu jicheng* categorize biographies of women according to virtue, talent, beauty, and other traits.
13. Wang Xiang's commentary: *Emperor Chengzu of Ming* 明成祖 *[then, Prince of Yan* 燕王*] initiated a military coup, overtaking the imperial palace's Jinchuan Gate* 金川門.

Emperor Jianwen 建文帝 *went into exile. Imperial official Huang Guan* 黃觀 *was out recruiting soldiers to work for Emperor Jianwen. When Huang heard that the regime had changed [because of the coup], he jumped into a river and committed suicide. Emperor Chengzu arranged to marry Huang's wife, Madame Weng* 翁氏, *and his daughter to a servant who took care of elephants (*xiangnu 象奴*). Madame Weng asked for proper wine rituals. Xiangnu went out to prepare the wine rituals. Both the mother and the daughter jumped into the river outside of the Tongji Gate* 通濟門 *to commit suicide. Their bodies went against the current of the water and arrived at the Qingxi River* 清溪 *in the city. Huang's body also floated along the river and arrived in the city in front of the imperial examination hall (Gongyuan* 貢院*). Three bodies met at this location. It amazed the public. They built a shrine south of the Gongyuan to commemorate the incident.* Translator's annotation: Emperor Chengzu of Ming was the husband of Empress Renxiaowen—she authored *Neixun* (one of the *Four Books for Women*). For more about Huang Guan and Madame Weng, see Zhang Tingyu, *Mingshi* (*History of Ming*), volume 31.

14. Wang Xiang's commentary: *Zhu Xu* 朱序 *of the Jin* 晉 *dynasty was the defense officer of Xiangyan* 襄陽. *Qin soldiers invaded Xiangyan. Madame Zhu* 朱夫人 *led maids and concubines from the Zhu household to defend the city. One side of the city wall was about to collapse. Madame Zhu used her own money to help repair the city wall overnight, thus warding off the invading Qin soldiers. The people called the wall "Madame Wall."* Translator's annotation: See Fang Xuanling, *Jinshu* (*Book of Jin*).
15. Wang Xiang's commentary: *Jin* 金 *soldiers [from the north] were invading the Song territory. [Song general] Han Shizhong* 韓世忠 *led his navy, fighting against Jin soldiers in the [Yangzi] River area. The Song soldiers were considerably outnumbered. Madame Liang* 梁夫人 *[, Han's wife,] climbed up to the Jin Mountain, beating the martial drums to cheer the spirits of the Song general and soldiers. They, thus, decisively defeated Jin Wuzhu* 金兀术 *[a Jin general] at the city of Zhenjiang* 鎮江. Translator's annotation: See Tuo Tuo et al., *Songshi* (*History of Song*). Madame Liang was a famous female general, Liang Hongyu 梁紅玉 .
16. Wang Xiang's commentary: *Madame Sun* 孫氏 *was the mother of a Jin* 晉 *[military official,] Yu Tan* 虞潭. *When Su Jun* 蘇峻 *was attacking the imperial capital city of Jin, Yu Tan was stationed to protect the Wuxin* 吳興 *area. His mother advised him to serve the state diligently, and not to worry about her old age. She furthermore sent her grandson Yu Chu* 虞楚 *to assist his father and to join the military, advising him to endeavor at both loyalty and filial piety. Yu Tan later was conferred the rank of marquis because of his merits. His mother passed away at the age of ninety-five. She was given the posthumous name Lady Xuan* 宣夫人. Translator's annotation: See Fang Xuanling et al., *Jinshu* (*Book of Jin*); and Wang Daokun, *Wangshi's Biographies of Women*, volume 6.
17. Wang Xiang's commentary: *Xie Fangde* 謝枋得 *of Song initiated a military revolt [to overturn the Mongol Yuan dynasty and] to resurrect the Song dynasty. He failed*

and died of starvation. His wife, Madame Li 李氏, *was hiding in the mountains with two young sons. They ate wild vegetation to survive. At the time, the Yuan general couldn't catch Madame Li; he thus issued the command: "If Li is not captured, I will kill all the residents in these mountains." Madame Li said: "These residents' lives should not be harmed for my sake." She thus surrendered herself; she was imprisoned in Jiankang* 建康. *When she heard that her husband had died, she hanged herself. Her two sons were released.* Translator's annotation: See Tuo Tuo et al., *Songshi* (*History of Song*). Jiankang, also known as Jinling or Nanjing, was the imperial capital city of several Chinese dynasties (including the Southern Song).

18. Wang Xiang's commentary: *Duke Huan of Qi* 齊桓公 *passed away. His five sons were in a power struggle for the throne. They locked the palace doors and did not bury their father's body for four months. Flies were coming out of the gates. A palace maid, Yan E* 晏娥, *could not bear to see her king's body being exposed like this. She thereby jumped over the wall to die for her king. She hanged herself next to the king's body.* Translator's annotation: It is not immediately clear why committing suicide was a solution in this case. Perhaps, she saw her death as a last resort to call attention to the princes' unfilial acts.
19. Wang Xiang's commentary: *When Emperor Yang of Sui* 隋煬帝 *stayed at the Jiangdu* 江都 *imperial palace, the kingdom was in grave chaos. [General] Yuwen Huaji* 宇文化及 *sent Pei Qiantong* 裴虔通 *to kill the emperor. All of the people inside the palace were running away for their own safety except Chu Guier* 朱貴兒. *She scolded the traitors: "Just a short while ago the emperor gifted you with warm clothes because of cold weather. Since when do you dare to plot against him?" When the party of Pei Qiantong attempted to hang the emperor, Guier used her body to shield the emperor. They therefore killed Guier first, then they assassinated the emperor.* Translator's annotation: Emperor Yangdi of Sui, known for being extravagant and wasteful, built several palaces for temporary stays. The Jiangdu palace was allegedly his favorite.
20. Wang Xiang's commentary: *Duke Xiao of the vassal state of Lu* 魯孝公 *(given name, Cheng* 稱*) was the youngest son of Duke Wu* 武公 *and the younger brother of Duke Yi* 懿公. *Duke Yi's older brother's son Bo Yu* 伯御 *murdered Duke Yi and proclaimed himself the new leader. Bo Yu's people planned to kill Duke Xiao [then only a little boy]. Duke Xiao's nanny, Madame Zang* 臧氏, *dressed her own son in the Duke's clothes and lay him down on the bed. Bo Yu killed her son. Nanny Zang carried young Duke Xiao and escaped to Duke Xiao's uncle's home. When Xiao became an adult, Xiao's uncle and nanny went to see King Xuan [of Zhou]. King Xuan executed Bo Yu and installed Duke Xiao as the new leader of Lu; the King also bestowed Xiao's nanny with the honorary title "Xiao's Righteous Nanny."* Translator's note: See Liu Xiang's *Biographies of Women*, volume 5, chapter 1.
21. Wang Xiang's commentary: *The Qin* 秦 *state abolished the Wei* 魏 *state and killed the king of Wei. Qin planned to execute all the princes. A young prince was hidden by his*

nursing nanny in the mountains. The king of Qin issued a command: "Whoever turns in the young prince will receive the reward of one-thousand pieces of gold. Whoever hides the prince will suffer the extinction of the whole clan." A former official of We said to the nanny: "Why don't you turn in the prince? You will be rewarded with one-thousand pieces of gold." The nanny did not yield. The former official informed the king of Qin. The king deployed soldiers to pursue them. The soldiers shot arrows at the prince while the nanny used her body to shield the prince. Several dozens of arrows landed on her. Both the nanny and the prince died. The king of Qin was moved by what had happened, arranged the burial rite appropriate for a minister to bury her, and bestowed on her the honorary title "Principled Nursing Nanny." Translator's annotation: For more information, see Liu Xiang's *Biographies of Women*, volume 5, chapter 11; and Wang Daokun's *Wangshi's Biographies of Women*, volume 4.

22. Wang Xiang's commentary: *[At the end of the Yuan dynasty,] a rebel force Chen Youliang* 陳友諒 *defeated Taiping* 太平 *[, a stronghold of another rebel force led by Zhu Yuanzhang* 朱元璋*, later the founding emperor of the Ming dynasty]. Chen killed the defense general Hua Yun* 花雲*. Hua Yun's wife, Madame Gao* 郜氏*, committed suicide to safeguard her integrity. Their maid, Madame Sun* 孫氏*, carried their three-year-old son, hid near a lake, behind tall grasses. She fed the little boy lotus seeds to survive. An old man, Lei* 雷, *guided them to Jinling* 金陵 *to see Ming Taizu* 明太祖 *(Emperor Taizu) [i.e., Zhu Yuanzhang]. As soon as the story about how they got there was told, Lei disappeared. Ming Taizhu bestowed on General Hua Yun's son the title of Marquis Dongqiu* 東丘侯 *and named him Hua Wei* 花煒*. He also conferred on Madame Sun the official title "Lady." [Hua] Wei served Madame Sun like his own mother.* Translator's note: See Chen Menglei, *Gujin tushu jicheng* (*Collection of Illustrations and Books from Antiquity to the Present*), volume 398, "Righteous Women," the entry for Hua Yun's Maid-servant, Madame Sun.

23. Wang Xiang's commentary: *Mao Xixi* 毛惜惜 *was a courtesan-prostitute in the Huaian area. Song official Li Quan* 李全 *surrendered to the invading Jin army. Later, when the Jin army attacked Huaian, the defense general also surrendered. Li Quan held a banquet for the guests. He summoned Xixi to sing and entertain the guests. She finally arrived only after several calls. She kept her head down and would not sing. The general asked: "I often requested you to sing and you did. Why are you not singing today?" Xixi replied: "The government entrusted you with a vast army. When you surrendered to invading traitors, you are also a traitor. Even though I am only a lowly courtesan-prostitute who entertains governmental officials, how can I sing for traitors?" The general was furious and killed her.* Translator's annotation: See Tuo Tuo et al., *Songshi* (*History of Song*); and Chen Menglei, *Gujin tushu jicheng* (*Collection of Illustrations and Books from Antiquity to the Present*), volume 398, "Righteous Women," the entry for Song dynasty, Mao Xixi.

24. Wang Xiang's commentary: *[During the period of Five Dynasties and Ten Kingdoms,] Liu Renzhan* 劉仁贍 *of Southern Tang* 南唐 *was stationed to protect*

Shouzhou 壽州. *The army of the state of Zhou attacked Shouzhou. Liu's son Congjian* 從諫 *planned to engage in a surprise attack on the Zhou camp. Without informing his father, [he and his troops left]. He returned after a terrible defeat. His father wanted to execute him for violating the military code. All the generals tried to dissuade Liu, but Liu would not yield. They went to see Liu's wife and pleaded with her to save her son. Madame Liu replied: "It is not that I do not love him. But the military code cannot be violated. It is not something that a woman should advise for a waiver." She closed the door, wailed, and did not come out. Thereupon, her son was executed.* Translator's annotation: See Chen Menglei, *Gujin tushu jicheng* (*Collection of Illustrations and Books from Antiquity to the Present*), volume 398, "Righteous Women," the entry for Southern Tang Liu Renzhan's Wife, Madame Xue 薛氏.

25. Wang Xiang's commentary: *[During the period of Five Dynasties and Ten Kingdoms,] Wang Jianfeng* 王建封 *was a junior officer under General Zhang* 章氏 *of the Kingdom of Min* 閩. *Wang often violated the military code and was supposed to be executed. One day when the general was drunk, the general's mother used the opportunity to release Wang. Wang escaped to the kingdom of Southern Tang; he later became a major general. One day, he led an army to attack the city of Jianzhou* 建州 *and the city was about to be conquered. [He heard that General Zhang's mother was in the city.] He sent a messenger carrying an arrow to be installed on the door of Zhang's mother's house. The messenger said to Madame Zhang: "Our general is going to wipe out the city. Whoever installs this arrow on the door will be spared. He wants to repay you his gratitude." Madame Zhang returned the arrow to the messenger and said: "I cannot bear to see all the lives in the city being terminated while my family alone is spared. I am willing to die with the city." [Wang] Jianfeng was moved by her righteousness. When he conquered the city, he spared all residents from death. The Zhang family was a notable and prosperous family in the Min area for generations.* Translator's annotation: see Chen Menglei, *Gujin tushu jicheng* (*Collection of Illustrations and Books from Antiquity to the Present*), volume 398, "Righteous Women," the entry for Southern Tang, Madame Lian 練夫人.

26. Translator's annotation: *Zhonggan yidan* 忠肝義膽 literally means "loyal liver, righteous gallbladder"; it is a Chinese idiom denoting exemplary loyalty and integrity.

【慈愛篇】

任恤睦婣，根於孝友；慈惠和讓，本於寬仁。是故螽斯緝羽，頌太姒之仁，銀鹿繞床，紀恭穆之德。士安好學，成於叔母之慈，伯道無兒，終獲子綏之報。義姑棄子留侄，而卻齊兵；覽妻與姒均役，以感朱母。趙姬不以公女之貴，而廢嫡庶之儀；衛宗不以君母之尊，而失夫人之禮。莊姜戴嬀，淑惠見於國風；京陵東海，雍睦著乎世範。是皆秉仁慈之懿，敦博愛之風，和氣萃於家庭，德教化於邦國者也，不亦可法歟！

7

Benevolent Love (Ciai pian 慈愛篇)

TRUSTWORTHINESS, CONSIDERATENESS, CONCILIATORINESS, and kindness all take root in filial piety and friendly affection.[1] Benevolence, gentleness, harmony, and yielding all have their foundations in leniency and humaneness.[2]

Therefore, [a poem, which describes] locusts flapping their wings together making loud sounds, praised Taisi's 太姒 humaneness.[3] Silver-plated deer surrounding the bedside memorialized Gongmu's 恭穆 virtue.[4] [Huangfu] Shian [皇甫] 士安 was diligent in his study; his accomplishments should be attributed to his aunt's benevolent love.[5] Bodao 伯道 [and his wife] did not have a son; their sacrifice was eventually repaid by [his young brother's] son Sui 綏.[6] A righteous aunt left behind her own son, but kept her nephew at her side; her righteous deed drove away the invading Qi 齊 soldiers.[7] [Wang] Lan's [王] 覽 wife voluntarily shared household labor with her sister-in-law Si 姒 ; her act moved her mother-in-law, Madame Zhu 朱母.[8] Lady Zhao 趙姬 did not use her status as the daughter of a duke to abolish proper ritual between a principal wife and a concubine.[9] The new king's mother of the state of Wei 衛 did not act contrary to ritual [toward the former king's principal wife] because of her new status.[10] The gentle kindness between Zhuangjiang 莊姜 and Daigui 戴媯 were seen in the Guofeng 國風 [of the *Classic of Poetry*].[11] [Two sisters-in-law,] one from Jingling 京陵 and the other from Donghai 東海, their harmonious way of interaction was a model for the world.[12]

These are all examples of upholding the beauty of humane kindness and of cultivating the culture of benevolent love. Harmonious peace begins with the family. Moral education transforms the state. Should we not emulate them?

Commentaries and Annotations

1. Wang Xiang's commentary: *filial piety (*xiao 孝*), friendly affection (*you 友*), conciliatoriness (*mu 睦*), kindness (*yin 婣*), trustworthiness (*ren 任*), and considerateness (*xu 恤*) are called the six conducts (*liuxing 六行*). Trustworthiness means to take seriously one's promise to care for another person's children or parents. Considerateness means to give special consideration to the widowed, the orphans, the childless, and the homeless. Conciliatoriness means to be harmonious and compliant in the management of the household and the family clans. Kindness means treating relatives and neighbors [in virtue of marriage] with grace and righteousness. Generally, these four kinds of virtuous conduct have their roots in the two words* xiao 孝 *("filial piety") and* you 友 *("friendly affection"). If one is filial, one will show respect to one's family members and dare not act arrogantly toward others; one would love one's family members and dare not despise others; one would extend the kind of care for the elderly members of one's family to the elderly of other families. If one exhibits friendly affection, one would love one's brothers, harmonize with one's wife and son, respect the older and the superior, care for the orphans and the young, and extend the kind of care for one's children to the children of others.* Translator's annotation: The concepts of six virtues (*liude* 六德), six conducts (*liuxing* 六行), and six arts (*liuyi* 六藝) first appeared in the *Zhouli* (*Zhou Rituals*), in the section entitled "Earth Official Situ" (Diguan Situ 地官司徒). The number 6 corresponds to Heaven, Earth, and the four seasons. The teaching that a morally ideal person and state should care for the widowed, the orphans, the childless, and the homeless (*jin lian guan gua gu du* 矜憐鰥寡孤獨) comes from the *Liji* (*Record of Rituals*), the Liyun 禮運 chapter. The statement about extending personal care to public and social care (*lao wu lao yiji ren zhi lao, you wu you yiji ren zhi you* 老吾老以及人之老，幼吾幼以及人之幼) comes from *Mencius* 1A:7.
2. Wang Xiang's commentary: *If one is lenient (*kuan 寬*), there is no person that one cannot forgive (*shu 恕*); if one is humane (*ren 仁*), there is no individual that one cannot love (*ai 愛*). Forgiveness gives birth to harmony (*he 和*) and yielding (*rang 讓*); love brings forth benevolence (*ci 慈*) and gentleness (*hui 惠*). Thus, it is said, leniency and humanness are the foundation of benevolence, gentleness, harmony, and yielding.* Translator's annotation: *Ci* 慈 may also be translated as "compassion, mercy" and *hui* 惠 as "giving benefits."

3. Wang Xiang's commentary: *The* Shijing *says: "Locusts flap their wings together, making loud* yiyi 缉缉 *sounds. Your offspring will be harmonious." This is speaking about the humaneness and kindness of empresses and royal consorts. They have many offspring. And yet, they do not make distinctions between who are the sons of the principal wife and who are the sons of concubines. All children are loved equally as one's own. It is as if locusts give birth to ninety-nine children and they flap their wings harmoniously as one.* Translator's annotation: These verses are from the Zhongsi 螽斯 poem in the Guofeng 國風 section the *Shijing* (*Classic of Poetry*). The correct words used in the poem for the *yiyi* sound are 揖揖, not 缉缉. Taisi 太姒 is the wife of Emperor Wen of Zhou. Her virtue is praised in Liu Xiang's *Biographies of Women*, volume 1, chapter 6; Wang Daokun's *Wangshi's Biographies of Women*, volume 1; Empress Renxiaowen's *Neixun* (*Teachings for the Inner Court*), chapters 11 and 19; and Liu Shi's *Nüfan jielu* (*Short Records of Models for Women*), chapter 2.
4. Wang Xiang's commentary: *Madame Ma* 馬氏 *was the consort of vassal King Wenmu* 文穆王, *Qian Yuanguan* 錢元瓘 *of Wuyue* 吳越 *[during the period of Five Dynasties and Ten Kingdoms]. She had no sons. She requested her father-in-law King Wusu* 武肅王 *(Liu* 鏐*) to issue an edict asking his son Wenmu to take concubines. Wusu said to her: "Surely, you are the one who will help extend my family line." Later, fifteen sons were born. She loved all of them affectionately and indiscriminately. She placed a large silver-plated deer on her bed surrounded by many little deer. Each son held one deer; they played on the bed.* Translator's annotation: Madame Ma 馬氏 was also known as Lady Zhuangmu 莊睦夫人. After she passed away, she was given the posthumous title of Lady Gongmu 恭穆夫人. For more information, see Fan Shang and Lin Yu, *Wuyue beishi* (*History of Wuyue*).
5. Wang Xiang's commentary: *In the Jin* 晉 *dynasty [during the Three Kingdoms period], Huangfu Shian* 皇甫士安 *(given name, Mi* 謐*), lost both his parents when he was young. His widowed aunt raised him. At the beginning, he was not fond of learning. His aunt wept and said: "Your family is dwindling in decline. Yet you are not fond of learning. How can you comfort your deceased parents and their hope? When I die, I would be ashamed in meeting my brother and sister-in-law in the underworld." Mi was moved to tears. He later became a great Confucian scholar. His courtesy name was Sir Xuanyan* 玄晏先生. Translator's note: Huangfu Shian (i.e., Huangfu Mi) was a learned scholar and a famous physician. Emperor Wu of Jin summoned him multiple times to serve in the imperial court, but he declined. He devoted his whole life to scholarship. For more, see Fang Xuanling et al., *Jinshu* (*Book of Jin*); and Wang Daokun, *Wangshi's Biographies of Women*, volume 7.
6. Wang Xiang's commentary: *Jin* 晉 *scholar Deng You* 鄧攸 *(learned name, Bodao* 伯道*) and his wife [during the period of the Three Kingdoms] fled to the mountains to escape the social chaos. He was carrying both his own son and his young brother's son. There was no food and they were exhausted. The situation would not allow them to continue to carry both. His wife said to him: "We will be able to have another son.*

But my deceased brother-in-law has only one son. His son should not be abandoned." Deng You therefore left behind their own son and kept their nephew Deng Sui 鄧綏 *at their side. Deng You later served Emperor Yuan of Jin and passed away without having another son. But his young brother's son Sui took good care of his uncle and aunt and was very filial. When his uncle and aunt passed away, Sui observed the three-year mourning rite for both.* Translator's annotation: The three-year mourning rite was the longest mourning period in funeral rituals. It was typically done by sons and daughters for their deceased parents, by a father when his oldest son passed away, or by ministers in mourning for the death of their emperors. For more, see the *Yili* (*Book of Ceremonial Rites*), the *Liji* (*Record of Rituals), Analects* 17.22, and *Mencius* 3A:2.

7. Wang Xiang's commentary: *[During the Eastern Zhou,] a marquis of a vassal state of Qi* 齊 *invaded Lu* 魯. *The Qi soldiers saw a woman fleeing from the calamity, but she abandoned her young son and was carrying an older son. They asked her: "There are no people who do not naturally love their younger sons more. But you abandoned your younger son and carried an older son instead. What is your reason?" The woman replied: "The younger child was my own son. The older child was the son of my deceased old brother. My older brother entrusted me to take care of his orphaned son. If I abandon his son when I encounter calamity, it is inhumane. I would rather leave behind my own son [if I am unable to rescue both]." Upon hearing this, the marquis of Qi sighed and said: "Even an ordinary woman knows what humaneness is. This is a country of ritual propriety and righteousness. How can we invade such a place?" They therefore initiated a peace agreement with Lu and withdrew the army.* Translator's annotation: See Liu Xiang's *Biographies of Women,* volume 5, chapter 6.
8. Wang Xiang's commentary: *Wang Xiang* 王祥 *of the Jin dynasty [during the period of the Three Kingdoms], had a stepmother Madame Zhu* 朱氏. *During the winter months, his stepmother missed the taste of fish. Xiang would lie down on the frozen river to thaw the water in order to catch carp for her. But his stepmother often abused him, contrary to ritual propriety. Her biological son Wang Lan* 王覽 *always voluntarily shared labor with his stepbrother. Madame Zhu then began to abuse Xiang's wife. Lan's wife also chose to labor together with her sister-in-law Si* 姒. *Their mother finally realized her errors and loved all of them.* Translator's annotation: This anecdote is among the well-known twenty-four exemplars of filial piety. See also Fang Xuanling et al., *Jinshu* (*Book of Jin*).
9. Wang Xiang's commentary: *Lady Zhao* 趙姬 *was the wife of Sir Zhao Chengzi* 趙成子 *(Shuai* 衰*), and the daughter of Duke Wen* 文公 *[of Jin* 晉 *in the period of Spring and Autumn]. At first, Shuai accompanied Duke Wen who fled to the tribal territory of Di* 狄. *Shuai married Jiwei* 季隗 *and gave birth to Zhao Ji* 趙姬. *Both the mother and the son stayed in Di. Later, Shuai became the minister of Jin and Duke Wen married her daughter [Lady Zhao] to Shuai. She gave birth to Tong* 同, *Gua* 括, *and Ying* 嬰. *Lady Zhao beseeched Shuai to welcome his oldest son Dun* 盾 *and*

his mother from Di. She honored Jiwei as Shuai's principal wife and Jiwei's son [Dun] as the son of the principal wife. Lady Zhao willingly took the position as a concubine. Translator's annotation: There are several typographic errors in the Zhuangyuange version of Wang Xiang's commentary. For instance, the name of Zhao Shuai's oldest son should be Zhao Dun 趙盾, not Zhao Ji 趙姬. Moreover, according to Liu Xiang's *Biographies of Women* (volume 2, chapter 8), Shuai's first wife's name should be Shuwei 叔隗, not Jiwei 季隗. See also Wang Daokun, *Wangshi's Biographies of Women*, volume 2.

10. Wang Xiang's commentary: *The birth mother of the new king of the vassal state of Wei 衛 was a concubine (shuqie 庶妾) of the former king. The first lady of the former king did not have a son. Therefore, the concubine's son was enthroned as the new king. The former first lady therefore wanted to move to a side residence. The new king's birth mother said [to the former first lady]: "The right way of distinction between the principal wife and the concubines cannot be abolished. How can I abolish proper rituals of serving my first lady because of my son? Today my first lady wants to move to another residence for my sake. This is to drive away the legal mother (dimu 嫡母), a violation of essential morality." Thereupon, she attempted suicide. Fearing her attempt of suicide, the legal mother of the new king accepted the new king's birth mother's request to stay and remained in the principal residence; she treated both of them with growing kindness and love. Both the new king and his birth mother also served his legal mother with increasing filial piety and reverence. The people of Wei honored their righteous conduct and called them "the two ladies from the Wei clan who follow ritual propriety."* Translator's annotation: See Liu Xiang's *Biographies of Women,* volume 4, chapter 12; and Wang Daokun's *Wangshi's Biographies of Women*, volume 1.
11. Wang Xiang's commentary: *Lady Zhuangjiang 莊姜 [of the period of Spring and Autumn] was from Qi. Madame Chen 陳氏 (Daigui 戴媯) was a concubine of their husband. Chen's son died and she was to return to her maternal home. Zhuangjiang could not bear to see Chen's departure and composed the Yanyan 燕燕 poem, of which two lines read as follows: "I sent you off until you were so far away that I can no longer see your back. My tears poured as if it has rained." The affectionate love between a principal wife and a concubine is as deep as this.* Translator's annotation: See the *Shijing* (*Classic of Poetry*), Guofeng section, the Yanyan poem.
12. Wang Xiang's commentary: *Madame Zhong 鍾氏, wife of Wang Hun 王渾 of Jin 晉, was from the Jingling 京陵 area. Hun's younger brother Cheng's 澄 wife, Madame Hao 郝氏, was from the Donghai 東海 region. Both sisters-in-law were harmonious, compliant, and friendly toward each other, and they managed their households with proper rituals. Households of the nobles and the commoners all followed their examples as norms.* Translator's annotation: The nuance of the story is that Madame Zhong was from an aristocratic family, whereas Madame Hao was a commoner. Because of the difference in their social status, their courteous interaction was regarded as especially praiseworthy. For more, see Fang Xuanling et al., *Jinshu* (*Book of Jin*), "Biographies of Women."

【秉禮篇】

德貌言工，婦之四行；禮義廉恥，國之四維。人而無禮，胡不遄死，言禮之不可失也。是故，文伯之母，不逾門而見康子；齊華夫人，不易駟而從孝公。孟子欲出妻，母責以非禮；申人欲娶婦，女恥其無儀。頃公吊杞梁之妻，必造廬以成禮；溧女哀子胥之餒，甯投溪而滅踪。羊子懷金，妻拏譏其不義；齊人乞墦，妾婦泣其無良。宋伯姬保傅不具不下堂，甯焚烈焰；楚貞姜符節不來不應召，甘沒狂瀾。是皆動必合義，居必中度，勉夫子以匡其失，守己身以善其道，秉禮而行，至死不變者，洵可法矣！

8

Upholding Ritual Propriety (Bingli pian 秉禮篇)

JUST LIKE VIRTUE, appearance, speech, and work are four principal conducts of a woman,[1] ritual propriety, righteousness, honesty, and a sense of shame are the four pillars of a country.[2] "If a person cannot observe ritual propriety, why not die quickly?" This speaks to the observance of ritual propriety, which must not be neglected.[3]

Therefore, [Gongfu] Wenbo's [公夫] 文伯 mother would not overstep the door threshold in receiving [her grandnephew], [Ji] Kangzi [季] 康子.[4] Lady Hua of Qi 齊華夫人 would not yield to Duke Xiao [of Qi] [齊] 孝公 to ride in a four-horse drawn carriage.[5] Mencius intended to divorce his wife. His mother reproached him for violating ritual propriety.[6] A man in the region of Shen 申 wanted to marry a woman [without following proper marriage rituals]. The woman [whom he wished to marry] shamed him for abandoning rituals.[7] Duke Qing [of Qi] [齊] 頃公 expressed his condolence to Qi Liang's 杞梁 wife [for Qi Liang's death]. The duke must do so in their residence to complete the proper ritual.[8] A woman from the River Li 溧 [水] area was saddened by [Wu] Zixu's

[伍] 子胥 lack of trust in her. She jumped into the river to die [rather than to survive in shame].[9] [Yue] Yangzi [樂] 羊子 brought home some gold [that he picked up from streets]. His wife and children ridiculed him for being unrighteous.[10] A man of the state of Qi 齊 begged for food in graveyards. His concubine and wife cried in contempt as if they had no husband.[11] Lady Boji of Song 宋伯姬 would not leave her residence hall without her woman guardians, *Bao* 保 and *Fu* 傅. She would rather perish in burning flame [than violate ritual propriety].[12] Lady Zhenjiang of Chu 楚貞姜 would not answer the king's summoning without seeing his amulet. She would rather drown in a raging flood [than violate ritual propriety].[13]

These are all examples of women who, when acting, comply with righteousness; when in residence, they follow the mean. These women admonished their husbands to rectify their husbands' mistakes and disciplined their persons to make good the Way. They upheld ritual propriety in their conduct and did not change their stand even when facing death. They are the examples that we ought to follow!

Commentaries and Annotations

1. Wang Xiang's commentary: *Filial piety, benevolence, chastity, and graciousness are women's virtues. Dignified quiet elegance is what is meant by women's appearance. Gentle words and euphemisms are what is meant by women's speech. Diligence, respect, and prudence are what is meant by women's work. These four are the constant principles of the way of a woman; they are the integrity and righteousness of a young lady.* Translator's annotation: "Four [womanly] conducts or virtues" (*sixing* 四行 or *side* 四德) occurred first in the *Zhouli* (*Zhou Rituals*) and the *Liji* (*Record of Rituals*). See Ban Zhao's *Lessons for Women*, chapter 4, for exposition.
2. Wang Xiang's commentary: Wei 維 *means "principle, bond" (*gang 綱*). The* Zhuan 《傳》 *(*Commentary*) says: "If the four pillars are not promulgated, a nation necessarily heads toward extinction." It means if a country does not abide by these four pillars, then ethical bonds will not prosper. Ministers and the common people will become lawless. This is the path to calamity and destruction.* Translator's annotation: The *Commentary* probably refers to the *Chunqiu zuozhuan* (*Zuo Commentary to the Spring and Autumn Annals*). The citation is from the *Xin Wudaishi* 《新五代史》 (*New History of the Five Dynasties*), authored by Ouyang Xiu 歐陽修. The concept of the "four pillars of a country" (*guozhi siwei* 國之四維) can be traced back to the *Guanzi* 管子, the Mumin 牧民 chapter.
3. Wang Xiang's commentary: *The* Shijing *(*Classic of Poetry*) says: "Look at mice, even they have proper limbs. If a person does not observe ritual propriety, why not die quickly?" It makes the point that such a person is not even comparable to an animal.* Translator's annotation: These verses are from the *Shijing*, Yongfeng 鄘風 section, Xiangshu 相鼠 poem.

4. Wang Xiang's commentary: *This is speaking about [Jingjiang 敬姜], mother of Gongfu Wenbo 公夫文伯 and grand-aunt of Ji Kangzi 季康子. She was already in her seventies. When Kangzi visited her, she would stand inside the door and install a handkerchief at the door. Kangzi would bow to her outside the door and speak to her where the handkerchief separated the space. They observed ritual propriety to such a great extent.* Translator's annotation: The custom of hanging a handkerchief at the door is found in the *Liji* (Record of Rituals). The Neize 內則 chapter reads: "When a child is born, if it is a boy, hang a wooden bow and arrow at the left side of the door. If it is a girl, hang a handkerchief at the right side of the door." For more about Lady Jingjiang, see Liu Xiang's *Biographies of Women*, volume 1, chapter 9; and Wang Daokun's *Wangshi's Biographies of Women*, volume 2. Liu Xiang cited Confucius's praise of her virtue four times. Ji Kangzi was a contemporary of Confucius and a minister of Lu during the Spring and Autumn period. *Analects* 12.17, 12.18, and 12.19 recorded the discussion between Ji Kangzi and Confucius on government. In 12.19, Ji Kangzi asked Confucius whether it was acceptable to kill those who violate the law in order to protect those who follow it. Confucius replied, "We are speaking about government. Why even mention killing? If you desire the good, the people will become good. The virtue of a gentleman is like the wind, and the virtue of a small man is like the grass. When the wind blows over the grass, the grass necessarily bends." Some contemporary scholars, e.g., Daniel A. Bell, interpret this passage as evidence supporting the view that a Confucian humane government would be very reluctant to use force or war.
5. Wang Xiang's Commentary: *The wife of Duke Xiao of the state of Qi 齊孝公 [in the Spring and Autumn period] was from the Hua family of the state of Wei. One day she rode in a covered carriage (*anche 安車*) on an outing with Duke Xiao. The carriage was running very fast. Suddenly the wheels slipped, the carriage turned over, and the curtains were torn. Lady Hua ordered her maids to hold up the curtain as a barrier. Duke Xiao sent a four-horse-drawn carriage for her. She declined and said: "To ride a carriage without a curtain violates proper rituals [for women]. My carriage was damaged which forced me to stay outside in a rural area; this also goes against proper rituals [for women]. To continue to live in violation of ritual propriety is not as good as sacrificing one's life in order to observe it." She then attempted suicide. Her maids were not able to revive her until a covered carriage finally arrived. She finally regained consciousness. Lady Hua observed ritual propriety to such a great extent.* Translator's annotation: According to the *Liji* (*Record of Rituals*), Qulishang 曲禮上 chapter, and the *Zhouli* (*Zhou Rituals*), Chunguan 春官 section, Zhongche 中車 chapter, women should ride in a one-horse-drawn covered carriage-sedan for seating—that is, *anche* 安車. Four-horse-drawn carriages were designed for men to ride in a standing position. For more, see Liu Xiang's *Biographies of Women*, volume 4, chapter 6; and Wang Daokun's *Wangshi's Biographies of Women*, volume 1.
6. Wang Xiang's commentary: *Mencius entered the room. He saw his wife exposing her upper body because of the summer heat. Mencius was unpleased and intended to divorce*

his wife. His wife said: "When a woman is in her private bedroom, there is no need for her to dress up. When she meets her husband here, she does not greet him with rituals proper for receiving a guest. Today you use guest rituals to reprimand me. I should leave." [When Mencius's mother heard of the incident,] she admonished Mencius: "According to the rituals, 'when one is about to ascend to the main hall, one calls out loudly.' This is done to warn others about one's presence. 'When one is about to enter the door of an inner room, one keeps one's eyes down.' This is to avoid seeing other's mistakes inadvertently. Today you are the one who does not know proper rituals, but on the contrary, you accused others of not following proper rituals. Is your own behavior not erroneous?" Thereupon, Mencius asked for forgiveness and asked his wife to stay. Translator's annotation: See Liu Xiang's *Biographies of Women*, volume 1, chapter 11; and Wang Daokun's *Wangshi's Biographies of Women*, volume 3.

7. Wang Xiang's commentary: *A man in the region of Shen 申 was going to marry a wife but did not prepare the six wedding rituals (*liuli 六禮*). He wanted to have the wedding very casually. The woman he wanted to marry would not comply. He sued her in court. The woman argued that the man was forcing the match without proper rituals; even if she dies, she would not comply. She wrote the poem* Xinglu 行露 *as her vow. Eventually the man arranged the six rituals. The marriage union of the two was completed. The poem is recorded in the* Shijing, Shaonan 召南 *section.* Translator's annotation: See Liu Xiang's *Biographies of Women*, volume 4, chapter 1; and Wang Daokun's *Wangshi's Biographies of Women*, volume 3.
8. Wang Xiang's commentary: *The state of Jin attacked the state of Qi. Qi Liang 杞梁, a military general of Qi, died in the battle. His wife encountered Duke Qing of Qi 齊頃公 on her way home to make funeral arrangements. The duke intended to conduct the rite of condolence right there at the road side. Qi Liang's wife said: "If you, Duke, think that my husband is guilty of a crime, I shall turn myself in to the Minister of Punishment (*Sikou 司寇*) for the death sentence. But if you conduct the rite of condolence out of commiseration, please consider doing so at his humble residence." The duke agreed. After she returned to their home, the duke personally came to express his condolences. The burial rite was completed. Qi Liang was then buried. After the burial, his wife passed away due to wailing in deep sorrow. The city wall collapsed because of it.* Translator's annotation: See Liu Xiang's *Biographies of Women*, volume 4, chapter 8; and Wang Daokun's *Wangshi's Biographies of Women*, volume 1. *Sikou* is an official title dated back to the Western Zhou dynasty (c. 1046–771 BCE). The title referred to the head minister in charge of investigation of crimes and enforcement of appropriate punishment. For more, consult the *Zhouli* (*Zhoul Rituals*), the Qiuguan 秋官 section, Sikou 司寇 chapter; the *Liji* (*Record of Rituals*), the Qulixia 曲禮下 chapter; and the *Shiji* (*Historical Records*), the Zhoubenji 周本紀 section.
9. Wang Xiang's commentary: *Wu Zixu 伍子胥 of the state of Chu 楚 was in exile. When he passed the River Li 溧水, he saw a woman washing linen in the river carrying a food basket. Zixu said to her: "I had not eaten for three days. Would Madame*

have pity on me and give me some food?" The woman kneeled and fed Zixu food. When he bid farewell, he said to her: "When those who try to capture me arrive, please do not tell them my whereabouts." The woman promised. Zixu still reminded her several times. The woman laughed and said: "I am thirty years old. In order to care for my mother, I remain unmarried. Am I the kind of person who will casually talk to anyone? I am a woman but I served a meal to a man. This has already violated proper rituals. I already gave you my word but you continue to remind me. This indicates that you suspect that I am untrustworthy. I cannot live untrustworthily and in violation of ritual propriety." She then threw herself into the river and drowned. Zixu was unable to rescue her in time. Later he arrived at the state of Wu 吳. He returned after defeating the state of Chu 楚. When en route the River Li, he threw a thousand pieces of gold into the water to repay the woman who helped him earlier. Translator's annotation: Wu Zixu was a famous statesman during the Spring and Autumn period. His father was the teacher of the crown prince of Chu but later, due to political turmoil, King Ping of Chu 楚平王 imprisoned and killed Zixu's father and his older brother. Zixu escaped from Chu and went to the state of Wu. He eventually defeated Chu. For more, see Sima Qian, *Shiji* (*Historical Records*), "Biography of Wu Zixu" 伍子胥列傳.

10. Wang Xiang's commentary: *[During the Warring States period,] Yue Yangzi* 樂羊子 *picked up someone's lost gold off the streets. He brought it home to show his wife. His wife said: "I have heard a wise learned person does not drink water from a stolen spring. A virtuous worthy person will not eat food handed to him in contempt. Why do you covet the gold that is contrary to ritual and are willing to act unrighteously?" Yangzi replied: "But the lost gold has no owner." His wife responded: "The gold has no owner. Does your conscience also have no owner?" Yue Yangzi felt ashamed. Thereupon, he waited on the street and returned the gold to its rightful owner.* Translator's annotation: For more, see Fan Ye, *Houhanshu* (*Book of Later Han*), "Biographies of Women."
11. Wang Xiang's commentary: *A man of the state of Qi had one wife and one concubine. Whenever he went out, he always returned home drunk and full. His wife asked him with whom he drank and ate. He always said that he was with the wealthy and the aristocrats. His wife doubted his words and said to herself: "He always drank with the nobles. Why [has] no one of high stature ever visited us?" She therefore followed her husband secretly. She saw him go outside of the city and into the area of graveyards. He begged for the leftovers from the worshipers. If one place did not have enough food, he would go to the next one. Upon seeing this, his wife was ashamed. She came home and told the concubine: "A husband should be someone whom you admire and devote your whole life to. Today it has become like this." They scorned their husband's shameful deeds and cried in the courtyard. Their husband did not know what happened; still carrying himself complacently, he returned home and bossed around his wife and concubine.* Translator's annotation: For more, see *Mencius*, 4B:33.

12. Wang Xiang's commentary: *Lady Boji* 伯姬 *was the wife of Duke Gong of Song* 宋共公 *and the daughter of Duke Xuan of Lu* 魯宣公. *After Duke Gong passed away, his brother Duke Yuan inherited the throne. Later, during the reign of Duke Jing, the palace caught fire. Lady Boji's attendants asked her to flee from the burning fire. Lady Boji said: "According to the right behavior of a woman, if her guardians Bao and Fu are not present, she should not leave her residence." Guardian Bao finally arrived and said: "My lady, please flee from the fire." Lady Boji responded: "Guardian Fu is not here yet. How can we panic and forget ritual propriety?" The fire approached rapidly. Court attendants were running away from the fire. Lady Boji did not leave her residence and died in the fire. She was sixty some years old.* Translator's annotation: See Liu Xiang, *Biographies of Women*, volume 4, chapter 2; Guliangzi, *Guliang Commentaries to the Spring and Autumn Annals*; and Gongyang Gao, *Gongyang Commentaries to the Spring and Autumn Annals* (under "Thirtieth Year of Duke Xiang [of Lu]"). For aristocratic ladies during the Spring and Autumn period (c. 771–476 BCE) to leave their residence at night, they must be accompanied by two women guardians, *bao mu* 保母 and *fu mu* 傅母. The *bao mu*'s work is to take care of the details of daily life, whereas the *fu mu*'s duty is to educate court ladies.
13. Wang Xiang's commentary: *Lady Zhen-Jiang* 貞姜, *the wife of King Zhao of Chu* 楚昭王, *was on an outing with the king. King Zhao asked Jiang to stay in the pavilion at the waterfront. He said to her if he sent anyone to summon her, the messenger would show her the king's amulet. Later, the river's water level suddenly rose rapidly. The king's messenger came to escort her to safety, but forgot to bring the king's amulet with him. She would not leave. The messenger said: "The water is rising rapidly. If I go back to bring the amulet, there will not be enough time. My lady, please leave immediately." Jiang responded: "The amulet is a sign of faithfulness. It is to safeguard faithfulness that ritual propriety is instituted. To survive without ritual propriety is not as good as to die for ritual propriety." The messenger returned to retrieve the amulet. But the flood water rose above the pavilion and Queen Jiang drowned in the water. King Zhao mourned her death and bestowed on her the title* Zhen Jiang 貞姜 *(Chaste Jiang).* Translator's annotation: See Liu Xiang's *Biographies of Women*, volume 4, chapter 10.

【智慧篇】

治安大道，固在丈夫。有智婦人，勝於男子。遠大之謀，預思而可料；倉卒之變，泛應而不窮。求之閨閫之中，是亦笄幃之傑。是故齊姜醉晉文而命駕，卒成霸業。有緡娠少康而出竇，遂致中興。顏女識聖人之後必顯，喻父擇壻而禱尼丘。陳母知先世之德甚微，令子因人以取侯爵。剪髮留賓，知吾兒之志大。隔屏窺客，識子友之不凡。楊敞妻促夫出而定策，以立一代之君。周顗母因客至而當庖，能具百人之食。晏御揚揚，妻恥之而令夫致貴。甯歌浩浩，姬識之而喻相尊賢。徒讀父書，知趙括之不可將。獨聞妾慟，識文伯之不好賢。樊女笑楚相之蔽賢，終舉賢而安萬乘。漂母哀王孫而進食，後封王以報千金。樂羊子能聽妻諫以成名；甯宸濠不用婦言而亡國。陶答子妻，畏夫之富盛而避禍，乃保幼以養姑。周才美婦，懼翁之橫肆而辭榮，獨全身以免子。漆室處女，不績其麻而憂魯國。巴家寡婦，能捐己產而保鄉民。凡此皆女子之嘉猷，婦人之明識。誠可謂知人免難，保家國而助夫子者歟。

9

Wisdom *(Zhihui pian 智慧篇)*

ALTHOUGH THE GREAT way of governing in peace rests on men,[1] yet a wise woman surpasses a man.[2] Grand long-term planning can be premeditated and predicted; changes due to sudden emergencies, however, are vastly varied and infinite.[3] If one seeks inside the inner quarters of women (*gui kun* 閨閫), one can surely find outstanding females.[4]

Therefore, Madame Jiang 姜 of the state of Qi 齊 purposefully intoxicated [her husband,] Duke Wen of Jin 晉文公, and arranged to have him driven away [from the state of Qi]. Duke Wen thus accomplished his kingly affairs.[5] You Min 有緡, who was pregnant with Prince Shao Kan 少康, escaped from a hole of a hideout. Later they restored their country.[6] Miss Yan 顏女 [Confucius's mother] knew that the offspring of a sage will necessarily be accomplished. She thus told her father whom he should select as his son-in-law. She then prayed to the god of Mountain Ni Qiu.[7] The mother of Chen [Ying] 陳 [嬰] 母 understood that the ancestors of the Chen family did not have great virtuous deeds. She therefore advised her son to follow a leader [instead of initiating an uprising on his own]. Later, he was bestowed the title of a marquis.[8] [Madame Tao 陶] cut [and sold] her hair [to buy food] in order to entertain the guests, for she knew her son's great ambition.[9] Observing the guests from behind the room divider, [Fang Xuanling's 房玄齡] mother discerned the unusual abilities of his friends.[10] Yang Chang's wife 楊敞妻 made him [overcome his fear and] come out of his room to decide on strategies to enthrone a [new] emperor.[11] Zhou Yi's mother 周顗母 took on the kitchen duty because unexpected guests arrived. She prepared food to feed a hundred people.[12] Yanzi's 晏子 carriage driver carried himself complacently. The driver's wife was ashamed of his complacency; it made her husband eventually become a distinguished man.[13] Ning [Qi] 甯 [戚] sang the song Haohao 浩浩. Lady [Jing 婧] alone understood his meaning and informed the minister [Guan Zhong 管仲] to use the worthy [as a minister of Qi 齊].[14] Zhao Kuo 趙括 studied his father's books [of military strategy] only superficially; his mother knew that Zhao Kuo should not be deployed as a general.[15] When [Gongfu] Wenbo [公夫] 文伯 passed away, his mother only heard the sorrowful weeping of his concubines. From this, she realized that Wenbo did not value the virtuous worthies [when he was alive].[16] Lady Fan 樊女 laughed at the Chu 楚 prime minister's avoidance of using the talented and the virtuous. Thereupon, the minister began to use the worthy. The state of Chu thus became greatly governed.[17] An elderly woman earning her living by washing cotton and silk threads in the river (*piao mu* 漂母) took pity on a young man and gave him food. He later was bestowed the title of a king and repaid her favor with a thousand pieces of gold.[18] Yue Yangzi 樂羊子 could listen to his wife's admonition; he thus became accomplished.[19] Ning Chenhao 甯宸濠 brought his state to destruction because he did not listen to a woman's warning.[20] Tao Dazi's wife 陶答子妻 shunned her husband's wealth and prosperity [acquired by unjust means]; she thus avoided calamity. Because of this, she could protect her son and care for her mother-in-law.[21] Zhou Caimei's wife 周才美 feared her father-in-law's intimidating lawless behavior; she thus left her prosperous household behind. She alone was able to preserve her life and her son's.[22] A young lady from Qishi 漆室 stopped spinning hemp because she was worried about [the future of] the state of Lu 魯.[23] A widow of the Ba 巴 area donated her personal fortunes in order to protect residents of her village.[24]

These are all examples of women's great strategies and plans in governance and their keen understanding. This is truly what is meant by "if one knows the people, one will be able to avoid calamity." These women are the protectors of their countries and families and the helpmates of their husbands!

Commentaries and Annotations

1. Wang Xiang's commentary: *Even though governing a country and maintaining peace under Heaven is a man's great path, the importance of rectifying one's person and regulating one's family also relates to the way of a woman. It is something indispensable.*
2. Wang Xiang's commentary: *A wise woman at home can correct and prevent a husband's mistakes, as well as respond to changes resulting from sudden emergencies. This is something that men cannot measure up to.*
3. Wang Xiang's commentary: *This is speaking about virtuous women from antiquity. Every time when something happened, they were able to deliberate concerning potential predicaments and to prevent problems beforehand. If the troubles were already there, they could respond to changes of sudden emergencies. If a crisis was not yet imminent, they were able to discern opportunities of a lifetime. [Men] cannot match this ability.*
4. Wang Xiang's commentary: *This is speaking about how women equipped with wise knowledge are rightly called outstanding persons among women.* Translator's annotation: *Gui kun* 閨閫 literally means "woman's bedroom"; it is used to refer to women generally.
5. Wang Xiang's commentary: *After Duke Wen of Jin* 晉文公 *just became a prince, he fled to the state of Qi in exile. Duke Huan of Qi* 齊桓公 *married his daughter to him. Duke Wen enjoyed his life so much that he forgot his responsibility to return to his home state of Jin. Ministers Zhao Shuai* 趙衰 *and Wei Chou* 魏犨, *who accompanied the prince into exile, had a meeting in the field of mulberry trees. They planned to kidnap the prince to return to Jin and to restore their home state. A woman working in the mulberry field heard this. She ran to report this to Madame Jiang of Qi* 齊姜. *Madame Jiang [Duke Wen's wife] killed her in order to prevent the information from leaking out. Jiang then intoxicated the prince and called Zhao Shuai and others to help the prince aboard the carriage. When the prince woke up, they had already left the territory of Qi. The prince afterwards went to the states of Chu* 楚 *and Qin* 秦, *borrowed their army, reclaimed his home state, and became king.* 犨 *pronounced as* 酬 (chou). Translator's annotation: See Zuo Qiuming, *Guoyu* 《國語》 (*Discourses of the States*), the section entitled Jinyu 晉語 ("Discourse of Jin").
6. Wang Xiang's commentary: 娠 *pronounced as* 身 (shen*). During the Xia* 夏 *dynasty, Han Zhuo* 寒浞 *killed Emperor Xiang of Xia* 夏帝相 *and usurped the throne. The emperor's consort, You Min* 有緡氏, *was pregnant at the time. She hid inside a hole in a wall and survived. She escaped to her maternal family and gave birth to Shao Kan* 少康. *Later, King [You] Yu* 虞 *married two daughters to Shao Kan. They had a*

territory of five hundred people. Eventually they destroyed Han Zhuo and revived the Xia dynasty.

7. Wang Xiang's commentary: *Kongzi's [i.e., Confucius's] father, Shuliang He* 叔梁紇, *wanted to remarry after his wife passed away. Confucius's mother Madame Yan's* 顏氏 *father one day said at home: "Kong Shuliang is old and ugly but strong and brave. He desires to remarry. But no one's daughter would marry him. [It's unfortunate,] but what can one do?" His youngest daughter Zhengzai [, later, Confucius's mother] replied: "I have heard that the Kong family is the offspring of a sage king. Their future generation will necessarily prosper. What's the harm of marrying him as a wife?" Her father said: "It will be all right to marry you to him." Thereupon, Yan married his daughter [Zhengzai] to Shuliang. [Zhengzai] was concerned that, because of Shuliang's old age, he would have no sons [to carry on family name]. She thus prayed to the god of Ni Qiu Mountain and later gave birth to Zhong Ni* 仲尼 *[i.e., Confucius].* Translator's annotation: Zhong Ni is Confucius's given name; Kong is his family name. For more information, see Sima Qian, *Shiji* 《史記》 (*Historical Records*), Kongzi shijia 孔子世家 ("Family Genealogy of Confucius"); Wang Shu, ed., *Kongzi jiayu* 《孔子家語》 (*Family Discourse of Confucius*), Benxingjie 本姓解 ("Explanation of the Family Name").
8. Wang Xiang's commentary: *At the end of Qin* 秦 *dynasty, the country was in grave chaos. Chen Ying* 陳嬰 *was quite talented. His people wanted to make him king. His mother said to him: "Your ancestors did not have great virtues. The uprising will not succeed if you rebel on your own. It is not as good as choosing a leader to serve. If the uprising succeeds, you may be rewarded with the title of a marquis. If it fails, you still can protect yourself from harm." Ying therefore joined Xiang Liang* 項梁 *in the uprising [against Qin]. He later pled allegiance to Han* 漢 *and was bestowed the title of Marquis Tangyi* 棠邑侯 *because of his contributions.* Translator's annotation: For more information, see Ban Gu et al., *Hanshu* (*Book of Han*); Liu Xiang, *Biographies of Women*, volume 8, chapter 5; and Wang Daokun, *Wangshi's Biographies of Women*, volume 5.
9. Wang Xiang's commentary: *Tao Kan* 陶侃 *had great ambition even when he was young. His friends were all outstanding people of the time. One day, Kan's friend Fan Kui* 范逵 *visited. But Kan's family was very poor and had nothing to serve. His mother cut her hair and secretly sold it to buy food. She also cut the straws off their sleeping mat to feed the guest's horse. Upon seeing this, Kui said in awe: "Without this mother, there will not be this son!"* Translator's annotation: Tao Kan (259–334 CE) was a renowned Jin 晉 dynasty (265–420 CE) general and governor.
10. Wang Xiang's commentary: *Fang Xuanling* 房玄齡 *studied under Wen Zhongzi* 文中子. *Fang's peers all had remarkable talents. They visited his home one time. His mother observed them from behind a room divider and said: "They are all talented men capable of becoming high-ranking officials and prime ministers. My son has friends of this caliber. What is there for me to be concerned about?" Later, Fang and*

his friends, such as Du Ruhui 杜如晦, *Xue Yuanjing* 薛元敬, *and so on, all served Emperor Taizhong of Tang* 唐太宗 *as top officials and ministers.* Translator's annotation: Wen Zhongzi 文中子 (584–617 CE) is the pen name of Wang Tong 王通, a renowned Confucian scholar during the Sui 隋 dynasty (581–618 CE).

11. Wang Xiang's commentary: *King Chang Yi* 昌邑王 *of Han was wanton. Grand General Huo Guang* 霍光 *was planning to remove him and enthrone Emperor Xuan* 宣帝. *He went to prime minister Yang Chang's* 楊敞 *home to discuss this. Chang was old and cowardly. When he heard of the plot, he trembled with fear and withdrew to his room. His wife made him come out and said: "To abolish a wanton king in order to enthrone a virtuous king is a grave matter. Why are you scared and retreat like this? If you do not come out today, when the plan is successfully carried out tomorrow, our family clans will be exterminated." Chang thereupon came out the room and decided with the others on the strategies to enthrone Emperor Xuan. On account of his merits, he was bestowed the title of Marquis Pingtong* 平通侯. Translator's annotation: See Liu Xiang's *Biographies of Women*, volume 8, chapter 9; and Wang Daokun's *Wangshi's Biographies of Women*, volume 5.
12. Wang Xiang's commentary: *Zhou Yi* 周顗, *courtesy name Bo Ren* 伯仁, *was a human-resources minister* 吏部尚書 *of Jin. His mother was Madame Li* 李氏, *given name Luo Xiu* 絡秀. *She was a daughter of a farming family. Yi's father was Andong General* 安東將軍 *Zhou Jun* 周浚, *who went hunting one day and sought shelter from the rain at Li's residence. That day Madame Li's father went out and her mother was ill. Madame Li, with the help of one maid and one servant, killed a pig and prepared a feast to feed one hundred people. Jun learned about what happened. He spoke in awe: "What a worthy lady!" He pled to marry Madame Li as his concubine. Her father initially hesitated and did not approve. She said to her father: "Our family clan is large but has low social status. Many people take advantage of us. If we do not establish relationship with the nobles, how do we protect our family?" Her father thus approved the marriage. She later gave birth to Bo Ren.*
13. Wang Xiang's commentary: *Yanzi* 晏子 *was the prime minister of the state of Qi. One day Yanzi's carriage driver drove Yangzi passing the driver's home. The driver acted complacently; the driver's wife felt ashamed of his complacency. When the driver returned home, she asked to leave him. The driver inquired about the reasons. His wife responded: "Yanzi is only five foot tall and yet he is the prime minister of Qi. I saw him carrying himself courteously, humbly, respectfully, and prudently, often as if [his talents and ability were] not sufficient. You are seven foot tall and are satisfied simply with being a carriage driver. When you passed our village gate, you carried yourself complacently. If this is your intention, you are not my husband." The driver thanked his wife and reproached himself. He learned to act humbly and courteously, often as if [his talent and ability were] not sufficient. Yanzi felt strange and asked. The driver told Yanzi what happened. Yanzi praised him for being able to take good advice and correct errors, and recommended the carriage driver to Duke Jing* 景公.

The duke bestowed on the driver the official title of Dafu 大夫 *and his wife, Mingfu* 命婦. Translator's annotation: Yanzi was a famous statesman during the Spring and Autumn period. Dafu was a title in the governmental system and the wife of a Dafu may be given the title Mingfu. For more information, see *Zhouli* (*Zhou Rituals*); Liu Xiang's *Biographies of Women*, volume 2, chapter 12; and Wang Daokun's *Wangshi's Biographies of Women*, volume 1.

14. Wang Xiang's commentary: *Duke Huan of Qi* 齊桓公 *was at an outing. He saw Ning Qi* 甯戚 *hitting an ox horn and singing. He knew this is a worthy man and deployed his minister Guan Zhong* 管仲 *to welcome Ning Qi. But Qi simply said: "How vast! The White River!" Guan Zhong could not penetrate the meaning; he did not attend the court meeting for five days, and looked worried. His concubine Jing* 婧 *asked about the reasons. [Guan] Zhong told her the story. Jing laughed and said: "That person had already expressed clearly his intention to you. Did you not know? An old poem read: 'Expansive is the White River. Black is the swimming fish. My King is summoning me. I shall reside here. The country is still not in peace. Why not follow me?' Ning Qi desires to be an official in the state of Qi." [Guan] Zhong was very pleased and conveyed the meaning to Duke Huan. Duke Huan engaged in fasting, performed rituals at the ancestral temple, and employed Ning Qi as a minister. The state of Qi thus became well governed and prosperous.* Translator's annotation: For more information, see Liu Xiang's *Biographies of Women*, volume 6, chapter 1; and Wang Daokun's *Wangshi's Biographies of Women*, volume 2.

15. Wang Xiang's commentary: *Zhao She* 趙奢 *of the state of Zhao* 趙 *was good at military strategy. After he passed away, the king of Zhao used his son Zhao Kuo* 趙括 *as a general to resist the Qin* 秦 *army. Kuo's mother went to see the king and said: "Kuo should not be appointed as a general. He only read his father's books superficially but does not know how to apply them. Once he discussed military strategies with my husband, he argued with such sophistry that my husband was unable to refute him. My husband later said to me, 'Kuo does not really know military strategy but only knows how to argue with sophistry. If one uses him as a general, his troops will necessarily be defeated and brings shame to the country.'" The king would not listen to her. Kuo's mother then said: "If Kuo is defeated, please do not blame or punish me." The king promised. Later, as predicated, Kuo was brutally defeated—he lost four hundred thousand men.*

16. Wang Xiang's commentary: *Gongfu Wenbo* 公父文伯 *of Lu* 魯 *passed away. His concubines wept in deep sorrow. Some even committed suicide. His mother [Jingjiang] was displeased and said: "My son died as a minister of the state of Lu. And yet, when worthy officials came to express their condolences, none of them appeared sad. Only his concubines and maids mourned sorrowfully. It must be the case that he only loved his concubines, but treated the worthy lightly and abandoned ritual propriety. It is fitting that he died as his did."* Translator's annotation: The story of Jingjiang is also cited in chapter 8. For more information, see Liu Xiang's *Biographies of Women*, volume 1, chapter 9; and Wang Daokun's *Wangshi's Biographies of Women*, volume 2.

17. Wang Xiang's commentary: *One day, King Zhuang of Chu* 楚莊王 *withdrew from the court after having an audience with his officials. Lady Fan* 樊姬 *asked him: "Why are you so late today?" The king replied: "I was engaging in a great conversation with my wise prime minister, Yu Qiuzi* 虞丘子. *I was not aware that it is so late." Lady Fan laughed and said: "Yu Qiuzi may be wise, but regrettably he is not loyal. I have served my king for eleven years. During this time, I have recruited nine ladies and they are all wiser than I. Yu Qiuzi has been the prime minister of Chu for ten years. People he promoted were all his children and relatives. I have never heard of him recommending someone worthy and virtuous." The king told Yu Qiuzi what Lady Fan said. Thereupon, Yu Qiuzi vacated his position and sought the wise. He found Sun Shuao* 孫叔敖 *and recommended him to serve as the prime minister. The state of Chu thus became greatly governed.* Translator's annotation: For more, see Liu Xiang's *Biographies of Women*, volume 2, chapter 5. This anecdote is also cited in Zheng Shi, *Nü xiaojing* 《女孝經》(*Classic of Filial Piety for Women*), in a chapter entitled "Wisdom."
18. Wang Xiang's commentary: *Han Xin* 韓信 *was fishing at the Hui River* 淮水. *An elderly woman, earning her living by washing cotton and silk threads, took pity on his poverty. She often gave him food. Han Xin said one day: "When I become accomplished, I will certainly repay your favor." The elderly woman responded: "I took pity on you—that's why I gave you food. Would I hope for any return?" Later, Han Xin helped Han* 漢 *defeat Chu* 楚. *He was bestowed the title of King Qi* 齊王. *He repaid the elderly woman's favor with a thousand pieces of gold.* Translator's note: Han Xin (231–196 BCE) was a famous Han military strategist and general. He played a decisive role in the victory of Han and the elimination of Chu for the eventual founding of the Han dynasty. He lived in poverty in his early years. For more, see Sima Qian, *Shiji* (*Historical Records*), "Biography of Marquis Huaiyin" 淮陰侯列傳 .
19. Wang Xiang's commentary: *Yue Yangzi* 樂羊子 *of Han* 漢 *returned home not long after he left home for his studies. His wife asked him the reason. He responded: "I missed you. That's why I returned." His wife was weaving at the time. She took a knife, cut off the fabric, and said: "One weaves threads into a fabric of inches. If one accumulates the work of inches, it will turn into a foot. If one does not stop at inches or at feet, the fabric will grow to ten feet long. Today you return home before you complete your studies. It is just like when I cut off the fabric, all previous efforts are wasted." Her husband was awakened by her words, returned to his studies, and later became a great scholar.* Translator's annotation: For more, consult Fan Ye, *Houhanshu* (*Book of Later Han*), "Biographies of Women." Yue Yangzi and his wife were also discussed in chapter 8. This anecdote reminds one of the well-known story about Mencius's mother.
20. Wang Xiang's commentary: *Chenhao* 宸濠, *vassal king Ning* 甯王 *of the Ming* 明 dynasty, *was thinking about usurping the throne. His consort, Madame Lou* 婁氏,

repeatedly warned him not to rebel. He would not listen and rebelled with his troops. Later, he was arrested by official Wang Shouren 王守仁*. Before he was executed, he sighed and said: "King Zhou* 紂 *destroyed his country because he listened to the words of a woman. I brought destruction to my state because I did not listen to the words of a woman."* Translator's annotation: For more, see Zhang Tingyu et al., *Mingshi* (*History of Ming*), "Biographies of Vassal Kings"; and Wang Daokun's *Wangshi's Biographies of Women*, volume 14.

21. Wang Xiang's commentary: *Dazi* 答子 *of the Tao* 陶 *area in the state of Qi* 齊 *was greedy when he was the governor of Tao. He returned home with a fortune ten times greater than before. His relatives came to his house to congratulate him. Only his wife held their young son and wept: "My husband has little virtue but occupies a high office. This is called the beginning of harm. He does not have merits but his household is prosperous. This is called the accumulating of disaster." Her mother-in-law was angry with her for saying these ominous things and banished her. She lived alone with her young son. Later, Dazi was killed by robbers. All his fortune was taken. Her mother-in-law alone survived because of her old age. She and her young son returned home to care for her mother-in-law.* Translator's annotation: See Liu Xiang's *Biographies of Women*, volume 2, chapter 9.
22. Wang Xiang's commentary: *Ming Official Zhou Caimei* 周才美 *was a governor. His father terrorized residents of the town. Caimei's wife was constantly unhappy at home. Her father-in-law asked her the reasons. She said: "My husband already occupies a high office. Our household does not have to worry about lacking wealth. But my father-in-law still amasses wealth unceasingly. Calamity is imminent." Her father-in-law was awakened by her words, changed his behavior, and began to do good deeds. Later, Caimei became blind and was dismissed from his official position. Her father-in-law took this to mean that doing good deeds does not bring good reward; he resorted back in doing evil deeds. Later, his son's eyesight suddenly recovered and was reassigned a governorship. The whole family was departing for the new post. Caimei's wife would not follow. She kept her son and lived alone. Her parents-in-law, her husband, his concubine and her child, and young servants all drowned in the river when the boat capsized. Only his wife and their young son survived.*
23. Wang Xiang's commentary: *A young woman from Qishi* 漆室 *in the state of Lu* 魯 *stopped spinning hemp and sighed. A neighboring woman asked: "Why are you so sad? Are you concerned that you are not yet married?" She replied: "No. I am worried about the fact that the king of Lu is in his old age but the prince is still very young." The neighboring woman laughed and said: "This belongs to state affairs. Why should you be concerned?" The young lady replied: "Not so. In the former times, a guest from Jin* 晉 *stayed at our house. His horse went loose, ran about, and destroyed our vegetable garden. For the rest of the year, we did not have vegetables to eat. Our neighboring girl eloped. The neighbors came to ask for my brother's help to chase her. When they crossed the river, the water level rose and my brother was drowned. For the rest of my*

life, I have no brother. Today, if Lu King passes away while the prince is still young, chaos and disaster will begin to rise. Revolts from the countryside will certainly harm the common people. How can our village be spared?" Later the state of Lu indeed went into catastrophe. Many people were killed. The main cause of death was military uprisings. Translator's annotation: See Liu Xiang's *Biographies of Women*, volume 3, chapter 13; and Wang Daokun's *Wangshi's Biographies of Women*, volume 2.

24. Wang Xiang's commentary: *The Qin dynasty was building the Great Wall. The Ba Shu* 巴蜀 *borough was supposed to provide ten thousand able bodies for compulsory labor. A widow named Qing* 清 *wrote a plea, stating that she would donate her family fortune to hire workers to build the border wall in the surrounding areas for the sake of relieving ten thousand villagers from compulsory labor. She gave millions of dollars and built hundreds of miles of the border wall. The project did not spend any government funds, the villagers did not have to leave their villages, and they were paid for their labor. Consequently, everyone worked their hardest. The border wall was completed within months. Emperor Shihuang* 始皇 *commended her act and built the Remembrance-of-Qing Pavilion to commemorate her contributions.*

【勤儉篇】

勤者女之職，儉者富之基。勤而不儉，枉勞其身；儉而不勤，甘受其苦。儉以益勤之有餘，勤以補儉之不足。若夫貴而能勤，則身勞而教以成；富而能儉，則守約而家日興。是以明德以太后之尊，猶披白練。穆姜以上卿之母，尚事紉麻。葛覃卷耳，咏后妃之賢勞。采蘩采蘋，述夫人之恭儉。七月之章，半言女職。五噫之咏，實賴妻賢。仲子辭三公之貴，己織屨而妻辟纑。少君卻萬貫之妝，共挽車而自出汲。是皆身執勤勞，躬行節儉，揚芳譽於詩書，播令名於史冊者也。女其勗諸。

10

Diligence and Frugality (Qinjian pian 勤儉篇)

DILIGENCE IS THE vocation of a woman. Frugality is the basis of wealth.[1] If a person is diligent but not frugal, then one labors in vain.[2] If a person is frugal but not diligent, then one wants to suffer.[3] Frugality benefits diligence's surplus. Diligence remedies frugality's deficit.[4] If one who holds a high position can be diligent, then by laboring with one's body, one has already accomplished the teaching. If one who has wealth can be frugal, then by limiting one's spending, the household will be prosperous day by day.[5]

Therefore, [Empress] Mingde 明德 even with the prestige of a dowager still wore plain white clothing.[6] Mu Jiang 穆姜, the mother of a prime minister, still did the work of spinning (*yin* 紉) hemp.[7] The poems Getan 葛覃 and Juaner 卷耳 praised the virtue and labor of empresses and royal consorts.[8] The poems Caifan 采蘩 and Caipin 采蘋 described aristocratic ladies' respectful manners and frugality.[9] The poem Qiyue 七月 largely depicted women's diligent work.[10] The author of the song Wuyi 五噫 in essence relied on his wife's virtue.[11] Zhongzi

仲子 declined the invitation to be a minister; he made shoes, and his wife made ropes from grass and threads from hemp, to make a living.[12] Shaojun 少君 returned vast dowries [to her maternal family]; she rode instead in a small carriage with her husband and fetched water on her own.[13]

These are all examples of persons who labored diligently and carried out deeds of frugality respectfully. These women's reputed names are well-known in literary works and in annals of histories. All women should be inspired and encouraged by them (*xu* 勗).[14]

Commentaries and Annotations

1. Wang Xiang's commentary: *If a woman is not diligent, production will be idle. If a person is not frugal, resources will be squandered. Neither is the way of managing a household.* Translator's annotation: Diligence and frugality pertain to the category of women's work (*fugong* 婦工) in the "four [womanly] virtues" (*side* 四德). These virtues are recommended in all four books of the *Nü sishu* (*Four Books for Women*).
2. Wang Xiang's commentary: *If a person is diligent, he/she necessarily toils. But if the person is unfrugal, his/her labor remedies nothing.*
3. Wang Xiang's commentary: *Frugality is to limit spending and to enjoy plainness and simplicity. But, if a person is not diligent in his work to supplement it, the person chooses to suffer.*
4. Wang Xiang's commentary: *If a person is not only diligent but also frugal, there will be daily increase and surplus. If a person is not only frugal but also diligent, the household will have plenty without deficit.*
5. Wang Xiang's commentary: *If a person already occupies a high rank and yet still works diligently, his/her family members would not dare to be lazy. This is teaching by the example of one's person. If a person already has wealth and yet still practices frugality, then even with daily use, there is no exhaustion. This is because limiting spending can bring forth wealth.*
6. Wang Xiang's commentary: *Empress Mingde Ma* 明德馬皇后 *was the royal consort of Emperor Ming of Han* 漢明帝 *and the mother of Emperor Zhang* 章帝. *Naturally respectful and frugal, she often wore clothing made of white fabric and disliked ornate, colorful clothes.* Translator's annotation: For more, see Fan Ye, *Houhanshu* (*Book of Later Han*), "Biography of Empress Ma."
7. Wang Xiang's commentary: 紉 *is pronounced as* 銀 (yin)*; it means "to spin." Mu Jiang* 穆姜 *was the mother of Gongfu Wenbo* 公父文伯, *a prime minister of Lu, and Mubo's* 穆伯 *wife, Jingjiang* 敬姜. *One day when Wenbo returned home from his court meeting, he saw his mother was spinning hemp. He said in an angry tone (*chu 歜*): "You are my mother, head of this household, why do you still labor over spinning?" His mother sighed and said: "The state of Lu is heading toward destruction! It uses*

you as the prime minister. But you have not learned the Great Way. For when a person labors with his body, he will think about the good; when he is idle, he will think about the evil. Today you are a prime minister but do not know how to be diligent. Contrarily, you blame me for working too hard at women's work. I am afraid that the state of Lu is going into obliteration and the family line of Mubo will be ruined." This anecdote can be found in [Zuo Qiuming's] Zuo Commentary to the Spring and Autumn Annals *(*Chunqiu [zuo]zhuan《春秋[左]傳》*). 歜 is pronounced as 畜 (*chu*).* Translator's annotation: Jingjiang is mentioned four times in Liu Shi's *Nüfan jielu* (*Short Records of Models for Women*), noted for her ritual propriety (chapter 8), wisdom (chapter 9), diligence and frugality (chapter 10), and talent (chapter 11). She appears to be an exemplar of multiple virtues. In Liu Xiang's *Biographies of Women*, Jingjiang was the only woman praised by Confucius on four occasions for her embodiment of multiple virtues (volume 1, chapter 9).

8. Wang Xiang's commentary: *[In the* Shijing,*] Zhounan* 周南 *section, the Getan* 葛覃 *poem portrayed how empresses and royal consorts personally went to mountains and valleys to harvest the vines of Ge plants, boiled them, and wove them into fine and coarse fabrics to make clothes. The Juaner* 卷耳 *poem described how empresses and royal consorts climbed the mountains to pick the Juaner plants to use as ritual offerings at the ancestral temples and how they missed their husbands [, who have traveled afar for state affairs]. Both poems depicted their diligence and travail.*
9. Wang Xiang's commentary: *[In the* Shijing,*] Shaonan* 召南 *section, the Caifan* 采蘩 *poem complimented aristocratic ladies' diligence despite their status of being nobles. The Caipin* 采蘋 *poem praised wives of governmental officials for their reverence and frugality, and their diligence in conducting ancestral temple rites.*
10. Wang Xiang's commentary: *In the Binfeng* 豳風 *section [of the* Shijing*], the Qiyue* 七月 *poem depicted aristocratic ladies not avoiding toils. They personally attended to agricultural work. When husbands were plowing the land, wives would prepare the meals. When husbands were harvesting the crops, wives would prepare the field. Even though they were the daughters of ministers and officials, they picked mulberry leaves to raise silkworms; they wove silk threads into fabric to make clothes for their husbands; they used the skins of fox and raccoon to make coats for their husbands. Their diligence, hard work, reverence, and frugality were to such a great extent.*
11. Wang Xiang's commentary: *Liang Hong* 梁鴻 *of the Han dynasty composed the song of Wuyu* 五噫 *when he withdrew from the chaos of the mundane world. He and his wife Meng Guang* 孟光 *went to the region of Wu* 吳*. They made their living by pounding rice. At mealtime, his wife always raised the bowl (*wan 案*) to her eyebrow level and knelt to offer the food to Hong.* 案 *is pronounced as* 碗 *(*wan*).* Translator's annotation: For more information, see Fan Ye, *Houhanshu*, "Biography of Liang Hong."
12. Wang Xiang's commentary: 纑 *is pronounced as* 盧 *(*lu*).* Lu 纑 *is to weave grass into a robe and hemp into thread. The king of the state of Qi* 齊 *wanted to employ Chen Zhongzi* 陳仲子 *as his prime minister, but Zhongzi would not accept the invitation.*

He left and settled in the town of Ling 陵. *His wife made rope from grass and thread from hemp. He made shoes to make a living.* Translator's annotation: For more information, see *Mencius* 3B:10. Mencius did not approve of Chen Zhongzi's choice to become a hermit. Here, the author of *Nüfan jielu* used this story to illustrate the virtue of frugality and diligence.

13. Wang Xiang's commentary: *Heng Shaojun* 桓少君 *was the wife of Bao Xuan* 鮑宣 *of the Han dynasty. When she was first married to Bao Xuan, she came with many servants and dowries. Xuan was displeased. He said to her: "You were born and raised in a wealthy high-ranking family but are now married to a poor and lowly household. I dare not to accept this marriage." His wife replied: "My father respects your virtue and frugality. He thus gave me in marriage to serve you." Thereupon, she followed Xuan's wishes and returned all servants, clothing, and accessories to her maternal family. She wore plain hairpins and rugged clothes, and rode in a small carriage (*luche 鹿車*) with her husband in returning to his village. After paying reverence to her parents-in-law, she picked up an urn and went outside to fetch water.* Translator's annotation: *Luche* 鹿車, "deer-drawn cart," means a small carriage. For more, see Fan Ye, *Houhanshu*, "Biographies of Women."
14. Wang Xiang's commentary: 勗 *(*xu*) means "to encourage."*

【才德篇】

男子有德便是才，斯言猶可。女子無才便是德，此語殊非。蓋不知才德之經，與邪正之辯也。夫德以達才，才以成德。故女子之有德者，固不必有才；而有才者，必貴乎有德。德本而才末，固理之宜然；若夫為不善，非才之罪也。故經濟之才，婦言猶可用；而邪僻之藝，男子亦非宜。禮曰：「奸聲亂色，不留聰明。淫樂慝禮，不役心志。」君子之教子也，獨不可以訓女乎? 古者后妃夫人，以逮庶妾匹婦，莫不知詩，豈皆無德者歟? 末世妒婦淫女，及乎悍妻潑嫗，大悖於禮，豈盡有才者耶? 曷觀齊妃有雞鳴之詩，鄭女有雁弋之警。緹縈上章以救父，肉刑用除。徐惠諫疏以匡君，窮兵遂止。宣文之授周禮，六官之鉅典以明。大家之續漢書，一代之鴻章以備。孝經著於陳妻。論語成於宋氏。女誡作於曹昭。內訓出於仁孝。敬姜紡績而教子，言標左史之章。蘇蕙織字以致夫，詩製迴文之錦。柳下惠之妻，能謚其夫。漢伏氏之女，傳經於帝。信宮闈之懿範，誠女學之芳規也。由是觀之，則女子之知書識字，達理通經，名譽著乎當時，才美揚乎後世，亶其然哉。若夫淫佚之書，不入於門。邪僻之言，不聞於耳。在父兄者，能思患而預防之。則養正以毓其才，師古以成其德，始為盡善而兼美矣。

女範捷錄終

II

Talent and Virtue
(Caide pian 才德篇)

A MAN'S VIRTUE is his talent: this saying is plausible.[1] Without talent is a woman's virtue: such a saying is certainly false.[2] Clearly, the speaker of this statement does not understand the guiding principle of talent and virtue and the distinction between an erroneous view and a correct view.[3]

For virtue will make talent successful, and talent should complete virtue.[4] Therefore, a woman who has virtue may not need talent; a woman, who has talent, however, must treasure virtue.[5] That virtue is the root and talent the branch is surely what reason demands. If someone does something evil, it is not the fault of talent itself.[6] Therefore, in regard to talents and skills in economics, governance, and salvation of the people, even a woman's advice ought to be taken seriously. Crafty skills in erroneous and evil matters, even for a man, they are inappropriate.[7]

The *Liji* (*Record of Rituals*) says, "Wicked sounds and distracting colors should not be retained in one's ears or eyes (*cong ming* 聰明). Lascivious music and flattering words that transgress ritual propriety will have detrimental effects on one's mind and will."[8] This is what gentlemen teach to their sons; why only not educate their daughters with the same teaching?[9]

In ancient times, from empresses, royal consorts, wives of officials, to the concubines and wives of common folk, all knew the *Shijing* (*Classic of Poetry*). Were they then all persons without virtue [because they have talent]?[10] When a dynasty is in decline, jealous women, wanton ladies, feisty overbearing wives, and brawling malicious old women populate the society. These women seriously violate ritual propriety. Were they all women with talent [because they lacked virtue]?[11]

[For women who had both talent and virtue,] why not look at the Jiming 雞鳴 poem composed by royal consort Qi 齊妃 and the Yanyi 雁弋 warning authored by Woman Zheng 鄭女?[12] Furthermore, Tiying 緹縈 wrote a letter, pleading with the imperial court to release her father; corporeal punishment was thus abolished.[13] Xu Hui 徐惠 remonstrated the emperor and consequently stopped him from exhausting the military in waging war frequently.[14] Xuanwen 宣文 taught the *Zhouli* (*Zhou Rituals*); the grand system of "six leading officials" was therefore illuminated.[15] [Cao] Taigu [曹] 大家 continued the compilation of the *Hanshu* (*Book of Han*); the monumental work of a dynasty was hence completed.[16] The [*Nü*] *xiaojing* (*Classic of Filial Piety* [*for Women*]) was authored by Chen [Miao]'s wife 陳 [邈] 妻. The [*Nü*] *lunyu* (*Analects* [*for Women*]) was the work of Madame(s) Song 宋氏.[17] The *Nüjie* (*Lessons for Women*) was composed by Cao Zhao 曹昭. The *Neixun* (*Teachings for the Inner Court*) was authored by [Empress] Renxiao 仁孝.[18] Jingjiang 敬姜 spun yarn to teach her son; her words were recorded in the canonical text by historian-official Zuo 左.[19] Su Hui 蘇蕙 sewed words [into a handkerchief] as a gift to her husband; the love poems were made of numerous palindromes.[20] Liu Xiahui's 柳下惠 wife was the best person to memorialize her husband's character with a fitting posthumous name.[21] In the Han dynasty, a [thirteen-year-old] girl from the Fu 伏 family passed on the canonical classic [of *Shangshu*] to Emperor [Wen].[22]

These are truly exemplary female role models; they are excellent examples of woman's learning. From these, we can conclude that women's knowledge of books and their literacy, their penetrating reason and their understanding of canonical classics, were remarkably known during their lifetimes, and the repute of their talents was passed on to later generations—all these did not happen accidentally.[23] If it is the case that lustful indecent books should not enter the household and malicious speeches should not be heard, fathers and older brothers should consider these problems and prevent them from happening beforehand. Accordingly, [female members of the household] can rectify their persons to guide their talents, and learn from the ancients to complete their virtues. Then, it will be doing the good to one's utmost while preserving what is beautiful![24]

The *Short Records of Models for Women* ends.

Commentaries and Annotations

1. Wang Xiang's commentary: *It says that it is more valuable for a person to have virtues than to have talents. Having talents without virtues, this person necessarily is not righteous. Having virtues without talents does not damage a person's ability to be good.*
2. Wang Xiang's commentary: *The previous two statements are from people of ancient times. The first statement does not go against right reason. The second statement, however, even though the meaning may be correct [in distinguishing men from women], its reason is false. Because even though men and women are different, their virtues are one. A woman should focus more on virtue, not talents—this reasoning is correct. But to simply say that without talent is virtue is false.*
3. Wang Xiang's commentary: *Talents are the function of virtues. Talents guided by virtues will be put to right use—they are the way to govern a country, regulate a family, and cultivate a person. Talents without virtues will be put to evil use—they are used only to make one's name, accumulate wealth, harm others, and benefit only the self.*
4. Wang Xiang's commentary: *Rectify one's mind and cultivate one's person. Then, one will be able to regulate the family and govern the state. This is what is meant by "virtue makes talent successful." Investigate things and pursue knowledge to its utmost. Then, one can make the will sincere and the mind rectified. This is speaking about "talent completes virtue."*
5. Wang Xiang's commentary: *A woman should regard virtue as essential. To have or not to have talent is not something that one should be overly concerned about.*
6. Wang Xiang's commentary: *Whoever possesses talent but does not strive to cultivate virtue abandons the essential in pursuit of the inessential. Such a person necessarily descends to the state of malice. Is this talent's fault?*
7. Wang Xiang's commentary: *If one can deploy one's talent to admonish one's king and rectify one's family so that virtue is promulgated and disaster is avoided, even in a woman this ability should be regarded as great skill in government and state affairs. Lascivious words and malicious speeches are not something which only women should avoid. Men should also despise and refrain from such things too.*

8. Wang Xiang's commentary: Cong ming 聰明 *refers to "ears and eyes." Ears should not listen to immoral sounds and eyes should not look at evil colors. This is the right teaching to follow. Lewd music such as today's lyrics and songs are licentious sounds that transgress ritual propriety. Just like over-the-top flattering compliments and excessive courtesy, they are all things that confuse our ears, eyes, mind, and will and things that all should take great caution about.* Translator's annotation: See *Analects* 5.25 for a discussion on insincerity in excessive courtesy (*zugong zhili* 足恭之禮). For more on wicked sounds, distracting colors, and lascivious music, consult the *Liji* (*Record of Rituals*), the Yueji 樂記 chapter.
9. Wang Xiang's commentary: *The previous four sentences speak about why a gentleman teaches others. If the lesson is something that men should adhere to, why shouldn't it be taught to women as well? If women understand the moral lesson, they will certainly not have the error of "having talent but without virtue."*
10. Wang Xiang's commentary: *Uninformed opinion says that if a woman has talent, such talent would corrupt her virtue. But they do not know that, of the three hundred plus poems in the* Shijing, *most of them were composed by women and young ladies. Their poems were accentuated with loyalty, considerateness, and peace. The contents were filled with remembrance of their husbands, yearning for the good, pleasing lyric without wantonness, and lamenting without anger. Were they all persons with talent but no virtue?*
11. Wang Xiang's commentary: *Uninformed opinion states that "without talent is a woman's virtue." Nowadays, lewd ladies and feisty women, who are illiterate but abusive toward their husbands and sons, disrespectful to their parents-in-laws, throwing temper tantrums and cursing at fellow villagers, are many. Are these the results of "without talent is virtue"?*
12. Wang Xiang's commentary: *A poem from the Qi* 齊 *region [in the* Shijing*] writes: "Roosters are already crowing. The imperial court is filled with officials. Ah, it actually is not the roosters' crowing. It was noise made by the flies." These lines describe a virtuous royal consort, who was afraid that her king would be late in having an audience with his ministers and officials, mistaking the noise made by flies for a rooster's crowing. A poem from the Zheng* 鄭 *region states: "The woman says, 'The rooster is crowing.' The man says, 'It is not dawn yet.' [She prompted,] 'Get up soon! Look at the skyline at night. The bright star is twinkling with brilliant sparks.' [He replied:] 'Wild ducks and geese are flying soon; I shall hunt them with bow and arrow.'" This is a poem depicting how a woman cautioned her husband that roosters were crowing and the dawn was fast approaching. The bright star was twinkling. She encouraged her husband to rise early so that he can wait for wild ducks and geese to fly by and to catch them.*
13. Wang Xiang's commentary: *For the anecdote about Tiying, see the earlier chapter entitled "Filial Conduct" [chapter 4].*
14. Wang Xiang's commentary: *At the end of Emperor Taizong of Tang's* 唐太宗 *reign, the emperor planned to resume its war with Gaoli* 高麗 *[Korea]. His consort, Lady*

Shu 淑妃 *(Xu Hui* 徐惠*), cautioned Taizong not to exhaust the military in engaging a war with a distant nation. Such a war would drain all military resources and wear out the citizens of China. Emperor Taizong thus stopped the war plan.*

15. Wang Xiang's commentary: *During the reign of Fu Jian* 苻堅 *(r. 357–385 CE) of Qian Qin* 前秦, *the* Zhouli *(*Zhou Rituals*) was badly damaged; its learning was lost. The Minister of Rituals (*Taichang 太常*), Wei Cheng's* 韋逞 *mother, Madame Song* 宋氏, *was eighty some years old. She was raised in a family of Zhouli scholars for generations [and had learned this school of thought since her childhood]. King Fu Jian bestowed on her the title of Sir/Teacher Xuanwen* 宣文君. *She ascended to the hall and gave lectures on the principles of the Zhou system of "six ministers." Several hundred students attended her lectures. Because of this, the learning of the Zhouli became prominent in the world.* Translator's annotation: The whole set of Confucian canons on rituals includes the *Liji* (*Record of Rituals*), the *Zhouli* (*Zhou Rituals*), and the *Yili* (*Book of Ceremonial Rituals*). *Liji* is translated into English, but the *Zhouli* and the *Yili* are not. For more about Madame Song, see Fang Xualing et al., *Jinshu* (*Book of Jin*), "Biographies of Women," in volume 96 of *Chizaotang siku quanshu huiyao* 《摛藻堂四庫全書薈要》 (China: China-America Digital Academic Library), 17b-18b, https://archive.org/details/06079119.cn.

16. Wang Xiang's commentary: 大家 *pronounced as* 太姑 *(*Taigu*). Ban Gu* 班固 *of the Later Han dynasty was the author of the* Qianhanshu *(*Book of Former Han*), but he passed away before he could finish the work. His young sister, Ban Zhao* 班昭, *continued and completed this work. People called her "Cao Taigu"* 曹大家. Translator's annotation: 大家 may be pronounced as 大姑 (*Dagu*) or 太姑 (*Taigu*). See translator's introduction (note 7) and Wang Xiang's biographic introduction (note 1) to Ban Zhao's *Nüjie (Lessons for Women)*.

17. Wang Xiang's commentary: *Tang scholar Chen Miao's wife, Madame Zheng* 鄭氏, *authored eighteen chapters of the* Nü xiaojing *(*Classic of Filila Piety for Women*). Imperial woman-teacher of the inner court (*Shanggong 尚宮*), Madame Song* 宋氏, *wrote twelve chapters of the* Nü lunyu *(*Analects for Women*). See the preceding books [of the* Nü sishu (Four Books for Women*)].* Translator's annotation: For more information about Madame Zheng, see Wang Daokun's *Wangshi's Biographies of Women*, volume 8.

18. Wang Xiang's commentary: *Cai Zhao* 曹昭 *is Ban Zhao* 班昭, *wife of Cao Shishu* 曹世叔, *also known as Cao Taigu* 曹大家, *who authored the seven chapters of the* Nüjie *(*Lessons for Women*). Madame Xu* 徐氏, *Empress Renxiaowen* 仁孝文皇后, *consort of Emperor Chengzu of Ming, wrote the twenty chapters of* Neixun *(*Teachings for the Inner Court*). Both works can be found in the preceding books [of the* Nü sishu *(*Four Books for Women*)].*

19. Wang Xiang's commentary: *For more about Madame Jingjiang* 敬姜, *see preceding chapters. Her words were recorded in Zuo Qiuming's* 左丘明 Guoyu 《國語》 *(Discourses of the States).* Translator's annotation: According to some accounts

including the *Shiji* (*Historical Records*), Zuo Qiuming 左丘明 was a historian, a writer, and probably a contemporary of Confucius. He was believed to be the author of the *Chunqiu zuozhuan* 《春秋左傳》 (*Zuo Commentary to the Spring and Autumn Annals*) and the *Guoyu* 《國語》 (*Discourses of the States*). In *Analects* 5.25, Confucius mentioned Zuo Qiuming as someone who is like-minded, with sound moral character. Details of his life and his surname were unclear. Some asserted that Zuo 左 is his last name, while others believe that Zuoqiu is, or that Zuo (meaning "left," as opposed to "right") is a title for a certain type of historian, not his surname.

20. Wang Xiang's commentary: *Official Dou Tao* 竇滔 *of Fu Qin* 苻秦 *[i.e., Qian Qin* 前秦*] was stationed in Xiangyang. He did not return home for a long period of time. His wife Su Hui* 蘇蕙 *sewed poems in palindromes into a handkerchief. These poems can be read from any direction, in three-word, five-word, or seven-word verses. All were self-contained poems. One can find five thousand plus poems on the handkerchief. When Tao saw these poems, he resigned from his post and returned home.* Translator's annotation: For more on Su Hui (also known as Su Ruolan 蘇若蘭), see Fang Xuanling et al., *Jinshu* (*Book of Jin*), "Biographies of Women," in volume 96 of *Chizaotang siku quanshu huiyao*, 20a–20b. This work of 840 words is also known as "Xuanji Diagram" (*Xuanji tu* 璇璣圖); it was cited in a well-known Qing 清 novel, Li Ruzhen's 李汝珍 *Jinghuayuan* 《鏡花緣》 (*Flowers in the Mirror*).

21. Wang Xiang's commentary: *Liu Xiahui* 柳下惠 *passed away. His students wanted to write a eulogy to express their sorrow and to commemorate his virtue. His wife said to the students: "To eulogize your teacher's virtue, none of you knows your teacher better than I do." Thereupon, she began to eulogize: "Sir Liu Xiahui, our teacher, was not boastful. His virtues were inexhaustible! He was faithful in keeping his words and honest in his dealing with others. He never harmed a single person. He yielded gently to adapt to the world without being stubborn or overbearing. Even with unjust and undeserved shame, he continued to help the multitude. Alas, his virtues were vast! Even though he was demoted three times, he never retracted his original intention to help others. He was a gentleman of generosity and kindness, someone who could always motivate himself to moral endeavor. What an untimely loss! He has passed away. It was hoped by many that he will have a long life but he died today. What a sorrow! His soul and spirit have left. Our teacher's posthumous commemorative name may appropriately be 'kind generous giving' (*hui 惠*)." Afterwards, his students followed this and were unable to change a single word. Their teacher was thus posthumously named "hui."* Translator's annotation: Liu Xiahui was an official of the state of Lu during the Spring and Autumn period. For more about him and his wife, see Liu Xiang's *Biographies of Women*, volume 2, chapter 10; and Wang Daokun's *Wangshi's Biographies of Women*, volume 2.

22. Wang Xiang's commentary: *During the reign of Emperor Wen of Han* 漢文帝*, the canonical classic* Shangshu 《尚書》 *(*Book of Documents*) was in desperate*

conditions of ruin. None of the Confucian official-scholars knew this work. An old Confucian scholar, Fu Sheng 伏生, *was ninety-some years old. He knew the Shangshu well, but his words were difficult to understand. Furthermore, his hands could no longer write. He had a granddaughter who was only thirteen years old, but she could understand her grandfather's speech and was capable of writing. Emperor Wen requested Fu Sheng to lecture on the* Shangshu *at the imperial court and his granddaughter to record the lectures. When the book was completed and presented to the emperor, the family was given a great reward of gold and silk. The text of* Shangshu *was thus preserved and promulgated around the world.*

23. Wang Xiang's commentary: *This speaks about how these women knew great books and carried themselves courteously. Their virtues were very impressive!*
24. Wang Xiang's commentary: *This speaks about if fathers and older brothers know that young women should not be exposed to malicious books or lustful music, they should themselves think about the problem and strictly prevent it from happening. They should teach young women proper rituals. Then, these young women would study the classics and know ritual propriety; they will be equipped with both talent and virtue. Isn't this a beautiful thing?*

APPENDIX

Liu Xiang's Biographies of Women (Lienü zhuan《列女傳》) *vis-à-vis the* Four Books for Women (Nü sishu《女四書》)

Comparative Table of Authors, Historical Timelines, and Categories of Women's Virtues

	Lienü zhuan 《列女傳》 (*Biographies of Women*)	*Nü sishu* 《女四書》 (*Four Books for Women*)			
Book title		*Nüjie* 《女誡》 (*Lessons for Women*)	*Nü lunyu* 《女論語》 (*Analects for Women*)	*Neixun* 《內訓》 (*Teachings for the Inner Court*)	*Nüfan jielu* 《女範捷錄》 (*Short Records of Models for Women*)
Author	Liu Xiang 劉向 (c. 77-6 BCE)	Ban Zhao 班昭 (c. 45–117 CE)	Song Ruoxin 宋若莘/華 (?–820) and Song Ruozhao宋若昭 (?–825 CE)	Empress Renxiaowen 仁孝文皇后 (1361–1407 CE)	Mme. Liu 劉氏 (c. 16th century CE)
Dynasty	Western Han 西漢 (206 BCE–9 CE)	Eastern Han 東漢 (25-220 CE)	Tang 唐 (618-907 CE)	Ming 明 (1368-1644 CE)	Ming 明 (1368-1644 CE)
Total # chapters	104 (7 volumes)*	7	12	20	11
	Volume # and title	Chapter # and title			
	Lienü zhuan 《列女傳》	*Nü sishu* 《女四書》 (*Four Books for Women*)			
		Nüjie	*Nü lunyu*	*Neixun*	*Nüfan jielu*
Category of women's virtues	1. *Muyi* 母儀 (Model Motherhood)	1. *Beiruo* 卑弱 (The Lowly and the Weak)	1. *Lishen* 立身 (Establishing One's Person)	1. *Dexing* 德性 (Virtuous Nature)	1. *Tonglun* 統論 (Unifying Thesis)
	2. *Xianming* 賢明 (Virtuous Intelligence)	2. *Fufu* 夫婦 (Husband and Wife)	2. *Xuezuo* 學作 (Learning the Work)	2. *Xiushen* 修身 (Self-Cultivation)	2. *Houde* 后德 (Queenly Virtues)

	3. *Renzhi* 仁智 (Humaneness and Wisdom)	3. *Jingshun* 敬順 (Respect and Compliance)	3. *Xueli* 學禮 (Learning the Rituals)	3. *Shenyan* 慎言 (Prudent Speech)	3. *Muyi* 母儀 (Model Motherhood)
	4. *Zenshun* 貞順 (Chastity and Obedience)	4. *Fuxing* 婦行 (Women's Conduct)	4. *Zaoqi* 早起 (Rising Early)	4. *Jinxing* 謹行 (Careful Conduct)	4. *Xiaoxing* 孝行 (Filial Conduct)
	5. *Jieyi* 節義 (Integrity and Righteousness)	5. *Zhuanxin* 專心 (One-Mindedness)	5. *Shifumu* 事父母 (Serving One's Parents)	5. *Qinli* 勤勵 (Diligence)	5. *Zhenlie* 貞烈 (Chastity and Ardency)
	6. *Biantong* 辯通 (Penetrating Rhetorical Skill)	6. *Qucong* 曲從 (Conceding Obedience)	6. *Shijiugu* 事姑舅 (Serving Parents-in-Law)	6. *Jiejian* 節儉 (Frugality)	6. *Zhongyi* 忠義 (Loyalty and Righteousness)
	7. *Niebi* 孽嬖 (The Evil and Spoiled)	7. *Heshumei* 和叔妹 (Harmony with Younger Brothers- and Sisters-in-Law)	7. *Shifu* 事夫 (Serving One's Husband)	7. *Jingjie* 警戒 (Watchfulness)	7. *Ciai* 慈愛 (Benevolent Love)
	*8. *Xu lienü zhuan* 續列女傳 (Supplemental Biographies of Women): Later authors wrote these twenty supplemental biographies. Thus, vol. 8's twenty chapters are not included in the above 104 chapters by Liu Xiang.		8. *Xunnannü* 訓男女 (Instructing Boys and Girls)	8. *Jishan* 積善 (Accumulating Good Deeds)	8. *Bingli* 秉禮 (Upholding Ritual Propriety)
			9. *Yingjia* 營家 (Managing the Household)	9. *Qianshan*遷善 (Becoming Good)	9. *Zhihui* 智慧 (Wisdom)
			10. *Daike* 待客 (Hosting Guests)	10. *Chongshengxun* 崇聖訓 (Revering Sagely Teachings)	10. *Qinjian* 勤儉 (Diligence and Frugality)

			11. *Herou* 和柔 (Harmony and Gentleness)	11. *Jingxianfan* 景賢範 (Admiring Wise Role Models)	11. *Caide* 才德 (Talent and Virtue)
			12. *Shoujie* 守節 (Guarding One's Integrity)	12. *Shifumu* 事父母 (Serving One's Parents)	
				13. *Shijun* 事君 (Serving One's Ruler)	
				14. *Shijiugu* 事舅姑 (Serving Parents-in-Law)	
				15. *Fengjisi* 奉祭祀 (Performing Religious Rites)	
				16. *Muyi* 母儀 (Model Motherhood)	
				17. *Muzong* 睦宗 (Friendly Relationship with Family Clans)	

				18. *Ciyou* 慈幼 (Benevolent Love for the Young)	
				19. *Daixia* 逮下 (Treating Imperial Concubines)	
				20. *Daiwaiqi* 待外戚 (Treating Imperial Consorts' Maternal Relatives)	

Bibliography

Ames, Roger T. "The Confucian World View: Uncommon Assumptions, Common Misconceptions." In *Asian Texts—Asian Contexts: Encounters with Asian Philosophies and Religions*, ed. David Jones and E. R. Klein, 30–46. Albany: State University of New York Press, 2010.

Ban, Gu 班固. *Baihu tongyi* 《白虎通義》 (*Comprehensive Discussions in the White Tiger Hall*). 1st century CE. http://ctext.org/bai-hu-tong. For English translation, see entries for Paul R. Goldin and Tjan Tjoe Som.

Ban, Gu 班固 et al. *Hanshu* 《漢書》 (*Book of Han*). [Also known as the *Qianhanshu* 《前漢書》 (*Book of Former Han*).] 1st century CE. 100 volumes. http://ctext.org/han-shu.

Ban, Zhao 班昭. *Nüjie* 《女誡》 (*Lessons for Women*). c. 1st century CE. In *Houhanshu* by Fan Ye, the *Nü sishu*, edited by Wang Xiang; and *Gujin tushu jicheng*, volume 395, edited by Chen Menglei et al. For more information, see entries for Fan Ye, Wang Xiang, and Chen Menglei. For 1932 translation without commentary, see entry for Nancy C. Swann.

Bell, Daniel A. *China's New Confucianism*. Princeton, NJ: Princeton University Press, 2008.

Benn, Charles. *China's Golden Age: Everyday Life in the Tang Dynasty*. Oxford: Oxford University Press, 2002.

Birch, Cyril, trans. *Peony Pavilion: Mudan ting*. 2nd ed. Bloomington: Indiana University Press, 2002.

Cao, Dagu/Taigu 曹大家. See Ban Zhao.

Chan, Sin Yee. "The Confucian Conception of Gender in the Twenty-First Century." In *Confucianism for the Modern World*, edited by Daniel A. Bell and Chaibong Hahm, 312–33. Cambridge: Cambridge University Press, 2003.

Chan, Wing-tsit, trans. and ed. *Reflections on Things at Hand: The Neo-Confucian Anthology Compiled by Chu Hsi and Lu Tsu-Chien*. New York: Columbia University Press, 1967.

Chan, Wing-tsit, trans. and ed. *A Source Book in Chinese Philosophy.* 4th printing. Princeton, NJ: Princeton University Press, 1973.

Chan, Wing-tsit 陳榮捷. *Zhuzi xintansuo* 《朱子新探索》 (*New Research on Zhu Xi*). Taipei: Xuesheng shuju 學生書局, 1988.

Chen, Dongyuan 陳東原. *Zhongguo funü shenghuo shi* 《中國婦女生活史》 (*History of Chinese Women's Daily Life*). Taipei: Shangwu yinshuguan 商務印書館 (台灣), 1997.

Chen, Hao 陳澔. *Liji jishuo* 《禮記集說》 (*Book of Rites, with Collected Commentaries*). Taipei: Shijie shuju 世界書局, 2009.

Chen, Hongmou 陳宏謀. *Jiaonü yigui* 《教女遺規》 (*Remaining Instructions for Teaching Women*). Tainan, Taiwan: Heyu chubanshe 和裕出版社, 2007.

Chen, Menglei 陳夢雷. *Gujin tushu jicheng* 《古今圖書集成》 (*Collection of Illustrations and Books from Antiquity to the Present*). 808 volumes. Reprint. Taipei: Dingwen shuju 鼎文書局, 1985. Also, http://ctext.org/library.pl?if=gb&res=81155.

Chen, Shou 陳壽. *Sanguozhi* 《三國志》 (*History of the Three Kingdoms*). c. 3rd century CE. 65 volumes. http://ctext.org/sanguozhi.

Chen, Yuan. "Legitimation Discourse and the Theory of Five Elements in Imperial China." *Journal of Song-Yuan Studies* 44 (2014): 325–64.

Ching, Julia. "Sung Philosophers on Women." *Monumenta Serica* 42 (1994): 259–74.

Chunangzhai Zhuren 處囊齋主人, ed. *Shinü shizuan* 《詩女史纂》 (*Compiled History of Women Poets*). c. 14th -17th centuries CE. http://ctext.org/wiki.pl?if=gb&res=509088.

Confucius (Kongzi 孔子). *Lunyu* 《論語》 (*Analects*). c. 5th century BCE. For English translation, see entry for Raymond Dawson.

Csikszentmihalyi, Mark, trans. and ed. *Readings in Han Chinese Thought*. Indianapolis, IN: Hackett, 2006.

Dadai liji 《大戴禮記》 (*Dadai Record of Rituals*). c. 1st-2nd centuries CE. http://ctext.org/da-dai-li-ji. Reprinted, with modern Chinese translation, introduction, notes, and commentary by Gao Ming 高明, *Dadai liji jinzhu jinyi* 《大戴禮記今註今譯》. Taipei: Shangwu yinshuguan 商務印書館 (台灣), 1993.

Dawson, Raymond, trans. *The Analects*. Oxford: Oxford University Press, 1993.

Daxue 《大學》 (*Great Learning*). In *A Source Book in Chinese Philosophy*, translated and edited by Wing-tsit Chan, 84–94. Princeton, NJ: Princeton University Press, 1973. Also, http://ctext.org/liji/da-xue, with translation by James Legge, originally published in *The Chinese Classics: with a Translation, Critical and Exegetical Notes, Prolegomena, and Copious Indexes*, volume 1 (London: Trübner, 1861–1872).

Ding, Weizhong 丁偉忠. "Mingdai de funü jiaoyu shi" 明代的婦女教育 ("Women's Education in the Ming Dynasty"). *Zhongguo dianji yu wenhua* 中國典籍與文化 3 (1994): 72–5.

Dong, Zhongshu 董仲舒. *Chunqiu fanlu* 《春秋繁露》 (*Luxuriant Dew of the Spring and Autumn Annals*). c. 2nd century BCE. http://ctext.org/chun-qiu-fan-lu/zh.

Reprinted, with modern Chinese translation, introduction, notes, and commentary by Lai Yanyuan 賴炎元, *Chunqiu fanlu jinzhu jinyi* 《春秋繁露今註今譯》. 2nd edition. Taipei: Shangwu yinshuguan 商務印書館 (台灣), 2010. English translation of some excerpts available in *A Source Book in Chinese Philosophy*, translated and edited by Wing-tsit Chan, 271–88. Princeton, NJ: Princeton University Press, 1973; and in *Images of Women in Chinese Thought and Cultures*, edited by Robin R. Wang, 162–9. Indianapolis, IN: Hackett, 2003.

Du, Xueyuan 杜學元. *Zhongguo nüzi jiaoyu tongshi* 《中國女子教育通史》 (*History of Chinese Women's Education*). Guiyang, China: Guizhou jiaoyu chubanshe 貴州教育出版社, 1995.

Ebrey, Patricia Buckley. *Chu Hsi's Family Rituals: A Twelfth-Century Chinese Manual for the Performance of Cappings, Weddings, Funerals, and Ancestral Rites*. Princeton, NJ: Princeton University Press, 1991.

Ebrey, Patricia Buckley. *The Inner Quarters: Marriage and the Lives of Chinese Women in the Sung Period*. Berkeley and Los Angeles: University of California Press, 1993.

Ebrey, Patricia Buckley. *The Cambridge Illustrated History of China*. Cambridge: Cambridge University Press, 1999.

Ebrey, Patricia Buckley, Anne Walthall, and James B. Palais. *East Asia: A Cultural, Social, and Political History*. Boston: Houghton Mifflin, 2006.

Fan, Ruiping, ed. *Confucian Bioethics*. Dordrecht: Kluwer, 1999.

Fan, Shang 范坰 and Lin Yu 林禹. *Wuyue beishi*《吳越備史》 (*History of Wuyue*). 4 volumes. c. 10th–13th centuries CE. http://ctext.org/library.pl?if=gb&res=527. Reprint. Shanghai: Shangwu yinshuguan 商務印書館 (上海), 1934.

Fan, Ye 范曄. *Houhanshu* 《後漢書》 (*Book of Later Han*). 5th century CE. 120 volumes. http://ctext.org/hou-han-shu/lie-nv-zhuan/zh. Reprinted, with modern Chinese translation, introduction, notes, and commentary by Wei Lianke 魏連科 et al., *Xinyi Houhanshu* 《新譯後漢書》. Taipei: Sanmin shuju 三民書局, 2013.

Fang, Xuanling 房玄齡 et al. *Jinshu* 《晉書》 (*Book of Jin*). c. 620 CE. 130 volumes. http://ctext.org/wiki.pl?if=en&res=788577. Also, in *Chizaotang siku quanshu huiyao* 《摛藻堂四庫全書薈要》. China: China-America Digital Academic Library, https://archive.org/details/06079080.cn.

Foust, Mathew A., and Sor-hoon Tan, eds. *Feminist Encounters with Confucius*. Leiden: Brill, 2016.

Gao, Shiyu 高世瑜. *Zhongguo gudai funü shenghuo* 《中國古代婦女生活》 (*Daily Life of Ancient Chinese Women*). Taipei: Shangwu yinshuguan 商務印書館 (台灣), 1998.

Goldin, Paul R. "The View of Women in Early Confucianism." In *The Sage and the Second Sex: Confucianism, Ethics, and Gender*, edited by Chenyang Li, 133–62. Chicago and La Salle, IL: Open Court, 2000.

Goldin, Paul R. *The Culture of Sex in Ancient China*. Honolulu: University of Hawaii Press, 2001.

Goldin, Paul R., trans. Excerpts from *Comprehensive Discussions in the White Tiger Hall*. In *Images of Women in Chinese Thought and Culture*, edited by Robin R. Wang, 170–6. Indianapolis, IN: Hackett, 2003.

Gongyang, Gao 公羊高. *Chunqiu gongyangzhuan* 《春秋公羊傳》 (*Gongyang Commentaries to the Spring and Autumn Annals*). c. 3rd century BCE. http://ctext.org/gongyang-zhuan/zh. For English translation, see entry for Harry Miller.

Guliangzi 穀梁子. *Chunqiu guliangzhuan* 《春秋穀梁傳》 (*Guliang Commentaries to the Spring and Autumn Annals*). c. 3rd–1st centuries BCE. http://ctext.org/guliang-zhuan/zh.

Guo, Jujing郭居敬. *Ershisi xiao* 《二十四孝》 (*Twenty-Four Exemplars of Filial Piety*). c. 14th century CE. http://ctext.org/wiki.pl?if=gb&chapter=824650.

Han, Ying 韓嬰. *Hanshi waizhuan* 《韓詩外傳》 (*Outer Commentary to the Classic of Poetry by Master Han*). c. 150 BCE. http://ctext.org/han-shi-wai-zhuan/zh.

Herr, Ranjoo Seodu. "Is Confucianism Compatible with Care Ethics? A Critique." *Philosophy East and West* 53, no. 4 (2003): 471–89.

Hong, Mai 洪邁. *Yijian zhi* 《夷堅志》. c. 1162－1202 CE. http://ctext.org/wiki.pl?if=gb&res=437573.

Hu, Wenkai 胡文楷. *Lidai funü zhuzuokao* 《歷代婦女著作考》 (*Verified Records of Women's Writings Through the Ages*). Shanghai: Shanghai guji chubanshe 上海古籍出版社, 1985.

Huang, Liling 黃麗玲. "*Nü sishu* yanjiu" 《女四書》研究 ("Research on *Four Books for Women*"). MA thesis, Taiwan Nanhua University 臺灣南華大學, 2003.

Huang, Qingquan 黃清泉. *Xinyi leinüu zhuan* 《新譯列女傳》 (*New Translation of Biographies of Women*). 2nd edition. Taipei: Sanmin shuju 三民書局, 2008.

Huang, Yanli 黃嫣梨, ed. *Nü sishu jizhu yizheng* 《女四書集注義證》 (*Four Books for Women, with Selections from Traditional Commentaries*). Hong Kong: Shangwu yinshuguan 商務印書館 (香港), 2008.

Huangdi neijing 《黃帝內經》 (*Yellow Emperor's Inner Canon*). c. 5th century BCE–2nd century CE. http://ctext.org/huangdi-neijing/zh. For English translation, see entry for Paul Unschuld.

Ivanhoe, Philip J, trans. with commentary. *The Daodejing of Laozi*. New York: Seven Bridges Press, 2002.

Ji, Yun 紀昀 et al., eds. *Siku quanshu* 《四庫全書》 (*Complete Library in Four Sections*). c. 36,000 volumes. Beijing, China: Qing Dynasty Imperial Library, 1773–1782 CE. Reprint, Taipei: Shangwu yinshuguan 商務印書館 (台灣), 1986.

Jiang, Xinyan. "Confucianism, Women, and Social Contexts." *Journal of Chinese Philosophy* 36, no. 2 (2009): 228–42.

Ke, Shaomin 柯劭忞 et al. *Xinyuanshi* 《新元史》 (*New History of Yuan*). 1920 CE. 257 volumes. http://ctext.org/wiki.pl?if=en&res=201395.

Kim, Hye-Kyung. "The Dream of Sagehood: A Re-Examination of Queen Sohae's *Naehoon* and Feminism." In *Bloomsbury Research Handbook of Chinese Philosophy and Gender*, edited by Ann A. Pang-White, 89–107. London: Bloomsbury, 2016.

Kinney, Ann Behnke, trans. and ed. *Exemplary Women of Early China: The Lienü zhuan of Liu Xiang*. New York: Columbia University Press, 2014.

Ko, Dorothy. *Teachers of the Inner Chambers: Women and Culture in Seventeenth-Century China*. Palo Alto, CA: Stanford University Press, 1994.

Kramers, Robert P., trans. and ed. *K'ung Tzu Chia Yü: The School Sayings of Confucius: Introduction and Translation of Sections 1-10 with Critical Notes*. Leiden: Brill, 1950.

Lai, Karyn L. *Learning from Chinese Philosophies: Ethics of Interdependent and Contextualised Self*. Aldershot and Burlington: Ashgate, 2006.

Lai, Yanyuan 賴炎元, ed. and tran. *Chunqiu fanlu jinzhu jinyi* 《春秋繁露今註今譯》(*Modern Translation of The Luxuriant Dew of the Spring and Autumn Annals with Commentary and Notes*). 2nd edition. Taipei: Shangwu yinshuguan 商務印書館 (台灣), 2010.

Laozi 老子. *Daodejing* 《道德經》, also known as *Laozi* 《老子》. c. 6th century BCE. For English translation, see entries for Philip J. Ivanhoe, D. C. Lau, and Stephen Mitchell.

Lau, D. C., trans. with commentary. *Lao Tzu—Tao Te Ching*. New York: Penguine, 1963.

Lau, D. C., trans. and ed. *The Book of Mencius* (*Mengzi* 孟子). Revised edition. New York: Penguin, 2005.

Lee, Hui-shu. "Empress Xu." In *Women Writers of Traditional China: An Anthology of Poetry and Criticism*, edited by Kang-i Sun Chang and Haun Saussy, 678–81. Stanford, CA: Stanford University Press, 1999.

Legge, James, trans. and ed. *The Chinese Classics: with a Translation, Critical and Exegetical Notes, Prolegomena, and Copious Indexes*. 5 volumes. Shanghai: Huadong shifan daxue chubanshe 華東師範大學出版社, 2011. Reprint, London: Trübner, 1861–1872.

Li, Chenyang. "The Confucian Concept of Jen and the Feminist Ethics of Care: A Comparative Study." *Hypatia: A Journal of Feminist Philosophy* 9, no. 1 (1994): 70–89.

Li, Chenyang. Introduction to *The Sage and the Second Sex: Confucianism, Ethics, and Gender*, edited by Chenyang Li, 1–21. Chicago and La Salle, IL: Open Court, 2000.

Li, Fang 李昉 et al. *Taiping yulan* 《太平御覽》(*Taiping Imperial Record and Collection of Books*). c. 10th century CE. http://ctext.org/taiping-yulan/zh. 5 volumes. Reprint. Taipei: Shangwu yinshuguan 商務印書館 (臺灣), 1965.

Li, Ju-Chen [Ruzhen] 李汝珍. *Jinghuayuan* 《鏡花緣》(*Flowers in the Mirror*). 1827 CE. Translated by Lin Tai-yi. Berkeley and Los Angeles: University of California Press, 1965.

Li, Shizhen 李時珍. *Bencao gangmu* 《本草綱目》(*Compendium of Materia Medica*). 1593 CE. http://ctext.org/wiki.pl?if=gb&res=8. Translated into English in 6 volumes. Beijing: Foreign Language Press, 2006.

Li, Yanshou 李延壽. *Beishi* 《北史》(*History of the Northern Dynasties*). c. 7th century CE. 100 volumes. http://ctext.org/wiki.pl?if=en&res=21033.

Liji 《禮記》 (*Record/Book/Classic of Rites/Rituals*). [Also known as *Xiaodai liji* 《小戴禮記》]. 5th–3rd centuries BCE. Reprinted, with modern Chinese translation, introduction, commentary, and notes by Jiang Yihua 姜義華, *Xinyi lijiduban* 《新譯禮記讀本》. 2 volumes. 2nd edition. Taipei: Sanmin shuju 三民書局, 2012. English translation with commentary and notes by James Legge, *The Li ki*, in *Sacred Books of the East*, volumes 27–8, edited by F. Max Müller. Oxford: Clarendon press, 19=79–1910. http://ctext.org/liji.

Liu, An 劉安. *Huainanzi* 《淮南子》. For English translation, see entry for John S. Major.

Liu, Renpeng 劉人鵬. *Jindai Zhongguo nüquan lunshu—guozu fanyi yu xingbie zhengshi* 《近代中國女權論述—國族、翻譯與性別政治》 (*Discourses on Modern Chinese Women's Rights—Nationality, Translation, and Gender Politics*). Taipei: Xuesheng shuju 學生書局 (台灣), 2000.

Liu, Shi 劉氏 [Madame Liu, also known as Wang Jiefu 王節婦, Chaste Widow Wang]. *Nüfan jielu* 《女範捷錄》 (*Short Records of Models for Women*). c. 16th century CE. In *Nü sishu*, edited by Wang Xiang; and *Gujin tushu jicheng*, volume 395, edited by Chen Menglei et al. For more information, see entries for Wang Xiang and Chen Menglei.

Liu, Xiang 劉向. *Lienü zhuan* 《列女傳》 (*Biographies of Women*). 1st century BCE. Reprinted, with modern Chinese translation, introduction, commentary, and notes by Huang Qingquan 黃清泉, *Xinyi leinü zhuan* 《新譯列女傳》. 2nd edition. Taipei: Sanmin shuju 三民書局, 2008. For English translation, see entry for Ann Kinney.

Liu, Xiang 劉向. *Shuoyuan* 《說苑》 (*Garden of Stories*). c. 1st century BCE. http://ctext.org/shuo-yuan.

Liu, Xu 劉昫 et al. *Tangshu* 《唐書》 (*Book of Tang*). [Also known as *Jiutangshu* 《舊唐書》 (*Old Book of Tang*)]. c. 945 CE. 200 volumes. http://ctext.org/wiki.pl?if=gb&res=456206.

Long, Wenbin 龍文彬. *Ming huiyao* 《明會要》 (*Essential Ming Laws and Regulations*). c. 1865 CE. http://ctext.org/library.pl?if=en&res=2377&by_author=%E9%BE%8D%E6%96%87%E5%BD%AC. Reprint. Beijing: Zhonghua shuju 中華書局, 1956.

Lorde, Audre. *Sister Outsider: Essays and Speeches*. Berkeley, CA: Crossing, 1984. Reprint, 2007.

Lu, Jiaqi 盧嘉琪. "*Siku quanshu* gengxuzhubian suoshou nüxing zhushu" 《四庫全書》賡續諸編所收女性著述 ("Women's Writings Included in Follow-up Volumes and Editions of the *Complete Library in Four Sections*"). *Chengda lishi xuebao* 成大歷史學報 32 (2007): 35–80.

Luo, Guanzhong 羅貫中. *Sanguo yanyi* 《三國演義》 (*Three Kingdoms*). c. 14th century CE. Edited by Ronald C. Iverson, translated by Yu Sumei. 3 volumes. North Clarendon, VT: Tuttle, 2014.

Luo, Shirong. "Relation, Virtue, and Relational Virtue: Three Concepts of Caring." *Hypatia* 22, no. 3 (2007): 92–110.

Mair, Victor H, trans. *Wandering on the Way: Early Taoist Tales and Parables of Chuang Tzu*. Honolulu, HI: University of Hawaii Press, 2000.

Major, John S., Sarah Queen, Andrew Meyer, and Harold D. Roth, trans. *The Huainanzi: A Guide to the Theory and Practice of Government in Early Han Chian*. New York: Columbia University Press, 2010.

Mann, Susan, and Yu-Yin Cheng, eds. *Under Confucian Eyes: Writings on Gender in Chinese History*. Berkeley and Los Angeles: University of California Press, 2001.

Mengzi 孟子. *Mengzi* 《孟子》 (*Mencius*). c. 4th-3rd centuries BCE. For English translation, see entries for D. C. Lau and Bryan Van Norden.

Miller, Harry, trans. *The Gongyang Commentaries on The Spring and Autumn Annals*. New York: Palgrave MacMillan, 2015.

Mitchell, Stephen. *Tao Te Ching: A New Translation*. New York: HarperCollins, 1994.

Mohanty, Chandra Talpade. *Feminism without Borders: Decolonizing Theory, Practicing Solidarity*. Durham, NC: Duke University Press, 2003.

Müller, F. Max, ed. *Sacred Books of the East*. 50 volumes. Oxford: Clarendon, 1879–1910.

Mou, Sherry J. *Gentlemen's Prescriptions for Women's Lives: A Thousand Years of Biographies of Chinese Women*. London: Routledge, 2015. Originally published by M. E. Sharpe, 2004.

Nie, Jing-Bao. " 'Human Drugs' in Chinese Medicine and the Confucian View: An Interpretive Study." In *Confucian Bioethics*, edited by Ruiping Fan, 167–206. Dordrecht: Kluwer, 1999.

Ouyang, Xiu 歐陽修, Song Qi 宋祁, et al. *Xintangshu* 《新唐書》 (*New Book of Tang*). c. 1060 CE. 225 volumes. http://ctext.org/wiki.pl?if=gb&res=182378. Reprint. Taipei: Dingwen shuju 鼎文書局, 1978.

Ouyang, Xiu 歐陽修. *Xin Wudaishi* 《新五代史》 (*New History of the Five Dynasties*). c. 11th century CE. 74 volumes. http://ctext.org/wiki.pl?if=en&res=626823.

Pang-White, Ann A. "Reconstructing Modern Ethics: Confucian Care Ethics." *Journal of Chinese Philosophy* 36, no. 2 (2009): 210–27.

Pang-White, Ann A. "Caring in Confucian Philosophy." *Philosophy Compass* 6, no. 6 (2011): 374–84.

Pang-White, Ann A. "Zhu Xi on Family and Women: Challenges and Potentials." *Journal of Chinese Philosophy* 40, no. 3–4 (2013): 436–55. Reprinted, with revision, in *The Bloomsbury Research Handbook of Chinese Philosophy and Gender*, edited by Ann A. Pang-White, 69–87. London: Bloomsbury, 2016.

Pang-White, Ann A., ed. *The Bloomsbury Research Handbook of Chinese Philosophy and Gender*. London and New York: Bloomsbury, 2016.

Pang-White, Ann A. "Confucius and the *Four Books for Women* (*Nü sishu* 《女四書》)." In *Feminist Encounters with Confucius*, edited by Mathew A. Foust and Sor-hoon Tan, 17–39. Leiden: Brill, 2016.

Pollard, Elizabeth, Clifford Rosenberg, Robert Tignor, Jeremy Adelman, Stephen Aron, Peter Brown, Benjamin Elman, Stephen Kotkin, Xinru Liu, Susanne Marchand, Holly Pittman, Gyan Prakash, Brent Shaw, and Michael Tsin. *Worlds Together, Worlds Apart—Volume 1: Beginnings Through the 15th Century*. New York: W. W. Norton, 2015.

Raphals, Lisa. "Gendered Virtue Reconsidered." In *The Sage and the Second Sex: Confucianism, Ethics, and Gender*, edited by Chenyang Li, 223–48. Chicago and La Salle, IL: Open Court, 2000.

Renxiaowen Huanghou 仁孝文皇后 (Empress Renxiaowen). *Neixun* 《內訓》 (*Teachings for the Inner Court*). c. 15th century CE. In *Nü sishu*, edited by Wang Xiang; *Gujin tushu jicheng*, volume 395, edited by Chen Menglei; and *Siku quanshu*, volume 709, edited by Ji Yun, et al. For more information, see entries for Wang Xiang, Chen Menglei, and Ji Yun.

Rosenlee, Li-Hsiang Lisa. *Confucianism and Women: A Philosophical Interpretation*. Albany: State University of New York Press, 2006.

Shangshu 《尚書》 (*Book of Documents*). [Also known as *Shujing* 《書經》 (*Classic of History*).] c. 8th–5th centuries BCE. Translated with commentary and notes by James Legge, *The Shu King or Book of Historical Documents*. Reprint. Whitefish, MT: Kessinger, 2004. Originally published as *The Shu King*, in *Sacred Books of the East*, volume 3, edited by F. Max Müller. Oxford: Clarendon Press, 1879–1910. Also, http://ctext.org/shang-shu.

Shaughnessy, Edward L. *Unearthing the Changes: Recently Discovered Manuscripts of the Yi Jing (I Ching) and Related Texts*. New York: Columbia University Press, 2014.

Shen, Shixing 申時行, Li Dongyang 李東陽, et al. *Daming huidian* 《大明會典》 (*Great Ming Laws*). c. 1587 CE. http://ctext.org/wiki.pl?if=g b&res=706630. Reprint. Taipei: Xinwenfeng chubangongsi 新文豐出版公司, 1976.

Shen, Shixing 申時行 et al. *Ming huidian* 《明會典》 (*Ming Laws*). c. 1587 CE. Reprint. 2nd printing. Beijing: Zhonghua shuju 中華書局, 2007.

Shijing 《詩經》 (*Classic of Poetry*). [Also known as the *Book of Songs*, the *Book of Odes*, the *Songs*, or the *Odes*.] c. 11th–8th centuries BCE. Reprinted, with modern Chinese translation, introduction, commentary, and notes by Teng Zhixian 滕志賢, *Xinyi shijing duben* 《新譯詩經讀本》. 2 volumes. 2nd edition. Taipei: Sanmin shuju 三民書局, 2016. Also, English translation of some parts with commentary and notes by James Legge, *The Shi king*, in *Sacred Books of the East*, volume 3, edited by F. Max Müller. Oxford: Clarendon Press, 1879–1910. http://ctext.org/book-of-poetry.

Sima, Qian 司馬遷. *Shiji* 《史記》 (*Historical Records*). [Also known as *Records of the Grand Historian*.] 1st century BCE. 130 volumes. Full classic Chinese text at http://ctext.org/shiji; *Kongzi shijia* 孔子世家 ("Family Genealogy of Confucius") at http://ctext.org/shiji/kong-zi-shi-jia/zh. Burton Watson translated some volumes; see entry for Burton Watson.

Som, Tjan Tjoe, trans. *Po Hu T'ung: The Comprehensive Discussions in the White Tiger Hall*. 2 volumes. Leiden: Brill, 1952.

Song, Lian 宋濂 et al. *Yuanshi* 《元史》 (*History of Yuan*). c. 14th century CE. 210 volumes. http://ctext.org/wiki.pl?if=en&res=603186.

Song, Ruoxing 宋若莘 [Ruohua 若華] and Song Ruozhao 宋若昭. *Nü lunyu* 《女論語》 (*Analects for Women*). c. 9th century CE. In *Nü sishu*, edited by Wang Xiang; *Gujin tushu jicheng*, volume 395, edited by Chen Menglei; and *Jiaonü yigui*, edited by Chen Hongmou. For more information, see entries for Wang Xiang, Chen Menglei, and Chen Hongmou. In addition to the new English translation provided in this volume, an earlier translation is available; see entry for Heying Zhan and Roger Bradshaw.

Spivak, Gayatri Charkravorty. *In Other Words: Essays in Culture and Politics*. New York: Methuen, 1987.

Standaert, Nicolas. *The Intercultural Weaving of Historical Texts: Chinese and European Stories*. Leiden: Brill, 2016.

Swann, Nancy Lee, trans. *Pan Chao: Foremost Woman Scholar of China*. New York: Russell & Russell, 1932. Reprinted in *Images of Women in Chinese Thought and Culture*, edited by Robin R. Wang, 177–88. Indianapolis, IN: Hackett, 2003.

Tao, Zongyi 陶宗儀. *Shuofu* 《說郛》 (*Compendium of Famous Writings*). c. 14th century CE. In *Siku quanshu* 《四庫全書》, edited by Ji Yun, et al. Also, http://ctext.org/library.pl?if=gb&res=6309.

Tong, Rosemarie. *Feminist Thought: A More Comprehensive Introduction*. 3rd ed. Boulder, CO: Westview, 2009.

Tsien, Tsuen-Hsuin. "Paper and Printing." In *Science and Civilization in China*, volume 5, part 1, edited by Joseph Needham, 201–17. Cambridge: Cambridge University Press, 1985. Also, Taipei: Caves Books, 1986.

Tu, Wei-ming. "Probing the 'Three Bonds' and 'Five Relationships' in Confucian Humanism." In *Confucianism and the Family*, edited by Walter H. Slote and George A. DeVos, 121–36. Albany: State University of New York Press, 1998.

Tuo, Tuo 脫脫 [Toqto'a, also known as 托克托] et al. *Songshi* 《宋史》 (*History of Song*). c. 1345 CE. 496 volumes. http://ctext.org/wiki.pl?if=en&res=975976.

Tuo, Tuo 脫脫 [Toqto'a, also known as 托克托] et al. *Jinshi* 《金史》 (*History of Jin*). c. 1345 CE. 135 volumes. http://ctext.org/wiki.pl?if=en&res=270779.

Unschuld, Paul U., trans. and ed. *Huang Di Nei Jing Ling Shu: The Ancient Classic on Needle Therapy*. 2nd edition. Berkeley and Los Angeles: University of California Press, 2016.

Unschuld, Paul U., and Hermann Tessenow, trans. and ed. *Huang Di Nei Jing Su Wen: An Annotated Translation of Huang Di's Inner Classic—Basic Questions*. 2 volumes. Berkeley and Los Angeles: University of California Press, 2011.

Van Norden, Bryan W., trans. *Mengzi: With Selections from Traditional Commentaries*. Indianapolis, IN: Hackett, 2008.

Wang, Daokun 汪道昆, ed. *Wangshi ji lienü zhuan* 《汪氏輯列女傳》 (*Wangshi's Biographies of Women*), with illustrations by Qiu Shizhou 仇十洲 [Qiu Ying 仇英]. [Also known as *Qiu Shizhou xiu xiang lienü zhuan* 《仇十洲綉像列女傳》 (*Qiu Shizhou's Illustrated Biographies of Women*).] c. 1573–1620 CE. China: Zhibuzu zhai 知不足齋, 1779. Full classic Chinese text at http://nrs.harvard.edu/urn-3:HUL.FIG:004758699. See also http://brbl-dl.library.yale.edu/vufind/Record/3543501.

Wang, Jiefu 王節婦. See Liu Shi.

Wang, Robin R., ed. *Images of Women in Chinese Thought and Cultures: Writings from the Pre-Qin Period through the Song Dynasty*. Indianapolis, IN: Hackett, 2003.

Wang, Robin R. *Yinyang: The Way of Heaven and Earth in Chinese Thought and Culture.* New York: Cambridge University Press, 2012.

Wang, Shu 王肅, ed. *Kongzi jiayu* 《孔子家語》 (*Family Discourse of Confucius*). 3rd century CE. Reprinted, with modern Chinese translation, introduction, commentary, and notes by Yang Chunqiu 羊春秋, *Xinyi Kongzi jiayu* 《新譯孔子家語》. 2nd edition. Taipei: Sanmin shuju 三民書局, 2008. Also, by Pan Shuren 潘樹仁, *Kongzi jiayu* 《孔子家語》. Hong Kong: Chunghwa shuju 中華書局 (香港), 2013. Full classic Chinese text at http://ctext.org/kongzi-jiayu/zh. For English translation of some sections, see entry for Robert Kramers.

Wang, Xiang 王相. *Nü sishu jizhu* 《女四書集註》 (*Four Books for Women, with Commentary*). c. 1580–1600 CE. Reprint, as *Zhuangyuange nü sishu jizhu* 《狀元閣女四書集註》 (*Zhuangyuange Edition of the Four Books for Women, with Commentary*). Beijing, China: Wenchengtang 文成堂, 1885.

Watson, Burton, trans. *The Tso Chuan: Selections from China's Oldest Narrative History*. Revised edition. New York: Columbia University Press, 1992.

Watson, Burton, trans. *Records of the Grand Historian: Han Dynasty I and II*. 3rd edition. New York: Columbia University Press, 1993.

Watson, Burton, trans. *Records of the Grand Historian: Qin Dynasty*. 3rd edition. New York: Columbia University Press, 1995.

Wawrytko, Sandra. "Kongzi as Feminist: Confucian Self-Cultivation in a Contemporary Context." *Journal of Chinese Philosophy* 27, no. 2 (2000): 171–86.

Wiley, Arthur, trans. *The Analects of Confucius*. New York: Random House, 1938.

Wiley, Arthur, trans. *The Book of Songs (Shijing): The Ancient Chinese Classic of Poetry*, edited by Joseph R. Allen, with additional translations. Subsequent edition. New York: Grove Press, 1996.

Woo, Tak-Ling Terry. "Emotions and Self-Cultivation in *Nü Lunyu* 《女論語》 (*Women's Analects*)." *Journal of Chinese Philosophy* 36, no. 2 (2009): 334–47.

Woo, Tak-Ling Terry. "Discourses on Women from the Classical Period to the Song: An Integrated Approach." In *The Bloomsbury Research Handbook of Chinese Philosophy and Gender*, edited by Ann A. Pang-White, 37–68. London: Bloomsbury, 2016.

Xiaojing 《孝經》 (*Classic of Filial Piety*). c. 5th–3rd centuries BCE. English translation with commentary and notes by James Legge, *The Hsiao king*, in *Sacred Books of the*

East, volume 3, edited by F. Max Müller (Oxford: Clarendon Press, 1879–1910). http://ctext.org/xiao-jing.

Yamazaki, Jun'ichi 山崎純一. *Kyōiku kara mita Chūgoku joseishi shiryo no kenkyu: "Onna shisho" to "Shinpufu" sanbusho* 《教育からみた中國女性史資料の研究：「女四書」と「新婦譜」三部書》 (*A View of Education from a Study of Documents on the History of Chinese Women: "Four Books for Women" and "Instructions for New Brides"*). Tokyo: Meiji shoin 明治書院, 1986.

Yangjie, Pan 陽節潘. *Gangjian zonglun* 《綱鑑總論》 (*General Discussion of the Main Points and Reflection*). c. 13th century CE. https://babel.hathitrust.org/cgi/pt?id=hvd.32044068371640;view=1up;seq=313;size=125

Yijing [*I Ching*] 《易經》 (*Classic of Changes*). [Also known as *Book of Changes*.] 11th–8th centuries BCE. Translated with commentary and notes by James Legge, *The Yi King*, in *Sacred Books of the East*, volume 16, edited by F. Max Müller. Oxford: Clarendon Press, 1879–1910. Also, http://ctext.org/book-of-changes.

Yili 《儀禮》 (*Book of Ceremonial Rituals/Rites*, or *Book of Etiquette and Ceremonial*). c. 5th–3rd centuries BCE. Full classic Chinese text at http://ctext.org/yili/shi-guan-li. Reprinted, with modern Chinese translation, introduction, commentary, and notes by Gu Baotian 顧寶田 and Zheng Shuyuan 鄭淑媛, *Xinyi yili duben* 《新譯儀禮讀本》. 2nd edition. Taipei: Sanmin shuju 三民書局, 2016.

Yuan, Lijun. "Ethics of Care and Concept of Jen: A Reply to Chenyang Li." *Hypatia* 17, no. 1 (2002): 107–29.

Zhan, Heying Jenny and Roger Bradshaw. "The Book of *Analects for Women*." *Journal of Historical Sociology* 9 (1996): 261–8. Reprinted in *Images of Women in Chinese Thought and Culture*, edited by Robin R. Wang, 327–40. Indianapolis, IN: Hackett, 2003.

Zhang, Tingyu 張廷玉 et al. *Mingshi* 《明史》 (*History of Ming*). c. 1739 CE. 332 volumes. http://ctext.org/wiki.pl?if=gb&res=410835.

Zheng Shi 鄭氏 [Madame Zheng]. *Nü xiaojing* 《女孝經》 (*Classic of Filial Piety for Women*). c. 8th century CE. In *Gujin tushu jicheng*, edited by Chen Menglei, volume 395. http://ctext.org/library.pl?if=gb&file=91781&page=21. Also in *Shuofu*, edited by Tao Zongyi; volume 880 of the *Siku quanshu*, edited by Ji Yun et al. About three-fourths of the text has been translated by Patricia Buckley Ebrey and is included in *Under Confucian Eyes*, edited by Susan Mann and Yu-Yin Cheng, 46–69. For more information, see entries for Chen Menglei, Tao Zongyi, Ji Yun et al., and Susan Mann and Yu-Yin Cheng.

Zhongyong 《中庸》 (*Doctrine of the Mean*). In *A Source Book in Chinese Philosophy*, translated and edited by Wing-tsit Chan, 95–114. 4th printing. Princeton, NJ: Princeton University Press, 1973. Also, English translation by James Legge at http://ctext.org/liji/zhong-yong. Originally published in James Legge, trans., *The Chinese Classics: With a Translation, Critical and Exegetical Notes, Prolegomena, and Copious Indexes*, volume 1. London: Trübner, 1861–1872.

Zhoubi suanjing 《周髀算經》(*Classic of Arithmetic from the Gnomon of the Zhou Sundial*). c. 1st century BCE. http://ctext.org/zhou-bi-suan-jing/zh.

Zhouli 《周禮》 (*Zhou Rituals/Rites*). c. 3rd–2nd centuries BCE. http://ctext.org/rites-of-zhou. Reprinted, with modern Chinese translation, commentary, and notes by Lin Yin 林尹, *Zhouli jinzhu jinyi* 《周禮今註今譯》. Taipei: Shangwu yinshuguan 商務印書館 (台灣), 1983.

Zhu, Xi 朱熹. *Jinsi lu* 《近思錄》 (*Reflections on Things at Hand*). c. 13th century CE. For English translation, see entry for Wing-tsit Chan.

Zhu, Xi 朱熹. *Xu jinsi lu* 《續近思錄》) (*Further Reflections on Things at Hand*). Excerpts translated into English by Allen Wittenborn. In *Images of Women in Chinese Thought and Cultures*, edited by Robin R. Wang, 321–6. Indianapolis, IN: Hackett, 2003.

Zhu, Xi 朱熹. *Zhuzi yulei* 《朱子語類》 (*Classified Conversations of Zhu Xi*). Beijing: Zhonghua shuju 中華書局, 1986.

Zhu, Xi. *Huian xiansheng Zhu wengong wenji* 《晦庵先生朱文公文集》 (*Collected Works of Sir Huian Zhu Wengong*). Beijing: Beijing tushuguan chubanshe 北京圖書館出版社, 2006.

Zhuangzi. *Zhuangzi* 《莊子》. c. 4th century BCE. For English translations, see entries for Victor H. Mair and Brook Ziporyn.

Ziporyn, Brook. *Zhuangzi: The Essential Writings with Selections from Traditional Commentaries*. Indianapolis, IN: Hackett, 2009.

Zuo, Qiuming 左丘明. *Chunqiu zuozhuan* 《春秋左傳》 (*Zuo Commentary to the Spring and Autumn Annals*). 5th–3rd centuries BCE. http://ctext.org/chun-qiu-zuo-zhuan. For English translation, see James Legge, *The Chinese Classics*, volume 5. London: Trübner, 1861–1872. For more recent translation of some parts, see Burton Watson, trans., *The Tso Chuan: Selections from China's Oldest Narrative History*. New York: Columbia University Press, 1992.

Zuo, Qiuming 左丘明. *Guoyu* 《國語》 (*Discourses of the States*). 5th–3rd centuries BCE. http://ctext.org/guo-yu/zh.

Index

Printed in the USA
CPSIA information can be obtained
at www.ICGtesting.com
CBHW070409130724
11541CB00010B/450

9 780190 460891